Microsoft® Visual C#® 2005
Step by Step

John Sharp

PUBLISHED BY
Microsoft Press
A Division of Microsoft Corporation
One Microsoft Way
Redmond, Washington 98052-6399

Library of Congress Control Number 2005933123

Printed and bound in the United States of America.

6 7 8 9   QWT   8 7

Distributed in Canada by H.B. Fenn and Company Ltd. A CIP catalogue record for this book is available from the British Library.

Microsoft Press books are available through booksellers and distributors worldwide. For further information about international editions, contact your local Microsoft Corporation office or contact Microsoft Press International directly at fax (425) 936-7329. Visit our Web site at www.microsoft.com/mspress. Send comments to mspinput@microsoft.com.

Microsoft, ActiveX, Excel, IntelliSense, JScript, Microsoft Press, MSDN, Visual Basic, Visual C#, Visual J#, Visual Studio, Windows, and Windows Server are either registered trademarks or trademarks of Microsoft Corporation in the United States and/or other countries. Other product and company names mentioned herein may be the trademarks of their respective owners.

The example companies, organizations, products, domain names, e-mail addresses, logos, people, places, and events depicted herein are fictitious. No association with any real company, organization, product, domain name, e-mail address, logo, person, place, or event is intended or should be inferred.

This book expresses the author's views and opinions. The information contained in this book is provided without any express, statutory, or implied warranties. Neither the authors, Microsoft Corporation, nor its resellers, or distributors will be held liable for any damages caused or alleged to be caused either directly or indirectly by this book.

Acquisitions Editor: Ben Ryan
Project Editor: Lynn Finnel
Technical Editors: Steve Lambert and Jon Kenoyer
Editorial and Production: Online Training Solutions, Inc.

Body Part No. X11-44955

Table of Contents

Part III **Creating Components**

14 Implementing Properties to Access Attributes 243

15 Using Indexers 259

16 Delegates and Events 273

Part IV   Working with Windows Applications

Acknowledgments

I am utterly amazed to find myself in this position! Writing a book takes a great deal of enthusiasm, together with the encouragement and skill of a surprisingly dedicated team of people. That I was asked to produce a second edition of this book showed that I had not tried sufficiently hard enough to upset them the first time around. Asking me for a third edition smacks of real staying power on their part. I would also like to thank Jon Jagger who co-authored the first edition of the book with me, and who remains the inspiration behind many of the exercises in the early sections in this book.

As time has gone by, I have found a real sense of comradeship with the editors and technical reviewers I have worked with. I owe them so much. In particular, for this edition of the book I would like to mention Steve Lambert and Jon Kenoyer, who put me and my code through the mill, uncovered all sorts of bugs in my programs, and made sure I corrected them. Susie Bayers and Lynn Finnel have performed sterling work in making sure what came out of the writing process was "book shaped" and made sense to someone other than myself.

As always, I would like to acknowledge the support given to me by my family: to Diana, who was able to judge how close I was to each deadline by the volume of my voice when pleading with the computer to "please work this time" and who had the good sense not to come too close when I reached 120 decibels; to James, who is convinced I am an unemployed layabout spending his time playing games on computers; and to Francesca, who is growing up so quickly that she can now type faster than I can.

And finally, "Up the Gills!" (OK, so we got relegated, but it's only a game.)

John Sharp

Introduction

Microsoft Visual C# is a powerful but simple language aimed primarily at developers creating applications by using the Microsoft .NET Framework. It inherits many of the best features of C++ and Microsoft Visual Basic, but few of the inconsistencies and anachronisms, resulting in a cleaner and more logical language. The advent of C# 2.0 has seen several important new features added to the language, including Generics, Iterators, and anonymous methods. The development environment provided by Microsoft Visual Studio 2005 makes these powerful features easy to use, and the many new wizards and enhancements included in Visual Studio 2005 can greatly improve your productivity as a developer.

The aim of this book is to teach you the fundamentals of programming with C# by using Visual Studio 2005 and the .NET Framework. You will learn the features of the C# language, and then use them to build applications running on the Microsoft Windows operating system. By the time you complete this book, you will have a thorough understanding of C# and will have used it to build Windows Forms applications, access Microsoft SQL Server databases, develop ASP.NET Web applications, and build and consume a Web service.

Finding Your Best Starting Point in This Book

This book is designed to help you build skills in a number of essential areas. You can use this book if you are new to programming or if you are switching from another programming language such as C, C++, Sun Microsystems Java, or Visual Basic. Use the following table to find your best starting point.

If you are	Follow these steps
New to object-oriented programming	1. Install the practice files as described in the next section, "Installing and Using the Practice Files."
	2. Work through the chapters in Parts I, II, and III sequentially.
	3. Complete Parts IV, V, and VI as your level of experience and interest dictates.
New to C#	1. Install the practice files as described in the next section, "Installing and Using the Practice Files." Skim the first five chapters to get an overview of C# and Visual Studio 2005, and then concentrate on Chapters 6 through 19.
	2. Complete Parts IV, V, and VI as your level of experience and interest dictates.

If you are	Follow these steps
Migrating from C, C++, or Java	1. Install the practice files as described in the next section, "Installing and Using the Practice Files."
	2. Skim the first seven chapters to get an overview of C# and Visual Studio 2005, and then concentrate on Chapters 8 through 19.
	3. For information about building Windows applications and using a database, read Parts IV and V.
	4. For information about building Web applications and Web services, read Part VI.
Switching from Visual Basic 6	1. Install the practice files as described in the next section, "Installing and Using the Practice Files."
	2. Work through the chapters in Parts I, II, and III sequentially.
	3. For information about building Windows applications, read Part IV.
	4. For information about accessing a database, read Part V.
	5. For information about creating Web applications and Web services, read Part VI.
	6. Read the Quick Reference sections at the end of the chapters for information about specific C# and Visual Studio 2005 constructs.
Referencing the book after working through the exercises	1. Use the index or the Table of Contents to find information about particular subjects.
	2. Read the Quick Reference sections at the end of each chapter to find a brief review of the syntax and techniques presented in the chapter.

Conventions and Features in This Book

This book presents information by using conventions designed to make the information readable and easy to follow. Before you start the book, read the following list, which explains conventions you'll see throughout the book and points out helpful features in the book that you might want to use.

Conventions

- Each exercise is a series of tasks. Each task is presented as a series of numbered steps (1, 2, and so on). A round bullet (•) indicates an exercise that has only one step.

- Notes labeled "tip" provide additional information or alternative methods for completing a step successfully.

- Notes labeled "important" alert you to information you need to check before continuing.

- A plus sign (+) between two key names means that you must press those keys at the same time. For example, "Press Alt+Tab" means that you hold down the Alt key while you press the Tab key.

Other Features

- Sidebars throughout the book provide more in-depth information about the exercise. The sidebars might contain background information, design tips, or features related to the information being discussed.

- Each chapter ends with a Quick Reference section. The Quick Reference section contains quick reminders of how to perform the tasks you learned in the chapter.

Online Companion Content

The online companion content page has content and links related to this book.

http://www.microsoft.com/mspress/companion/0-7356-2129-2/

Technology Updates

As technologies related to this book are updated, links to additional information will be added to the Microsoft Press Technology Updates Web page. Visit this page periodically for updates on Visual Studio 2005 and other technologies.

http://www.microsoft.com/mspress/updates/

> **Note** Practice files for this book are on the companion CD.

System Requirements

You'll need the following hardware and software to complete the exercises in this book:

- Microsoft Windows XP Professional Edition with Service Pack 2, Microsoft Windows Server 2003 with Service Pack 1, or Windows 2000 with Service Pack 4. (Microsoft Windows 2000 Datacenter Server is not supported.)

- Microsoft Visual Studio 2005 Standard or Professional Edition, including SQL Server 2005 Express.

- 766 MHz Pentium or compatible processor (1.5 GHz Pentium recommended).

- 256 MB RAM (512 MB or more recommended).

- Video monitor (800 × 600 or higher resolution) with at least 256 colors (1024 × 768 High Color 16-bit recommended).

- CD-ROM or DVD-ROM drive.

- Microsoft Mouse or compatible pointing device.

You will also need to have Administrator access to your computer to configure SQL Server 2005 Express Edition and to modify the Windows Registry in Chapter 28, "Creating and Using a Web Service."

Prerelease Software

This book was reviewed and tested against the August 2005 Community Technical Preview (CTP) of Visual Studio 2005. The August CTP was the last preview before the final release of Visual Studio 2005. This book is expected to be fully compatible with the final release of Visual Studio 2005. If there are any changes or corrections for this book, they will be collected and added to a Microsoft Knowledge Base article. See the "Support for this Book" section in this Introduction for more information.

Installing and Using the Practice Files

The companion CD inside this book contains the practice files that you'll use as you perform the exercises in the book. By using the practice files, you won't waste time creating files that aren't relevant to the exercise. The files and the step-by-step instructions in the lessons also let you learn by doing, which is an easy and effective way to acquire and remember new skills.

Installing the Practice Files

Follow these steps to install the practice files on your computer's hard disk so that you can use them with the exercises in this book.

1. Remove the CD from the package inside this book, and insert it into your CD-ROM drive.

> **Note**   An end user license agreement should open automatically. If this agreement does not appear, open My Computer on the desktop or Start menu, double-click the icon for your CD-ROM drive, and then double-click StartCD.exe.

2. Review the end user license agreement. If you accept the terms, select the accept option and then click Next.

   A menu will appear with options related to the book.

3. Click Install Practice Files.

4. Follow the onscreen instructions.

   The practice files are installed to the following location on your computer:

   My Documents\Microsoft Press\Visual CSharp Step by Step

Configuring SQL Server Express Edition

The exercises in Part V of this book require that you have access to SQL Server Express Edition to create and use the Northwind Traders database. If you are using SQL Server 2005 Express Edition, log in as Administrator on your computer and follow these steps to grant access to the user account that you will be using for performing the exercises in these chapters.

1. On the Windows Start menu, click All Programs, click Accessories, and then click Command Prompt to open a command prompt window.

2. In the command prompt window, type the following command:

   ```
   sqlcmd -S YourServer\SQLExpress -E
   ```

   Replace *YourServer* with the name of your computer.

   You can find the name of your computer by running the *hostname* command in the command prompt window, before running the *sqlcmd* command.

3. At the 1> prompt, type the following command, including the square brackets, and then press Enter:

   ```
   sp_grantlogin [YourServer\UserName]
   ```

   Replace *YourServer* with the name of your computer, and replace *UserName* with the name of the user account you will be using.

4. At the 2> prompt, type the following command and then press Enter:

   ```
   go
   ```

   If you see an error message, ensure you have typed the **sp_grantlogin** command correctly, including the square brackets.

5. At the 1> prompt, type the following command, including the square brackets, and then press Enter:

   ```
   sp_addsrvrolemember [YourServer\UserName], dbcreator
   ```

6. At the 2> prompt, type the following command and then press Enter:

   ```
   go
   ```

   If you see an error message, make sure you have typed the **sp_addsrvrolemember** command correctly, including the square brackets.

7. At the 1> prompt, type the following command and then press Enter:

   ```
   exit
   ```

8. Close the command prompt window.

Using the Practice Files

Each chapter in this book explains when and how to use any practice files for that chapter. When it's time to use a practice file, the book will list the instructions for how to open the file. The chapters are built around scenarios that simulate real programming projects, so you can easily apply the skills you learn to your own work.

For those of you who like to know all the details, here's a list of the Visual C# projects on the practice disk.

Project	Description
Chapter 1	
TextHello	This project gets you started. It steps through the creation of a simple program that displays a text-based greeting.
WinFormHello	This project displays the greeting in a window by using Windows Forms.
Chapter 2	
PrimitiveDataTypes	This project demonstrates how to declare variables of each of the primitive types, how to assign values to these variables, and how to display their values in a window.
MathsOperators	This program introduces the arithmetic operators (+ − * / %).
Chapter 3	
Methods	In this project, you'll re-examine the code in the previous project and investigate how it is structured by using methods.
DailyRate	This project walks you through writing your own methods (both manually and by using a wizard), running the methods, and stepping through the method calls by using the Visual Studio debugger.
Chapter 4	
Selection	This project shows how a cascading *if* statement is used to compare two dates.
switchStatement	This simple program uses a *switch* statement to convert characters into their XML representations.
Chapter 5	
Iteration	This project displays code fragments for each of the different iteration statements and the output that each generates.
whileStatement	This project uses a *while* statement to read the contents of a source file one line at a time and display each line in a Windows text box.
doStatement	This project uses a *do* statement to convert a number to its string representation.

Project	Description
Chapter 6	
MathsOperators	This project re-examines the MathsOperators project from Chapter 2, "Working with Variables, Operators, and Expressions," and causes various unhandled exceptions to make the program fail. The *try* and *catch* keywords then make the application more robust so that it no longer fails.
Chapter 7	
Classes	This project covers the basics of defining your own classes, complete with public constructors, methods, and private fields. It also covers creating class instances by using the *new* keyword and by using static methods and fields.
Chapter 8	
Parameters	This program investigates the difference between value parameters and reference parameters. It demonstrates how to use the *ref* and *out* keywords.
Chapter 9	
StructsAndEnums	This project uses an *enum* type to represent the four different suits of a playing card, and then uses a *struct* type to represent a calendar date.
Chapter 10	
Aggregates	This project builds on the previous project by using the *ArrayList* collection class to group together playing cards in a hand.
Chapter 11	
ParamsArrays	This project demonstrates how to use the *params* keyword to create a single method that can accept any number of *int* arguments and find and return the one with the smallest value.
Chapter 12	
CSharp	This project uses a hierarchy of interfaces and classes to simulate both reading a C# source file and classifying its contents into various kinds of tokens (identifiers, keywords, operators, and so on). As an example of use, it also derives classes from the key interfaces to display the tokens in a rich text box in color syntax.
Chapter 13	
UsingStatement	This project revisits a small piece of code from the previous chapter and reveals that it is not exception-safe. It shows you how to make the code exception-safe with a *using* statement.

Project	Description
Chapter 14	
Properties	This project presents a simple Windows application that uses several properties to continually display the size of its main window.
Chapter 15	
Indexers	This project uses two indexers: one to look up a person's phone number when given a name, and the other to look up a person's name when given a phone number.
Chapter 16	
Delegates	This project displays the time in digital format by using delegate callbacks. The code is then simplified by using events.
Chapter 17	
BinaryTree	This project shows you how to use Generics to build a *typesafe* structure that can contain elements of any type.
BuildTree	This project demonstrates how to use Generics to implement a *type-safe* method that can take parameters of any type.
Chapter 18	
BinaryTree	This project shows you how to implement the generic *IEnumerator<T>* interface to create an enumerator for the generic BinaryTree class.
IteratorBinaryTree	This project uses an Iterator to generate an enumerator for the generic BinaryTree class.
Chapter 19	
Operators	This project builds three structs, called *Hour*, *Minute*, and *Second*, that contain user-defined operators. The code is then simplified by using a conversion operator.
Chapter 20	
BellRingers	This project is a Windows Forms application demonstrating basic Windows Forms controls.
Chapter 21	
BellRingers	This project is an extension of the application created in Chapter 20, "Introducing Windows Forms," but with drop-down and pop-up menus added to the user interface.
Chapter 22	
CustomerDetails	This project demonstrates how to validate user input, using customer information as an example.

Project	Description
Chapter 23	
DisplayProducts	This project shows you how to use Microsoft ADO.NET to connect to the Northwind Traders database, and retrieve information from the Products table. The project uses the Data Source Configuration Wizard to generate a data source to connect to the database, and *DataSet*, *DataTable*, and *TableAdapter* objects to bind the data source to a *DataGridView* control. The *DataGridView* control displays the data in a Windows Form.
ReportOrders	This project shows how to access a database by using ADO.NET code rather than by using the components generated by the Data Source Configuration Wizard. The application retrieves information from the Orders table in the Northwind Traders database.
Chapter 24	
ProductsMaintenance	This project demonstrates how to use the *DataSet*, *DataTable*, and *TableAdapter* components to update information in a database. The application uses a *DataGridView* control on a Windows Form and enables the user to modify information in the Products table in the Northwind Traders database.
Chapter 25	
HonestJohn	This project creates a simple Microsoft ASP.NET Web site that enables the user to input information about employees working for a fictitious software development company.
Chapter 26	
HonestJohn	This project is an extended version of the HonestJohn project from the previous chapter and shows how to validate user input in an ASP.NET Web application.
Chapter 27	
Northwind	This project shows how to use Forms-based security for authenticating the user. The application also demonstrates how to use ADO.NET from an ASP.NET Web form, showing how to query and update a database in a scalable manner.
Chapter 28	
NorthwindServices	This project implements a Web service, providing remote access across the Internet to data in the Products table in the Northwind Traders database.
ProductInfo	This project shows how to create a Windows application that consumes a Web service. It shows how to invoke the Web methods in the NorthwindServices Web service.

In addition to these projects, several projects have solutions available for the practice exercises. The solutions for each project are included on the CD in the folder for each chapter and are labeled Complete.

Uninstalling the Practice Files

Follow these steps to remove the practice files from your computer.

1. In Control Panel, open Add Or Remove Programs.

2. From the Currently Installed Programs list, select Microsoft Visual C# 2005 Step By Step.

3. Click Remove.

4. Follow the onscreen instructions to remove the practice files.

Support for this Book

Every effort has been made to ensure the accuracy of this book and the contents of the companion CD. As corrections or changes are collected, they will be added to a Microsoft Knowledge Base article. To view the list of known corrections for this book, visit the following article:

http://support.microsoft.com/kb/905035/

Microsoft Press provides support for books and companion CDs at the following Web site:

http://www.microsoft.com/learning/support/books/

Questions and Comments

If you have comments, questions, or ideas regarding the book or this companion CD, or questions that are not answered by visiting the sites above, please send them to Microsoft Press via e-mail to:

mspinput@microsoft.com

Or via postal mail to:

Microsoft Press

Attn: Step by Step Series Editor

One Microsoft Way

Redmond, WA 98052-6399

Please note that product support is not offered through these mail addresses.

Microsoft Press Online:
Resources for Microsoft Visual Studio 2005

This site provides you with resources that work with your Microsoft Press books to keep you current and help you develop your skills as you quickly learn about the latest versions of Microsoft software.

Go to to *http://www.microsoft.com/learning/books/visualstudio2005/* to find:

- Updated information for your Visual Studio 2005 books, when available.
- Sample content from additional Microsoft Press books.
- A brief survey to provide feedback about your books.
- Special offers

At the site, you may also join the Microsoft Press Insiders' club, with the following additional benefits:

- a Microsoft Press book in searchable e- reference form
- Discounts on popular Microsoft Press books
- Updates on changes to the certification exam that you are pursuing, when available
- Charter membership in the Microsoft Press Insiders' club, which includes e-mail updates about the latest offerings in learning products, special offers, advance notices about discounts at participating booksellers, and exclusive offers. It is the one e-mail you'll be glad to see in your Inbox!

Visit *http://www.microsoft.com/learning/books/visualstudio2005/*.

Part I
Introducing Microsoft Visual C# and Microsoft Visual Studio 2005

Chapter 1
Welcome to C#

After completing this chapter, you will be able to:

■ Use the Visual Studio 2005 programming environment.

■ Create a C# console application.

■ Use namespaces.

■ Create a C# Windows Forms application.

Microsoft Visual C# is Microsoft's powerful, component-oriented language. C# plays an important role in the architecture of the Microsoft .NET Framework, and some people have drawn comparisons to the role that C played in the development of UNIX. If you already know a language such as C, C++, or Java, you'll find the syntax of C# reassuringly familiar because it uses the same curly brackets to delimit blocks of code. However, if you are used to programming in other languages, you should soon be able to pick up the syntax and feel of C#; you just need to learn to put the curly brackets and semi-colons in the right place. Hopefully this is just the book to help you!

In Part I, you'll learn the fundamentals of C#. You'll discover how to declare variables and how to use operators such as plus (+) and minus (-) to create values. You'll see how to write methods and pass arguments to methods. You'll also learn how to use selection statements such as *if* and iteration statements such as *while*. Finally, you'll understand how C# uses exceptions to handle errors in a graceful, easy-to-use manner. These topics form the core of C#, and from this solid foundation, you'll progress to more advanced features in Part II through Part VI.

Beginning Programming with the Visual Studio 2005 Environment

Visual Studio 2005 is a tool-rich programming environment containing all the functionality you'll need to create large or small C# projects. You can even create projects that seamlessly combine modules from different languages. In the first exercise, you'll start the Visual Studio 2005 programming environment and learn how to create a console application.

Create a console application in Visual Studio 2005

1. In Microsoft Windows, click the Start button, point to All Programs, and then point to Microsoft Visual Studio 2005.

2.   Click the Microsoft Visual Studio 2005 icon. Visual Studio 2005 starts.

> **Note**   If this is the first time that you have run Visual Studio 2005, you might see a dialog box prompting you to choose your default development environment settings. Visual Studio 2005 can tailor itself according your preferred development language. The various dialog boxes and tools in the integrated development environment (IDE) will have their default selections set for the language you choose. Select Visual C# Development Settings from the list, and then click the Start Visual Studio button. After a short delay, the Visual Studio 2005 IDE appears.

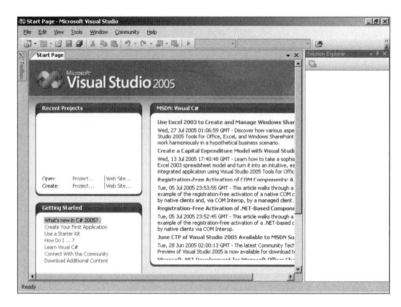

3.   On the File menu, point to New, and then click Project. The New Project dialog box opens. This dialog box allows you to create a new project using various templates, such as Windows Application, Class Library, and Console Application, that specify the type of application you want to create.

> **Note**   The actual templates available depend on the version of Visual Studio 2005 you are using. It is also possible to define new project templates, but that is beyond the scope of this book.

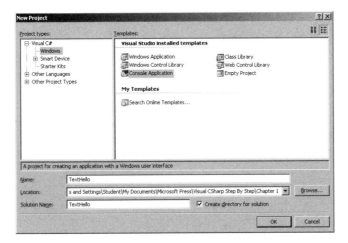

4. In the Templates pane, click the Console Application icon.

5. In the Location field, type **C:\Documents and Settings***YourName***\
    My Documents\Microsoft Press\Visual CSharp Step by Step\Chapter 1**.

    Replace the text *YourName* in this path with your Windows user name. To save a bit of
    space throughout the rest of this book, we will simply refer to the path "C:\Documents
    and Settings\YourName\My Documents" as your "\My Documents" folder.

> **Note**   If the folder you specify does not exist, Visual Studio 2005 creates it for you.

6. In the Name field, type **TextHello**.

7. Ensure that the Create Directory for Solution check box is checked and then click OK.
    The new project opens.

The *menu bar* at the top of the screen provides access to the features you'll use in the programming environment. You can use the keyboard or the mouse to access the menus and commands exactly as you can in all Windows-based programs. The *toolbar* is located beneath the
menu bar and provides button shortcuts to run the most frequently used commands. The
Code and Text Editor window occupying the main part of the IDE displays the contents of
source files. In a multi-file project, each source file has its own *tab* labeled with the name of
the source file. You can click the tab once to bring the named source file to the foreground
in the Code and Text Editor window. The *Solution Explorer* displays the names of the files associated with the project, among other items. You can also double-click a file name in the
Solution Explorer to bring that source file to the foreground in the Code and Text Editor
window.

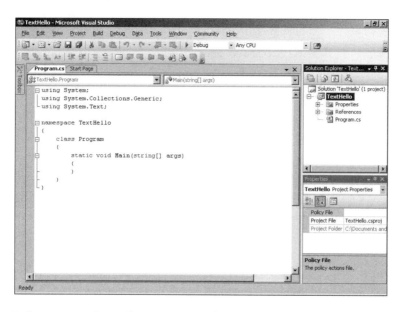

Before writing the code, examine the files listed in the Solution Explorer, which Visual Studio 2005 has created as part of your project:

- **Solution 'TextHello'**   This is the top level solution file, of which there is one per application. If you use Windows Explorer to look at your \My Documents\Microsoft Press\ Visual CSharp Step by Step\Chapter 1\TextHello folder, you'll see that the actual name of this file is TextHello.sln. Each solution file contains references to one or more project files.

- **TextHello**   This is the C# project file. Each project file references one or more files containing the source code and other items for the project. All the source code in a single project must be written in the same programming language. In Windows Explorer, this file is actually called TextHello.csproj, and it is stored in your \My Documents\Microsoft Press\Visual CSharp Step by Step\Chapter 1\TextHello\TextHello folder.

- **Properties**   This is a folder in the TextHello project. If you expand it, you will see that it contains a file called AssemblyInfo.cs. AssemblyInfo.cs is a special file that you can use to add *attributes* to a program, such as the name of the author, the date the program was written, and so on. There are additional attributes that you can use to modify the way in which the program will run. These attributes are outside the scope of this book.

- **References**   This is a folder that contains references to compiled code that your application can use. When code is compiled, it is converted into an *assembly* and given a unique name. Developers use assemblies to package up useful bits of code that they have written for distribution to other developers that might want to use them in their applications. Many of the features that you will be using when writing applications using this book will make use of assemblies provided by Microsoft with Visual Studio 2005.

■ **Program.cs**   This is a C# source file, and is the one displayed in the Code and Text Editor window when the project is first created. You will write your code in this file. It contains some code that Visual Studio 2005 provides automatically, which you will examine shortly.

Writing Your First Program

The Program.cs file defines a class called Program that contains a method called *Main*. All methods must be defined inside a class. The *Main* method is special—it designates the program's entry point. It must be a static method. (Methods are discussed in Chapter 3, "Writing Methods and Applying Scope." Static methods are discussed in Chapter 7, "Creating and Managing Classes and Objects." The *Main* method is discussed in Chapter 11, "Understanding Parameter Arrays.")

 Important   C# is a case-sensitive language. You must spell *Main* with a capital *M*.

In the following exercises, you'll write the code to display the message *Hello World* in the console; you'll build and run your Hello World console application; you'll learn how namespaces are used to partition code elements.

Write the code using IntelliSense technology

1. In the Code and Text Editor window displaying the Program.cs file, place the cursor in the *Main* method after the opening brace, and type **Console**. As you type the letter C at the start of the word *Console* an IntelliSense list appears. This list contains all of the valid C# keywords and data types that are valid in this context. You can either continue typing, or scroll through the list and double-click the Console item with the mouse. Alternatively, after you have typed *Con*, the Intellisense list will automatically home in on the *Console* item and you can press the Tab, Enter, or Spacebar key to select it.

   Main should look like this:

   ```
   static void Main(string[] args)
   {
       Console
   }
   ```

    Note   *Console* is a built-in class that contains the methods for displaying messages on the screen and getting input from the keyboard.

2. Type a period immediately after *Console*. Another Intellisense list appears displaying the methods, properties, and fields of the *Console* class.

3. Scroll down through the list until *WriteLine* is selected, and then press Enter. Alternatively, you can continue typing until *WriteLine* is selected and then press Enter.

   The IntelliSense list closes, and the *WriteLine* method is added to the source file. *Main* should now look like this:

   ```
   static void Main(string[] args)
   {
       Console.WriteLine
   }
   ```

4. Type an open parenthesis. Another IntelliSense tip appears.

   This tip displays the parameters of the *WriteLine* method. In fact, *WriteLine* is an *over-loaded method*, meaning that *Console* contains more than one method named *Write Line*. Each version of the *WriteLine* method can be used to output different types of data. (Overloaded methods are discussed in Chapter 3.) *Main* should now look like this:

   ```
   static void Main(string[] args)
   {
       Console.WriteLine(
   }
   ```

   You can click the tip's up and down arrows to scroll through the overloaded versions of *WriteLine*.

5. Type a close parenthesis, followed by a semicolon.

   Main should now look like this:

   ```
   static void Main(string[] args)
   {
       Console.WriteLine();
   }
   ```

6. Type the string *"Hello World"* between the left and right parentheses.

   Main should now look like this:

   ```
   static void Main(string[] args)
   {
       Console.WriteLine("Hello World");
   }
   ```

> **Tip**   Get into the habit of typing matched character pairs, such as (and) and { and }, *before* filling in their contents. It's easy to forget the closing character if you wait until after you've entered the contents.

IntelliSense Icons

IntelliSense displays the name of every member of a class. To the left of each member name is an icon that depicts the type of member. The icons and their types include the following:

Icon	Meaning
	C# keyword
	method (discussed in Chapter 3)
	property (discussed in Chapter 14)
	class (discussed in Chapter 7)
	struct (discussed in Chapter 9)
	enum (discussed in Chapter 9)
	interface (discussed in Chapter 12)
	delegate (discussed in Chapter 16)
{}	Namespace

Note You will frequently see lines of code containing two forward slashes followed by ordinary text. These are comments. They are ignored by the compiler, but are very useful for developers because they help document what a program is actually doing. For example:

```
Console.ReadLine(); // Wait for the user to press the Enter key
```

All text from the two slashes to the end of the line will be skipped by the compiler. You can also add multi-line comments starting with /*. The compiler will skip everything until it finds a */ sequence, which could be many lines lower down. You are actively encouraged to document your code with as many comments as necessary.

Build and run the console application

1. On the Build menu, click Build Solution. This action causes the C# code to be compiled, resulting in a program that you can run. The Output windows appears below the Code and Text Editor window.

> **Tip**   If the Output window does not appear, click the View menu, and then click Output
> to display it.

In the Output window, messages similar to the following show how the program is
being compiled and display the details of any errors that have occurred. In this case
there should be no errors or warnings, and the program should build successfully:

```
------ Build started: Project: TextHello, Configuration: Debug Any CPU ----
Csc.exe /config /nowarn:"1701;1702" /errorreport: prompt /warn:4 …

Compile complete -- 0 errors, 0 warnings

TextHello -> C:\Documents and Settings\John\My Documents\Microsoft Press\…
============ Build: 1 succeeded or up-to-date, 0 failed, 0 skipped ========
```

> **Note**   An asterisk after the file name in the tab above the Code and Text Editor window
> indicates that the file has been changed since it was last saved. There is no need to man-
> ually save the file before building because the Build Solution command automatically
> saves the file.

   2.   On the Debug menu, click Start Without Debugging. A Command window opens and
        the program runs. The message *Hello World* appears, and then the program waits for the
        user to press any key, as shown in the following graphic:

   3.   Ensure that the Command window displaying the program has the focus, and then
        press Enter. The Command window closes and you return to the Visual Studio 2005
        programming environment.

> **Note**   If you run the program using Start Debugging on the Debug menu, the appli-
> cation runs but the Command window closes immediately without waiting for you to
> press a key.

4. In the Solution Explorer, click the TextHello project (not the solution), and then click Show All Files button. Entries named *bin* and *obj* appear above the C# source filenames. These entries correspond directly to folders named bin and obj in the project folder (\My Documents\Microsoft Press\Visual CSharp Step by Step\Chapter 1\TextHello\TextHello). These folders are created when you build your application, and they contain the executable version of the program and some other files.

5. In the Solution Explorer, click the + to the left of the bin entry. Another folder named Debug appears.

6. In the Solution Explorer, click the + to the left of the Debug entry. Three entries named TextHello.exe, TextHello.pdb, and TextHello.vshost.exe appear. The file TextHello.exe is the compiled program, and it is this file that runs when you click Start Without Debugging in the Debug menu. The other two files contain information that is used by Visual Studio 2005 if you run your program in Debug mode (when you click Start Debugging in the Debug menu).

Command Line Compilation

You can also compile your source files into an executable file manually by using the csc command-line C# compiler. You must first complete the following steps to set up your environment:

1. On the Windows Start menu, point to All Programs, point to Microsoft Visual Studio 2005, point to Visual Studio Tools, and click Visual Studio 2005 Command Prompt. A Command window opens, and the envionment variables *PATH*, *LIB*, and *INCLUDE* are configured to include the locations of the various .NET Framework libraries and utilities.

> **Tip**   You can also run the vcvarsall.bat script, located in the C:\Program Files\Microsoft Visual Studio 8\VC folder, if you want to configure the environment variables while running in an ordinary Command Prompt window.

2. In the Visual Studio 2005 Command Prompt window, type the following command to go to the \My Documents\Microsoft Press\Visual CSharp Step by Step\Chapter 1\TextHello\TextHello project folder:

   ```
   cd \Documents and Settings\YourName\My Documents\Microsoft Press\Visual CSharp
   Step by Step\Chapter 1\TextHello\TextHello
   ```

3. Type the following command:

   ```
   csc /out:TextHello.exe Program.cs
   ```

   This command creates the executable file TextHello.exe from the C# source file. If you don't use the */out* command-line option, the executable file takes its name from the source file and is called Program.exe.

4. Run the program by typing the following command:

   ```
   TextHello
   ```

   The program should run exactly as before, except that you will not see the "Press any key to continue" prompt.

Using Namespaces

The example you have seen so far is a very small program. However, small programs can soon grow into bigger programs. As a program grows, it creates two problems. First, more code is harder to understand and maintain than less code. Second, more code usually means more names; more named data, more named methods, and more named classes. As the number of names increases so does the likelihood of the project build failing because two or more names clash (especially when the program uses third-party libraries).

In the past, programmers tried to solve the name-clashing problem by prefixing names with some sort of qualifier (or set of qualifiers). This solution is not a good one because it's not scalable; names become longer and you spend less time writing software and more time typing (there is a difference) and reading and re-reading incomprehensibly long names.

Namespaces help solve this problem by creating a named container for other identifiers, such as classes. Two classes with the same name will not be confused with each other if they live in different namespaces. You can create a class named *Greeting* inside the namespace named *TextHello*, like this:

```
namespace TextHello
{
    class Greeting
    {
        ...
    }
}
```

You can then refer to the *Greeting* class as *TextHello.Greeting* in your own programs. If someone else also creates a *Greeting* class in a different namespace and installs it on your computer, your programs will still work as expected because they are using the *TextHello.Greeting* class. If you want to refer the new *Greeting* class, you must specify that you want the class from the new namespace.

It is good practice to define all your classes in namespaces, and the Visual Studio 2005 environment follows this recommendation by using the name of your project as the top-level namespace. The .NET Framework Software Developer Kit (SDK) also adheres to this recommendation; every class in the .NET Framework lives inside a namespace. For example, the *Console* class lives inside the *System* namespace. This means that its fully qualified name is actually *System.Console*.

Of course, if you had to write the fully qualified name of a class every time, it would be no better that just naming the class *SystemConsole*. Fortunately, you can solve this problem with a *using* directive. If you return to the TextHello program in Visual Studio 2005 and look at the file Program.cs in the Code and Text Editor window, you will notice the following statements:

```
using System;
using System.Collections.Generic;
using System.Text;
```

The *using* statement brings a namespace into scope, and you no longer have to explictly qualify objects with the namespace they belong to in the code that follows. The three namespaces shown contain classes that are used so often that Visual Studio 2005 automatically adds these *using* statements every time you create a new project. You can add further *using* directives to the top of a source file.

The following exercise demonstrates the concept of namespaces further.

Try longhand names

1. In the Code And Text Editor window, comment out the *using* directive at the top of Program.cs:

    ```
    //using System;
    ```

2. On the Build menu, click Build Solution. The build fails, and the Output pane displays the following error message twice (once for each use of the *Console* class):

    ```
    The name 'Console' does not exist in the current context.
    ```

3. In the Output pane, double-click the error message. The identifier that caused the error is selected in the Program.cs source file.

> **Tip** The first error can affect the reliability of subsequent diagnostic messages. If your build has more than one diagnostic message, correct only the first one, ignore all the others, and then rebuild. This strategy works best if you keep your source files small and work iteratively, building frequently.

4. In the Code and Text Editor window, edit the *Main* method to use the fully qualified name *System.Console*.

   Main should look like this:

   ```
   static void Main(string[] args)
   {
       System.Console.WriteLine("Hello World");
   }
   ```

> **Note** When you type *System.*, notice how the names of all the items in the *System* namespace are displayed by IntelliSense.

5. On the Build menu, click Build Solution. The build succeeds this time. If it doesn't, make sure *Main* is *exactly* as it appears in the preceding code, and then try building again.

6. Run the application to make sure it still works by clicking Start Without Debugging on the Debug menu.

In the Solution Explorer, click the + to the left of the References entry. This displays the assemblies referenced by the Solution Explorer. An assembly is a library containing code written by other developers (such as the .NET Framework). In some cases, the classes in a namespace are stored in an assembly that has the same name (such as *System*), although this does not have to be the case—some assemblies hold more than one namespace. Whenever you use a namespace, you also need to make sure that you have referenced the assembly that contains the classes for that namespace; otherwise your program will not build (or run).

Creating a Windows Forms Application

So far you have used Visual Studio 2005 to create and run a basic Console application. The Visual Studio 2005 programming environment also contains everything you'll need to create graphical Windows applications. You can design the form-based user interface of a Windows application interactively by using the Visual Designer. Visual Studio 2005 then generates the program statements to implement the user interface you've designed.

From this explanation, it follows that Visual Studio 2005 allows you to maintain two views of the application: the Design View and the Code View. The Code and Text Editor window (showing the program statements) doubles as the Design View window (allowing you to lay out your user interface), and you can switch between the two views whenever you want.

In the following set of exercises, you'll learn how to create a Windows program in Visual Studio 2005. This program will display a simple form containing a text box where you can enter your name and a button that, when clicked, displays a personalized greeting in a message box. You will use the Visual Designer to create your user interface by placing controls on a form; inspect the code generated by Visual Studio 2005; use the Visual Designer to change the control properties; use the Visual Designer to resize the form; write the code to respond to a button click; and run your first Windows program.

Create a Windows project in Visual Studio 2005

1. On the File menu, point to New, and then click Project. The New Project dialog box opens.

2. In the Project Types pane, click Visual C#.

3. In the Templates pane, click the Windows Application icon.

4. Ensure that the Location field refers to your **\My Documents\Microsoft Press\Visual CSharp Step by Step\Chapter 1** folder.

5. In the Name field, type **WinFormHello**.

6. In the Solutions field, ensure that **Create new Solution** is selected. This action creates a new solution for holding the Windows application. The alternative, **Add to Solution**, will add the project to the TextHello solution.

7. Click OK. Visual Studio 2005 closes your current application (prompting you to save it first of necessary) and creates and displays an empty Windows form in the Design View window.

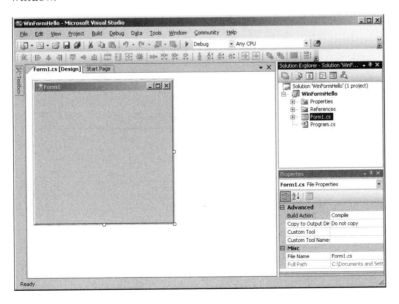

In the following exercise, you'll use the Visual Designer to add three controls to the Windows form and examine some of the C# code automatically generated by Visual Studio 2005 to implement these controls.

Create the user interface

1. Click the Toolbox tab that appears to the left of the form in the Design View. The Toolbox appears, partially obscuring the form and displaying the various components and controls that you can place on a Windows form.

2. In the Toolbox, click the + sign by Common Controls to display a list of controls that are used by most Windows Forms applications.

3. Click Label, and then click the visible part of the form. A *Label* control is added to the form, and the Toolbox disappears from view.

> **Tip**   If you want the Toolbox to remain visible but not hide any part of the form, click the Auto Hide button to the right in Toolbox title bar (it looks like a pin). The Toolbox appears permanently on the left side of the Visual Studio 2005 window, and the Design View shrinks to accommodate it. (You might lose a lot of space if you have a low-resolution screen.) Clicking the Auto Hide button once more causes the Toolbox to disappear again.

4. The *Label* control on the form is probably not exactly where you want it. You can click and drag the controls you have added to a form to reposition them. Using this technique, move the *Label* control so that it is positioned towards the upper-left corner of the form. (The exact placement is not critical for this application.)

5. On the View menu, click Properties Window. The Properties window appears on the right side of the screen. The Properties window allows you to set the properties for items in a project. It is context sensitive, in that it displays the properties for the currently selected item. If you click anywhere on the form displayed in the Design View, you will see that the Properties windows displays the properties for the form itself. If you click the *Label* control, the window displays the properties for the label instead.

6. Click the *Label* control on the form. In the Properties window, locate the *Text* property, change it from **label1** to **Enter your name**, and then press Enter. On the form, the label's text changes to *Enter Your Name*.

> **Tip**   By default, the properties are displayed in categories. If you prefer to display the properties in alphabetical order, click the Alphabetical button that appears above the properties list.

7. Display the Toolbox again. Click TextBox, and then click the form. A *TextBox* control is added to the form. Move the *TextBox* control so that it is directly underneath the *Label* control.

> **Tip**   When you drag a control on a form, alignment handles appear automatically when the control becomes aligned vertically or horizontally with other controls. This give you a quick visual cue for making sure that controls are lined up neatly.

8. While the *TextBox* control is selected, locate the *Text* property in the Properties window, type **here**, and then press Enter. On the form, the word *here* appears in the text box.

9. In the Properties window, find the *(Name)* property. Visual Studio 2005 gives controls and forms default names, which, although they are a good starting point, are not always very meaningful. Change the name of the *TextBox* control to **userName**.

> **Note**   We will talk more about naming conventions for controls and variables in Chapter 2, "Working with Variables, Operators, and Expressions."

10. Display the Toolbox again, click Button, and then click the form. Drag the *Button* control to the right of the *TextBox* control on the form so that it is aligned horizontally with the text box.

11. Using the Properties window, change the *Text* property of the *Button* control to **OK**. Change its *(Name)* property to **ok**. The caption on the button changes.

12. Click the Form1 form in the Design View window. Notice that resize handles (small squares) appear on the lower edge, the right-hand edge, and the right-hand bottom corner of the form.

13. Move the mouse pointer over the resize handle. The pointer changes to a diagonal double-headed arrow.

14. Hold down the left mouse button, and drag the pointer to resize the form. Stop dragging and release the mouse button when the spacing around the controls is roughly equal.

> **Tip**   You can resize many controls on a form by selecting the control and dragging one of the resize handles that appears in the corners of the control. Note that a form has only one resize handle, whereas most controls have four (one on each corner). On a form, any resize handles other than the one in the lower-right corner would be superfluous. Also note that some controls, such as *Label* controls, are automatically sized based on their contents and cannot be resized by dragging them.

The form should now look similar to the one in the following graphic.

15. In the Solution Explorer, right-click the file Form1.cs, and then click View Code. The Form1.cs source file appears in the Code and Text Editor window.

    There are now two tabs named Form1.cs above the Code and Text Editor/Design View window. You can click the one suffixed with [Design] to return to Design View window at any time.

    Form1.cs contains some of the code automatically generated by Visual Studio 2005. You should note the following elements:

■ *using* **directives**   Visual Studio 2005 has written a number of *using* directives at the top of the source file (more than for the previous example). For example:

```
using System.Windows.Forms;
```

The additional namespaces contain the classes and controls used when building graphical applications—for example, the *TextBox*, *Label*, and *Button* classes.

■ **The namespace**   Visual Studio 2005 has used the name of the project as the name of the top-level namespace:

```
namespace WinFormHello
{
    ...
}
```

■ **A class**   Visual Studio 2005 has written a class called *Form1* inside the *WinForm Hello* namespace:

```
namespace WinFormHello
{
    partial class Form1 ...
    {
        ...
    }
}
```

> **Note**   For the time being, ignore the partial keyword in this class. I will describe its purpose shortly.

This class implements the form you created in the Design View. (Classes are discussed in Chapter 7.)

There does not appear to be much else in this class—there is a little bit of code known as a *constructor* that calls a method called *InitializeComponent*, but nothing else. (A constructor is a special method with the same name as the class. It is executed when the form is created and can contain code to initialize the form. Constructors are also discussed in Chapter 7.) However, Visual Studio 2005 is performing a sleight of hand and is hiding a few things from you, as I will now demonstrate.

In a Windows Forms application, Visual Studio 2005 actually generates a potentially large amount of code. This code performs operations such as creating and displaying the form when the application starts, and creating and positioning the various controls on the form. However, this code can change as you add controls to a form and change their properties. You are not expected to change this code (indeed, any changes you make are likely to be overwritten the next time you edit the form in the Design View), so Visual Studio 2005 hides it from you.

To display the hidden code, return to the Solution Explorer, and click the Show All Files button. The bin and obj folders appear, much as they did with the Console application you developed in the first part of this chapter. However, notice that Form1.cs now has a + sign next to it. If you click this + sign, you see a file called Form1.Designer.cs, and a file called Form1.resx.

Double-click the file Form1.Designer.cs to display its contents in the Code and Text Editor window. You will see the remaining code for the Form1 class in this file. C# allows you to split the code for a class across multiple source files, as long as each part of the class is marked with the partial keyword. This file includes a region labelled *Windows Form Designer generated code*. Expanding this region by clicking the + sign reveals the code created and maintained by Visual Studio 2005 when you edit a form using the Design View window. The actual contents of this file include:

■ **The *InitializeComponent* method**   This method is mentioned in the file Form1.cs. The statements inside this method set the properties of the controls you added to the form in the Design View. (Methods are discussed in Chapter 3.) Some of the statements in this method that correspond to the actions you performed using the Properties window are shown below:

```
...
private void InitializeComponent()
{
    this.label1 = new System.Windows.Forms.Label();
    this.userName = new System.Windows.Forms.TextBox();
    this.ok = new System.Windows.Forms.Button();
    ...
    this.label1.Text = "Enter your name";
    ...
    this.userName.Text = "here";
```

```
        . . .
        this.ok.Text = "OK";
        . . .
    }
    . . .
```

- **Three fields**   Visual Studio 2005 has created three fields inside the *Form1* class. These
  fields appear near the end of the file:

```
private System.Windows.Forms.Label label1;
private System.Windows.Forms.TextBox userName;
private System.Windows.Forms.Button ok;
. . .
```

These fields implement the three controls you added to the form in Design View. (Fields
are discussed in Chapter 7.)

It is worth restating that although this file is interesting to look at, you should never edit its
contents yourself. Visual Studio 2005 automatically updates this file when you make changes
in the Design View. Any code that you need to write yourself should be placed in the Form1.cs
file.

At this point you might well be wondering where the *Main* method is and how the form gets
displayed when the application runs; remember that *Main* defines the point at which the program starts. In the Solution Explorer, you should notice another source file called Program.cs.
If you double-click this file the following code appears in the Code and Text Editor window:

```
namespace WinFormHello
{
    static class Program
    {
        /// <summary>
        /// The main entry point for the application.
        /// </summary>
        [STAThread]
        static void Main()
        {
            Application.EnableVisualStyles();
            Application.Run(new Form1());
        }
    }
}
```

You can ignore most of this code. However, the key statement is:

```
Application.Run(new Form1());
```

This statement creates the form and displays it, whereupon the form takes over.

In the following exercise, you'll learn how to add code that runs when the OK button on the
form is clicked.

Write the code for the OK button

1. Click the Form1.cs[Design] tab above the Code and Text Editor window to display Form1 in the Design View.

2. Move the mouse pointer over the OK button on the form, and then double-click the button. The Form1.cs source file appears in the Code and Text Editor window. Visual Studio 2005 has added a method called *ok_Click* to the *Form1* class. (It has also added a statement to the *InitializeComponent* method in the Form1.Designer.cs file to automatically call *ok_Click* when the OK button is clicked. It does this by using a *delegate* type; *delegates* are discussed in Chapter 16, "Delegates and Events.")

3. Type the *MessageBox* statement shown below inside the *ok_Click* method. The complete method should look like this:

```
private void ok_Click(object sender, System.EventArgs e)
{
    MessageBox.Show("Hello " + userName.Text);
}
```

Make sure you have typed this code exactly as shown, including the trailing semicolon.

You're now ready to run your first Windows program.

Run the Windows program

1. On the Debug menu, click Start Without Debugging. Visual Studio 2005 saves your work, compiles your program, and runs it. The Windows form appears:

2. Enter your name, and then click OK. A message box appears welcoming you by name.

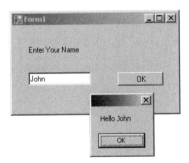

3. Click OK in the message box. The message box closes.

4. In the Form1 window, click the Close button (the X in the upper-right corner of the form). The Form1 window closes.

■ **If you want to continue to the next chapter**

   Keep Visual Studio 2005 running, and turn to Chapter 2.

■ **If you want to exit Visual Studio 2005 now**

   On the File menu, click Exit. If you see a Save dialog box, click Yes to save your work.

Chapter 1 Quick Reference

To	Do this	Key combination
Create a new console application	On the File menu, point to New, and then click Project to open the New Project dialog box. For the project type, select Visual C#. For the template, select Console Application. Select a directory for the project files in the Location box. Choose a name for the project. Click OK.	
Create a new Windows application	On the File menu, point to New, and then click Project to open the New Project dialog box. For the project type, select Visual C#. For the template, select Windows Application. Select a directory for the project files in the location box. Choose a name for the project. Click OK.	
Build the application	On the Build menu, click Build Solution.	F6
Run the application	On the Debug menu, click Start Without Debugging.	Ctrl+F5

Chapter 2

Working with Variables, Operators, and Expressions

After completing this chapter, you will be able to:

- Understand statements, identifiers, and keywords.
- Use variables to store information.
- Work with primitive data types.
- Use arithmetic operators such as the plus sign (+) and the minus sign (–).
- Increment and decrement variables.

In Chapter 1, "Welcome to C#," you learned how to use the Microsoft Visual Studio 2005 programming environment to build and run a console program and a Windows Forms application. In this chapter, you'll be introduced to the elements of Microsoft Visual C# syntax and semantics, including statements, keywords, and identifiers. You'll study the primitive types that are built into the C# language and the characteristics of the values that each type holds. You'll also see how to declare and use local variables (variables that exist only within a function or other small section of code), learn about the arithmetic operators that C# provides, learn how to use operators to manipulate values, and learn how to control expressions containing two or more operators.

Understanding Statements

A *statement* is a command that performs an action. Statements are found inside methods. You'll learn more about methods in Chapter 3, "Writing Methods and Applying Scope," but for now, think of a method as a named sequence of statements inside a class. *Main*, which was introduced in the previous chapter, is an example of a method. Statements in C# must follow a well-defined set of rules. These rules are collectively known as *syntax*. (In contrast, the specification of what statements *do* is collectively known as *semantics*.) One of the simplest and most important C# syntax rules states that you must terminate all statements with a semicolon. For example, without its terminating semicolon, the following statement won't compile:

```
Console.WriteLine("Hello World");
```

> **Tip**   C# is a "free format" language, which means that white space, such as a space character or a new line, is not significant except as a separator. In other words, you are free to lay out your statements in any style you choose. A simple, consistent layout style makes a program easier to read and understand.

The trick to programming well in any language is learning its syntax and semantics and then using the language in a natural and idiomatic way. This approach makes your programs readable and easy to modify. In the chapters throughout this book, you'll see examples of the most important C# statements.

Using Identifiers

Identifiers are the names you use to identify the elements in your programs. In C#, you must adhere to the following syntax rules when choosing identifiers:

- You can use only letters (uppercase and lowercase), digits, and underscore characters.
- An identifier must start with a letter (an underscore is considered a letter).

For example, *result*, *_score*, *footballTeam*, and *plan9* are all valid identifiers, whereas *result%*, *footballTeam$*, and *9plan* are not.

> **Important**   C# is a case-sensitive language: *footballTeam* and *FootballTeam* are not the same identifier.

Identifying Keywords

The C# language reserves 77 identifiers for its own use, and you should not reuse these identifiers for your own purposes. These identifiers are called *keywords*, and each has a particular meaning. Examples of keywords are *class*, *namespace*, and *using*. You'll learn the meaning of most of the keywords as you proceed through this book. The keywords are listed in the following table.

abstract	as	base	bool
break	byte	case	catch
char	checked	class	const
continue	decimal	default	delegate
do	double	else	enum
event	explicit	extern	false
finally	fixed	float	for
foreach	goto	if	implicit

in	int	interface	internal
is	lock	long	namespace
new	null	object	operator
out	override	params	private
protected	public	readonly	ref
return	sbyte	sealed	short
sizeof	stackalloc	static	string
struct	switch	this	throw
true	try	typeof	uint
ulong	unchecked	unsafe	ushort
using	virtual	void	volatile
while			

Tip   In the Visual Studio 2005 Code and Text Editor window, keywords are colored blue when you type them.

Using Variables

A *variable* is a storage location that holds a value. You can think of a variable as a box holding temporary information. You must give each variable in a program a unique name. You use a variable's name to refer to the value it holds. For example, if you want to store the value of the cost of an item in a store, you might create a variable simply called *cost*, and store the item's cost in this variable. Later on, if you refer to the *cost* variable, the value retrieved will be the item's cost that you put there earlier.

Naming Variables

You should adopt a naming convention for variables that help you avoid confusion concerning the variables you have defined. The following list contains some general recommendations:

■ Don't use underscores.

■ Don't create identifiers that differ only by case. For example, do not create one variable named *myVariable* and another named *MyVariable* for use at the same time, because it is too easy to get them confused.

Note   Using identifiers that differ only by case can limit the ability to reuse classes in applications developed using other languages that are not case sensitive, such as Visual Basic.

■ Start the name with a lowercase letter.

- In a multiword identifier, start the second and each subsequent word with an uppercase letter. (This is called *camelCase* notation.)

- Don't use Hungarian notation. (Microsoft Visual C++ developers reading this book are probably familiar with Hungarian notation. If you don't know what Hungarian notation is, don't worry about it!)

> **Important**   You should treat the first two recommendations as compulsory because they relate to Common Language Specification (CLS) compliance. If you want to write programs that can interoperate with other languages, such as Microsoft Visual Basic .NET, you need to comply with these recommendations.

For example, *score*, *footballTeam*, *_score*, and *FootballTeam* are all valid variable names, but only the first two are recommended.

Declaring Variables

Remember that variables are like boxes in memory that can hold a value. C# has many different types of values that it can store and process—integers, floating-point numbers, and strings of characters, to name three. When you declare a variable, you must specify what type of data it will hold.

> **Note**   Microsoft Visual Basic programmers should note that C# does not allow implicit declarations. You must explicitly declare all variables before you can use them if you want your code to compile.

You declare the type and name of a variable in a declaration statement. For example, the following statement declares that the variable named *age* holds *int* (integer) values. As always, the statement must be terminated with a semi-colon.

```
int age;
```

The variable type *int* is the name of one of the *primitive* C# types—*integer* which is a whole number. (You'll learn about several primitive data types later in this chapter.) After you've declared your variable, you can assign it a value. The following statement assigns *age* the value 42. Again, you'll see that the semicolon is required.

```
age = 42;
```

The equal sign (=) is the *assignment* operator, which assigns the value on its right to the variable on its left. After this assignment, the *age* variable can be used in your code to refer to the value it holds. The next statement writes the value of the *age* variable, 42, to the console:

```
Console.WriteLine(age);
```

> **Tip** If you leave the mouse pointer over a variable in the Visual Studio 2005 Code and Text Editor window, a ToolTip appears telling you the type of the variable.

Working with Primitive Data Types

C# has a number of built-in types called *primitive data types*. The following table lists the most commonly used primitive data types in C#, and the ranges of values that you can store in them.

Data type	Description	Size (bits)	*Range	Sample usage
int	Whole numbers	32	$<->2^{31}$ through $2^{31}<->1$	`int count;` `count = 42;`
long	Whole numbers (bigger range)	64	$<->2^{63}$ through $2^{63}<->1$	`long wait;` `wait = 42L;`
float	Floating-point numbers	32	$\pm3.4 \times 10^{38}$	`float away;` `away = 0.42F;`
double	Double precision (more accurate) floating-point numbers	64	$\pm1.7 \times 10^{308}$	`double trouble;` `trouble = 0.42;`
decimal	Monetary values	128	28 significant figures	`decimal coin;` `coin = 0.42M;`
string	Sequence of characters	16 bits per character	Not applicable	`string vest;` `vest = "42";`
char	Single character	16	0 through $2^{16}<->1$	`char grill;` `grill = '4';`
bool	Boolean	8	*true* or *false*	`bool teeth;` `teeth = false;`

* The value of 2^{16} is 65,536; the value of 2^{31} is 2,147,483,648; and the value of 2^{63} is 9,223,372,036,854,775,808.

Unassigned Local Variables

When you declare a variable, it contains a random value until you assign a value to it. This behavior was a rich source of bugs in C and C++ programs that created a variable and used it as a source of information before giving it a value. C# does not allow you to use an unassigned variable. You must assign a value to a variable before you can use it, otherwise your program will not compile. This requirement is called the *Definite Assignment Rule*. For example, the following statements will generate a compile-time error because *age* is unassigned:

```
int age;
Console.WriteLine(age); // compile time error
```

Displaying Primitive Data Type Values

In the following exercise, you'll use a C# program named *PrimitiveDataTypes* to demonstrate how several primitive data types work.

Display primitive data type values

1. Start Visual Studio 2005.

2. On the File menu, point to Open, and then click Project/Solution.

   The Open Project dialog box appears.

3. Move to the \Microsoft Press\Visual CSharp Step by Step\Chapter 2\Primitive-DataTypes folder in your My Documents folder. Select the file PrimitiveDataTypes.sln and then click Open.

   The solution loads, and the Solution Explorer displays the solution and Primitive-DataTypes project.

> **Note**   Solution file names have the .sln suffix, such as PrimitiveDataTypes.sln. A solution can contain one or more projects. Project files have the .csproj suffix. If you open a project rather than a solution, Visual Studio 2005 will automatically create a new solution file for it. If you build the solution, Visual Studio 2005 automatically saves any updated or new files, and you will be prompted to provide a name and location for the new solution file.

4. On the Debug menu, click Start Without Debugging.

   The following application window appears:

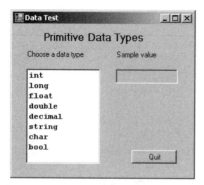

5. In the Choose A Data type list, click the *string* type.

   The value 42 appears in the Sample value box.

6. Click the *int* type in the list.

The value *to do* appears in the Sample value box, indicating that the statements to display an *int* value still need to be written.

7. Click each data type in the list. Confirm that the code for the *double* and *bool* types also needs to be completed.

8. Click Quit to close the window and stop the program.

Control returns to the Visual Studio 2005 programming environment.

Use primitive data types in code

1. Right-click the Form1.cs file in the Solution Explorer and then click View Code.

    The Code and Text Editor window opens displaying the Form1.cs file.

2. In the Code and Text Editor window, find the *showFloatValue* method listed here:

```
private void showFloatValue()
{
    float var;
    var = 0.42F;
    value.Text = "0.42F";
}
```

> **Tip**   To locate an item in your project, point to Find And Replace on the Edit menu and click Quick Find. A dialog box opens asking what you want to search for. Type the name of the item you're looking for, and then click Find Next. By default, the search is not case-sensitive. If you want to perform a case-sensitive search, click the + button next to the Find Options label to display additional options, and check the Match Case check box. If you have time, you can experiment with the other options as well.
>
> You can also press Ctrl+F (press the Control key, and then press F) to display the Quick Find dialog box rather then using the Edit menu. Similarly, you can press Ctrl+H to display the Quick Find and Replace dialog box.

The *showFloatValue* method runs when you click the *float* type in the list box. This method contains three statements:

■ The first statement declares a variable named *var* of type *float.*

■ The second statement assigns *var* the value 0.42F. (The *F* is a type suffix specifying that 0.42 should be treated as a *float* value. If you forget the *F*, the value 0.42 will be treated as a *double*, and your program will not compile because you cannot assign a value of one type to a variable of a different type in this way.)

■ The third statement displays the value of this variable in the *value* TextBox on the form. This statement requires a little bit of your attention. The way in which you display an item in a TextBox is to set its *Text* property. You did this at design time in Chapter 1 using the Properties window. This statement shows you how to perform the same task programmatically, using the expression *value.Text*. The data that you put in the *Text* property must be a string (a sequence of characters), and not a number. If you try and assign a number to the *Text* property your program will not compile. For this reason, the statement simply displays the text "0.42F" in the TextBox (anything in double-quotes is text, otherwise known as a *string*). In a real-world application, you would add statements that convert the value of the variable *var* into a string and then put this into the *Text* property, but you need to know a little bit more about C# and the .NET Framework before we can do that (we will cover data type conversions in Chapter 11, "Understanding Parameter Arrays," and Chapter 19, "Operator Overloading").

3. In the Code and Text Editor window, locate the *showIntValue* method listed here:

```
private void showIntValue()
{
    value.Text = "to do";
}
```

The *showIntValue* method is called when you click the *int* type in the list box.

> **Tip**   Another way to find a method in the Code and Text Editor window is to click the Members list that appears above the window, to the right. This window displays a list of all the methods (and other items). You can click the name of a member, and you will be taken directly to it in the Code and Text Editor window.

4. Type the following two statements at the start of the *showIntValue* method, after the open curly brace:

```
int var;
var = 42;
```

The *showIntValue* method should now look like this:

```
private void showIntValue()
{
    int var;
    var = 42;
    value.Text = "to do";
}
```

5. On the Build menu, click Build Solution.

The build will display some warnings, but no errors. You can ignore the warnings for now.

6. In the original statement, change the string "*to do*" to "*42*".

The method should now look exactly like this:

```
private void showIntValue()
{
    int var;
    var = 42;
    value.Text = "42";
}
```

7. On the Debug menu, click Start Without Debugging.

   The form appears again.

> **Tip** If you have edited the source code since the last build, the Start Without Debugging command automatically rebuilds the program before starting the application.

8. Select the *int* type in the list box. Confirm that the value 42 is displayed in the Sample value text box.

9. Click Quit to close the window and stop the program.

10. In the Code and Text Editor window, find the *showDoubleValue* method.

11. Edit the *showDoubleValue* method exactly as follows:

```
private void showDoubleValue()
{
    double var;
    var = 0.42;
    value.Text = "0.42";
}
```

12. In the Code and Text Editor window, locate the *showBoolValue* method.

13. Edit the *showBoolValue* method exactly as follows:

```
private void showBoolValue()
{
    bool var;
    var = false;
    value.Text = "false";
}
```

14. On the Debug menu, click Start Without Debugging.

    The form appears.

15. In the list, select the *int*, *double*, and *bool* types. In each case, verify that the correct value is displayed in the Sample value text box.

16. Click Quit to stop the program.

Using Arithmetic Operators

C# supports the regular arithmetic operations you learned in your childhood: the plus sign (+) for addition, the minus sign (−) for subtraction, the asterisk (*) for multiplication, and the forward slash (/) for division. These symbols (+, −, *, and /) are called *operators* as they "operate" on values to create new values. In the following example, the variable *moneyPaidTo Consultant* ends up holding the product of 750 (the daily rate) and 20 (the number of days the consultant was employed):

```
long moneyPaidToConsultant;
moneyPaidToConsultant = 750 * 20;
```

> **Note**   The values that an operator operates on are called *operands*. In the expression 750 * 20, the * is the operator, and 750 and 20 are the operands.

Determining an Operator's Values

Not all operators are applicable to all data types, so whether you can use an operator on a value depends on the value's type. For example, you can use all the arithmetic operators on values of type *char*, *int*, *long*, *float*, *double*, or *decimal*. However, with one exception, you can't use the arithmetic operators on values of type *string* or *bool*. So the following statement is not allowed because the *string* type does not support the minus operator (subtracting one string from another would be meaningless):

```
// compile time error
Console.WriteLine("Gillingham" - "Manchester City");
```

The exception is that the + operator can be used to concatenate string values. The following statement writes 431 (not 44) to the console:

```
Console.WriteLine("43" + "1");
```

> **Tip**   You can use the method *Int32.Parse* to convert a string value to an integer if you need to perform arithmetic computations on values held as strings.

You should also be aware that the type of the result of an arithmetic operation depends on the type of the operands used. For example, the value of the expression 5.0 / 2.0 is 2.5; the type of both operands is *double* (in C#, literal numbers with decimal points are always *double*, not *float*, in order to maintain as much accuracy as possible), and so the type of the result is also *double*. However, the value of the expression 5 / 2 is 2. In this case, the type of both operands is *int*, and so the type of the result is also *int*. C# always rounds values down in circumstances like this. The situation gets a little more complicated if you mix the types of the operands. For example, the expression 5 / 2.0 consists of an *int* and a *double*. The C# compiler detects the mismatch and generates code that converts the *int* into a *double* before performing the operation. The result of the operation is therefore a *double* (2.5). However, although this works, it is considered poor practice to mix types in this way.

C# also supports one less-familiar arithmetic operator: the remainder, or modulus, operator, which is represented by the percent symbol (%). The result of *x* % *y* is the remainder after dividing *x* by *y*. For example, 9 % 2 is 1 since 9 divided by 2 is 8, remainder 1.

> **Note** In C and C++, you can't use the % operator on floating-point values, but you can use it in C#.

Examining Arithmetic Operators

The following exercise demonstrates how to use the arithmetic operators on *int* values using a previously written C# program named *MathsOperators*.

Work with arithmetic operators

1. On the File menu, point to Open, and then click Project/Solution. Open the *MathsOperators* project, located in the \Microsoft Press\Visual CSharp Step by Step\Chapter 2\MathsOperators folder in your My Documents folder.

2. On the Debug menu, click Start Without Debugging.

   A form appears on the screen.

3. Type **54** in the left operand text box.

4. Type **13** in the right operand text box.

   You can now apply any of the operators to the values in the text boxes.

5. Click the − Subtraction option, and then click Calculate.

   The text in the Expression box changes to 54 − 13, and 41 appears in the Result box, as shown in the following graphic:

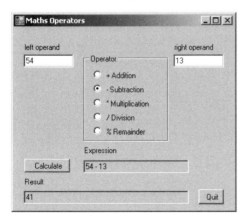

6. Click the / Division option, and then click Calculate.

The text in the Expression text box changes to 54 / 13, and the number 4 appears in the Result box. In real life, 54 / 13 is 4.153846 recurring, but this is not real life; this is C#! In C#, when you divide one integer by another integer, the answer you get back is an integer, as explained earlier.

7. Select the % Remainder option, and then click Calculate.

The text in the Expression text box changes to 54 % 13, and the number 2 appears in the Result box. This is because the remainder after dividing 54 by 13 is 2 (54 – ((54 / 13) * 13) is 2 if you do the arithmetic rounding down to an integer at each stage— my old maths master at school would be horrified to be told that (54 / 13) * 13 does not equal 54!).

8. Practice with other combinations of numbers and operators. When you're finished, click Quit.

The program stops, and you return to the Visual Studio 2005 programming environment.

Now take a look at the *MathsOperators* program code.

Examine the *MathsOperators* program code

1. Display the Form1 form in the Design View window (click the Form1.cs[Design] tab if necessary).

> **Tip**   You can quickly switch between the Design View window and the Code and Text Editor displaying the code for a form by pressing the **F7** key.

2. In the View menu, point to Other Windows and then click Document Outline.

The Document Outline window appears showing the names and types of the controls on the form. If you click each of the controls on the form, the name of the control is highlighted in the Document Outline window.

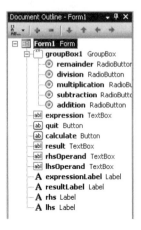

> **Important**   Be careful not to accidentally delete or change the names of any controls on the form while viewing them in the Document Outline window. The application will no longer work if you do.

3. Click the the two *TextBox* controls that the user types numbers into on the form. In the Document Outline window, verify that they are named *lhsOperand* and *rhsOperand*.

    When the form runs, the *Text* property of each of these controls holds (as strings) the numeric values you enter.

4. Towards the bottom of the form, verify that the *TextBox* control used to display the expression being evaluated is named *expression*, and that the *TextBox* control used to display the result of the calculation is named *result*.

    At runtime, setting the *Text* property of a *TextBox* control to a string value causes that value to be displayed.

5. Close the Document Outline window.

6. Press F7 to display the Form1.cs source file in the Code and Text Editor window.

7. In the Code and Text Editor window, locate the *subtractValues* method:

    ```
    private void subtractValues()
    {
        int lhs = int.Parse(lhsOperand.Text);
        int rhs = int.Parse(rhsOperand.Text);
        int outcome;
        outcome = lhs - rhs;
        expression.Text = lhsOperand.Text + " - " + rhsOperand.Text;
        result.Text = outcome.ToString();
    }
    ```

The first statement in this method declares an *int* variable called *lhs* and initializes it to the result of the explicit conversion of the *lhsOperand.Text* property to an *int*. (The *Text* property of a *TextBox* is a string, and must be converted to an integer before you can store it in an *int*. This is what the *int.Parse* method does) The second statement declares an *int* variable called *rhs* and initializes it to the result of the explicit conversion of the *rhsOperand.Text* property to an *int*. The third statement declares an *int* variable called *outcome*. The fourth statement subtracts the value of the *rhs* variable from the value of the *lhs* variable, and the result is assigned to *outcome*. The fifth statement concatenates three strings (using the + operator) and assigns the result to the *expression.Text* property. The sixth statement converts the *int* value of *outcome* to a *string* by using the *ToString* method, and assigns the string to the *result.Text* property.

The *Text* Property and the *ToString* Method

I mentioned earlier that *TextBox* controls displayed on a form have a *Text* property that allows you to access the displayed contents. For example, the expression *result.Text* refers to the contents of the *result* text box on the form. Text boxes also have many other properties, such as the location and size of the text box on the form. You will learn more about properties in Chapter 14, "Implementing Properties to Access Attributes."

Every class has a *ToString* method. The purpose of *ToString* is to convert an object into its string representation. In the previous example, the *ToString* method of the integer object, *outcome*, is used to convert the integer value of *outcome* into the equivalent string value. This conversion is necessary because the value is displayed in the *Text* property of the *result* field—the *Text* property can only contain strings. When you create your own classes, you can also define your own implementation of the *ToString* method. Methods are discussed in Chapter 3.

Controlling Precedence

Precedence governs the order in which an expression's operators are evaluated. Consider the following expression, which uses the + and * operators:

```
2 + 3 * 4
```

This expression is potentially ambiguous; does 3 bind to the + operator on its left or to the * operator on its right? The order of the operations matters because it changes the result:

- If the + operator takes precedence over the * operator, 3 binds to the + operator, the result of the addition (2 + 3) forms the left operand of the * operator, and the result of the whole expression is 5 * 4, which is 20.

- If the * operator takes precedence over the + operator, 3 binds to the * operator, the result of the multiplication (3 * 4) forms the right operand of the + operator, and the result of the whole expression is 2 + 12, which is 14.

In C#, the multiplicative operators (*, /, and %) have precedence over the additive operators (+ and −). The answer to 2 + 3 * 4 is therefore 14. As each new operator is discussed in later chapters, its precedence will be explained.

You can use parentheses to override precedence and force operands to bind to operators in a different way. For example, in the following expression, the parentheses force the 2 and the 3 to bind to the + operator (making 5), and the result of this addition forms the left operand of the * operator to produce the value 20:

```
(2 + 3) * 4
```

> **Note**   The term *parentheses* or *round brackets* refers to ( ). The term *braces* or *curly brackets* refers to { }. The term *square brackets* refers to [ ].

Using Associativity to Evaluate Expressions

Operator precedence is only half the story. What happens when an expression contains different operators that have the same precedence? This is where associativity becomes important. *Associativity* is the direction (left or right) to which an expression's operators are bound. Consider the following expression that uses the / and the * operators:

```
4 / 2 * 6
```

This expression is still potentially ambiguous. Does 2 bind to the / operator to its left or to the * operator to its right? The precedence of both operators is the same (they are both multiplicative), but the order in which the expression is evaluated is important because you get one of two possible results:

- If the 2 binds to the / operator, the result of the division (4 / 2) forms the left hand operand of the * operator, and the result of the whole expression is (4 / 2) * 6, or 12.

- If the 2 binds to the * operator, the result of the multiplication (2 * 6) forms the right hand operand of the / operator and the result of the whole expression is 4 / (2 * 6), or 4/12.

Because the * and / operators have the same precedence, you cannot use precedence to determine whether the 2 binds to the * operator or to the / operator. However, operators also have associativity to determine how they are evaluated. The * and / operators are both left-associative, which means that the operands are evaluated from left to right. In this case, 4 / 2 will be evaluated before multiplying by 6, giving the result 12. As each new operator is discussed in later chapters, its associativity will also be covered.

Incrementing and Decrementing Variables

If you wanted to add 1 to a variable, you could use the + operator:

```
count = count + 1;
```

However, it is unlikely that an experienced programmer would write code like this. Adding 1 to a variable is so common that in C#, you can do it with the ++ operator. To increment the variable *count* by 1, write the following statement:

```
count++;
```

Similarly, subtracting 1 from a variable is so common that in C# you can do it with the -- operator. To decrement the variable *count* by one, write this statement:

```
count--;
```

> **Note**   The ++ and -- operators are *unary* operators, meaning that they take only a single operand. Theyshare the same precedence and left associativity as the ! unary operator, which is discussed in Chapter 4, "Using Decision Statements."

The following table shows you how to use these two operators.

Don't write this	Write this
`variable = variable + 1;`	`variable++;`
`variable = variable - 1;`	`variable--;`

Prefix and Postfix

The increment (++) and decrement (--) operators are unusual in that you can place them either before or after the variable. Using the operator symbol before the variable is called the prefix form of the operator, and using the operator symbol after the variable is called the postfix form. Here are examples:

```
count++; // postfix increment
++count; // prefix increment
count--; // postfix decrement
--count; // prefix decrement
```

Whether you use the prefix or postfix form of the ++ or -- operator makes no difference to the variable being incremented or decremented. For example, if you write *count++*, the value of count increases by 1, and if you write *++count*, the value of count also increases by 1. Knowing this, you're probably wondering why there are two ways to write the same thing. To understand the answer, you must remember that ++ and -- are operators, and that all operators produce a value. The value produced by *count++* is the value of count before the increment takes place, whereas the value produced by *++count* is the value of count after the increment takes place. Here is an example:

```
int x;
x = 42;
Console.WriteLine(x++); // x is now 43, 42 written out
x = 42;
Console.WriteLine(++x); // x is now 43, 43 written out
```

The way to remember which operand does what is to look at the order of the elements (the operand and the operator) in a prefix or postfix expression. In the expression *x++*, the variable *x* occurs first, so its value is used as the value of the expression before *x* is incremented. In the expression ++*x*, the operator occurs first, so it is performed before the the value of *x* is evaluated as the result.

These operators are most commonly used in *while* and *do* statements, which will be presented in Chapter 5, "Using Compound Assignment and Iteration Statements." If you are using the increment and decrement operators in isolation, stick to the postfix form and be consistent.

■ **If you want to continue to the next chapter**

Keep Visual Studio 2005 running, and turn to Chapter 3.

■ **If you want to exit Visual Studio 2005 now**

On the File menu, click Exit. If you see a Save dialog box, click Yes to save your work.

Chapter 2 Quick Reference

To	Do this
Declare a variable	Write the name of the data type, followed by the name of the variable, followed by a semicolon. For example: `int outcome;`
Change the value of a variable	Write the name of the variable on the left, followed by the assignment operator, followed by the expression calculating the new value, followed by a semicolon. For example: `outcome = 42;`
Convert a *string* to an *int*	Call the *System.Int32.Parse* method. For example: `System.Int32.Parse("42");`
Override precedence	Use parentheses in the expression to force operands to bind to specific operators. For example: `(3 + 4) * 5`
Increment or decrement a variable	Use the ++ or -- operator. For example: `count++;`

Chapter 3
Writing Methods and Applying Scope

After completing this chapter, you will be able to:

- Declare and call methods.

- Pass information to a method.

- Return information from a method.

- Define local and class scope.

- Use the integrated debugger to step in and out of methods as they run.

In Chapter 2, "Working with Variables, Operators, and Expressions," you learned how to declare variables, how to create expressions using operators, and how precedence and associativity control expressions containing multiple operators. In this chapter, you'll learn about methods. You'll also learn how to use arguments and parameters to pass information to a method and how to return information from a method by using return statements. Finally, you'll see how to step in and out of methods by using the Microsoft Visual Studio 2005 integrated debugger. This information is useful when you need to trace the execution of your methods because they do not work quite as you expected.

Declaring Methods

A *method* is a named sequence of statements. If you have previously programmed using languages such as C or Visual Basic, a method is very similar to a function or a subroutine. Each method has a name and a body. The method name should be a meaningful identifier that indicates the overall purpose of the method (*CalculateIncomeTax*, for example). The method body contains the actual statements to be run when the method is called. Most methods can be given some data for processing and can return information, which is usually the result of the processing. Methods are a fundamental and powerful mechanism.

Specifying the Method Declaration Syntax

The syntax of a Microsoft Visual C# method is as follows:

```
returnType methodName ( parameterList )
{
    // method body statements go here
}
```

- The *returnType* is the name of a type and specifies what kind of information the method returns. This can be the name of any type, such as *int* or *string*. If you're writing a method that does not return a value, you must use the keyword *void* in place of the return type.

- The *methodName* is the name used to call the method. Method names must follow the same identifier rules as variable names. For example, *addValues* is a valid method name, whereas *add$Values* is not valid. For now, you should use camelCase for method names, and you should start them with a verb to make them descriptive—for example, *display-Customer*.

- The *parameterList* is optional and describes the types and names of the information that you can pass into the method. You write the parameters between the left and right parentheses as though you're declaring variables, with the name of the type followed by the name of the parameter. If the method you're writing has two or more parameters, you must separate them with commas.

- The method body statements are the lines of code that are run when the method is called. They are enclosed between opening and closing curly braces ({ }).

Important C, C++, and Microsoft Visual Basic programmers should note that C# does not support global methods. You must write all your methods inside a class, or your code will not compile.

Here's the definition of a method called *addValues* that returns an *int* result and has two *int* parameters called *leftHandSide* and *rightHandSide*:

```
int addValues(int leftHandSide, int rightHandSide)
{
    // ...
    // method body statements go here
    // ...
}
```

Here's the definition of a method called *showResult* that does not return a value and has a single *int* parameter called *answer*:

```
void showResult(int answer)
{
    // ...
}
```

Notice the use of the keyword *void* to indicate that the method does not return anything.

Important Visual Basic programmers should notice that C# does not use different keywords to distinguish between a method that returns a value (a function) and a method that does not return a value (a procedure or subroutine). You must always specify either a return type or *void*.

Writing *return* Statements

If you want a method to return information (in other words, its return type is not *void*), you must write a return statement inside the method. You do this using the keyword *return* followed by an expression that calculates the returned value and a semicolon. The type of expression must be the same as the type specified by the function. In other words, if a function returns an *int*, the return statement must return an *int*; otherwise your program will not compile. Here is an example:

```
int addValues(int leftHandSide, int rightHandSide)
{
    // ...
    return leftHandSide + rightHandSide;
}
```

The *return* statement should be at the end of your method because it causes the method to finish. Any statements after the *return* statement are not executed (though the compiler warns you about this problem if you put statements after the *return* statement).

If you don't want your method to return information (in other words, its return type is *void*), you can use a variation of the return statement to cause an immediate exit from the method. You write the keyword *return*, immediately followed by a semicolon. For example:

```
void showResult(int answer)
{
    // display the answer
    ...
    return;
}
```

If your method does not return anything, you can also omit the return statement, because the method finishes automatically when execution arrives at the closing curly brace at the end of the method. Although this practice is common, it is not always considered good style.

In the following exercise, you will examine another version of the MathsOperators application from Chapter 2. This version has been improved by the careful use of some small methods.

> **Tip**   There is no minimum size for a method. If a method helps to avoid repetition and makes your program easier to understand, the method is useful regardless of how small it is.
>
> There is also no maximum line length for a method, but usually you want to keep your method code small enough to get the job done. If your method is more than one screen in length, consider breaking it into smaller methods for readability.

Examine method definitions

1. Start Visual Studio 2005.

2. Open the *Methods* project in the \Microsoft Press\Visual CSharp Step by Step\Chapter 3\Methods folder in your My Documents folder.

3. On the Debug menu, click Start Without Debugging.

   Visual Studio 2005 builds and runs the application.

4. Re-familiarize yourself with the application and how it works, and then click Quit.

5. Display the code for Form1.cs in the Code and Text Editor window (right-click Form1.cs in the Solution Explorer and click View Code).

6. In the Code and Text Editor window, locate the *addValues* method.

   The method looks like this:

```
private int addValues(int leftHandSide, int rightHandSide)

{

    expression.Text = leftHandSide.ToString() + " + " + rightHandSide.ToString();

    return leftHandSide + rightHandSide;

}
```

   The *addValues* method contains two statements. The first statement displays the calculation being performed in the *expression* TextBox on the form. The values of the parameters *leftHandSide* and *rightHandSide* are converted into strings (using the *ToString* method you met in Chapter 2), and concatenated together with a "+" sign in the middle.

   The second statement uses the + operator to add the values of the *leftHandSide* and *rightHandSide int* variables together and returns the result of this addition. Remember that adding two *int* values together creates another *int* value, so the return type of *addValues* is *int*.

7. In the Code and Text Editor window, locate the *showResult* method.

   The *showResult* method looks like this:

```
private void showResult(int answer)

{

    result.Text = answer.ToString();

}
```

   This method contains one statement that displays a string representation of the *answer* parameter in the *result* TextBox.

Calling Methods

Methods exist to be called! You call a method by name to ask it to perform its task. If the method requires information (as specified by its parameters), you must supply the information requested. If the method returns information (as specified by its return type), you should arrange to capture this information somehow.

Specifying the Method Call Syntax

The syntax of a C# method call is as follows:

```
methodName ( argumentList )
```

- The *methodName* must exactly match the name of the method you're calling. Remember, C# is a case-sensitive language.

- The *argumentList* supplies the optional information that the method accepts. You must supply an argument for each parameter, and the value of each argument must be compatible with the type of its corresponding parameter. If the method you're calling has two or more parameters, you must separate the arguments with commas.

> **Important** You must include the parentheses in every method call, even when calling a method that has no arguments.

Here is the *addValues* method again:

```
int addValues(int leftHandSide, int rightHandSide)
{
    // ...
}
```

The *addValues* method has two *int* parameters, so you must call it with two comma-separated *int* arguments:

```
addValues(39, 3);    // okay
```

You can also replace the literal values 39 and 3 with the names of *int* variables. The values in those variables are then passed to the method as its arguments, like this:

```
int arg1 = 99;

int arg2 = 1;

addValues(arg1, arg2);
```

If you try to call *addValues* in some other way, you will probably not succeed, for the reasons described in the following examples:

```
addValues;              // compile time error, no parentheses
addValues();            // compile time error, not enough arguments
addValues(39);          // compile time error, not enough arguments
addValues("39", "3");   // compile time error, wrong types
```

The *addValues* method returns an *int* value. This *int* value can be used wherever an *int* value can be used. Consider these examples:

```
result = addValues(39, 3);      // on right hand side of an assignment
showResult(addValues(39, 3));   // as argument to another method call
```

The following exercise continues using the MathsOperators application. This time you will examine some method calls.

Examine method calls

1. Return to the Methods project. (This project is already open in Visual Studio 2005 if you're continuing from the previous exercise. If you are not, open it from the \Microsoft Press\Visual CSharp Step by Step\Chapter 3\Methods folder in your My Documents folder.

2. Display the code for Form1.cs in the Code and Text Editor window.

3. Locate the *calculate_Click* method, and look at the first two statements of this method after the *try* statement and opening curly brace. (We will cover the purpose of *try* statements in Chapter 6, "Managing Errors and Exceptions.")

   The statements are as follows:

   ```
   int leftHandSide = System.Int32.Parse(leftHandSideOperand.Text);
   int rightHandSide = System.Int32.Parse(rightHandSideOperand.Text);
   ```

   These two statements declare two *int* variables called *leftHandSide* and *rightHandSide*. However, the interesting parts are the way in which the variables are initialized. In both cases, the *Parse* method of the *System.Int32* class is called (*System* is a namespace, *Int32* is the name of the class in this namespace). This method takes a single *string* parameter and converts it to an *int* value. These two lines of code take whatever the user has typed into the *leftHandSideOperand* and *rightHandSideOperand* *TextBox* controls on the form and converts them into *int* values.

4. Look at the fourth statement in the *calculate_Click* method (after the *if* statement and another opening curly brace):

   ```
   calculatedValue = addValues(leftHandSide, rightHandSide);
   ```

This statement calls the *addValues* method, passing the values of the *leftHandSide* and *rightHandSide* variables as its arguments. The value returned by the *addValues* method is stored in the *calculatedValue* variable.

5. Look at the next statement:

```
showResult(calculatedValue);
```

This statement calls the *showResult* method, passing the value in the *calculatedValue* variable as its argument. The *showResult* method does not return a value.

6. In the Code and Text Editor window, find the *showResult* method you looked at earlier. The only statement of this method is this:

```
result.Text = answer.ToString();
```

Notice that the *ToString* method call uses parentheses even though there are no arguments.

> **Tip** You can call methods belonging to other objects by prefixing the method with the name of the object. In the previous example, the expression *answer.ToString()* calls the method named *ToString* belonging to the object called *answer*.

Applying Scope

You have seen in some of the examples that you can create a variable inside a method. The variable comes into existence at the point where a statement defines it, and subsequent statements in the same method can then use the variable. In other words, a variable can be used only after it has been created. After the method has finished, the variable disappears completely.

If a variable can be used at a particular location in a program, the variable is said to be in *scope* at that location. To put it another way, the scope of a variable is simply the region of the program in which that variable is usable. Scope applies to methods as well as variables. The scope of an identifier (of a variable or method) is linked to the location of the declaration that introduces the identifier into the program, as you'll now learn.

Defining Local Scope

The opening and closing curly braces that form the body of a method define a scope. Any variables you declare inside the body of a method are scoped to that method; they disappear when the method ends and can be accessed only by code running within that method. These variables are called *local variables* because they are local to the method in which they are declared; they are not in scope in any other method. This arrangement means that you cannot use local variables to share information between methods. Consider this example:

```
class Example
{
    void firstMethod()
    {
        int myVar;
        ...
    }
    void anotherMethod()
    {
        myVar = 42; // error - variable not in scope
        ...
    }
}
```

This code would fail to compile because *anotherMethod* is trying to use the variable *myVar* which is not in scope. The variable *myVar* is available only to statements in *firstMethod*.

Defining Class Scope

The opening and closing curly braces that form the body of a class also create a scope. Any variables you declare inside the body of a class (but not inside a method) are scoped to that class. The proper C# name for the variables defined by a class is *fields*. Unlike local variables, you can use fields to share information between methods. Here is an example:

```
class Example
{
    void firstMethod()
    {
        myField = 42; // ok
        ...
    }

    void anotherMethod()
    {
        myField = 42; // ok
        ...
    }

    int myField = 0;
}
```

The variable *myField* is defined within the class, but outside of the methods *firstMethod* and *anotherMethod*. Therefore, *myField* has class scope and is available for use by all methods in the class.

There is one other point to notice about this example. In a method, you must declare a variable before you can use it. Fields are a little different. A method can use a field before the statement that defines the field—the compiler sorts out the details for you!

Overloading Methods

If two identifiers have the same name and are declared in the same scope, they are said to be *overloaded*. Often an overloaded identifier is a bug that gets trapped as a compile-time error. For example, if you declare two local variables with the same name in the same method, you get a compile-time error. Similarly, if you declare two fields with the same name in the same class or two identical methods in the same class, you also get a compile-time error. This fact might seem hardly worth mentioning, given that everything so far has turned out to be a compile-time error. However, there is a way that you can overload an identifier, and that way is both useful and important.

Consider the *WriteLine* method of the *Console* class. You have already used this method for outputting a string to the screen. However, when you type *WriteLine* in the Code and Text Editor window when writing C# code, you will notice that IntelliSense gives you 19 different options! Each version of the *WriteLine* method takes a different set of parameters; one implementation takes no parameters and simply outputs a blank line, another implementation takes a bool parameter and outputs a string representation of its value (*true* or *false*), yet another implementation takes a decimal parameter and outputs it as a string, and so on. At compile time, the compiler looks at the types of the arguments you are passing in and then calls the version of the method that has a matching set of parameters. Here is an example:

```
static void Main()
{
    Console.WriteLine("The answer is ");
    Console.WriteLine(42);
}
```

Overloading is primarily useful when you need to perform the same operation on different data types. You can overload a method when the different implementations have different sets of parameters; that is, when they have the same name but a different number of parameters, or when the types of the parameters differ. This capability is allowed so that, when you call a method, you can supply a comma-separated list of arguments, and the number and type of the arguments is used by the compiler to select one of the overloaded methods. However, note that although you can overload the parameters of a method, you can't overload the return type of a method. In other words, you can't declare two methods with the same name that differ only in their return type. (The compiler is clever, but not that clever.)

Writing Methods

In the following exercises, you'll create an application method that calculates how much a consultant would charge for a given number of consultancy days at a fixed daily rate. You will start by developing the logic for the application and then use the Generate Method Stub Wizard to help you write the methods that are used by this logic. Next, you'll run these methods in a console application to get a feel for the program. Finally, you'll use the Visual Studio 2005 debugger to step in and out of the method calls as they run.

Develop the logic for the application

1. Using Visual Studio 2005, open the DailyRate project in the \Microsoft Press\Visual CSharp Step by Step\Chapter 3\DailyRate folder in your My Documents folder.

2. In the Solution Explorer, double-click the file Program.cs to display the program in the Code and Text Editor window.

3. Add the following statements to the body of the *run* method:

```
double dailyRate = readDouble("Enter your daily rate: ");
int noOfDays = readInt("Enter the number of days: ");
writeFee(calculateFee(dailyRate, noOfDays));
```

The *run* method is called by the *Main* method when the application starts (the way in which it is called requires an understanding of classes, which we will look at in Chapter 7, "Creating and Managing Classes and Objects") .

The block of code you have just added to the *run* method calls the *readDouble* method (which you will write shortly) to ask the user for the daily rate for the consultant. The next statement calls the *readInt* method (which you will also write) to obtain the number of days. Finally, the *writeFee* method (to be written) is called to display the results on the screen. Notice that the value passed to *writeFee* is the value returned by the *calculateFee* method (the last one you will need to write), which takes the daily rate and the number of days and calculates the total fee payable.

> **Note** Because you have not yet written the *readDouble*, *readInt*, *writeFee*, or *calculateFee* methods, IntelliSense does not display them when you type this code. Also, do not try to build the application yet, because it will fail.

Write the methods using the Generate Method Stub Wizard

1. In the Code and Text Editor window, click the *readDouble* method call in the *run* method.

A small underscore character appears underneath the first letter ("r") of *readDouble*. If you move the cursor over the letter "r", an icon appears. If you hover the mouse over this icon,the tooltip "Options to generate a method stub (Shift + Alt + F10)" appears, with a drop-down menu. Click the drop-down menu, and the option "Generate method stub for 'readDouble' in 'DailyRate.Program'" apppears, as shown here:

2. Click Generate method stub for 'readDouble' in 'DailyRate.Program'.

   The Generate Method Stub Wizard examines the call to the *readDouble* method, ascertains the type of its parameters and return value, and generates a method with a default implementation, like this:

```
private double readDouble(string p)

{

    throw new Exception("The method or operation is not implemented.");

}
```

   The new method is created with the *private* qualifier, which will be described in Chapter 7. The body of the method currently just throws an *Exception*. (Exceptions will be described in Chapter 6.) You will replace the body with your own code in the next step.

3. Delete the *throw new Exception(...);* statement from the *readDouble* method, and replace it with the following lines of code:

```
Console.Write(p);
string line = Console.ReadLine();
return double.Parse(line);
```

   This block of code outputs the string in variable *p* to the screen. This variable is the string parameter passed in when the method is called, and contains a message prompting the user to type in their daily rate. The user types in a value, which is read into a *string* by using the *ReadLine* method and converted into a *double* by using the *double.Parse* method. The result is passed back as the return value of the method call.

> **Note**   The *ReadLine* method is the companion method to *WriteLine*; it reads user input from the keyboard, finishing when the user presses the **Enter** key. The text typed by the user is passed back as the return value.

4. Click the call to the *readInt* method in the *run* method, and use the same process as before to generate a method stub for the *readInt* method.

   The *readInt* method is generated with a default implementation.

> **Tip**   You can also generate a method stub by right-clicking a method call and selecting Generate Method Stub from the context menu.

5. Replace the body of the *readInt* method with the following statements:

```
Console.Write(p);
string line = Console.ReadLine();
return int.Parse(line);
```

   This block of code is very similar to the *readDouble* method. The only difference is that the method returns an *int* value, so the *string* is converted into a number by using the *int.Parse* method.

6. Right-click the call to the *calculateFee* method in the *run* method, and then click Generate Method Stub.

   The *calculateFee* method is generated:

```
private object calculateFee(double dailyRate, int noOfDays)
{
    throw new Exception("The  method or operation is not implemented");
}
```

   Notice that the Generate Method Stub Wizard uses the name of the arguments passed in to generate names for the parameters. (You can of course change the parameter names if they are not suitable.) What is more intriguing is the type returned by the method, which is *object*. The Generate Method Stub Wizard is unable to determine exactly what type of value should be returned by the method from the context in which it is called. The *object* type just means a "thing," and you should change it to the type you require when you add the code to the method. The *object* type will be described in more detail in Chapter 7.

7. Change the definition of the *calculateFee* method so that it returns a *double*:

```
private double calculateFee(double dailyRate, int noOfDays)
{
    throw new Exception("The  method or operation is not implemented");
}
```

8. Replace the body of the *calculateFee* method with the following statement, which calulates the fee payable by multiplying the two parameters together and then returns it:

```
return dailyRate * noOfDays;
```

9. Right-click the call to the *writeFee* method in the *run* method, then click Generate Method Stub.

   The *writeFee* method is generated. Note that the Generate Method Stub Wizard uses the definition of the *calculateFee* method to work out that its parameter should be a *double*. Also, the method call does not use a return value, so the type of the method is *void*:

```
private void writeFee(double p)
{
    ...
}
```

10. Type the following statements inside the *writeFee* method:

```
Console.WriteLine("The consultant's fee is: {0}", p * 1.1);
```

> **Note** This version of the *WriteLine* method demonstrates the use of a simple format string. The text *{0}* is a placeholder that is replaced with the value of the expression following the string (*p * 1.1*) when it is evaluated at runtime.

11. On the Build menu, click Build Solution.

> **Tip** If you feel sufficiently comfortable with the syntax, you can also write methods by typing them directly in the Code and Text Editor window. You do not always have to use the Generate Method Stub menu option.

Refactoring Code

A very useful feature of Visual Studio 2005 is the ability to refactor code.

Occasionally you will find yourself writing the same (or very similar) code in more than one place in an application. When this occurs, highlight the block of code you have just typed, and click Extract Method on the Refactor menu. The Extract Method dialog box appears, prompting you for the name of a new method to create containing this code. Type a name and click OK. The new method is created containing your code, and the code you typed is replaced with a call to this method. The Extract Method is also intelligent enough to work out whether the method should take any parameters and return a value.

Test the program

1. On the Debug menu, click Start Without Debugging.

   Visual Studio 2005 builds the program and then runs it. A console window appears.

2. At the Enter Your Daily Rate prompt, type **525**, and then press Enter.

3. At the Enter The Number Of Days prompt, type **17**, and then press Enter.

   The program writes the following message to the console window:

   ```
   The consultant's fee is: 9817.5
   ```

4. Press the Enter key to return control to the Visual Studio 2005 programming environment.

In the final exercise, you'll use the Visual Studio 2005 debugger to run your program in slow motion. You'll see when each method is called (this action is referred to as *stepping into the method*) and then see how each return statement transfers control back to the caller (also known as *stepping out of the method*). While you are stepping in and out of methods, you'll use the tools on the Debug toolbar. However, the same commands are also available on the Debug menu when an application is running in Debug mode.

Step through the methods using the Visual Studio 2005 debugger

1. In the Code and Text Editor window, find the *run* method.

2. Move the mouse pointer to the first statement in the *run* method.

   The first statement in the *run* method is as follows:

   ```
   double dailyRate = readDouble("Enter your daily rate: ");
   ```

3. Right-click anywhere on this line, and on the context menu, click Run To Cursor.

   The program runs until it reaches the first statement in the *run* method, and then it pauses. A yellow arrow in the left margin of the Code and Text Editor window indicates the current statement, which is also highlighted with a yellow background.

4. On the View menu, point to Toolbars, and then make sure the Debug toolbar is checked.

   If it was not already visible, the Debug toolbar opens. It might appear docked with the other toolbars. If you cannot see the toolbar, try using the Toolbars command on the View menu to hide it, and notice which buttons disappear. Then display the toolbar again. The Debug toolbar looks like this:

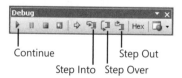

> **Tip**   To make the Debug toolbar appear in its own window, use the handle at the left end of the toolbar to drag it over the Code and Text Editor window.

5. On the Debug toolbar, click Step Into.

    This action causes the debugger to step into the method being called. The yellow cursor jumps to the opening curly brace at the start of the *readDouble* method. Click Step Into again. The cursor advances to the first statement:

```
Console.Write(p);
```

> **Tip**   You can also press F11 rather than clicking Step Into on the Debug toolbar.

6. On the Debug toolbar, click Step Over.

    This action causes the method to execute the next statement without debugging it (stepping into it). The yellow cursor moves to the second statement of the method, and the program displays the Enter Your Daily Rate prompt in a Console window before returning to Visual Studio 2005 (the Console window may be hidden behind Visual Studio).

> **Tip**   You can also press F10 rather than clicking Step Over.

7. On the Debug toolbar, click Step Over.

    This time the yellow cursor disappears and the Console window gets the focus because the program is executing the *Console.ReadLine* method and is waiting for you to type something in.

8. Type **525** in the Console window, and then press Enter.

    Control returns to Visual Studio 2005. The yellow cursor appears on the third line of the method.

9. Without clicking, move the mouse over the reference to the *line* variable on either the second or the third line of the method (it doesn't matter which).

    A ScreenTip appears, displaying the current value of the *line* variable ("525"). You can use this feature to make sure that a variable has been set to an expected value while stepping through methods.

10. On the Debug toolbar, click Step Out.

    This action causes the current method to continue running uninterrupted to its end. The *readDouble* method finishes, and the yellow cursor is placed back at the first statement of the *run* method.

> **Tip**   You can also press Shift+F11 rather than clicking Step Out.

11. On the Debug toolbar, click Step Into.

    The yellow cursor moves to the second statement in the *run* method:

    ```
    int noOfDays = readInt("Enter the number of days: ");
    ```

12. On the Debug toolbar, click Step Over.

    This time you have chosen to run the method without stepping through it. The Console window appears again prompting you for the number of days.

13. In the Console window, type **17,** and then press Enter.

    Control returns to Visual Studio 2005. The yellow cursor moves to the third statement of the *run* method:

    ```
    writeFee(calculateFee(dailyRate, noOfDays));
    ```

14. On the Debug toolbar, click Step Into.

    The yellow cursor jumps to the opening curly brace at the start of the *calculateFee* method. This method is called first, before *writeFee*.

15. On the Debug toolbar, click Step Out.

    The yellow cursor jumps back to the third statement of the *run* method.

16. On the Debug toolbar, click Step Into.

    This time, the yellow cursor jumps to the opening curly brace at the start of the *writeFee* method.

17. Place the mouse over the *p* variable in the method definition.

    The value of *p*, 8925.0, is displayed.

18. On the Debug toolbar, click Step Out.

    The message *The consultant's fee is: 9817.5* is displayed in the Console window. (You might need to bring the Console window to the foreground to display it if it is hidden behind Visual Studio 2005). The yellow cursor returns to the third statement in the *run* method.

19. On the Debug toolbar, click Continue to cause the program to continue running without stopping at each statement.

> **Tip**   You can also press F5 to continue execution in the Debugger.

The application finishes running.

Congratulations! You've successfully written and called methods and used the Visual Studio 2005 debugger to step in and out of methods as they run.

■ **If you want to continue to the next chapter**

Keep Visual Studio 2005 running, and turn to Chapter 4.

■ **If you want to exit Visual Studio 2005 now**

On the File menu, click Exit. If you see a Save dialog box, click Yes to save your work.

Chapter 3 Quick Reference

To	Do this

Declare a method	Write the method inside a class. For example:
	
	```int addValues(int leftHandSide, int rightHandSide)```
	```{```
	``` ...```
	```}```

Return a value from inside a method	Write a *return* statement inside the method. For example: ```return leftHandSide + rightHandSide;```
Return from a method before the end of the method	Write a *return* statement inside the method. For example: ```return;```
Call a method	Write the name of the method, together with any arguments between parentheses. For example: ```addValues(39, 3);```
Use the Generate Method Stub Wizard	Highlight a call to the method, and then click Generate Method Stub on the IntelliSense menu.
Display the Debug toolbar	On the View menu, point to Toolbars, and then click Debug.
Step into a method	On the Debug toolbar, click Step Into. or On the Debug menu, click Step Into.
Step out of a method	On the Debug toolbar, click Step Out. or On the Debug menu, click Step Out.

Chapter 4
Using Decision Statements

After completing this chapter, you will be able to:

- Declare *bool* variables.

- Use Boolean operators to create expressions whose outcome is either true or false.

- Write if statements to make decisions based on the result of a Boolean expression.

- Write switch statements to make more complex decisions.

In Chapter 3, "Writing Methods and Applying Scope," you learned how to group related statements into methods. You also learned how to use arguments and parameters to pass information to a method and how to use *return* statements to pass information out of a method. Dividing a program up into a set of discrete methods, each designed to perform a specific task or calculation, is a recommended design strategy. Many programs need to solve large and complex problems. Breaking up a program into methods helps you understand these problems and focus on how to solve them one piece at a time. You also need to be able to write methods that selectively perform different actions depending on the circumstances. In this chapter, you'll see how to accomplish these tasks.

Declaring *bool* Variables

In the world of programming (unlike in the real world), everything is black or white, right or wrong, true or false. For example, if you create an integer variable called *x*, assign the value 99 to *x*, and then ask, "Does *x* contain the value 99?", the answer is definitely true. If you ask, "Is *x* less than 10?", the answer is definitely false. These are examples of *Boolean expressions*. A Boolean expression always evaluates to true or false.

Note   The answers to these questions are not definitive for all programming languages. An unassigned variable has an undefined value, and you cannot, for example, say that it is definitely less than 10. Issues such as this one are a common source of errors in C and C++ programs. The Microsoft Visual C# compiler solves this problem by ensuring that you always assign a value to a variable before examining it. If you try to examine the contents of an unassigned variable, your program will not compile.

Microsoft Visual C# provides a data type called *bool*. A *bool* variable can hold one of two values: *true* or *false*. For example, the following three statements declare a *bool* variable called *areYouReady*, assign *true* to the variable, and then write its value to the console:

```
bool areYouReady;
areYouReady = true;
Console.WriteLine(areYouReady); // writes True
```

Using Boolean Operators

A *Boolean operator* is an operator whose result is either true or false. C# has several very useful Boolean operators, the simplest of which is the NOT operator, which is represented by the exclamation point symbol (!). The *!* operator negates a Boolean value, yielding the opposite of that value. In the previous example, if the value of the variable *areYouReady* is *true*, the value of the expression *!areYouReady* is *false*.

Understanding Equality and Relational Operators

Two much more commonly used Boolean operators are the equality (==) and inequality (!=) operators. You use these binary operators to find out whether a value is the same as another value of the same type. The following table summarizes how these operators work, using an *int* variable called *age* as an example.

Operator	Meaning	Example	Outcome if age is 42
==	Equal to	age == 100	*false*
!=	Not equal to	age != 0	*true*

Closely related to these two operators are the *relational* operators. You use these operators to find out whether a value is less than or greater than another value of the same type. The following table shows how to use these operators.

Operator	Meaning	Example	Outcome if age is 42
<	Less than	age < 21	*false*
<=	Less than or equal to	age <= 18	*false*
>	Greater than	age > 16	*true*
>=	Greater than or equal to	age >= 30	*true*

Note   Don't confuse the *equality* operator == with the *assignment* operator =. Code such as *x==y* compares *x* to *y* and has the value *true* if the values are the same. Code such as *x=y* assigns the value of *y* to *x*.

Understanding Conditional Logical Operators

C# also provides two other Boolean operators: the logical AND operator, which is represented by the *&&* symbol, and the logical OR operator, which is represented by the *||* symbol. Collectively, these are known as the conditional logical operators. Their purpose is to combine Boolean expressions together into bigger expressions. These binary operators are similar to the equality and relational operators in that their outcome is either *true* or *false*, but they differ in that the values they operate on must themselves be either *true* or *false.*

The outcome of the *&&* operator is *true* if and only if both of the Boolean expressions it operates on are *true.* For example, the following statement assigns the value *true* to *validPercentage* if and only if the value of *percent* is greater than or equal to zero and the value of *percent* is less than or equal to 100:

```
bool validPercentage;
validPercentage = (percent >= 0) && (percent <= 100);
```

> **Tip**   A common beginner's error is to try to combine the two tests by naming the percent variable only once, like this:
>
> ```
> percent >= 0 && <= 100 // this statement will not compile.
> ```
>
> Using parentheses helps avoid this type of mistake and also clarifies the purpose of the expression. For example, compare these two expressions:
>
> ```
> validPercentage = percent >= 0 && percent <= 100
> ```
>
> and
>
> ```
> validPercentage = (percent >= 0) && (percent <= 100)
> ```
>
> Both expressions return the same value, because the precedence of the *&&* operator is less than that of *>=* and *<=*. However, the second expression conveys its purpose in a more readable manner.

The outcome of the *||* operator is *true* if either of the Boolean expressions it operates on is *true.* You use the *||* operator to determine whether any one of a combination of Boolean expressions is *true.* For example, the following statement assigns the value *true* to *invalidPercentage* if the value of *percent* is less than zero, or the value of *percent* is greater than 100:

```
bool invalidPercentage;
invalidPercentage = (percent < 0) || (percent > 100);
```

Short Circuiting

The *&&* and *||* operators both exhibit a feature called *short circuiting*. Sometimes it is not necessary to evaluate both operands. For example, if the left operand of the *&&* operator evaluates to *false*, then the result of the entire expression is *false* regardless of the value of the right operand. Similarly, if the value of the left operand of the *||* operator evaluates to *true*, the result of the entire expression is *true*. In these cases, the *&&* and *||* operators bypass the evaluation of the right Boolean expressions. Here are some examples:

```
(percent >= 0) && (percent <= 100)
```

In this expression, if the value of *percent* is less than zero, the Boolean expression on the left side of *&&* evaluates to *false*. This value means that the result of the entire expression must be *false*, regardless of the remaining expression; therefore, the Boolean expression on the right side of *&&* is not evaluated.

```
(percent < 0) || (percent > 100)
```

In this expression, if the value of *percent* is less than zero, the Boolean expression on the left side of *||* evaluates to *true*. This value means that the result of the entire expression must be *true*; therefore, the Boolean expression on the right side of *||* is not evaluated.

If you carefully design expressions that use the conditional logical operators, you can boost the performance of your code by avoiding unnecessary work. Place simple Boolean expressions that can be evaluated easily on the left side of a conditional logical operator and put more complex expressions on the right side. In many cases, you will find that the program does not need to evaluate the more complex expressions.

Summarizing Operator Precedence and Associativity

The following table summarizes the precedence and associativity of all the operators you have learned about so far. Operators in the same category have the same precedence. Operators in a higher category take precedence over operators in a lower category.

Category	Operators	Description	Associativity
Primary	()	Precedence override	Left
	++	Post-increment	
	--	Post-decrement	
Unary	!	Logical NOT	Left
	+	Addition	
	-	Subtraction	
	++	Pre-increment	
	--	Pre-decrement	

Category	Operators	Description	Associativity
Multiplicative	* / %	Multiply Divide Division remainder	Left
Additive	+ -	Addition Subtraction	Left
Relational	< < = > > =	Less than Less than or equal Greater than Greater than or equal	Left
Equality	= = !=	Equal to Not equal to	Left
Conditional AND	&&	Logical AND	Left
Conditional OR	||	Logical OR	Left
Assignment	=		Right

Using *if* Statements to Make Decisions

You use an *if* statement when you want to choose between executing two different blocks of code depending on the result of a Boolean expression.

Understanding *if* Statement Syntax

The syntax of an *if* statement is as follows (*if* and *else* are keywords):

```
if ( booleanExpression )
    statement-1;
else
    statement-2;
```

If *booleanExpression* evaluates to *true*, then *statement-1* runs; otherwise *booleanExpression* is *false*, and *statement-2* runs. The *else* keyword and the following *statement-2* are optional. If there is no *else* clause, nothing happens when the *booleanExpression* is *false*.

For example, here's an *if* statement that increments the seconds hand of a stopwatch (minutes are ignored for now). If the value of the *seconds* variable is 59, it is reset to 0, otherwise it is incremented using the ++ operator:

```
int seconds;
...
if (seconds == 59)
    seconds = 0;
else
    seconds++;
```

Boolean Expressions Only Please!

The expression in an *if* statement must be enclosed in parentheses. Additionally, the expression must be a Boolean expression. In some other languages (notably C and C++), you can write an integer expression, and the compiler will silently convert the integer value to *true* (nonzero) or *false* (zero). C# does not support this behavior, and the compiler reports an error if you write such an expression.

If you accidentally write an assignment instead of an equality test in an *if* statement, the C# compiler recognizes your mistake. For example:

```
int seconds;
...
if (seconds = 59)  // compile-time error
...
if (seconds == 59) // ok
```

Accidental assignments were another common source of bugs in C and C++ programs, which would silently convert the value assigned (59) into a Boolean expression (anything non-zero was considered to be true), with the result that the code following the *if* statement would be performed every time.

Finally, you can use a Boolean variable as the expression, as in this example:

```
bool inWord;
...
if (inWord == true) // ok, but not commonly used
...
if (inWord)         // better
```

Using Blocks to Group Statements

Sometimes you'll want to run two or more statements when a Boolean expression is true. You could group the statements inside a new method and then call the new method, but a simpler solution is to group the statements inside a *block*. A block is simply a sequence of statements grouped between an opening and a closing curly brace. In the following example, two statements that reset the *seconds* variable to zero and increment the *minutes* variable are grouped inside a block, and the whole block executes if the value of *seconds* is equal to 59:

```
int seconds = 0;
int minutes = 0;
...
if (seconds == 59)
{
    seconds = 0;
    minutes++;
}
else
    seconds++;
```

> **Important**   If you omit the curly braces, the C# compiler associates only the first statement (seconds = 0) with the *if* statement. The subsequent statement (minutes++) will not be recognized by the compiler as part of the *if* statement when the program is compiled. Furthermore, when the compiler reaches the *else* keyword, it will not associate it with the previous *if* statement, so it reports a syntax error instead.

Cascading *if* Statements

You can nest *if* statements inside other *if* statements. In this way, you can chain together a sequence of Boolean expressions, which are tested one after the other until one of them evaluates to *true*. In the following example, if the value of *day* is 0, the first test evaluates to *true* and *dayName* is assigned *Sunday*. If the value of *day* is not 0, the first test fails and control passes to the *else* clause, which runs the second *if* statement and compares the value of *day* with 1. The second *if* statement is reached only if the first test is *false*. Similarly, the third *if* statement is reached only if the first and second tests are *false*.

```
if (day == 0)
    dayName = "Sunday";
else if (day == 1)
    dayName = "Monday";
else if (day == 2)
    dayName = "Tuesday";
else if (day == 3)
    dayName = "Wednesday";
else if (day == 4)
    dayName = "Thursday";
else if (day == 5)
    dayName = "Friday";
else if (day == 6)
    dayName = "Saturday";
else
    dayName = "unknown";
```

In the following exercise, you'll write a method that uses a cascading *if* statement to compare two dates.

Write *if* statements

1. Start Microsoft Visual Studio 2005.

2. Open the Selection project, located in the \Microsoft Press\Visual CSharp Step by Step\Chapter 4\Selection folder in your My Documents folder.

3. On the Debug menu, click Start Without Debugging.

   Visual Studio 2005 builds and runs the application. There are two *DateTimePicker* controls on the form called *first* and *second*. (These controls display a calendar allowing you to select a date when you click the drop-down arrow.) Both controls are currently set to today's date.

4. Click Compare.

   The following text appears in the text box:

   ```
   first == second : False
   first != second : True
   first <  second : False
   first <= second : False
   first >  second : True
   first >= second : True
   ```

   The Boolean expression first == second should be true because both *first* and *second* are set to today's date. In fact, only the less than operator and the greater than or equal to operator seem to be correct!

5. Click Quit.

   You return to the Visual Studio 2005 programming environment.

6. Display the code for Form1.cs in the Code and Text Editor window. Locate the *compare_Click* method, which looks like this:

   ```
   private int compare_Click(object sender, System.EventArgs e)
   {
       int diff = dateCompare(first.Value, second.Value);

       info.Text = "";

       show("first == second", diff == 0);

       show("first != second", diff != 0);

       show("first < second", diff < 0);

       show("first <= second", diff <= 0);

       show("first > second", diff > 0);

       show("first >= second", diff >= 0);
   }
   ```

This method runs whenever the user clicks the *Compare* button on the form. It retrieves the values of the dates displayed in the *first* and *second* DateTimePicker controls on the form and calls another method called *dateCompare* to compare them. You will examine the *dateCompare* method in the next step, but its purpose is to examine its arguments and return an integer value based on their relative values; it returns zero if they have the same value, -1 if the value of *first* is less than the value of *second*, and +1 if the value if *first* is greater than the value of *second*. (A date is considered greater than another date if it comes after it chronologically.)

The *show* method summarizes the results of the comparison in the *info* TextBox control on the form.

7. Locate the *dateCompare* method, which looks like this:

```
private int dateCompare(DateTime leftHandSide, DateTime rightHandSide)
{
    // TO DO
    return 42;
}
```

This method currently returns the same value whenever it is called, rather than 0, -1, or +1 depending on the values of its parameters. This explains why the application is not working as expected! You need to implement this method to correctly compare two dates.

8. Remove the // TO DO comment and the *return* statement from the *dateCompare* method.

9. Type the following statements in the body of the *dateCompare* method:

```
int result;
if (leftHandSide.Year < rightHandSide.Year)
    result = -1;
else if (leftHandSide.Year > rightHandSide.Year)
    result = +1;
else if (leftHandSide.Month < rightHandSide.Month)
    result = -1;
else if (leftHandSide.Month > rightHandSide.Month)
    result = +1;
else if (leftHandSide.Day < rightHandSide.Day)
    result = -1;
else if (leftHandSide.Day > rightHandSide.Day)
    result = +1;
else
    result = 0;
return result;
```

If the expressions leftHandSide.Year < rightHandSide.Year and leftHandSide.Year > rightHandSide.Year are false, then leftHandSide.Year == rightHandSide.Year must be true, and the program flow correctly moves on to compare the *Month* property of *lhs* and *rhs*. Similarly, if leftHandSide.Month < rightHandSide.Month and leftHandSide.Month > rightHandSide.Month are false, then leftHandSide.Month == rightHandSide.Month must be true, and the program flow again correctly moves on to compare the *Day* property of *lhs* and *rhs*. Lastly, if leftHandSide.Day < rightHandSide.Day and leftHandSide.Day > rightHandSide.Day are false, then leftHandSide.Day == rightHandSide.Day must be true, and, because the *Month* and *Year* properties must also be true, the two dates must be the same.

10.   On the Debug menu, click Start Without Debugging.

The application is rebuilt and restarted. Once again, the two *DateTimePicker* controls, *first* and *second*, are set to today's date.

11.   Click Compare.

The following text appears in the text box:

```
first == second : True
first != second : False
first <  second : False
first <= second : True
first >  second : False
first >= second : True
```

These are the correct results.

12.   Move the second *DateTimePicker* control onto tomorrow's date.

13.   Click Compare.

The following text appears in the text box:

```
first == second : False
first != second : True
first <  second : True
first <= second : True
first >  second : False
first >= second : False
```

Again, these are the correct results.

14.   Click Quit.

Using *switch* Statements

Sometimes when you write a cascading *if* statement, all the *if* statements look very similar, because they all evaluate an identical expression. The only difference is that each *if* compares the result of the expression with a different value. For example:

```
if (day == 0)
    dayName = "Sunday";
else if (day == 1)
    dayName = "Monday";
else if (day == 2)
    dayName = "Tuesday";
else if (day == 3)
    ...
else
    dayName = "Unknown";
```

In these situations, you can often rewrite the cascading *if* statement as a *switch* statement to make your program more efficient and more readable.

Understanding *switch* Statement Syntax

The syntax of a *switch* statement is as follows (*switch*, *case*, and *default* are keywords):

```
switch ( controllingExpression )
{
case constantExpression :
    statements
    break;
case constantExpression :
    statements
    break;
...
default :
    statements
    break;
}
```

The *controllingExpression* is evaluated once, and the statements below the *case* whose *constantExpression* value is equal to the result of the controllingExpression run as far as the *break* statement. The *switch* statement then finishes, and the program continues at the first statement after the closing brace of the *switch* statement.

If none of the *constantExpression* values are equal to the value of the *controllingExpression*, the statements below the optional *default* label run.

> **Note**   If the value of the *controllingExpression* does not match any of the *case* labels and there's no *default* label, program execution continues with the first statement after the closing brace of the *switch* statement.

For example, you can rewrite the previous cascading *if* statement as the following *switch* statement:

```
switch (day)
{
case 0 :
    dayName = "Sunday";
    break;
case 1 :
    dayName = "Monday";
    break;
case 2 :
    dayName = "Tuesday";
    break;
...
default :
    dayName = "Unknown";
    break;
}
```

Following the *switch* Statement Rules

The *switch* statement is very useful, but, unfortunately, you can't always use it when you might like to. Any *switch* statement you write must adhere to the following rules:

- You can use *switch* only on primitive data types, such as *int* or *string*. With any other types, you'll have to use an *if* statement.

- The *case* labels must be constant expressions, such as 42 or "42". If you need to calculate your *case* label values at run time, you must use an *if* statement.

- The *case* labels must be unique expressions. In other words, two *case* labels cannot have the same value.

- You can specify that you want to run the same statements for more than one value by providing a list of *case* labels and no intervening statements, in which case, the code for the final label in the list is executed for all cases. However, if a label has one or more associated statements, execution cannot fall through to subsequent labels, and the compiler generates an error. For example:

```
switch (trumps)
{
case Hearts :
case Diamonds :      // Fall-through allowed - no code between labels
    color = "Red";   // Code executed for Hearts and Diamonds
    break;
```

```
case Clubs :
    color = "Black";
case Spades :          // Error - code between labels
    color = "Black";
    break;
}
```

> **Note**   The *break* statement is the most common way to stop fall-through, but you can also use a *return* statement or a *throw* statement. The *throw* statement is described in Chapter 6, "Managing Errors and Exceptions."

No Fall-Through

Because of the no fall-through rule, you can freely rearrange the sections of a *switch* statement without affecting its meaning (including the *default* label, which by convention is usually placed as the last label, but does not have to be).

C and C++ programmers should note that the *break* statement is mandatory for every case in a *switch* statement (even the default case). This requirement is a good thing; it is very common in C or C++ programs to forget the *break* statement, allowing execution to fall through to the next label and leading to bugs that are very difficult to spot.

If you really want to, you can mimic fall-through in C# by using a *goto* statement to go to the following *case* or *default* label. This usage is not recommended though, and this book does not show you how to do it!

In the following exercise, you will complete a program that reads the characters of a string and maps each character to its XML representation. For example, the '<' character has a special meaning in XML (it's used to form elements) and must be translated into "<". You will write a *switch* statement that tests the value of the character and traps the special XML characters as *case* labels.

Write *switch* statements

1. Start Visual Studio 2005.

2. Open the SwitchStatement project, located in the \Microsoft Press\Visual CSharp Step by Step\Chapter 4\SwitchStatement folder in your My Documents folder.

3. On the Debug menu, click Start Without Debugging.

   Visual Studio 2005 builds and runs the application. There are two text boxes separated by a Copy button.

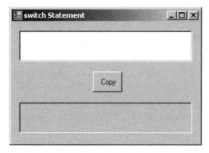

4. Type the following sample text into the upper text box:

    ```
    inRange = (lo <= number) && (number <= hi);
    ```

5. Click Copy.

    The statement is copied verbatim into the lower text box, and no translation of the '<' character occurs.

6. Close the form.

7. Display the code for Form1.cs in the Code and Text Editor window. Locate the *copyOne* method.

    The *copyOne* method copies one character from the upper text box to the lower text box. At the moment, *copyOne* contains a *switch* statement with a single *default* section.

    In the following few steps, you will modify this *switch* statement to convert characters that are significant in XML to their XML mapping. For example, the '<' character will be converted to the string "<".

8. Add the following statements to the *switch* statement, above the *default* label:

    ```
    case '<' :
        target.Text += "&lt;";
        break;
    case '>' :
        target.Text += "&gt;";
        break;
    case '&' :
        target.Text += "&amp;";
        break;
    case '\"' :
        target.Text +=   "&#34;";
        break;
    case '\'' :
        target.Text += "&#39;";
        break;
    ```

> **Note** The back-slash (\) in the final two cases is an escape character that causes the following characters (" and ') to be treated literally, rather than as characters delimiting a string or character constant.

9. On the Debug menu, click Start Without Debugging.

    Visual Studio 2005 builds and runs the application.

10. Type the following statement into the upper text box:

```
inRange = (lo <= number) && (number <= hi);
```

11. Click Copy.

    The statement is copied into the lower text box. This time, each character undergoes the XML mapping implemented in the *switch* statement.

12. Close the form.

■ **If you want to continue to the next chapter**

    Keep Visual Studio 2005 open, and turn to Chapter 5.

■ **If you want to exit Visual Studio 2005 now**

    On the File menu, click Exit. If you see a Save dialog box, click Yes.

Chapter 4 Quick Reference

To	Do this	Example
Determine whether two values are equivalent	Use the == or != operator.	`answer == 42`
Compare the value of two expressions	Use the <, <=, >, or >= operator.	`age >= 21`
Declare a Boolean variable	Use the *bool* keyword as the type of the variable.	`bool inRange;`
Create a Boolean expression that is true only if two other conditions are true	Use the && operator.	`inRange = (lo <= number)` `        && (number <= hi) ;`
Create a Boolean expression that is true if either of two other conditions is true	Use the || operator.	`outOfRange = (number < lo)` `        || (hi < number);`
Run a statement if a condition is true	Use an *if* statement.	`if (inRange)` `    process();`

Run more than one statement if a condition is true	Use a block.	`if (seconds == 59)`
		`{`
		`    seconds = 0;`
		`    minutes++;`
		`}`

Associate different statements with different values of a controlling expression	Use a *switch* statement.	`switch (current)`
		`{`
		`    case '<':`
		`        ...`
		`        break;`
		`    default :`
		`        ...`
		`        break;`
		`}`

Chapter 5

Using Compound Assignment and Iteration Statements

After completing this chapter, you will be able to:

- Update the value of a variable by using compound assignment operators.

- Write *while*, *for*, and *do* iteration statements.

- Step through a *do* method, and watch as the values of the variables change.

In Chapter 4, "Using Decision Statements," you learned how to use the *if* and *switch* constructs to selectively run statements. In this chapter, you'll see how to use a variety of iteration (or *looping*) statements to repeatedly run one or more statements. When you write iteration statements, you usually need to control the number of iterations that you perform. You can achieve this by using a variable, updating its value with each iteration, and stopping the process when the variable reaches a particular value. Therefore, you'll also learn about the special assignment operators that you should use to update the value of a variable in these circumstances.

Using Compound Assignment Operators

You've already seen how to use arithmetic operators to create new values. For example, the following statement uses the + operator to create a value that is 42 greater than the variable *answer*. The new value is then written to the console:

```
Console.WriteLine(answer + 42);
```

You've also seen how to use assignment statements to change the value of a variable. The following statement uses the assignment operator to change the value of *answer* to 42:

```
answer = 42;
```

If you want to add 42 to the value of a variable, you can combine the assignment operator and the addition operator. For example, the following statement adds 42 to *answer*. In other words, after this statement runs, the value of *answer* is 42 more than it was before:

```
answer = answer + 42;
```

Although this statement works, you'll probably never see an experienced programmer write this. Adding a value to a variable is so common that Microsoft Visual C# lets you perform this task in shorthand manner by using the compound assignment operator, +=. To add 42 to *answer*, an experienced programmer would write the following statement:

```
answer += 42;
```

You can use this shortcut to combine any arithmetic operator with the assignment operator, as the following table shows. These operators are collectively known as the *compound assignment operators*.

Don't write this	Write this
variable = variable * number;	variable *= number;
variable = variable / number;	variable /= number;
variable = variable % number;	variable %= number;
variable = variable + number;	variable += number;
variable = variable - number;	variable -= number;

Tip The compound assignment operators share the same precedence and right associativity as the simple assignment operator.

The += operator also functions on strings; it appends one string to the end of another. For example, the following code displays "Hello John" on the console:

```
string name = "John";
string greeting = "Hello ";
greeting += name;
Console.WriteLine(greeting);
```

You cannot use any of the other compound assignment operators on strings.

Note Use the ++ and -- operators instead of a compound assignment operator when incrementing or decrementing a variable by 1. For example, replace:

```
count += 1;
```

with

```
count++;
```

Writing *while* Statements

You use a *while* statement to repeatedly run a statement while a Boolean expression is true. The syntax of a *while* statement is:

```
while ( booleanExpression )
    statement
```

The Boolean expression is evaluated and, if it's true, the statement runs and the Boolean expression is evaluated again. If the expression is still true, the statement is repeated and the expression evaluated again. This process continues until the Boolean expression evaluates to false when the *while* statement exits; execution then continues with the first statement after the *while* statement. A *while* statement shares many syntactic similarities with an *if* statement (in fact, the syntax is identical except for the keyword):

- The expression must be a Boolean expression.

- The Boolean expression must be written inside parentheses.

- If the Boolean expression evaluates to false when first evaluated, the statement does not run.

- If you want to perform two or more statements under the control of a *while* statement, you must use curly braces to group those statements in a block.

Here's a *while* statement that writes the values 0 through 9 to the console:

```
int i = 0;
while (i != 10)
{
    Console.WriteLine(i);
    i++;
}
```

All *while* statements should terminate at some point. A common beginner's mistake is forgetting to include a statement to eventually cause the Boolean expression to evaluate to false and terminate the loop. In the example, the *i++* statement performs this role.

> **Note**   The variable, *i*, in the *while* loop controls the number of iterations that are performed. This is a very common idiom, and the variable that performs this role is sometimes called the *Sentinel* variable.

In the following exercise, you will write a *while* loop to read the contents of a source file one line at a time and write each line to a text box in a Windows application.

Write a *while* statement

1. Using Visual Studio 2005, open the *WhileStatement* project, located in the \Microsoft Press\Visual CSharp Step by Step\Chapter 5\WhileStatement folder in your My Documents folder.

2. On the Debug menu, click Start Without Debugging.

   Visual Studio 2005 builds and runs the Windows application. The application itself is a simple text file viewer, allowing you to select a file and display its contents.

3. Click Open File.

   The Open dialog box opens.

4. Navigate to the \Microsoft Press\Visual CSharp Step by Step\Chapter 5\ WhileStatement\WhileStatement folder in your My Documents folder.

5. Select the Form1.cs file, and then click Open.

   The name of the source file, Form1.cs, appears in the small text box, but the contents of Form1.cs do not appear in the large text box. This is because the code that reads the contents of the source file and displays it in the large text box has not yet been implemented. You will add this functionality in the following steps.

6. Close the form and return to Visual Studio 2005.

7. Display the code for the file Form1.cs in the Code and Text Editor window. Locate the *openFileDialog_FileOk* method.

   This method is called when the user clicks the Open button after selecting a file in the Open dialog box. The body of the method is currently implemented as follows:

   ```
   string fullPathname = openFileDialog.FileName;
   FileInfo src = new FileInfo(fullPathname);
   filename.Text = src.Name;
   /* add while loop here */
   ```

   The first statement declares a *string* variable called *fullPathname* and initializes it to the *FileName* property of the *openFileDialog* object. This statement initializes *fullPathname* to the full name (including the folder) of the source file selected in the Open dialog box.

> **Note**   The *openFileDialog* object is an instance of the *OpenFileDialog* component that is available in the Toolbox. This component provides methods that you can use to display the standard Windows Open dialog box, select a file, and retrieve name and path of the selected file.

The second statement declares a *FileInfo* variable called *src* and initializes it to an object that represents the file selected in the Open dialog box. (*FileInfo* is a class provided by the Microsoft .NET Framework that allows you to manipulate files.)

The third statement assigns the *Text* property of the *filename* control to the *Name* property of the *src* variable. The *Name* property of the *src* variable holds the name of the file selected in the Open dialog box without its folder. This assignment makes the name of the file appear in the filename component of the Windows form.

8. Replace the */* add while loop here */* comment with the following statement:

```
source.Text = "";
```

The *source* field is the large text box on the form. Setting its *Text* property to the empty string ("") clears any text that is currently displayed.

9. Type the following statement after the line you just added to the *openFileDialog_FileOk* method:

```
TextReader reader = src.OpenText();
```

This statement declares a *TextReader* variable called *reader*. (*TextReader* is another class, provided by the .NET Framework, that you can use for reading streams of characters from sources such as files. It is located in the System.IO namespace) The *FileInfo* class provides the *OpenText* method for opening the file selected by the user in the Open dialog. The *OpenText* method returns a *TextReader* object. This statement initializes *reader* to the *TextReader* object returned from the *src.OpenText* method call. The *reader* variable can now be used to read the file chosen by the user.

10. Type the following statements after the previous line you added to the *openFileDialog_FileOk* method:

```
string line = reader.ReadLine();
while (line != null)
{
    source.Text += line + '\n';
    line = reader.ReadLine();
}
reader.Close();
```

This code declares a *string* variable called *line* which is used to hold each line of text as the reader reads it from the file. The statement calls the *reader.ReadLine* method to read the first line from the file. This method returns either the next line of text, or a special value called *null* if there are no more lines to read. The result of this call is assigned to the *line* variable.

The Boolean expression at the start of the *while* loop examines the value in the *line* variable. If it is not null, the body of the loop displays the line of text by appending it to the end of the *Text* property of the *source* TextBox, together with a newline character ('\n' – the *ReadLine* method of the *TextReader* object strips out the newline characters as it reads each line, so the code needs to add it back in again). The *while* loop then reads in the next line of text (this is the update part of the loop) before performing the next iteration.

When the loop finishes, the call to the *Close* method of the *TextReader* object closes the file.

> **Tip**   As you become more experienced with C# syntax, you will find that you can abbreviate the code in the *while* loop as follows:
>
> ```
> string line;
> while ((line = reader.ReadLine()) != null) {        source.Text += line + '\n';  }
> reader.Close();
> ```
>
> In this case, the Boolean expression at the start of the loop also performs the initialization and update. The *ReadLine* method is called, and the return value assigned to the *line* variable. However, an assignment statement actually yields a value—the value of the expression being assigned. Therefore, you can compare the result of an assignment expression by using a relational operator to produce a Boolean result. In this example, if the value assigned is *null*, the value of the assignment expression is *null*, and the comparison to *null* is true.

11. On the Debug menu, click Start Without Debugging.

12. Click Open File.

The Open dialog box opens.

13. Navigate to the \Microsoft Press\Visual CSharp Step by Step\Chapter 5\WhileStatement\WhileStatement folder in your My Documents folder. Select the Form1.cs file and then click Open.

This time the contents of the selected file are displayed in the text box:

14. In the text box, locate the *openFileDialog_FileOk* method. Verify that this method contains the code you just added.

15. Click Close.

    You return to the Visual Studio 2005 programming environment.

Writing *for* Statements

Most *while* statements have the following general structure:

```
initialization
while (Boolean expression)
{
  statement
  update control variable
}
```

A *for* statement allows you to write a more formal version of this kind of construct by combining the initialization, the Boolean expression, and the update (the loop's "housekeeping"). You'll find the *for* statement useful because it is much harder to forget any one of the three parts. Here is the syntax of a *for* statement:

```
for (initialization; Boolean expression; update control variable)
    statement
```

The *while* loop shown earlier, that displays the integers from 0 to 9, can be reconstructed as the following *for* loop:

```
for (int i = 0; i != 10; i++)
{
    Console.WriteLine(i);
}
```

The initialization occurs once at the start of the loop. If the Boolean expression evaluates to true, the statement runs. The control variable update occurs and the Boolean expression is re-evaluated. If the condition is still true, the statement is executed again, the control variable is updated, the Boolean expression is evaluated again, and so on.

Notice that the initialization occurs only once, and that the statement in the body of the loop always executes before the update occurs, and that the update occurs before the Boolean expression evaluates.

You can omit any of the three parts of a *for* statement. If you omit the Boolean expression, it defaults to true. The following *for* statement runs forever:

```
for (int i = 0; ;i++)
{
    Console.WriteLine("somebody stop me!");
}
```

If you omit the initialization and update parts, you have a strangely spelled *while* loop:

```
int i = 0;
for (; i != 10; )
{
    Console.WriteLine(i);
    i++;
}
```

> **Note**   The initialization, Boolean expression, and update control variable parts of a *for* statement must always be separated by semicolons.

If necessary, you can provide multiple initializations and multiple updates in a *for* loop (you can only have one Boolean expression). To achieve this, separate the various initializations and updates with commas, as shown in the following example:

```
for (int i = 0, j = 10; i <= j; i++, j--)
{
    ...
}
```

> **Tip**   It's considered good style to use an explicit statement block for the body of *if, while,* and *for* statements even when the block contains only one statement. By writing the block, you make it easier to add statements to the block at a later date. Without the block, to add another statement, you'd have to remember to add both the extra statement *and* the braces, and it's very easy to forget the braces.

Understanding *for* Statement Scope

You might have noticed that you can declare a variable in the initialization part of a *for* statement. That variable is scoped to the body of the *for* statement and disappears when the *for* statement finishes. This rule has two important consequences. First, you cannot use that variable after the *for* statement has ended, because it's no longer in scope. Here's an example:

```
for (int i = 0; i != 10; i++)
{
    ...
}
Console.WriteLine(i); // compile time error
```

Second, you can write two or more *for* statements next to each other that use the same variable name, because each variable is in a different scope. Here's an example:

```
for (int i = 0; i != 10; i++)
{
    ...
}
 for (int i = 0; i != 20; i += 2) // okay
{
    ...
}
```

Writing *do* Statements

The *while* and *for* statements both test their Boolean expression at the start of the loop. This means that if the expression evaluates to *false* on the very first test, the body of the loop does not run, not even once. The *do* statement is different; its Boolean expression is evaluated after each iteration, and so the body always executes at least once.

The syntax of the *do* statement is as follows (don't forget the final semicolon):

```
do
    statement
while (booleanExpression);
```

Use a statement block if the body of the loop comprises more than one statement. Here's a version of the previous example that writes the values 0 through 9 to the console, this time using a *do* statement:

```
int i = 0;
do
{
    Console.WriteLine(i);
    i++;
}
while (i != 10);
```

The *break* and *continue* Statements

In Chapter 4, you saw the *break* statement being used to jump out of a *switch* statement. You can also use a *break* statement to jump out of the body of an iteration statement. When you break out of a loop, the loop exits immediately and execution continues at the first statement after the loop. Neither the update nor the continuation condition of the loop is re-run.

In contrast, the *continue* statement causes the program to immediately perform the next iteration of the loop (after re-evaluating the Boolean expression). Here's a version of the previous example that writes the values 0 through 9 to the console, this time using *break* and *continue* statements:

```
int i = 0;
while (true)
{
    Console.WriteLine("continue " + i);
    i++;
    if (i != 10)
        continue;
    else
        break;
}
```

This code is absolutely ghastly. Many programming guidelines recommend using *continue* cautiously or not at all because it is often associated with hard-to-understand code. The behavior of *continue* is also quite subtle. For example, if you execute a *continue* statement from inside a *for* statement, the update part runs before performing the next iteration of the loop.

In the following exercise, you will write a *do* statement to convert a number to its string representation.

Write a *do* statement

1. Using Visual Studio 2005, open the *DoStatement* project, located in the \Microsoft Press\Visual CSharp Step by Step\Chapter 5\DoStatement folder in your My Documents folder.

2. On the Debug menu, click Start Without Debugging.

    Visual Studio 2005 builds and runs the Windows application.

    The application displays a form that has two text boxes and the Show Steps button. When you type a positive number (the algorithm used doesn't work with negative numbers) in the upper text box, and click the Show Steps button, the lower text box shows the steps used to create a string representation of this number.

> **Note** This is simply an example showing you how to convert a number to a string using a *do* loop. The .NET Framework provides the *Convert.ToString* method which does the same thing, and is the method you should really use to perform this task if you need it in your own applications.

3. As an example, type **2693** in the upper text box, and then click Show Steps.

   The lower text box displays the steps used to create a string representation of 2693:

4. Close the window to return to the Visual Studio 2005 programming environment.

5. Display the code for Form1.cs in the Code and Text Editor window.

6. Locate the *showSteps_Click* method. This method runs when the user clicks the Show Steps button on the form.

   This method contains the following statements:

```
int amount = System.Int32.Parse(number.Text);
steps.Text = "";
string current = "";
do
{
    int digitCode = '0' + amount % 10;
    char digit = Convert.ToChar(digitCode);
    current = digit + current;
    steps.Text += current + "\r\n";
    amount /= 10;
}
while (amount != 0);
```

> **Note**   \r indicates a carriage return. When writing text to a multiline *TextBox* con-
> trol, you need to output a carriage return and a newline to proceed to the next line
> and return the cursor to the start of the line. Without it, the text will all appear on
> the same line.

The first statement converts the string value in the *Text* property of the *number* text box
into an *int* using the *Parse* method of the *System.Int32* class:

```
int amount = System.Int32.Parse(number.Text);
```

The second statement clears the text displayed in the lower text box (called *steps*) by setting its *Text* property to the empty string:

```
steps.Text = "";
```

The third statement declares a *string* variable called *current* and initializes it to the empty
string:

```
string current = "";
```

The real work in this method is performed by the *do* statement which begins at the
fourth statement.

```
do
{
    ...
}
while (amount != 0);
```

The algorithm repeatedly uses integer arithmetic and the modulus operator to divide
the *amount* variable by 10; the remainder after each successive division constitutes the
next digit in the string being built. Eventually *amount* is reduced to zero, and the loop
finishes. Notice that the body must run at least once. This behavior is exactly what is
required because even the number 0 has one digit.

The first statement inside the *do* loop is:

```
int digitCode = '0' + amount % 10;
```

This statement declares an *int* variable called *digitCode* and initializes it to the result of
the following expression:

```
'0' + amount % 10
```

This expression requires a little explanation! The value of '0' is the zero character. In the
character set used by Windows, this character equates to the integer value 48 (each character has its own unique character code which is an integer value). Similarly, the character code for '1' is 49, the character code for '2' is 50, and so on.

The value of amount % 10 is the remainder you get when you divide *amount* by 10. For example, if *amount* contains the value 2693, then 2693 % 10 is 3. (2693 divided by 10 is 269 with a remainder of 3.) Therefore, if *amount* equals 2693, then the expression '0' + amount % 10 is the same as '0' + 3, which is 51. This is the code for the character **'3'**. (The + operator performs an implicit cast, converting **'0'** to the integer value 48 to allow this expression to be evaluated.)

The second statement inside the *do* loop is:

```
char digit = Convert.ToChar(digitCode);
```

This statement declares a *char* variable called *digit* and initializes it to the result of the *Convert.ToChar(digitCode)* method call. This method call returns the *char* with the integer character code value of the argument. In other words, the value of Convert.ToChar('0' + 3) is the value of '3'.

The third statement inside the *do* loop is:

```
current = digit + current;
```

This statement *prepends* the *char digit* just calculated to the *current* string. Notice that this statement cannot be replaced by current += digit, because that would *append* the digit.

The fourth statement inside the *do* loop is:

```
steps.Text += current + "\r\n";
```

This statement appends another step to the *Text* property of the Steps text box.

The final statement inside the *do* loop is:

```
amount /= 10;
```

This statement is the same as amount = amount / 10;. If the value of *amount* is 2693, the value of *amount* after this statement runs is 269. Notice that each iteration through the *do* statement removes the last digit from *amount* and prepends that digit to the *current* string.

In the final exercise, you will use the Visual Studio 2005 debugger to step through the previous *do* statement to help you understand how it works.

Step through the *do* statement

1. In the Code and Text Editor window, find the *showSteps_Click* method.

2. Move the cursor to the first statement of the *showSteps_Click* method.

   The first statement is as follows:

   ```
   int amount = System.Int32.Parse(number.Text);
   ```

3. Right-click anywhere in the first statement and click Run To Cursor.

Visual Studio 2005 builds and runs the application.

4. When the form appears, type **2693** in the upper text box, and then click Show Steps.

The program stops and you are placed in Visual Studio 2005 in debug mode. A yellow arrow in the left margin of the Code and Text Editor window indicates the current statement.

5. Display the Debug toolbar if it is not visible (on the View menu, point to Toolbars and then select Debug). On the Debug toolbar, click the Windows drop-down arrow.

The following menu appears:

6. On the menu, click Locals.

The Locals window appears. This window displays the name, value, and type of the local variables in the current method, including the *amount* local variable. Notice that the value of *amount* is currently zero:

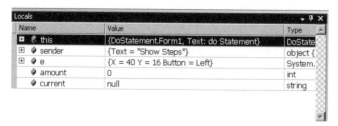

7. On the Debug toolbar, click the Step Into button.

    The debugger runs the current statement:

    ```
    int amount = System.Int32.Parse(number.Text);
    ```

    The value of *amount* in the Locals window changes to 2693 and the yellow arrow moves to the next statement.

8. Click the Step Into button.

    The debugger runs the statement:

    ```
    steps.Text = "";
    ```

    This statement does not affect the Locals window because *steps* is a field of the form and not a local variable. The yellow arrow moves to the next statement.

9. Click the Step Into button.

    The debugger runs the statement:

    ```
    string current = "";
    ```

    The yellow arrow moves to the opening curly brace at the start of the *do* loop.

10. Click the Step Into button.

    The yellow arrow moves to the first statement inside the *do* loop. The *do* loop contains two local variables of its own, *digitCode* and *digit*. Notice that these local variables have appeared in the Locals window and that the value of *digitCode* is zero.

11. Click the Step Into button.

    The debugger runs the statement:

    ```
    int digitCode = '0' + amount % 10;
    ```

    The value of *digitCode* in the Locals window changes to 51. This is because the value of the expression amount % 10 is 3 (the value of *amount* is 2693), and the code for character '3' is 51 (48 + 3).

12. Click the Step Into button.

    The debugger runs the statement:

    ```
    char digit = Convert.ToChar(digitCode);
    ```

    The value of *digit* changes to '3' in the Locals window. The Locals window shows *char* values using both the underlying numeric value (in this case, 51) and also the character representation ('3'). The yellow arrow moves to the next statement inside the *do* loop.

    Note that in the Locals window, the value of the *current* variable is "".

13. Click the Step Into button.

The debugger runs the statement:

```
current = current + digit;
```

The value of *current* changes to "3" in the Locals window.

14. Click the Step Into button.

The debugger runs the statement:

```
steps.Text += current + "\r\n";
```

This statement displays the text "3" in the *steps* text box, followed by a carriage return and newline character, to cause subsequent output to be displayed on the next line in the text box.

In the Locals window, the value of *amount* is still 2693.

15. Click the Step Into button.

The debugger runs the statement:

```
amount /= 10;
```

The value of *amount* changes to 269 in the Locals window. The yellow arrow moves to the curly brace at the end of the *do* loop.

16. Click the Step Into button

The yellow arrow moves to the *while* statement.

17. Click the Step Into button.

The debugger runs the statement:

```
while (amount != 0);
```

The value of *amount* is 269, and the expression **269 != 0** evaluates to *true*, so the *do* loop should perform another iteration. The yellow arrow jumps back to open curly brace at the start of the *do* loop.

18. Click the Step Into button.

The yellow arrow moves to the first statement inside the *do* loop again.

19. Click the Step Into button 22 more times and watch the values of the local variables change in the Locals window.

In the Locals window, the value of *amount* is now zero and the value of *current* is "2693". The yellow arrow is on the continuation condition of the *do* loop:

```
while (amount != 0);
```

The value of *amount* is now 0, so the expression **amount != 0** evaluates to *false*, so the *do* loop should terminate.

20. Click the Step Into button.

The debugger runs the statement:

```
while (amount != 0);
```

As predicted the *do* loop terminates, and the yellow arrow moves to the closing brace at the end of the *showSteps_Click* method.

21. Click the Continue button.

The form appears, displaying the four steps used to create a string representation of 2693: "3", "93", "693", and "2693".

22. Close the form to return to the Visual Studio 2005 programming environment.

Congratulations! You have successfully written meaningful *while* and *do* statements and used the Visual Studio 2005 debugger to step through the *do* statement.

■ **If you want to continue to the next chapter**

Keep Visual Studio 2005 running and turn to Chapter 6, "Managing Errors and Exceptions."

■ **If you want to exit Visual Studio 2005 now**

On the File menu, click Exit. If you see a Save dialog box, click Yes.

Chapter 5 Quick Reference

To	Do this
Add an amount to a variable	Use the compound addition operator. For example: ```variable += amount;```
Subtract an amount from a variable	Use the compound subtraction operator. For example: ```variable -= amount;```

Run one or more statements while a condition is true	Use a *while* statement. For example:
	
	```int i = 0;```
	```while (i != 10)```
	```{```
	``` Console.WriteLine(i);```
	``` i++;```
	```}```
	
	Alternatively, use a *for* statement. For example:
	
	```for (int i = 0; i != 10; i++)```
	```{```
	``` Console.WriteLine(i);```
	```}```

Repeatedly execute statements one or more times	Use a *do* statement. For example:
	
	```int i = 0;```
	```do```
	```{```
	``` Console.WriteLine(i);```
	``` i++;```
	```}```
	```while (i != 10);```

Chapter 6
Managing Errors and Exceptions

After completing this chapter, you will be able to:

- Handle exceptions by using the *try*, *catch*, and *finally* statements.
- Control integer overflow by using the checked and unchecked keywords.
- Raise exceptions from your own methods by using the throw keyword.
- Ensure that code always runs, even after an exception has occurred, by using a *finally* block.

You have now seen the core C# statements you need to know to read and write methods; declare variables; use operators to create values; write *if* and *switch* statements to selectively run code; and write *while*, *for*, and *do* statements to repeatedly run code. However, the previous chapters haven't considered the possibility (or probability) that things can go wrong. It is very difficult to ensure that a piece of code always works as expected. Failures can occur for a large number of reasons, many of which are beyond your control as a programmer. Any applications that you write must be capable of detecting failures and handling them in a graceful manner. In this final chapter of Part I, "Introducing Microsoft Visual C# and Microsoft Visual Studio 2005," you'll learn how C# throws exceptions to signal that an error has occurred, and how to use the *try*, *catch*, and *finally* statements to catch and handle the errors that these exceptions represent. By the end of this chapter, you'll have a solid foundation in C#, which you will build on in Part II, "Understanding the C# Language."

Coping with Errors

It's a fact of life that bad things sometimes happen. Tires get punctured, batteries run down, screwdrivers are never where you left them, and users of your applications behave in an unpredictable manner. Errors can occur at almost any stage when a program runs, so how do you detect them and attempt to recover? Over the years, a number of mechanisms have evolved. A typical approach adopted by older systems such as Unix involved arranging for the operating system to set a special global variable whenever a method failed. Then, after each call to a method, you checked the global variable to see whether the method failed. This solution has a number of shortcomings:

- The main program logic becomes intertwined with alternating code to check and handle the errors. The program quickly becomes hard to understand.

- The error checking and handling code is typically very repetitive and can easily double the size of the program. A large program is harder to understand than a small program simply because it's larger. Duplicate code is always a warning sign that an application can be structured in a better manner.

- The error codes used by a global variable, such as −1 used by Unix systems, are not inherently meaningful. What does −1 mean? Integer error codes don't describe the errors they represent. They're very programmatic. Once again, the program becomes harder to understand and maintain.

- It's just too easy to ignore the error condition and assume that a method being called works every time. Many programmers don't like to read documentation, and fewer like to write it, so the method might not be documented with information about the errors it can cause.

For these reasons, C# and most other modern object-oriented languages don't handle errors in this way. It's just too painful. They use *exceptions* instead. If you want to write robust C# programs, you need to know about exceptions.

Trying Code and Catching Exceptions

C# makes it easy to separate the code that implements the main flow of the program from the error handling code, by using exceptions and exception handlers. To write exception-aware programs, you need to do two things:

1. Write your code inside a *try* block (*try* is a keyword). When the code runs, it attempts to execute all the statements inside the *try* block, and if none of the statements generates an exception, they all run, one after the other, to completion. However, if an error condition occurs, execution jumps out of the *try* block and into a *catch* handler.

2. Write one or more *catch* handlers (*catch* is a keyword) immediately after the *try* block to handle any possible error conditions. If any one of the statements inside the *try* block causes an error, the runtime generates and throws an exception. The runtime then examines the *catch* handlers after the *try* block and transfers control directly to a matching handler. *Catch* handlers are designed to trap particular exceptions, allowing you to provide different handlers for the different errors that can happen.

Here's an example that uses a *try* block to attempt to convert some text fields into integer values, call a method to calculate a value, and write the result to a text field. Converting a string to an integer requires that the string contains a valid representation and not some arbitrary sequence of characters. If the string contains invalid characters, the *Int32.Parse* method throws a *FormatException*, and execution transfers to the corresponding *catch* handler. When the *catch* handler finishes, the program continues with the first statement after the handler:

```
try
{
    int leftHandSide = Int32.Parse(leftHandSideOperand.Text);
    int rightHandSide = Int32.Parse(rightHandSideOperand.Text);
    int answer = doCalculation(leftHandSide, rightHandSide);
    result.Text = answer.ToString();
}
catch (FormatException fEx)
{
    // Handle the exception
    ...
}
```

Handling an Exception

The *catch* handler uses syntax similar to that used by a method parameter to specify the exception to be caught. In the previous example, when a *FormatException* is thrown, the *fEx* variable is populated with an object containing the details of the exception. The *FormatException* type has a number of fields that you can examine to determine the exact cause of the exception. Many of these fields are common to all exceptions. For example, the *Message* field contains a text description of the error that caused the exception. You can use this information when handling the exception, recording the details to a log file, or outputting a meaningful message to the user and asking them to try again, for example.

Unhandled Exceptions

What happens if a *try* block throws an exception and there is no corresponding *catch* handler? In the previous example, it is possible that the *leftHandSideOperand* field contains the string representation of a valid integer, but the integer that it represents is outside of the range of valid integers supported by C# (for example, "2147483648"). In this case, the *Int32.Parse* statement will throw an *OverflowException*, which will not be caught by the *catch* handler as it specifies that it catches *FormatException*. If the *try* block is part of a method, the method finishes and returns to the calling method. If the calling method uses a *try* block, the common language runtime attempts to locate a matching *catch* handler after the *try* block and execute it. If the calling method does not use a *try* block, or there is no matching *catch* handler, the calling method terminates and returns to its caller where the process is repeated. If a matching *catch* handler is eventually found, it runs and execution continues with the first statement after the *catch* handler in the catching method.

Important   Notice that after catching an exception, execution continues in the method containing the *catch* block that caught the exception. Control does *not* return to the method that caused the exception.

If, after cascading back through the list of calling methods, the common language runtime is unable to find a matching catch handler, the program terminates with an unhandled exception. If you are running the application in Visual Studio 2005 in Debug mode (you selected Start Debugging in the Debug menu to run the application), the following information dialog box appears and the application drops into the debugger, allowing you to determine the cause of the exception:

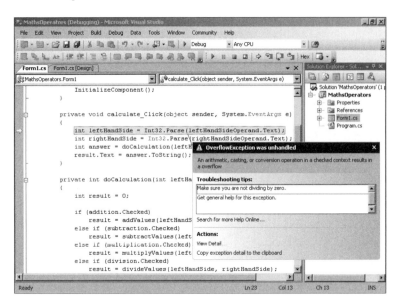

Using Multiple *catch* Handlers

The previous discussion highlighted how different errors throw different kinds of exceptions to represent different kinds of failure. To cope with these situations, you can supply multiple *catch* handlers, one after the other, like this:

```
try
{
    int leftHandSide = Int32.Parse(leftHandSideOperand.Text);
    int rightHandSide = Int32.Parse(rightHandSideOperand.Text);
    int answer = doCalculation(leftHandSide, rightHandSide);
    result.Text = answer.ToString();
}
catch (FormatException fEx)
{
    //...
}
catch (OverflowException oEx)
{
    //...
}
```

Catching Multiple Exceptions

The exception-catching mechanism of the common language runtime is pretty comprehensive. There are many different exceptions defined in the .NET Framework, and any programs you write will be able to throw most of them! It is highly unlikely that you will want to write *catch* handlers for every possible exception that your code can throw. So how do you ensure that all possible exceptions are caught and handled?

The answer to this question lies in the way the different exceptions are related to each other. Exceptions are organized into families called inheritance hierarchies (you will learn about inheritance in Chapter 12, "Working with Inheritance"). *FormatException* and *OverflowException* both belong to a family called *SystemException*, as do a number of other exceptions. Rather than catching each of these exceptions individually, you can create a handler that catches *SystemException*. *SystemException* is itself a member of a family simply called *Exception*, which is the great-grandaddy of all exceptions. If you catch *Exception*, the handler traps every possible exception that can occur.

> **Note**   The *Exception* family includes a wide variety of exceptions, many of which are intended for use by various parts of the common language runtime. Some of these are somewhat esoteric, but it is still useful to understand how to catch them.

The next example shows how to catch all possible system exceptions:

```
try
{
    int leftHandSide = Int32.Parse(leftHandSideOperand.Text);
    int rightHandSide = Int32.Parse(rightHandSideOperand.Text);
    int answer = doCalculation(leftHandSide, rightHandSide);
    result.Text = answer.ToString();
}
catch (Exception ex) // this is a general catch handler
{
    //...
}
```

> **Tip**   If you wish to catch *Exception*, you can actually omit its name from the *catch* handler, because it is the default exception:
>
> ```
> catch  {      // ... }
> ```
>
> However, this is not always recommended. The exception object passed in to the *catch* handler can contain useful information concerning the exception, which is not accessible when using this version of the *catch* construct.

There is one final question you should be asking at this point: What happens if the same exception matches multiple *catch* handlers at the end of a *try* block? If you catch *FormatException* and *Exception* in two different handlers, which one will run (or will both execute)?

When an exception occurs, the first handler found by the common language runtime that matches the exception is used, and the others are ignored. What this means is, if you place a handler for *Exception* before a handler for *FormatException*, the *FormatException* handler will never run. Therefore you should place more specific *catch* handlers above a general *catch* handler after a *try* block. If none of the specific *catch* handlers matches the exception, the general *catch* handler will.

In the following exercise, you will write a *try* block and catch an exception.

Write a *try/catch* statement

1. Start Visual Studio 2005.

2. Open the *MathsOperators* solution located in the \Microsoft Press\Visual CSharp Step By Step\Chapter 6\MathsOperators folder in your My Documents folder.

   This is a variation on the program that you first saw in Chapter 2, "Working with Variables, Operators, and Expressions." It was used to demonstrate the different arithmetic operators.

3. On the Debug menu, click Start Without Debugging.

> **Note**   If you run the application in Debug mode, it drops into the debugger when an unhandled exception occurs. This is not what we want in this example, so ensure that you click Start Without Debugging.

   Visual Studio 2005 builds and runs the Windows application. The Exceptions Form appears.

   You are now going to deliberately enter some text that is not valid in the left operand text box. This operation will demonstrate the lack of robustness in the current version of the program.

4. Type **John** in the left operand text box, and then click Calculate.

   A dialog box reports an unhandled exception; the text you entered in the left operand text box caused the application to fail.

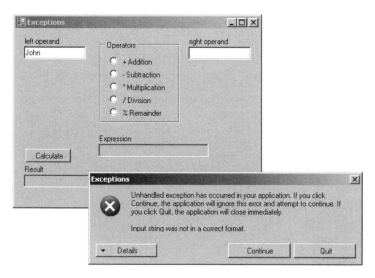

5. Click Details in the Exception dialog box to display the information concerning the exception:

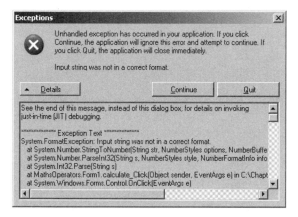

From the first few lines of text, you can ascertain that the exception was thrown by the call to *Int32.Parse* inside the *calculate_Click* method.

6. Click Quit to close the Exceptions dialog box and return to Visual Studio 2005.

7. Display the code for the file Form1.cs in the Code pane.

8. Locate the *calculate_Click* method. Add a *try* block around the four statements inside this method, so that the code looks exactly as follows:

```
try
{
    int leftHandSide = Int32.Parse(leftHandSideOperand.Text);
    int rightHandSide = Int32.Parse(rightHandSideOperand.Text);
    int answer = doCalculation(leftHandSide, rightHandSide);
    result.Text = answer.ToString();
}
```

9. Add a *catch* block after this new *try* block, as follows:

```
catch (FormatException fEx)
{
    result.Text = fEx.Message;
}
```

This *catch* handler catches the *FormatException* thrown by *Int32.Parse*, and then writes its *Message* text to the *Text* property of the *result* text box at the bottom of the form.

10. On the Debug menu, click Start Without Debugging.

11. Type **John** in the left operand text box, and then click Calculate.

The *catch* handler successfully catches the *FormatException*, and the message "Input string was not in a correct format." is written to the Result text box. The application is now a bit more robust.

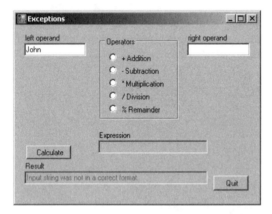

12. Click Quit to return to the Visual Studio 2005 programming environment.

Using Checked and Unchecked Integer Arithmetic

In Chapter 2, you learned how to use binary arithmetic operators such as + and * on primitive data types such as *int* and *double*. You also saw that the primitive data types have a fixed size. For example, a C# *int* is 32 bits. Because *int* has a fixed size, you know exactly the range of value that it can hold: it is −2147483648 to 2147483647.

> **Tip**   If you want to determine the minimum or maximum value of *int* in code, you can use the *Int32.MinValue* or *Int32.MaxValue* fields.

The fixed size of the *int* type creates a problem. For example, what happens if you add 1 to an *int* whose value is currently 2147483647? The answer is that it depends on how the application is compiled. By default, the C# compiler generates code that allows the calculation to silently overflow. In other words, you get the wrong answer. (In fact, the calculation wraps around to the largest negative integer value and the result generated is −2147483648.) The reason for this behavior is performance: integer arithmetic is a common operation in almost every program, and adding the overhead of overflow checking to each integer expression could lead to very poor performance. In many cases, the risk is acceptable because you know (or hope!) that your *int* values won't reach their limits. If you don't like this approach, you can turn on overflow checking by setting.

> **Tip**   You can enable and disable overflow checking in Visual Studio 2005 by setting the project properties. On the Project menu, click *YourProject* Properties (where *YourProject* is the name of your project). In the project properties dialog box, click the Build tab. Click the Advanced button in the lower-right corner of the page. In the Advanced Build Settings dialog box, select or clear the "Check for arithmetic overflow/underflow" check box.

Regardless of how you compile an application, you can use the *checked* and *unchecked* keywords to selectively turn on and off integer arithmetic overflow checking in parts of an application that you think need it. These keywords override the compiler option.

Writing *checked* Statements

A *checked statement* is a block preceded by the *checked* keyword. All integer arithmetic in a checked statement always throws an *OverflowException* if an integer calculation in the block overflows, as shown in this example:

```
int number = Int32.MaxValue;
checked
{
    int willThrow = number++;
    Console.WriteLine("this won't be reached");
}
```

> **Important**   Only integer arithmetic directly inside the *checked* block is checked. For example, if one of the checked statements is a method call, the checking does not encapsulate the method call.

You can also use the *unchecked* keyword to create an *unchecked* block statement. All integer arithmetic in an *unchecked* block is not checked and never throws an *OverflowException*. For example:

```
int number = Int32.MaxValue;
unchecked
{
    int wontThrow = number++;
    Console.WriteLine("this will be reached");
}
```

> **Important**   You cannot use the *checked* and *unchecked* keywords to control floating point (non-integer) arithmetic. The *checked* and *unchecked* keywords control only integer arithmetic. Floating point arithmetic never throws *OverflowException*—not even when you divide by 0.0 (the .NET Framework has a representation for infinity).

Writing Checked Expressions

You can also use the *checked* and *unchecked* keywords to control overflow checking on integer expressions by preceding just the individual parenthesized expression with the *checked* or *unchecked* keyword, as shown in this example:

```
int wontThrow = unchecked(Int32.MaxValue + 1);
int willThrow = checked(Int32.MaxValue + 1);
```

The compound operators (such as += and -=) and the increment (++) and decrement (–) operators are arithmetic operators and can be controlled by using the *checked* and *unchecked* keywords. Remember, x += y; is the same as x = x + y;.

In the following exercise, you will see how to perform checked arithmetic when using Visual Studio 2005.

Use checked expressions

1. Return to Visual Studio 2005, and display the MathsOperators solution.

2. On the Debug menu, click Start Without Debugging.

    You will now attempt to multiply two large values.

3. Type **9876543** in the left operand text box, type **9876543** in the right operand text box, select the Multiplication option under Operators, and then click Calculate.

    The value –1195595903 appears in the Result text box on the form. This is a negative value, which cannot possibly be correct. This value is the result of a multiplication operation that silently overflowed the 32-bit limit of the *int* type.

4. Click Quit to return to the Visual Studio 2005 programming environment.

5. In the Code pane displaying Form1.cs, locate the *multiplyValues* method:

    ```
    private int multiplyValues(int leftHandSide, int rightHandSide)
    {
        expression.Text = leftHandSide.ToString() + " * " + rightHandSide.ToString();
        return leftHandSide * rightHandSide;
    }
    ```

    The *return* statement contains the multiplication operation that is silently overflowing.

6. Edit the *return* statement so that the return value is checked. The *multiplyValues* method should look exactly as follows:

```
private int multiplyValues(int leftHandSide, int rightHandSide)
{
    expression.Text = leftHandSide.ToString() + " * " + rightHandSide.ToString();
    return checked(leftHandSide * rightHandSide);
}
```

The multiplication is now checked and will throw an *OverflowException* rather than silently returning the wrong answer.

7. In the Code pane, locate the *calculate_Click* method.

8. Add the following *catch* handler immediately after the existing *FormatException catch* handler in the *calculate_Click* method:

```
catch (OverflowException oEx)
{
    result.Text = oEx.Message;
}
```

> **Tip** The logic of this *catch* handler is the same as that for the *FormatException catch* handler. However, it is still worth keeping these handlers separate rather than simply writing a generic *Exception catch* handler as you might decide to handle these exceptions differently in the future.

9. On the Debug menu, click Start Without Debugging to build and run the application.

10. Type **9876543** in the left operand text box, type **9876543** in the right operand text box, select the Multiplication option under Operators, and then click Calculate.

The second *catch* handler successfully catches the *OverflowException* and displays the message "Arithmetic operation resulted in an overflow" in the Result text box.

11. Click Quit to return to the Visual Studio 2005 programming environment.

Throwing Exceptions

Suppose you are implementing a method called *monthName* that accepts a single *int* argument and returns the name of the corresponding month. For example, *monthName(1)* returns "January." The question is: what should the method return when the integer argument is less than 1 or greater than 12? The best answer is that the method shouldn't return anything at all; it should throw an exception. The .NET Framework class libraries contain lots of exception classes specifically designed for situations such as this. Most of the time, you will find that one of these classes describes your exceptional condition. (If not, you can easily create your own exception class, but you need to know a bit more about the C# language before you can do that.) In this case, the existing .NET Framework *ArgumentOutOfRangeException* class is just right:

```
public static string monthName(int month)
{
    switch (month)
    {
        case 1 :
            return "January";
        case 2 :
            return "February";
        ...
        case 12 :
            return "December";
        default :
            throw new ArgumentOutOfRangeException("Bad month");
    }
}
```

Notice how the *default* case uses a *throw* statement to generate an exception. The *throw* statement needs an exception to throw. This example uses an expression that creates a new *ArgumentOutOfRangeException* object. The object is initialized with a string that will populate its *Message* property, by using a constructor. Constructors are covered in detail in Chapter 7, "Creating and Managing Classes and Objects."

In the following exercises, you will add code that throws and catches exceptions to the MathsOperators project.

Throw your own exception

1. Return to Visual Studio 2005, and make sure the MathsOperators solution is still open.

2. On the Debug menu, click Start Without Debugging.

3. Type **24** in the left operand text box, type **36** in the right operand text box, and then click Calculate.

   The value *0* ppears in the Result text box. The fact that you have not selected an operator option is not immediately obvious. It would be useful to write a diagnostic message in the Result text box.

4. Click Quit to return to the Visual Studio 2005 programming environment.

5. In the Code pane displaying Form1.cs, locate and examine the *doCalculation* method. It looks like this:

   ```
   private int doCalculation(int leftHandSide, int rightHandSide)
   {
       int res = 0;
       if (addition.Checked)
           res = addValues(leftHandSide, rightHandSide);
       else if (subtraction.Checked)
           res = subtractValues(leftHandSide, rightHandSide);
   ```

```
    else if (multiplication.Checked)
        res = multiplyValues(leftHandSide, rightHandSide);
    else if (division.Checked)
        res = divideValues(leftHandSide, rightHandSide);
    else if (remainder.Checked)
        res = remainderValues(leftHandSide, rightHandSide);
    return res;
}
```

The *addition*, *subtraction*, *multiplication*, *division*, and *remainder* fields are the radio buttons that appear in the Operators group on the form. Each radio button has a *Checked* Boolean property that has the value *true* if the option is selected. The cascading *if* statement examines each radio button in turn to find out which one is selected. If none of the options are selected, none of the *if* statements will be true and the *res* variable will remain at its initial value (0). This variable holds the value that is returned by the method.

> **Important**   Do not confuse the C# *checked* keyword with the *Checked* property of a radio button—they are not related in any way.

You could try to solve the problem by adding one more *else* statement to the *if-else* cascade, to write a message to the *result* text box, as follows:

```
if (addition.Checked)
    res = addValues(leftHandSide, rightHandSide);
...
else if (remainder.Checked)
    res = remainderValues(leftHandSide, rightHandSide);
else
    result.Text = "no operator selected";
```

However, this solution is not a good idea as it is not really the purpose of this method to output messages. With this code, you would have two methods in the program that write diagnostic messages to the *result* text box— *calculate_Click* and *doCalculation*. It is better to separate the detection and signaling of an error from the catching and handling of that error.

6. Add one more *else* statement to the list of *if-else* statements (immediately before the *return* statement) and throw an *InvalidOperationException* exactly as follows:

```
else
    throw new InvalidOperationException("no operator selected");
```

7. On the Debug menu, click Start Without Debugging to build and run the application.

8. Type **24** in the left operand text box, type **36** in the right operand text box, and then click Calculate.

An Exception message box appears.

9. Click Details.

The message tells you that an *InvalidOperationException* has been thrown with the string "no operator selected."

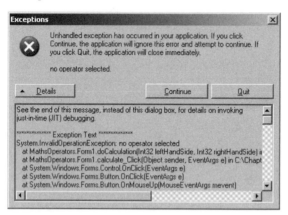

10. Click Quit in the Exceptions message box.

The application terminates and you return to Visual Studio 2005.

Now that you have written a *throw* statement and verified that it throws an exception, you will write a *catch* handler to catch this exception.

Catch your own exception

1. In the Code pane displaying Form1.cs, locate the *calculate_Click* method.

2. Add the following catch handler immediately below the existing two catch handlers in the *calculate_Click* method:

```
catch (InvalidOperationException ioEx)
{
    result.Text = ioEx.Message;
}
```

This code will catch the *InvalidOperationException* that is thrown when no operator option is selected.

3. On the Debug menu, click Start Without Debugging.

4. Type **24** in the left operand text box, type **36** in the right operand text box, and then click Calculate.

The message "no operator selected" appears in the Result text box.

5. Click Quit.

The application is now a lot more robust than it was. However, several exceptions could still arise that would not be caught and might cause the application to fail. For example, if you attempt to divide by zero, an unhandled *DivideByZeroException* will be thrown (integer division by zero does throw an exception, unlike floating point division by zero). One way to solve this would be to write an ever larger number of *catch* handlers inside the *calculate_Click* method. However, a better solution would be to add a general *catch* handler that catches *Exception* to the end of the list of *catch* handlers. This will trap all unhandled exceptions.

> **Tip**   The decision of whether to explicitly catch all unhandled exceptions in a method depends on the nature of the application you are building. In some cases, it makes sense to catch exceptions as close to the point that they occur as possible, but in other situations it is more useful to let an exception propagate back up the method call stack to be handled by the method that invoked the routine that threw the exception.

6. In the Code pane displaying Form1.cs, locate the *calculate_Click* method.

7. Add the following *catch* handler to the end of the list of existing *catch* handlers:

```
catch (Exception ex)
{
    result.Text = ex.Message;
}
```

This *catch* handler will catch all hitherto unhandled exceptions, whatever their specific type.

8. On the Debug menu, click Start Without Debugging.

You will now attempt some calculations known to cause exceptions and confirm that they are all caught.

9. Type **24** in the left operand text box, type **36** in the right operand text box, and then click Calculate. Confirm that the diagnostic message "no operator selected" still appears in the Result text box. This message was generated by the *InvalidOperationException* handler.

10. Type **John** in the left operand text box, and then click Calculate. Confirm that the diagnostic message "Input string was not in a correct format" appears in the Result text box. This message was generated by the *FormatException* handler.

11. Type **24** in the left operand text box, type **0** in the right operand text box, select the Divide option under Operators, and then click Calculate. Confirm that the diagnostic message "Attempted to divide by zero" appears in the Result text box. This message was generated by the general *Exception* handler.

12. Click Quit.

Using a *finally* Block

It is important to remember that when an exception is thrown, it changes the flow of execution through the program. This means you can't guarantee that a statement will always run
when the previous statement finishes, because the previous statement might throw an exception. Look at the following example. It's very easy to assume the call to *reader.Close* will always
occur. After all, it's right there in the code:

```
TextReader reader = src.OpenText();
string line;
while ((line = reader.ReadLine()) != null)
{
    source.Text += line + "\n";
}
reader.Close();
```

Sometimes it's not an issue if one particular statement does not run, but on many occassions
it can be a big problem. If the statement releases a resource that was acquired in a previous
statement, then failing to execute this statement results in the resource being retained. This
example is just such a case: If the call to *src.OpenText* succeeds, then it acquires a resource (a
file handle) and you must ensure that you call *reader.Close* to release the resource. If you don't,
sooner or later you'll run out of file handles and be unable to open more files (if you find file
handles too trivial, think of database connections instead).

The way to ensure a statement is always run, whether or not an exception has been thrown, is
to write that statement inside a *finally* block. A *finally* block occurs immediately after a *try*
block, or immediately after the last *catch* handler after a *try* block. As long as the program
enters the *try* block associated with a *finally* block, the *finally* block will always be run, even if
an exception occurs. If an exception is thrown and caught locally, the exception handler executes first, followed by the *finally* block. If the exception is not caught locally (the common
language runtime has to search through the list of calling methods to find a handler), the
finally block runs first. In any case, the *finally* block always executes.

The solution to the *reader.Close* problem is as follows:

```
TextReader reader = null;
try
{
    reader = src.OpenText();
    string line;
    while ((line = reader.ReadLine()) != null)
    {
        source.Text += line + "\n";
    }
}
finally
{
    if (reader != null)
    {
```

```
        reader.Close();
    }
}
```

Even if an exception is thrown, the *finally* block ensures that the *reader.Close* statement always executes. You'll see another way to solve this problem in Chapter 13, "Using Garbage Collection and Resource Management."

■ **If you want to continue to the next chapter**

Keep Visual Studio 2005 running and turn to Chapter 7.

■ **If you want to exit Visual Studio 2005 now**

On the File menu, click Exit. If you see a Save dialog box, click Yes.

Chapter 6 Quick Reference

To	Do this

Throw an exception	Use a *throw* statement. For example:
	
	``csharp
	throw new FormatException(source);
	``

Ensure that integer arithmetic is always checked for overflow	Use the *checked* keyword. For example:
	
	``csharp
	int number = Int32.MaxValue;
	checked
	{
	    number++;
	}
	``

Catch a specific exception	Write a *catch* handler that catches the specific exception class. For example:
	
	``csharp
	try
	{
	    ...
	}
	catch (FormatException fEx)
	{
	    ...
	}
	``

Catch all exceptions in a single *catch* handler	Write a *catch* handler that catches *Exception*. For example:
	
	``csharp
	try
	{
	    ...
	}
	catch (Exception ex)
	{
	    ...
	}
	``

Ensure that some code will always be run, even if an exception is thrown	Write the code inside a *finally* block. For example:
	
	``csharp
	try
	{
	    ...
	}
	finally
	{
	    // always run
	}
	``

Part II
Understanding the C# Language

In this part:

Chapter 7
Creating and Managing Classes and Objects

After completing this chapter, you will be able to:

- Define a class containing a related set of methods and data items.

- Control the accessibility of a class's members by using the public and private keywords.

- Create objects by using the *new* keyword and a constructor.

- Write and call your own constructors.

- Create methods and data that can be shared by all instances of the same class, by using the *static* keyword.

In Part I, "Introducing Microsoft Visual C# and Microsoft Visual Studio 2005," you learned how to declare variables, use operators to create values, call methods, and write many of the statements you need when implementing a method. You now know enough to progress to the next stage—combining methods and data into your own classes.

The Microsoft .NET Framework contains thousands of classes, and you have used a number of them already, including *Console* and *Exception*. Classes provide a convenient mechanism for modeling the entities manipulated by applications. An *entity* can represent a specific item, such as a customer, or something more abstract, such as a transaction. Part of the design process of any system is concerned with determining the entities that are important, and then performing an analysis to see what information they need to hold and what functions they should perform. You store the information that a class holds as fields, and implement the functions of a class by using methods.

The chapters in Part II, "Understanding the C# Language," provide you with all you need to know to create your own classes.

Understanding Classification

Class is the root word of classification. When you design a class, you systematically arrange information into a meaningful entity. This arranging is an act of classification and is something that everyone does—not just programmers. For example, all cars share common behaviors (they can be steered, stopped, accelerated, and so on) and common attributes (they have a steering wheel, an engine, and so on). People use the word *car* to mean objects that share these common behaviors and attributes. As long as everyone agrees on what a word means, it all works well; you can express complex but precise ideas in a concise form. Without classification, it's hard to imagine how people could think or communicate at all.

Given that classification is so deeply ingrained into the way we think and communicate, it makes sense to try to write programs by classifying the different concepts inherent in a problem and its solution, and then modeling these classes in a programming language. This is exactly what modern object-oriented programming languages, such as Microsoft Visual C#, allow you to do.

The Purpose of Encapsulation

Encapsulation is an important principle when defining classes. The idea is that a program that uses a class should not have to worry how that class actually works internally; the program simply creates an instance of a class, and calls the methods of that class. As long as those methods do what they say they will do, the program does not care how they are implemented. For example, when you call the *Console.WriteLine* method, you don't want to be bothered with all the intricate details of how the Console class physically arranges for data to be output to the screen. A class might need to maintain all sorts of internal state information in order to perform its various methods. This additional state information and activity is hidden from the program that is using the class. Therefore, encapsulation is sometimes referred to as information-hiding. Encapsulation actually has two purposes:

1. To combine methods and data inside a class; in other words, to support classification.

2. To control the accessibility of the methods and data; in other words, to control the use of the class.

Defining and Using a Class

In C#, you use the *class* keyword, a name, and a pair of curly braces to define a new class. The data and methods of the class occur in the body of the class, between the curly braces. Here is a C# class called *Circle* that contains one method (to calculate the circle's area) and one piece of data (the circle's radius):

```
class Circle
{
    double Area()
    {
        return 3.141592 * radius * radius;
    }

    double radius;
}
```

The body of a class contains ordinary methods (such as *Area*) and fields (such as *radius*)—remember that variables in a class are called fields. You've already seen how to declare variables in Chapter 2, "Working with Variables, Operators, and Expressions," and how to write methods in Chapter 3, "Writing Methods and Applying Scope"; in fact, there's almost no new syntax here.

Using the *Circle* class is similar to using other types that you have already met; you create a variable specifying *Circle* as its type, and then you initialize the variable with some valid data. Here is an example:

```
Circle c;// Create a Circle variable
c = new Circle();// Initialize it
```

Note the use of the *new* keyword. Previously, when you initialized a variable such as an *int* or a *float,* you simply assigned it a value:

```
int i;
i = 42;
```

You cannot do the same with variables of class types. One reason is that C# just doesn't provide the syntax for assigning literal class values to variables. (What is the *Circle* equivalent of 42?) Another reason concerns the way in which memory for variables of class types is allocated and managed by the common language runtime—this will be discussed further in Chapter 8, "Understanding Values and References." For now, just accept that the *new* keyword creates a new instance of a class (more commonly called an object).

> **Important** Don't get confused between the terms *class* and *object*. A class is the definition of a type. An object is an instance of that type, created when the program runs. For example, it is possible to create many instances of the *Circle* class in a program by using the *new* keyword, just as you can create many *int* variables in a program. Each instance of the *Circle* class is an object that occupies its own space in memory, and runs independently of all the other instances.

Controlling Accessibility

Surprisingly, the *Circle* class is currently of no practical use. When you encapsulate your methods and data inside a class, the class forms a boundary to the outside world. Fields (such as *radius*) and methods (such as *Area*) defined in the class can be seen by other methods inside the class, but not by the outside world—they are private to the class. In other words, although you can create a Circle object in a program, you cannot access its *radius* field or call its *Area* method, which is why the class is not of much use—yet! However, you can modify the definition of a field or method with the *public* and *private* keywords to control whether it is accessible from the outside:

- A method or field is said to be *private* if it is accessible only from the inside of the class. To declare that a method or field is *private*, you write the keyword *private* before its declaration. This is actually the default, but it is good practice to explicitly state that fields and methods are private to avoid any confusion.

- A method or field is said to be *public* if it is accessible from both the inside and the outside of the class. To declare that a method or field is *public*, you write the keyword *public* before its declaration.

Here is the *Circle* class again. This time *Area* is declared as a public method and *radius* is declared as a private field:

```
class Circle
{
    public double Area()
    {
        return 3.141592 * radius * radius;
    }

    private double radius;
}
```

> **Note**   C++ programmers should note that there is no colon after the *public* or *private* keywords. You must repeat the keyword on every declaration.

Note that *radius* is declared as a private field; it is not accessible from outside the class. However, *radius* is accessible from inside the *Circle* class. This is why the *Area* method can access the *radius* field; *Area* is inside the *Circle* class, so the body of *Area* has access to *radius*. However, the class is still of limited value as there is no way of initializing the *radius* field. To fix this, we will use a constructor.

> **Tip**   The fields in a class are automatically initialized to *0, false,* or *null* depending on their type. However, it is still good practice to provide an explicit means of initializing fields.

> **Important**   Don't declare two *public* class members whose names differ only in case. If you do, your class will not conform to the Common Language Specification (CLS), and will not be usable from other languages that are not case sensitive, such as Microsoft Visual Basic.

Working with Constructors

When you use the *new* keyword to create an object, the common language runtime has to construct that object by using the definition of the class. The common language runtime has to grab a piece of memory from the operating system, fill it with the fields defined by the class, and then call the constructor to perform any initialization required.

A *constructor* is a special method; it has the same name as the class, it can take parameters, but it cannot return a value (not even a void). Every class must have a constructor. If you don't write one yourself, the compiler automatically generates a default constructor for you (however, it doesn't actually do anything!). You can write your own default constructor quite easily—just add a public method with the same name as the class, that does not return a value. The following example shows the *Circle* class with a default constructor that initializes the *radius* field to 0:

```
class Circle
{
    public Circle()  // default constructor
    {
        radius = 0.0;
    }

    public double Area()
    {
        return 3.141592 * radius * radius;
    }

    private double radius;
}
```

> **Note**   In C# parlance, the *default* constructor is a constructor that does not take any parameters. It does not matter whether the compiler generates it or you write it yourself, it is still the default constructor. You can also write non-default constructors, as you will see in the section titled "Overloading Constructors" later in this chapter.

Note that the constructor is marked as public. If this keyword is omitted, the constructor will be private (just like any other methods and fields). If the constructor is private, it cannot be used outside of the class, which will prevent you from being able to create *Circle* objects from methods that are not part of the *Circle* class. You might therefore think that private constructors are not that valuable. They do have their uses, but they are beyond the scope of the current discussion.

You can now use the *Circle* class and exercise its *Area* method. Notice how you use dot notation to invoke the *Area* method on a *Circle* object:

```
Circle c;
c = new Circle();
double areaOfCircle = c.Area();
```

Overloading Constructors

You're almost finished, but not quite. You can now declare a *Circle* variable, point it to a newly created *Circle* object, and then call its *Area* method. However, there is still one last problem. The area of all *Circle* objects will always be 0 because the default constructor sets the radius to 0 and it stays at 0 (it's private, and there is no way of changing its value once it has been initialized). One way to solve this problem is to realize that a constructor is just a special kind of method and it—like all methods—can be overloaded. Just as there are several versions of the *Console.WriteLine* method, each of which takes different parameters, so you can also write different versions of a constructor. You can add a constructor to the *Circle* class, with the radius as its parameter, like this:

```
class Circle
{

    public Circle()  // default constructor
    {
        radius = 0.0;
    }

    public Circle(double initialRadius) // overloaded constructor
    {
        radius = initialRadius;
    }

    public double Area()
    {
        return 3.141593 * radius * radius;
    }

    private double radius;
}
```

 Note   The order of the constructors in a class is immaterial; you can define them in whatever order you feel most comfortable with.

There is a quirk of the C# language that you should be aware of: If you write your own constructor for a class, the compiler does not generate a default constructor. Therefore, if you've written your own constructor that accepts one or more parameters and you also want a default constructor, you'll have to write the default constructor yourself.

Partial Classes

A class can contain a number of methods, fields, and constructors, as well as other items that we will discuss in later chapters. A highly functional class can become quite large. A new feature of C# 2.0 allows you to split the source code for a class into separate files, so you can organize the definition of a large class into smaller, easier to manage pieces. This feature is used by Visual Studio 2005 for Windows Forms applications, where the source code that the developer can edit is maintained in a separate file from the code that is generated by Visual Studio whenever the layout of a form changes.

When you split a class across multiple files, you define the parts of the class by using the *partial* keyword in each file. For example, if the *Circle* class was split between two files called circ1.cs (containing the constructors), and circ2.cs (containing the methods and fields, the contents of circ1.cs would look like this:

```
partial class Circle
{
    public Circle()  // default constructor
    {
        this.radius = 0.0;
    }

    public Circle(double initialRadius) // overloaded constructor
    {
        this.radius = initialRadius;
    }
}
```

The contents of circ2.cs would look like this:

```
partial class Circle
{
     public double Area()
    {
        return Math.PI * radius * radius;
    }

    private double radius;
}
```

When you compile a class that has been split into separate files, you must provide all the files to the compiler.

In the following exercise, you will declare a class with two public constructors and two private fields. You will create instances of the class by using the *new* keyword and calling the constructors.

Write constructors and create objects

1. Start Microsoft Visual Studio 2005.

2. Open the Classes project, located in the \Microsoft Press\Visual CSharp Step by Step\Chapter 7\Classes folder in your My Documents folder.

3. Display the file Program.cs in the Code and Text Editor window, and locate the Main method of the Program class.

   The *Main* method calls the *Entrance* method, wrapped in a *try* block and followed by a *catch* handler. This *try/catch* block allows you to write the code that would normally go inside *Main* in the *Entrance* method instead, safe in the knowledge that any exceptions will be caught.

4. Display the file Point.cs in the Code and Text Editor window.

   The *Point* class is currently empty. There is no constructor, so the compiler will write one for you. You will now invoke this compiler-generated constructor.

5. Return to the Program.cs file, and locate the *Entrance* method of the *Application* class. Edit the body of the *Entrance* method to contain the following statement:

   ```
   Point origin = new Point();
   ```

6. On the Build menu, click Build Solution.

   The code builds without error because the compiler generates the code for a default constructor for the *Point* class. However, you cannot see the C# code for this constructor as the compiler does not generate any source language statements.

7. Return to the *Point* class in Point.cs. Add a *public* constructor that accepts two *int* arguments, and calls *Console.WriteLine* to display the values of the arguments to the console.

   The *Point* class should look like this:

   ```
   class Point
   {
       public Point(int x, int y)
       {
           Console.WriteLine("x:{0}, y:{1}", x, y);
       }
   }
   ```

   Note   Remember that the *Console.WriteLine* method uses *{0}* and *{1}* as placeholders. In the statement shown, *{0}* will be replaced with the value of *x*, and *{1}* will be replaced with the value of *y* when the program runs.

8. On the Build menu, click Build Solution.

The compiler now reports an error:

```
No overload for method 'Point' takes '0' arguments
```

The call to the default constructor in *Entrance* no longer works because there is no longer a default constructor. Because you have written your own constructor for the *Point* class, the compiler has not automatically generated the default constructor. You will now fix this by writing your own default constructor.

9. Edit the *Point* class and add a *public* default constructor that calls *Console.WriteLine* to write the string *"default constructor called"* to the console.

   The *Point* class should now look like this:

```
class Point
{
    public Point()
    {
        Console.WriteLine("default constructor called");
    }

    public Point(int x, int y)
    {
        Console.WriteLine("x:{0}, y:{1}", x, y);
    }
}
```

10. In the Program.cs file, edit the body of the *Entrance* method. Declare a variable called *bottomRight* of type *Point* and initialize it to a new *Point* object by using the constructor with two arguments. Supply the values 1024 and 1280.

   The *Entrance* method should now look like this:

```
static void Entrance()
{
    Point origin = new Point();
    Point bottomRight = new Point(1024, 1280);
}
```

11. On the Debug menu, click Start Without Debugging.

   The code now builds without errors, and runs. The following messages are written to the console:

```
default constructor called
x:1024, y:1280
```

12. Press the Enter key.

   The console window closes, and you return to the Visual Studio 2005 programming environment. You will now add two *int* fields to the *Point* class and modify the constructors to initialize these fields.

13. Edit the *Point* class and add two *private* instance fields called *x* and *y* of type *int*.

    The *Point* class should now look like this:

    ```
    class Point
    {
        public Point()
        {
            Console.WriteLine("default constructor called");
        }

        public Point(int x, int y)
        {
            Console.WriteLine("x:{0}, y:{1}", x, y);
        }

        private int x, y;
    }
    ```

    You will now edit the second *Point* constructor to initialize the *x* and *y* fields to the values of the *x* and *y* parameters. There is a potential trap when you do this. If you are not careful, the constructor will look like this:

    ```
    public Point(int x, int y) // Don't type this in!
    {
        x = x;
        y = y;
    }
    ```

    Although this code will compile, these statements appear to be ambiguous. How does the compiler know in the statement x = x; that the first x is the field, and the second x is the parameter? It doesn't! A parameter to a method with the same name as a field overrides the field in any statements the method. All this constructor actually does is assign the parameters to themselves; it does not modify the fields at all. This is clearly not what we want.

    The solution is to use the *this* keyword to qualify which variables are parameters and which are fields. Prefixing a variable with *this* means "the field in this object."

14. Modify the *Point* constructor as follows:

    ```
    public Point(int x, int y)
    {
        this.x = x;
        this.y = y;
    }
    ```

15. Edit the default *Point* constructor to initialize the *x* and *y* fields to −1 (and remove the *Console.WriteLine* statement). Note that although there are no parameters to cause confusion, it is still good practice to qualify the field references with *this*:

```
public Point()
{
    this.x = -1;
    this.y = -1;
}
```

16. On the Build menu, click Build Solution. Confirm that the code compiles without errors or warnings (you can run it, but it does not produce any output yet).

Naming and Accessibility

The following .NET Framework recommendations relate to the naming conventions for fields and methods based upon the accessibility of class members:

■ Identifiers that are *public* should start with a capital letter. For example, *Area* starts with A (not a) because it's *public*. This system is known as the *PascalCase* naming scheme (it was first used in the Pascal language).

■ Identifiers that are not *public* (which include local variables) should start with a lowercase letter. For example, *radius* starts with r (not R) because it's *private*. This system is known as the *camelCase* naming scheme.

There's only one exception to this rule: class names should start with a capital letter and constructors must match the name of their class exactly; therefore, a *private* constructor must start with a capital letter.

Methods that belong to a class and that operate on the data belonging to a particular instance of a class are called *instance methods*. In the following exercise, you will write an instance method for the *Point* class, called *DistanceTo*, that calculates the distance between two points.

Write and call instance methods

1. In the Classes project in Visual Studio 2005, add the following public instance method called *DistanceTo* to the *Point* class, between the constructors and the private variables. The method accepts a single *Point* argument called *other* and returns a *double*.

The *DistanceTo* method should look like this:

```
class Point
{
    ...

    public double DistanceTo(Point other)
    {
    }
    ...

}
```

In the next steps, you will edit the body of the *DistanceTo* instance method to calculate and return the distance between the *Point* object being used to make the call and the

Point object passed as a parameter. To do this, you will need to calculate the difference between the *x* coordinates and the *y* coordinates.

2. In the *DistanceTo* method, declare a local *int* variable called *xDiff*, and initialize it to the difference between *this.x* and *other.x*:

```
int xDiff = this.x - other.x;
```

3. Declare another local *int* variable called *yDiff*, and initialize it to the difference between *this.y* and *other.y*.

The *DistanceTo* method should now look like this:

```
public double DistanceTo(Point other)
{
    int xDiff = this.x - other.x;
    int yDiff = this.y - other.y;
}
```

To calculate the distance, you can use a method based on Pythagoras' theorem: Work out the square root of the sum of the square of *xDiff* and the square of *yDiff*. The *System.Math* class provides the *Sqrt* method which you can use to calculate square roots.

4. Add the following return statement to perform the calculation:

```
return Math.Sqrt(xDiff * xDiff + yDiff * yDiff);
```

The *DistanceTo* method should now look like this:

```
public double DistanceTo(Point other)
{
    int xDiff = this.x - other.x;
    int yDiff = this.y - other.y;
    return Math.Sqrt(xDiff * xDiff + yDiff * yDiff);
}
```

You will now test the *DistanceTo* method.

5. Return to the *Entrance* method in the *Program* class. After the statements that declare and initialize the *origin* and *bottomRight Point* variables, declare a variable called *distance* of type *double*. Initialize this *double* variable to the result obtained when you call the *DistanceTo* method on the *origin* object and when you pass the *bottomRight* object to it as an argument.

The *Entrance* method should now look like this:

```
static void Entrance()
{
    Point origin = new Point();
    Point bottomRight = new Point(1024, 1280);
    double distance = origin.DistanceTo(bottomRight);
}
```

> **Note** IntelliSense should display the *DistanceTo* method when you type the period character after *origin*.

6. Add another statement to the *Entrance* method that writes the value of the *distance* variable to the console by using the *Console.WriteLine* method.

   The *Entrance* method should now look like this:

   ```
   static void Entrance()
   {
       Point origin = new Point();
       Point bottomRight = new Point(1024, 1280);
       double distance = origin.DistanceTo(bottomRight);
       Console.WriteLine("Distance is : {0}", distance);
   }
   ```

7. On the Debug menu, click Start Without Debugging.

   The program builds and runs.

8. Confirm that the value of 1640.605 (approximately) is written to the console window. Press Enter to close the application and return to Visual Studio 2005.

Understanding *static* Methods and Data

In the previous exercise you used the *Sqrt* method of the *Math* class. If you think about it, the way in which you called the method was slightly odd. You invoked the method on the class itself, not an object of type *Math*. So, what's happening and how does this work?

You will often find that not all methods naturally belong to an instance of a class; they are utility methods inasmuch as they provide a useful utility that is independent of any specific class instance. The *Sqrt* method is just such an example. If *Sqrt* were an instance method of *Math*, you'd have to create a *Math* object to call *Sqrt* on:

```
Math m = new Math();
double d = m.Sqrt(42.24);
```

This would be cumbersome. The *Math* object would play no part in the calculation of the square root. All the input data that *Sqrt* needs is provided in the parameter list, and the single result is returned to the caller by using the method's return value. Classes are not really needed here, so forcing *Sqrt* into an instance straitjacket is just not a good idea. The *Math* class also contains many other mathematical utility methods such as *Sin*, *Cos*, *Tan*, and *Log*. Incidentally, the *Math* class also contains a utility field called *PI* that we could have used in the *Area* method of the *Circle* class:

```
public double Area()
{
    return Math.PI * radius * radius;
}
```

In C#, all methods must be declared inside a class. However, if you declare a method or a field as *static*, you can call the method or access the field by using the name of the class. No instance is required. This is how the *Sqrt* method of the real *Math* class is declared:

```
class Math
{
    public static double Sqrt(double d) { ... }
    ...
}
```

Bear in mind that a *static* method is not called on an object. When you define a *static* method, it does not have access to any instance fields defined for the class; it can only use fields that are marked as *static*. Furthermore, it can only directly invoke other methods in the class that are marked as *static*; non-static (instance) methods require creating an object to call them on first.

Creating a Shared Field

As mentioned in the previous section, you can also use the *static* keyword when defining a field. This allows you to create a single field that is shared between all objects created from a single class, (non-static fields are local to each instance of an object). In the following example, the *static* field *NumCircles* in the *Circle* class is incremented by the *Circle* constructor every time a new *Circle* object is created:

```
class Circle
{

    public Circle()  // default constructor
    {
        radius = 0.0;
        NumCircles++;
    }

    public Circle(double initialRadius) // overloaded constructor
    {
        radius = initialRadius;
        NumCircles++;
    }

    ...
    private double radius;
    public static int NumCircles = 0;
}
```

All *Circle* objects share the same *NumCircles* field, and so the statement *NumCircles++;* increments the same data every time a new instance is created. You access the *NumCircles* field specifying the *Circle* class rather than an instance. For example:

```
Console.WriteLine("Number of Circle objects: {0}", Circle.NumCircles);
```

> **Tip**   Static methods are also called *class* methods. However, *static* fields tend not to be called *class* fields; they're just called *static* fields (or sometimes *static* variables).

Creating a *static* Field with the *const* Keyword

You can also declare that a field is static but that its value can never change by prefixing the field with the *const* keyword. *Const* is short for "constant." A *const* field does not use the *static* keyword in its declaration, but is nevertheless static. However, for reasons that are beyond the scope of this book to describe, you can declare a field as *const* only when the field is an enum, a primitive type, or a string. For example, here's how the real *Math* class declares *PI* as a *const* field (it declares *PI* to many more decimal places than shown here):

```
class Math
{
    ...
    public const double PI = 3.14159265358979;
}
```

Static Classes

Another feature of the C# language is the ability to declare a class as *static*. A *static* class can contain only *static* members (all objects that you create using the class will share a single copy of these members). The purpose of a *static* class is purely to act as a holder of utility methods and fields. A *static* class cannot contain any instance data or methods, and it does not make sense to try and create an object from a *static* class by using the *new* operator. In fact, you can't actually create an instance of an object using a *static* class by using *new* even if you wanted to (the compiler will report an error if you try). If you need to perform any initialization, a *static* class can have a default constructor, as long as it is also declared as *static*. Any other types of constructor are illegal and will be reported as such by the compiler.

If you were defining you own version of the *Math* class, containing only *static* members, it could look like this:

```
public static class Math
{
    public static double Sin(double x) {…}
    public static double Cos(double x) {…}
    public static double Sqrt(double x) {…}
    ...
}
```

Note, however, that the real *Math* class is not defined this way as it actually does have some instance methods.

In the final exercise in this chapter, you will add a *private static* field to the *Point* class and initialize the field to 0. You will increment this count in both constructors. Finally, you will write a *public static* method to return the value of this *private static* field. This field will enable you to find out how many *Point* objects have been created.

Write *static* members and call *static* methods

1. Using Visual Studio 2005, display the *Point* class in the Code and Text Editor window.

2. Add a *private static* field called *objectCount* of type *int* to the end of the *Point* class. Initialize it to 0 as you declare it.

   The *Point* class should now look like this:

   ```
   class Point
   {
       ...;
       private static int objectCount = 0;
   }
   ```

> **Note**   You can write the keywords *private* and *static* in any order. The preferred order is *private* first, *static* second.

3. Add a statement to both *Point* constructors to increment the *objectCount* field.

   Each time an object is created, its constructor will be called. As long as you increment the *objectCount* in each constructor (including the default constructor), *objectCount* will hold the number of objects created so far. This strategy works only because *objectCount* is a shared *static* field. If *objectCount* was an instance field, each object would have its own personal *objectCount* field which would be set to 1. The *Point* class should now look like this:

   ```
   class Point
   {
       public Point()
       {
           this.x = -1;
           this.y = -1;
           objectCount++;
       }

       public Point(int x, int y)
       {
           this.x = x;
           this.y = y;
           objectCount++;
       }

       ...
       private static int objectCount = 0;
   }
   ```

Notice that you cannot prefix *static* fields and methods with the *this* keyword as they do not belong to the current instance of the class (they do not actually belong to any instance).

The question now is this: How can users of the *Point* class find out how many *Point* objects have been created? At the moment, the *objectCount* field is *private* and not available outside the class. A poor solution would be to make the *objectCount* field publicly accessible. This strategy would break the encapsulation of the class; you would then have no guarantee that its value was correct because anything could change the value in the field. A much better idea is to provide a *public static* method that returns the value of the *objectCount* field. This is what you will do now.

4. Add a *public static* method to the *Point* class called *ObjectCount* that returns an *int* but does not take any parameters. In this method, return the value of the *objectCount* field.

   The *Point* class should now look like this:

```
class Point
{
    public static int ObjectCount()
    {
        return objectCount;
    }
    ...
}
```

5. Display the *Program* class in the Code and Text Editor window, and locate the *Entrance* method.

6. Add a statement to the *Entrance* method to write the value returned from the *Object-Count* method of the *Point* class to the screen.

   The *Entrance* method should look like this:

```
static void Entrance()
{
    Point origin = new Point();
    Point bottomRight = new Point(600, 800);
    double distance = origin.distanceTo(bottomRight);
    Console.WriteLine("Distance is :{0}", distance);
    Console.WriteLine("No of Point objects :{0}", Point.ObjectCount());
}
```

The *ObjectCount* method is called by using *Point*, the name of the class, and not the name of a *Point* variable (such as *origin* or *bottomRight*). Because two *Point* objects have been created by the time *ObjectCount* is called, the method should return a value of 2.

7. On the Debug menu, click Start Without Debugging.

8. Confirm that the value of 2 is written to the console window (after the message displaying the value of the *distance* variable). Press Enter to finish the program and return to Visual Studio 2005.

Congratulations. You have successfully created a class, and used constructors to initialize the fields in a class. You have created instance and *static* methods, and called both of these types of methods. You have also implemented instance and *static* fields. You have seen how to make fields and methods accessible by using the *public* keyword, and how to hide them using the *private* keyword.

- **If you want to continue to the next chapter**

  Keep Visual Studio 2005 running, and turn to Chapter 8.

- **If you want to exit Visual Studio 2005 now**

  On the File menu, click Exit. If you see a Save dialog box, click Yes.

Chapter 7 Quick Reference

To	Do this
Declare a class	Write the keyword *class*, followed by the name of the class, followed by an opening and closing brace. The methods and fields of the class are declared between the opening and closing brace. For example: ```\nclass Point\n{\n ...\n}\n```
Declare a constructor	Write a method whose name is the same as the name of the class and that has no return type (not even *void*). For example: ```\nclass Point\n{\n public Point(int x, int y)\n {\n ...\n }\n}\n```
Call a constructor	Use the *new* keyword, and specify the constructor with an appropriate set of parameters. For example: ```\nPoint origin = new Point(0, 0);\n```
Declare a *static* method	Write the keyword *static* before the declaration of the method. For example: ```\nclass Point\n{\n public static int ObjectCount()\n {\n ...\n }\n}\n```
Call a *static* method	Write the name of the class, followed by a period, followed by the name of the method. For example: ```\nint pointsCreatedSoFar = Point.ObjectCount();\n```
Declare a *static* field	Write the keyword *static* before the declaration of the field. For example: ```\nclass Point\n{\n ...\n private static int objectCount;\n}\n```

To	Do this

Declare a *const* field	Write the keyword *const* before the declaration of the field, and omit the *static* keyword For example:
	
	``
	class Math
	{
	    ...
	    public const double PI = ...;
	}
	``

Access a *static* field	Write the name of the class, followed by a period, followed by the name of the *static* field. For example:
	
	``
	double area = Math.PI * radius * radius;
	``

Chapter 8

Understanding Values and References

After completing this chapter, you will be able to:

- Explain the differences between a value type and a reference type.
- Modify the way in which arguments are passed as method parameters, by using the *ref* and *out* keywords.
- Box a value by initializing or assigning a variable of type *object*.
- Unbox a value by casting the object reference that refers to the boxed value.

In Chapter 7, "Creating and Managing Classes and Objects," you learned how to declare your own classes and create objects by using the *new* keyword. You also saw how to build an object by using a constructor. In this chapter, you will learn about the very different characteristics of the primitive types (such as *int*) and class types (such as *Circle*).

Copying *int* Variables and Classes

All primitive types such as *int* are called value types. When you declare an *int* variable, the compiler generates code that allocates a block of memory big enough to hold an integer. A statement that assigns a value (such as 42) to the *int* causes the value to be copied to this block of memory.

Class types, such as *Circle* (described in Chapter 7), are handled differently. When you declare a *Circle* variable, the compiler *does not* generate code that allocates a block of memory big enough to hold a *Circle*; all it does is allot a small piece of memory that can potentially hold the address of (or a reference to) another block of memory containing a *Circle*. The memory for the *Circle* object itself is only allocated when the *new* keyword is used to create the object.

This demonstrates that value types are so called because they hold values directly. Reference types (such as classes) hold references to blocks of memory.

> **Note**   If you are a C or C++ programmer you might be tempted to think of reference types simply as pointers. While reference types in C# exhibit many similarities to pointers, they provide far more functionality. For example, in a C or C++ application it is possible to make a pointer reference almost any block of memory regardless of the type of data the block is holding. Sometimes this is useful, but more often than not it is the cause of many insidious programming errors. In C#, all references are *strongly typed*; you cannot declare a reference variable that refers to one type (such as *Circle*), and then use the variable to access a block of memory holding a different type. There are other differences as well, concerning the way in which the common language runtime manages and reclaims memory. These features are discussed in Chapter 13, "Using Garbage Collection and Resource Management."

Because of the different ways that they hold data, value types are sometimes called *direct* types, and reference types are sometimes called *indirect* types. You need to fully understand the difference between value types and reference types.

Consider the situation where you declare a variable named *i* as an *int* and assign it the value 42. If you declare another variable *copyi* as an *int*, and initialize or assign *copyi* to *i*, *copyi* will hold the same value as *i* (42). However, the fact that *copyi* and *i* happen to hold the same value does not alter the fact that there are two copies of the value 42: one inside *i* and the other inside *copyi*. If you modify the value in *i*, the value in *copyi* does not change. Let's see this in code:

```
int i = 42;// declare and initialize i
int copyi = i;// copyi contains a copy of the data in i
i++;// incrementing i has no effect on copyi
```

The effect of declaring *c* as a *Circle* (the name of a class) is very different. When you declare *c* as a *Circle*, *c* can refer to a *Circle* object. If you declare *refc* as another *Circle*, it can also refer to a *Circle* object. If you choose to initialize or assign *refc* to *c*, *refc* will refer to the same *Circle* object that *c* does; there is only one *Circle* object, and *refc* and *c* both refer to it. Let's see this in code:

```
Circle c = new Circle(42);
Circle refc = c;
```

The following graphic illustrates both examples:

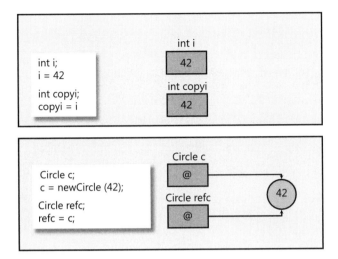

The difference explained above is very important. In particular, it means that the behavior of method parameters depends on whether they are value types or reference types. You'll explore this difference in the following exercise.

Use value parameters and reference parameters

1. Start Microsoft Visual Studio 2005.

2. Open the *Parameters* project, located in the \Microsoft Press\Visual CSharp Step by Step\Chapter 8\Parameters folder in your My Documents folder.

3. Display the Pass.cs source file in the Code and Text Editor window. Locate the *Pass* class. Add a *public static* method called *Value* to the *Pass* class. This method should accept a single *int* parameter (a value type) called *param* and have a return type of *void*. The body of *Value* should simply assign 42 to *param*.

   The *Pass* class should look exactly like this:

```
namespace Parameters
{
    class Pass
    {
        public static void Value(int param)
        {
            param = 42;
        }
    }
}
```

4. Display the Program.cs source file in the Code and Text Editor window, and then locate the *Entrance* method of the *Program* class.

The *Entrance* method is called by the *Main* method when the program starts running. As explained in Chapter 7, the method call is wrapped in a *try* block and followed by a *catch* handler.

5. Add four statements to the *Entrance* method to perform the following tasks:

    a. Declare a local *int* variable called *i* and initialize it to 0.

    b. Write the value of *i* to the console by using *Console.WriteLine*.

    c. Call *Pass.Value*, passing *i* as an argument.

    d. Write the value of *i* to the console again.

The calls to *Console.WriteLine* before and after the call to *Pass.Value* allow you to see whether the call to *Pass.Value* actually modifies the value of *i*. The *Entrance* method should look exactly like this:

```
static void Entrance()
{
    int i = 0;
    Console.WriteLine(i);
    Pass.Value(i);
    Console.WriteLine(i);
}
```

6. On the Debug menu, click Start Without Debugging to build and run the program.

7. Confirm that the value of 0 is written to the console window twice.

The assignment inside *Pass.Value* was made by using a copy of the argument, and the original argument *i* is completely unaffected.

8. Press the Enter key to close the application.

You will now see what happens when you pass an *int* parameter that is wrapped inside a class.

9. Display the WrappedInt.cs source file in the Code and Text Editor window. Add a *public* instance field called *Number* of type *int* to the *WrappedInt* class.

The *WrappedInt* class should look exactly like this:

```
namespace Parameters
{
    class WrappedInt
    {
        public int Number;
    }
}
```

10. Display the Pass.cs source file in the Code and Text Editor window. Add a *public static* method called *Reference* to the *Pass* class. This method should accept a single *WrappedInt*

parameter called *param* and have a return type of *void*. The body of the *Reference* method should assign 42 to *param.Number*.

The *Pass* class should look exactly like this:

```
namespace Parameters
{
    class Pass
    {
        public static void Value(int param)
        {
            param = 42;
        }

        public static void Reference(WrappedInt param)
        {
            param.Number = 42;
        }
    }
}
```

11. Display the Program.cs source file in the Code and Text Editor window. Add four more statements to the *Entrance* method to perform the following tasks:

   a.   Declare a local *WrappedInt* variable called *wi* and initialize it to a new *WrappedInt* object by calling the default constructor.

   b.   Write the value of *wi.Number* to the console.

   c.   Call the *Pass.Reference* method, passing *wi* as an argument.

   d.   Write the value of *wi.Number* to the console again.

As before, the calls to *Console.WriteLine* allow you to see whether the call to *Pass.Reference* modifies the value of *wi.Number*. The *Entrance* method should now look exactly like this:

```
static void Entrance()
{
    int i = 0;
    Console.WriteLine(i);
    Pass.Value(i);
    Console.WriteLine(i);

    WrappedInt wi = new WrappedInt();
    Console.WriteLine(wi.Number);
    Pass.Reference(wi);
    Console.WriteLine(wi.Number);
}
```

12. On the Debug menu, click Start Without Debugging to build and run the application.

As before, the first two values written to the console window are 0 and 0, before and after the call to *Pass.Value*. For the next two values, which correspond to value *wi.Number* before and after *Pass.Reference*, confirm that the value of 0 and then the value of 42 are written to the console window.

13.   Press the Enter key to close the application.

In the previous exercise, the value of *wi.Number* is initialized to 0 by the compiler-generated code. The *wi* variable contains a reference to the newly created *WrappedInt* object (which contains an *int*). The *wi* variable is then copied as an argument to the *Pass.Reference* method. Because *WrappedInt* is a class (a reference type), *wi* and *param* both refer to the same *Wrapped-Int* object. Any changes made to the contents of the object through the *param* variable in the *Pass.Reference* method are visible by using the *wi* variable when the method completes. The following diagram illustrates what happens when a *WrappedInt* object is passed as an argument to the *Pass.Reference* method:

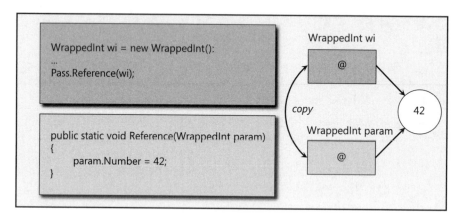

Using *ref* and *out* Parameters

When you pass an argument to a method, the corresponding parameter is initialized with a copy of the argument. This is true regardless of whether the parameter is a value type (such as an *int*), or a reference type (such as a *WrappedInt*). This arrangement means it's impossible for any change to the parameter to affect the value of the argument passed in. For example, in the following code, the value output to the console is 42 and not 43. The *DoWork* method increments a *copy* of the argument (*arg*), and *not* the original argument:

```
static void DoWork(int param)
{
    param++;
}

static void Main()
{
    int arg = 42;
    DoWork(arg);
    Console.WriteLine(arg); // writes 42 not 43
}
```

In the previous exercise you saw that if the parameter to a method is a reference type, then any changes made by using that parameter change the data referenced by the argument passed in. The key point is that, although the data that was referenced changed, the parameter itself did not—it still referenced the same object. In other words, although it is possible to modify the object that the argument refers to through the parameter, it's not possible to modify the argument itself (for example, to set it to refer to a completely new object). Most of the time, this guarantee is very useful and can help to reduce the number of bugs in a program. Occasionally, however, you might want to write a method that actually needs to modify an argument. C# provides the *ref* and *out* keywords to allow you to do this.

Creating *ref* Parameters

If you prefix a parameter with the *ref* keyword, the parameter becomes an alias for (or a reference to) the actual argument rather than a copy of the argument. When using a *ref* parameter, anything you do to the parameter, you also do to the original argument, because the parameter and the argument both reference the same object. When you pass an argument to a *ref* parameter, you must also prefix the argument with the *ref* keyword. This syntax provides a useful visual indication that the argument might change. Here's the previous example again, this time modified to use the *ref* keyword:

```
static void DoWork(ref int param) // using ref
{
    param++;
}

static void Main()
{
    int arg = 42;
    DoWork(ref arg);          // using ref
    Console.WriteLine(arg); // writes 43
}
```

This time, because the *DoWork* method is passed a reference to the original argument rather than a copy, any changes it makes by using this reference also change the original argument, so the value 43 is displayed on the console.

The rule that you must assign a value to a variable before you can use it still applies to *ref* arguments. For example, in the following example, *arg* is not initialized, so this code will not compile. This failure is because *param++* inside *DoWork* is really *arg++*, and *arg++* is allowed only if *arg* has a defined value:

```
static void DoWork(ref int param)
{
    param++;
}

static void Main()
{
```

```
        int arg;                    // not initialized
        DoWork(ref arg);
        Console.WriteLine(arg);
}
```

Creating *out* Parameters

The compiler checks that a *ref* parameter has been assigned a value before calling the method. However, there may be times when you want the method itself to initialize the parameter, and so pass an uninitialized argument to the method. The *out* keyword allows you to do this.

The *out* keyword is very similar to the *ref* keyword. You can prefix a parameter with the *out* keyword so that the parameter becomes an alias for the argument. As when using *ref*, anything you do to the parameter, you also do to the original argument. When you pass an argument to an *out* parameter, you must also prefix the argument with the *out* keyword.

The keyword *out* is short for *output*. When you pass an *out* parameter to a method, the method has to assign a value to it. The following example does not compile because *DoWork* does not assign a value to *param*:

```
static void DoWork(out int param)
{
    // Do nothing
}
```

However, the following example does compile because *DoWork* assigns a value to *param*:

```
static void DoWork(out int param)
{
    param = 42;
}
```

Because an *out* parameter must be assigned a value by the method, you're allowed to call the method without initializing its argument. When the method call has finished, the argument must have been assigned a value. For example, the following code calls *DoWork* to initialize the variable *arg*, which is then displayed on the console:

```
static void DoWork(out int param)
{
    param = 42;
}


static void Main()
{
    int arg;                    // not initialized
    DoWork(out arg);
    Console.WriteLine(arg); // writes 42
}
```

Use *ref* parameters

1. Return to the *Parameters* project in Visual Studio 2005.

2. Display the Pass.cs source file in the Code and Text Editor window.

3. Edit the *Value* method to accept its *int* parameter as a *ref* parameter.

   The *Value* method should look like this:

```
class Pass
{
    public static void Value(ref int param)
    {
        param = 42;
    }
    ...
}
```

4. Display the Program.cs source file in the Code and Text Editor window.

5. Edit the third statement of the *Entrance* method so that the *Pass.Value* method call passes its argument as a *ref* parameter.

   The *Entrance* method should now look like this:

```
class Application
{
    static void Entrance()
    {
        int i = 0;
        Console.WriteLine(i);
        Pass.Value(ref i);
        Console.WriteLine(i);
        ...
    }
}
```

6. On the Debug menu, click Start Without Debugging to build and run the program.

   This time, the first two values written to the console window are 0 and 42. This result shows that the call to the *Pass.Value* method has modified the argument *i*.

7. Press the Enter key to close the application.

> **Note**   You can use the *ref* and *out* modifiers on reference type parameters as well as value type parameters. The effect is exactly the same. The parameter becomes an alias for the argument. If you reassigned the parameter to a newly constructed object, you would actually be reassigning the argument to the newly constructed object.

How Computer Memory is Organized

Computers use memory to hold programs being executed, and the data that these programs use. In order to understand the differences between value and reference types, it is helpful to understand how data is organized in memory.

Operating systems and runtimes (such as the common language runtime) frequently divide the memory used for holding data into two separate chunks, each of which is managed in a distinct manner. These two chunks of memory are traditionally called *the stack* and *the heap*. The stack and the heap serve very different purposes:

■ When you call a method, the memory required for its parameters and its local variables is always acquired from the stack. When the method finishes (because it either returns or throws an exception), the memory acquired for the parameters and local variables is automatically released back to the stack and is available for reuse when another method is called.

■ When you create an object (an instance of a class) by using the *new* keyword and a constructor call, the memory required to build the object is always acquired from the heap. You have seen that the same object can be referenced from several places by using reference variables. When the last reference to an object disappears, the memory used by the object becomes available for reuse (although it might not be reclaimed immediately). Chapter 13 includes a more detailed discussion of how heap memory is reclaimed.

> **Note**   All value types are created on the stack. All reference types (objects) are created on the heap.

The names *stack* and *heap* come from the way in which the runtime organizes memory:

■ Stack memory is organized like a stack of boxes piled on top of each other. When a method is called, each parameter is put in a box which is placed on top of the stack. Each local variable is likewise assigned a box, and these are placed on top of the boxes already on the stack. When a method finishes, all its boxes are removed from the stack.

■ Heap memory is like a large pile of boxes strewn around a room rather than stacked neatly on top of each other. Each box has a label indicating whether it is in use or not. When a new object is created, the runtime searches for an empty box and allocates it to the object. The reference to the object is stored in a local variable on the stack. The runtime keeps track of the number of references to each box (remember that two variables can refer to the same object). When the last reference disappears, the runtime marks the box as not in use, and at some point in the future will empty the box and make it available for reuse.

Using the Stack and the Heap

Now let's examine what happens when the following *Method* is called:

```
void Method(int param)
{
    Circle c;
    c = new Circle(param);
    ...
}
```

Suppose the value passed into *param* is the value 42. A piece of memory (just enough for an *int*) is allocated from the stack, and initialized with the value 42. Inside the method, another piece of memory big enough to hold a reference is also allocated from the stack, but left uninitialized (this is for the *Circle* variable, *c*). Next, another piece of memory big enough for a *Circle* object is allocated from the heap. This is what the *new* keyword does. The *Circle* constructor runs to convert this raw heap memory into a *Circle* object. A reference to this *Circle* object is stored in the variable *c*. The following graphic illustrates the situation:

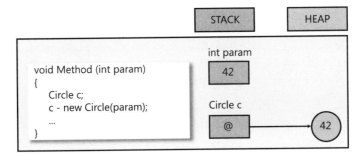

At this point, you should note two things:

1. Although the object itself is stored on the heap, the reference to the object (variable *c*) is stored on the stack.

2. Heap memory is not infinite. If heap memory is exhausted, the *new* operator will throw an *OutOfMemoryException* and the object will not be created.

> **Note** The *Circle* constructor could also throw an exception. If it does, the memory allocated to the *Circle* object will be reclaimed and the value returned by the constructor will be a null reference.

When the function ends, the parameters and local variables go out of scope. The memory acquired for *c* and the memory acquired for *param* is automatically released back to the stack. The runtime notes that the *Circle* object is no longer referenced, and at some point in the future will arrange for its memory to be reclaimed by the heap (see Chapter 13).

The *System.Object* Class

One of the most important reference types in the .NET Framework is the *Object* class in the *System* namespace. To fully appreciate the significance of the *System.Object* class requires that you understand inheritance, which is described in Chapter 12, "Working with Inheritance." For the time being, simply accept that all classes are specialized types of *System.Object*, and that you can use *System.Object* to create a variable that can refer to any reference type. *System.Object* is such an important class that C# provides the *object* keyword as an alias for *System.Object*. In your code, you can use *object* or you can write *System.Object*; they mean exactly the same thing.

> **Tip**   Use the *object* keyword in preference to *System.Object*. It's more direct and it's also consistent with using other keywords that have longer synonyms, as you'll discover in Chapter 9, "Creating Value Types with Enumerations and Structs." If your program contains a using System; directive, you could also write *Object* with a capital O (without the *System.* prefix), but it's best to consistently use the simpler keyword *object*.

In the following example, the variables *c* and *o* both refer to the same *Circle* object. The fact that the type of *c* is *Circle* and the type of *o* is *object* (the alias for *System.Object*) in effect provides two different views of the same object:

```
Circle c;
c = new Circle(42);

object o; o = c;
```

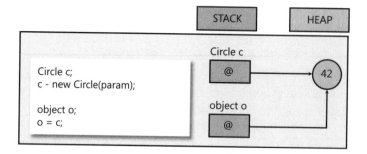

Boxing

As you have just seen, variables of type *object* can refer to any object of any reference type. That is, they can refer to any instance of a class. However, variables of type *object* can also refer to a value type. For example, the following two statements initialize the variable *i* (of type *int*, a value type) to 42 and then initialize the variable *o* (of type *object*, a reference type) to *i*:

```
int i = 42;
object o = i;
```

The effect of the second statement is subtle. Remember that *i* is a value type and it exists in the stack. If the reference inside *o* referred directly to *i*, the reference would be referring to the stack. However, all references refer to objects on the heap. Instead, a piece of memory is allocated from the heap, an exact copy of the value inside *i* is stored in this piece of memory, and the reference inside *o* is pointed to the copy. (Creating references to items on the stack could seriously compromise the robustness of the runtime, and create a potential security flaw, so it is not allowed.) This automatic copying of an item from the stack to the heap is called *boxing*. The following graphic shows the result:

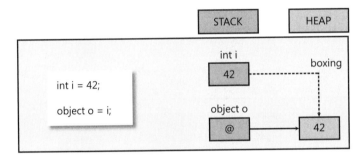

Important   If you modify the original value of a variable, you are not modifying the value that now exists on the heap, because it's just a copy.

Unboxing

Because a variable of type *object* can refer to a boxed copy of a value, it's only reasonable to allow you to get at that boxed value through the variable. You might expect to be able to access the boxed *int* value that a variable *o* refers to by using a simple assignment statement such as:

```
int i = o;
```

However, if you try this syntax, you'll get a compile time error. If you think about it, it's pretty sensible that you can't use the int i = o; syntax. After all, *o* could be referencing absolutely anything and not just an *int*. Consider what would happen in the following code if this statement was allowed:

```
Circle c = new Circle();
int i = 42;
object o;

o = c;  // o refers to a circle
i = o;  // what is stored in i?
```

To obtain the value of the boxed copy, you must use what is known as a *cast*, an operation that checks that it is safe to convert one type to another, and then does the conversion. You prefix the *object* variable with the name of the type, in parentheses, as in this example:

```
int i = 42;
object o = i;  // boxes
i = (int)o;    // compiles okay
```

The effect of this cast is subtle. The compiler notices that you've specified the type *int* in the cast. Next, the compiler generates code to check what *o* actually refers to, at runtime. It could be absolutely anything. Just because your cast says *o* refers to an *int*, that doesn't mean it actually does. If *o* really does refer to a boxed *int* and everything matches, the cast succeeds and the compiler-generated code extracts the value from the boxed *int*. (In this example, the boxed value is then used to initialize *i*.) This is called *unboxing*. The following diagram shows what is happening:

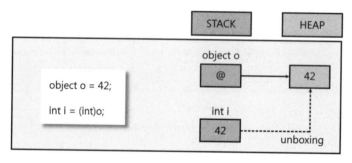

However, if *o* does not refer to a boxed *int* there is a type mismatch, causing the cast to fail. The compiler-generated code throws an *InvalidCastException* at runtime. Here's an example of an unboxing cast that fails:

```
Circle c = new Circle(42);
object o = c;        // doesn't box because Circle is a class
int i = (int)o;      // compiles okay, but throws at runtime
```

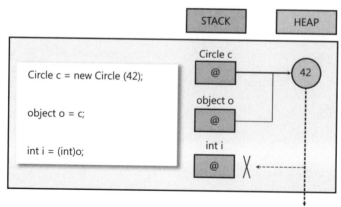

> **Note** The type you specify in the unboxing cast must exactly match the type actually in the box. For example, if the box holds a copy of an *int* and you try to unbox it into a *long*, you will get an *InvalidCastException*. The fact that there is a built-in implicit conversion from an *int* to a *long* is irrelevant. The match must be exact.

You will use boxing and unboxing in later exercises. Keep in mind that boxing and unboxing are expensive operations because of the amount of checking required, and the need to allocate additional heap memory. Boxing has its uses, but injudicious use can severely impair the performance of a program. You will see an alternative to boxing in Chapter 17, "Introducing Generics."

Pointers and Unsafe Code

This section is purely for your information and is aimed at developers who are familiar with C or C++. If you are new to programming, feel free to skip this section!

If you have already developed in languages such as C or C++, much of the preceding discussion concerning object references might be familiar. Although neither C nor C++ have explicit reference types, both languages have a construct that provides similar functionality—pointers.

A *pointer* is a variable that holds the address of, or a reference to, an item in memory (on the heap or on the stack). A special syntax is used to identify a variable as a pointer. For example, the following statement declares the variable *pi* as a pointer to an integer:

```
int *pi;
```

Although the variable *pi* is declared as a pointer, it does not actually point anywhere until you initialize it. For example, to use *pi* to point to the integer variable *i*, you can use the following statements, and the & operator, which returns the address of a variable:

```
int *pi;

int i = 99;
...
pi = &i;
```

You can access and modify the value held in the variable *i* through the pointer variable *pi* like this:

```
*pi = 100;
```

This code updates the value of the variable *i* to 100, because *pi* points to the same memory location as the variable *i*.

One of the main problems that developers learning C and C++ have is understanding the syntax used by pointers. The * operator has at least two meanings (in addition to being the arithmetic multiplication operator), and there is often great confusion about when to use & rather than *. The other issue with pointers is that it is very easy to point somewhere invalid, or to forget to point somewhere at all, and then try to reference the data pointed to. The result will be either garbage or a program that fails with an error because the operating system detects an attempt to access an illegal address in memory. There is also a whole range of security flaws in many existing systems resulting from the mismanagement of pointers; some environments (not Microsoft Windows) fail to enforce checks that a pointer does not refer to memory that belongs to another process, opening up the possibility that confidential data could be compromised.

Reference variables were added to C# to avoid all these problems. If you really want to, you can continue to use pointers in C#, but you must mark the code as *unsafe*. The *unsafe* keyword can be used to mark a block of code, or an entire method, as shown here:

```
public static void Main(string [] args)
{
    int x = 99, y = 100;
    unsafe
    {
        swap (&x, &y);
    }
    Console.WriteLine("x is now {0}, y is now {1}", x, y);
}

public static unsafe void swap(int *a, int *b)
{
    int temp;
    temp = *a;
    *a = *b;
    *b = temp;
}
```

When you compile programs containing unsafe code, you must specify the /*unsafe* option.

Unsafe code also has a bearing on how memory is managed; objects created in unsafe code are said to be unmanaged. We discuss this issue in more detail in Chapter 13.

In this chapter, you have learned some important differences between value types that hold their value directly on the stack and reference types that refer indirectly to their objects on the heap. You have also learned how to use the *ref* and *out* keywords on method parameters to gain access to the arguments. You have seen how assigning a variable of the *System.Object* class to a value (such as 42) causes the variable to refer to a boxed copy of the value made on the heap. You have seen how assigning a variable of a value type to a variable of the *System.Object* class causes the boxed copy to refer to a variable of a value type (such as *int*).

- **If you want to continue to the next chapter**

  Keep Visual Studio 2005 running and turn to Chapter 9.

- **If you want to exit Visual Studio 2005 now**

  On the File menu, click Exit. If you see a Save dialog box, click Yes.

Chapter 8 Quick Reference

To	Do this

Copy a value type variable	Simply make the copy. Because the variable is a value type, you will have two copies of the same value. For example:
	
	 ```int i = 42;```
	```int copyi = i;```

Copy a reference type variable	Simply make the copy. Because the variable is a reference type, you will have two references to the same object. For example:
	
	 ```Circle c = new Circle(42);```
	```Circle refc = c;```

Pass an argument to a *ref* parameter	Prefix the argument with the *ref* keyword. This makes the parameter an alias for the actual argument rather than a copy of the argument. For example:
	
	 ```static void Main()```
	```{```
	``` int arg = 42;```
	``` DoWork(ref arg);```
	``` Console.WriteLine(arg);```
	```}```

Pass an argument to an *out* parameter	Prefix the argument with the *out* keyword. This makes the parameter an alias for the actual argument rather than a copy of the argument. For example:
	
	 ```static void Main()```
	```{```
	``` int arg = 42;```
	``` DoWork(out arg);```
	``` Console.WriteLine(arg);```
	```}```

Box a value	Initialize or assign a variable of type object to the value. For example: ```object o = 42;```
Unbox a value	Cast the object reference that refers to the boxed value to the type of the value. For example: ```int i = (int)o;```

Chapter 9

Creating Value Types with Enumerations and Structs

After completing this chapter, you will be able to:

- Declare an enumeration type.

- Create and use an enumeration type.

- Declare a structure type.

- Create and use a structure type.

In Chapter 8, "Understanding Values and References," you learned about the two fundamental kinds of types that exist in Microsoft Visual C#: value types and reference types. A value type variable holds its value directly on the stack, whereas a reference type variable holds a reference to an object on the heap. In Chapter 7, "Creating and Managing Classes and Objects," you learned how to write your own classes, thus creating your own reference types. In this chapter, you'll learn how to write your own value types.

C# supports two kinds of value types: enumerations and structures.

Working with Enumerations

Suppose you want to represent the seasons of the year in a program. You could use the integers 0, 1, 2, and 3 to represent Spring, Summer, Fall, and Winter, respectively. This system would work, but it's not very intuitive. If you used the integer value 0 in code, it wouldn't be obvious that a particular 0 represented Spring. It also wouldn't be a very robust solution. For example, nothing would stop you from using any integer value rather than just 0, 1, 2, and 3. C# offers a better solution. You can use the enum keyword to create an enumeration type (sometimes called an enum type) whose values are limited to a set of symbolic names.

Declaring an Enumeration Type

Here's how to declare an enumeration type, called *Season*, whose literal values are limited to the symbolic names *Spring*, *Summer*, *Fall*, and *Winter*:

```
enum Season { Spring, Summer, Fall, Winter }
```

The symbolic names must appear between a pair of braces in a comma-separated list. Internally, an enumeration associates an integer value with each element. By default, the numbering starts at 0 for the first element and goes up in steps of 1.

Using an Enumeration

Once you have declared your enumeration type, you can use it in exactly the same way as any other type. If the name of your enumeration type is *Season*, you can create variables of type *Season*, fields of type *Season*, and parameters of type *Season*, as shown in this example:

```
enum Season { Spring, Summer, Fall, Winter }

class Example
{
    public void Method(Season parameter)
    {
        Season localVariable;
        ...
    }

    private Season currentSeason;
}
```

An enumeration type is a value type. Enumeration variables live on the stack (as discussed in Chapter 8). This is not really surprising when you remember that the underlying type of an enumeration is always an integral type.

Before you can use the value of an enumeration variable, it must be assigned a value. You can only assign valid values to an enumeration variable. For example:

```
Season colorful = Season.Fall;
Console.WriteLine(colorful);  // writes out 'Fall'
```

Notice that you have to write *Season.Fall* rather than *Fall*. All enumeration literal names are scoped by their enumeration type. This is very useful because it allows different enumeration types to coincidentally contain literals with the same name. Also, notice that when you display an enumeration variable by using *Console.WriteLine*, the compiler generates code that writes out the name of the literal whose value matches the value of the variable.

If needed, you can explictly convert an enumeration variable to a string that represents its current value by using the built-in *ToString* method that all enumeration types automatically inherit from the *System.Enum* type. For example:

```
string name = colorful.ToString();
Console.WriteLine(name);      // also writes out 'Fall'
```

It's also possible to retrieve the underlying integer value of an enumeration variable. To do this, you must cast it to its underlying type. Remember from the discussion of unboxing in Chapter 8 that casting a type converts the data from one type to another, as long as the conversion is valid and meaningful. For example, the following code fragment will write out the value 2 and not the word *Fall* (*Spring* is 0, *Summer* 1, *Fall* 2, and *Winter* 3):

```
enum Season { Spring, Summer, Fall, Winter }
...
Season colorful = Season.Fall;
Console.WriteLine((int)colorful); // writes out '2'
```

Many the standard operators that you can use on integral variables can also be used on enumeration variables (except the *bitwise* and *shift* operators, which are covered in Chapter 15, "Using Indexers"). For example, you can compare two enumeration variables of the same type for equality by using the == operator, and you can even perform arithmetic on an enumeration variable (although the result might not always be meaningful!).

Choosing Enumeration Literal Values

Each enumeration has a set of integer values associated with its elements, starting with 0 for the first element. If you prefer, you can associate a specific integer constant (such as 1) with an enumeration literal (such as *Spring*), as in the following example:

```
enum Season { Spring = 1, Summer, Fall, Winter }
```

Important   The integer value that you initialize an enumeration literal with must be a compile-time constant value (such as 1). That is, it must be a constant whose value does not depend on any run-time behavior (such as a method call).

If you don't explicitly give an enumeration literal a constant integer value, the compiler gives it a value that is one more than the value of the previous enumeration literal, except for the very first enumeration literal, to which the compiler gives a default value of 0. In the previous example, the underlying values of Spring, Summer, Fall, and Winter are 1, 2, 3, and 4.

You are allowed to give more than one enumeration literal the same underlying value. For example, in the United Kingdom, *Fall* is referred to as *Autumn*. You can cater for both cultures as follows:

```
enum Season { Spring, Summer, Fall, Autumn = Fall, Winter }
```

Choosing an Enumeration's Underlying Type

When you declare an enumeration type, the enumeration literals are given values of type *int*. In other words, the underlying type defaults to an *int*. You can also choose to base your enumeration type on a different underlying integer type. For example, to declare that *Season*'s underlying type is a *short* rather than an *int*, you can write this:

```
enum Season : short { Spring, Summer, Fall, Winter }
```

The main reason for doing this is to save memory; an *int* occupies more memory than a *short*, and if you do not need the entire range of values available to an *int* it can make sense to use a smaller data type.

You can base an enumeration on any of the eight integer types: *byte, sbyte, short, ushort, int, uint, long,* or *ulong*. The values of all the enumeration literals must fit inside the range of the chosen base type. For example, if you base an enumeration on the *byte* data type you can have a maximum of 256 literals (starting at zero).

Now that you know how to create an enumeration type, the next step is to use it.

In the following exercise, you will work with a console application to declare and use an enumeration class that represents the months of the year.

Create and use an enumeration type

1. Start Microsoft Visual Studio 2005.

2. Open the *StructsAndEnums* project, located in the \Microsoft Press\Visual CSharp Step by Step\Chapter 9\StructsAndEnums folder in your My Documents folder.

3. In the Code and Text Editor window, display the Month.cs source file.

   The source contains an empty namespace called *StructsAndEnums*.

4. Add an enumeration type called *Month* inside the *StructsAndEnums* namespace, for modeling the months of the year.

   The 12 enumeration literals for *Month* are January through December. The *Month* enumeration should look exactly like this:

```
namespace StructsAndEnums
{
    enum Month
    {
        January, February, March, April,
        May, June, July, August,
        September, October, November, December
    }
}
```

5. Display the Program.cs source file in the Code and Text Editor window.

As in the exercises in previous chapters, the *Main* method calls the *Entrance* method and traps any exceptions that occur.

6. In the Code and Text Editor window, add a statement to the *Entrance* method to declare a variable called *first* of type *Month* and initialize it to *Month.January*. Add another statement to write the value of the *first* variable to the console.

The *Entrance* method should look like this:

```
static void Entrance()
{
    Month first = Month.January;
    Console.WriteLine(first);
}
```

> **Note**   When you type the period following *Month*, Intellisense will automatically display all the values in the *Month* enumeration.

7. On the Debug menu, click Start Without Debugging.

Visual Studio 2005 builds and runs the program. Confirm that the word 'January' is written to the console.

8. Press Enter to close the program and return to the Visual Studio 2005 programming environment.

9. Add two more statements to the *Entrance* method to increment the *first* variable and display its new value to the console.

The *Entrance* method should look like this:

```
static void Entrance()
{
    Month first = Month.January;
    Console.WriteLine(first);
    first++;
    Console.WriteLine(first);
}
```

10. On the Debug menu, click Start Without Debugging.

Visual Studio 2005 builds and runs the program. Confirm that the words 'January' and 'February' are written to the console. Notice how performing a mathematical operation (such as the increment operation) on an enumeration variable changes the internal integer value of the variable. When it is displayed, the corresponding enumeration value is output.

11. Press Enter to close the program and return to the Visual Studio 2005 programming environment.

12. Modify the first statement in the *Entrance* method to initialize the *first* variable to *Month.December*.

The *Entrance* method should look like this:

```
static void Entrance()
{
    Month first = Month.December;
    Console.WriteLine(first);
    first++;
    Console.WriteLine(first);
}
```

13. On the Debug menu, click Start Without Debugging.

Visual Studio 2005 builds and runs the program. This time the word 'December' is written to the console, followed by the number 12. Although you can perform arithmetic on an enumeration, if the results of the operation are outside the range of values defined for the enumerator, then all the runtime can do is treat the variable as the corresponding integer value.

14. Press Enter to close the program and return to the Visual Studio 2005 programming environment.

Working with Structure Types

You saw in Chapter 8 that classes define reference types that are always created on the heap. In some cases, the class can contain so little data that the overhead of managing the heap becomes disproportionate. In these cases it is better to define the type as a structure. Because structures are stored on the stack, the memory management overhead is often reduced (as long as the structure is reasonably small).

A structure can have its own fields, methods, and constructors just like a class (and unlike an enumeration), but it is a value type and not a reference type.

Common Structure Types

You may not have realized it, but you have already used structures in previous exercises in this book. In C#, the primitive numeric types *int*, *long*, and *float*, are aliases for the structures *System.Int32*, *System.Int64*, and *System.Single*, respectively. This means that you can actually call methods on variables and literals of these types. For example, all of

---

these structures provide a *ToString* method that can convert a numeric value to its string representation. The following statements are all legal statements in C#:

```
int i = 99;
Console.WriteLine(i.ToString());
Console.WriteLine(55.ToString());
float f = 98.765F;
Console.WriteLine(f.ToString());
Console.WriteLine(98.765F.ToString());
```

You don't see this use of the *ToString* method very often, because the *Console.WriteLine* method calls it automatically when it is needed. Use of the static methods exposed by these structures is much more common. For example, in earlier chapters the static *Int32.Parse* method was used to convert a string to its corresponding integer value:

```
string s = "42";
int i = Int32.Parse(s);
```

> **Note**   Because *int* is simply an alias for *Int32*, you can also use *int.Parse*.

These structures also include some useful static fields. For example, *Int32.MaxValue* is the maximum value that an *int* can hold, and *Int32.MinValue* is the smallest value you can store in an *int*.

The following table shows the primitive types in C#, their equivalent types in the .NET Framework, and whether each type is a class or structure.

Keyword	Type equivalent	Class or structure
bool	*System.Boolean*	Structure
byte	*System.Byte*	Structure
decimal	*System.Decimal*	Structure
Double	*System.Double*	Structure
Float	*System.Single*	Structure
Int	*System.Int32*	Structure
Long	*System.Int64*	Structure
Object	*System.Object*	Class
Sbyte	*System.SByte*	Structure
Short	*System.Int16*	Structure
String	*System.String*	Class
Uint	*System.UInt32*	Structure
Ulong	*System.UInt64*	Structure
Ushort	*System.UInt16*	Structure

Declaring Structure Types

To declare your own structure value type, you use the *struct* keyword followed by the name of the type, followed by the body of the structure between opening and closing braces. For example, here is a *struct* called *Time* that contains three *public int* fields called *hours*, *minutes*, and *seconds*:

```
struct Time
{
    public int hours, minutes, seconds;
}
```

As with classes, making the fields of a structure *public* is not advisable in most cases; there is no way to ensure that *public* fields contain valid values. For example, anyone could set the value of *minutes* or *seconds* to a value greater than 60. A better idea is to make the fields *private* and provide your structure with constructors and methods, as shown in this example:

```
struct Time
{
    public Time(int hh, int mm, int ss)
    {
        hours = hh % 24;
        minutes = mm % 60;
        seconds = ss % 60;
    }

    public int Hours()
    {
        return hours;
    }
    ...
    private int hours, minutes, seconds;
}
```

> **Note**   By default, you cannot use many of the common operators on your own structure types. For example, you cannot use operators such as == and != on your own *struct* type variables. However, you can explicitly declare and implement operators for your own *struct* types. The syntax for doing this is covered in Chapter 19.

Use structs to implement simple concepts whose main feature is their value. For example, an *int* is a value type because its main feature is its value. If you have two *int* variables that contain the same value (such as 42), one is as good as the other. When you copy a value type variable, you get two copies of the value. In contrast, when you copy a reference type variable, you get two references to the same object. In summary, use structs for lightweight concepts where it makes sense to copy the value, and use classes for more heavyweight concepts where it doesn't make sense to copy the value.

Understanding Structure and Class Differences

A structure and a class are syntactically very similar but there are a few important differences. Let's look at some of these differences.

- You can't declare a default constructor (a constructor with no parameters) for a *struct*. The following example would compile if *Time* were a class, but because *Time* is a *struct* it fails to compile:

```
struct Time
{
    public Time() { ... } // compile time error
    ...
}
```

The reason you can't declare your own default constructor in a *struct* is because the compiler *always* generates one. In a class, the compiler generates the default constructor only if you don't write a constructor yourself.

The compiler-generated default constructor for a structure always sets the fields to 0, *false*, or *null*—just like for a class. Therefore, you should ensure that a structure value created by the default constructor behaves logically and makes sense with these default values. If you don't want to use these default values, you can initialize fields to different values by providing a non-default constructor. However, if you don't initialize a field in the constructor, the compiler won't initialize it for you. This means you must explicitly initialize all the fields in all the structure constructors or you'll get a compile-time error. For instance, although the following example would compile and silently initialize *seconds* to 0 if *Time* were a class, because *Time* is a struct, it fails to compile:

```
struct Time
{
    public Time(int hh, int mm)
    {
        hours = hh;
        minutes = mm;
    }   // compile time error: seconds not initialized
    ...
    private int hours, minutes, seconds;
}
```

- In a class, you can initialize instance fields at their point of declaration. In a struct, you cannot. For instance, the following example would compile if *Time* were a class, but because *Time* is a struct, it causes a compile-time error (reinforcing the rule that every structure must initialize all its fields in all its constructors):

```
struct Time
{
    ...
    private int hours = 0; // compile time error
    private int minutes;
    private int seconds;
}
```

The following table summarizes the main differences between a structure and a class.

Question	Struct	Class
Is this a value type or a reference type?	A structure is a value type.	A class is a reference type.
Do instances live on the stack or the heap?	Structure instances are called *values* and live on the stack.	Class instances are called *objects* and live on the heap.
Can you declare a default constructor?	No	Yes
If you declare your own constructor, will the compiler still generate the default constructor?	Yes	No
If you don't initialize a field in your own constructor, will the compiler automatically initialize it for you?	No	Yes
Are you allowed to initialize instance fields at their point of declaration?	No	Yes

There are other differences between classes and structures concerning inheritance. For example, a class can inherit from a base class, but a structure cannot. These differences are covered in Chapter 12, "Working with Inheritance." Now that you know how to declare structures, the next step is to use them to create values.

Declaring Structure Variables

After you have defined a *struct* type, you can use it in exactly the same way as any other type. For example, if you have defined the *Time* struct, you can create variables, fields, and parameters of type *Time*, as shown in this example:

```
struct Time
{
    ...
    private int hours, minutes, seconds;
}

class Example
{
    public void Method(Time parameter)
    {
        Time localVariable;
        ...
    }

    private Time currentTime;
}
```

Understanding Structure Initialization

The earlier discussion described how the fields in a structure are initialized by using a constructor. However, because structs are value types, you can create *struct* type variables without calling a constructor, as shown in the following example:

```
Time now;
```

In this example, the variable is created but its fields are left in their uninitialized state. Any attempt to access the values in these fields will result in a compiler error. The following graphic depicts the state of the fields in the *now* variable:

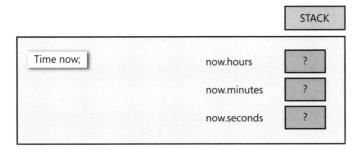

If you call a constructor, the various rules of structure constructors described earlier guarantee that all the fields in the structure will be initialized:

```
Time now = new Time();
```

This time, the default constructor initializes the fields in the structure as shown in the following graphic:

Note that in both cases, the *Time* variable is created on the stack.

If you've written your own structure constructor, you can also use that to initialize a *struct* variable. As explained earlier in this chapter, a structure constructor must always explicitly initialize all its fields. For example:

```
struct Time
{
    public Time(int hh, int mm)
```

```
    {
        hours = hh;
        minutes = mm;
        seconds = 0;
    }
    ...
    private int hours, minutes, seconds;
}
```

The following example initializes *now* by calling a user-defined constructor:

```
Time now = new Time(12, 30);
```

The following graphic shows the effect of this example:

Copying Structure Variables

You're allowed to initialize or assign one *struct* variable to another *struct* variable, but only if the *struct* variable on the right side is completely initialized (that is, if all its fields are initialized). For instance, the following example compiles because *now* is fully initialized (the graphic shows the results of performing the assignment):

```
Time now = new Time(12, 30);
Time copy = now;
```

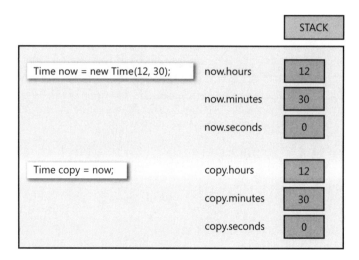

The following example fails to compile because *now* is not initialized:

```
Time now;
Time copy = now; // compile time error: now unassigned
```

When you copy a *struct* variable, each field on the left side is copied directly from its corresponding field on the right side. This copying is done as a fast single-block copy that never throws an exception. It is worth emphasizing that this form of assignment copies the entire struct. Compare this behavior to the equivalent action if *Time* was a class, in which case both variables (*now* and *copy*) would reference the *same* object on the heap.

> **Note**   C++ programmers should note that this copy behavior cannot be changed.

It's time to put this knowledge into practice. In the following exercise, you will create and use a *struct* type to represent a date.

Create and use a struct type

1. Open the *StructsAndEnums* project, located in the \Microsoft Press\Visual CSharp Step by Step\Chapter 9\StructsAndEnums folder in your My Documents folder, if it is not already open.

2. Display the Date.cs source file in the Code and Text Editor window.

3. Add a *struct* called *Date* inside the *StructsAndEnums* namespace.

    This structure should contain three private fields: one called *year* of type *int*, one called *month* of type *Month* (as declared in the previous exercise), and one called *day* of type *int*. The *Date* structure should look exactly as follows:

    ```
    struct Date
    {
        private int year;
        private Month month;
        private int day;
    }
    ```

    Now consider the default constructor that the compiler will generate for *Date*. This constructor will set the *year* to 0, the *month* to 0 (the value of January), and the *day* to 0. The *year* value of 0 is not valid (there was no year 0), and the *day* value of 0 is also not valid (each month starts on day 1). One way to fix this problem is to translate the *year* and *day* values by implementing the *Date* structure so that when the *year* field holds the value Y, this value represents the year Y + 1900, and when the *day* field holds the value D, this value represents the day D + 1. The default constructor will then set the three fields to values that represent the *Date* 1 January 1900.

4. Add a *public* constructor to the *Date* struct. This constructor should take three parame-
    ters: an *int* called *ccyy* for the *year*, a *Month* called *mm* for the *month*, and an *int* called *dd*
    for the *day*. Use these three parameters to initialize the corresponding fields. A *year* field
    of *Y* represents the year *Y* + 1900, so you need to initialize the *year* field to the value *ccyy*
    − 1900. A *day* field of *D* represents the day *D* + 1, so you need to initialize the *day* field
    to the value *dd* − 1.

    The *Date* structure should now look like this:

    ```
    struct Date
    {
        public Date(int ccyy, Month mm, int dd)
        {
            this.year = ccyy - 1900;
            this.month = mm;
            this.day = dd - 1;
        }

        private int year;
        private Month month;
        private int day;
    }
    ```

5. Add a *public* method called *ToString* to the *Date* structure after the constructor. This
    method takes no arguments and returns a string representation of the date. Remember,
    the value of the *year* field represents *year* + 1900, and the value of the *day* field repre-
    sents *day* + 1.

> **Note**   The *ToString* method is a little different from the methods you have seen so far.
> Every type, including structs and classes that you define, automatically has a *ToString*
> method whether you want it or not. Its default behavior is to convert the data in a vari-
> able into a string representation of that data. Sometimes the default behavior is mean-
> ingful, other times it is less so. For example, the default behavior of the *ToString* method
> generated for the *Date* class simply generates the string "StructsAndEnums.Date". To
> quote Zaphod Beeblebrox in *The Restaurant at the End of the Universe* (Douglas Adams),
> this is "shrewd, but dull." You need to define a new version of this method that overrides
> the default behavior, by using the *override* keyword. Overriding methods are discussed in
> more detail in Chapter 12.

The *ToString* method should look as follows:

```
public override string ToString()
{
    return this.month + " " + (this.day + 1) + " " + (this.year + 1900);
}
```

> **Note**   The + signs in the parentheses are the arithmetic addition operator. The others are the string concatenation operator. Without the parentheses, all occurrences of the + sign will be treated as the string concenation operator because the expression being evaluated is a string. It can be a little confusing when the same symbol in a single expression denotes different operators!

6. Display the Program.cs source file in the Code and Text Editor window.

7. Add a statement to the end of the *Entrance* method to declare a local variable called *defaultDate* and initialize it to a *Date* value constructed by using the default Date constructor. Add another statement to *Entrance* to write *defaultDate* to the console by calling *Console.WriteLine*.

> **Note**   The *Console.WriteLine* method automatically calls the *ToString* method of its argument to format the argument as a string.

The *Entrance* method should now look like this:

```
static void Entrance()
{
    ...
    Date defaultDate = new Date();
    Console.WriteLine(defaultDate);
}
```

8. On the Debug menu, click Start Without Debugging to build and run the program. Confirm that January 1 1900 is written to the console (the original output of the *Entrance* method will be displayed first).

9. Press the Enter key to return to the Visual Studio 2005 programming environment.

10. In the Code and Text Editor window, return to the *Entrance* method, and add two more statements. The first statement should declare a local variable called *halloween* and initialize it to October 31 2005. The second statement should write the value of *halloween* to the console.

The *Entrance* method should now look like this:

```
static void Entrance()
{
    ...
    Date halloween = new Date(2005, Month.October, 31);
    Console.WriteLine(halloween);
}
```

> **Note** When you type the *new* keyword, Intellisense will automatically detect that there are two constructors available for the *Date* type.

11. On the Debug menu, click Start Without Debugging. Confirm that October 31 2005 is written to the console after the previous information.

12. Press Enter to close the program.

You have successfully used the *enum* and *struct* keywords to declare your own value types and then used these types in code.

- **If you want to continue to the next chapter**

  Keep Visual Studio 2005 running and turn to Chapter 10.

- **If you want to exit Visual Studio 2005 now**

  On the File menu, click Exit. If you see a Save dialog box, click Yes.

Chapter 9 Quick Reference

To	Do this
Declare an enumeration type	Write the keyword *enum*, followed by the name of the type, followed by a pair of braces containing a comma-separated list of the enumeration literal names. For example: ```enum Season {Spring, Summer, Fall, Winter }```
Declare an enumeration variable	Write the name of the enumeration type on the left followed by the name of the variable, followed by a semicolon. For example: ```Season currentSeason;```

Initialize or assign an enumeration variable to a value	Write the name of the enumeration literal name in combination with the name of the enumeration type it belongs to. For example:
	
	```currentSeason = Spring; // compile time error```
	```currentSeason = Season.Spring; // okay```

Declare a *struct* type	Write the keyword *struct*, followed by the name of the *struct* type, followed by the body of the *struct* (the constructors, methods, and fields). For example:
	
	```struct Time```
	```{```
	``` public Time(int hh, int mm, int ss)```
	``` { ... }```
	``` ...```
	``` private int hours, minutes, seconds;```
	```}```

Declare a *struct* variable	Write the name of the *struct* type, followed by the name of the variable, followed by a semicolon. For example: ```Time now;```

Initialize or assign a *struct* variable to a value	Initialize or assign the variable to a *struct* value created by calling a structure constructor. For example:
	
	```Time lunch = new Time(12, 30, 0);```
	```lunch = new Time(12, 30, 0);```

Chapter 10
Using Arrays and Collections

After completing this chapter, you will be able to:

- Declare, initialize, copy, and use array variables.
- Declare, initialize, copy, and use variables of various collection types.

So far, you have seen how to create and use variables of many different types. However, all the examples of variables you have seen so far have one thing in common—they hold information about a single item (an *int*, a *float*, a *Circle*, a *Time*, and so on). What happens if you need to manipulate sets of items? One solution would be to create a variable for each item in the set, but this leads to a number of further questions: How many variables do you need? How should you name them? If you need to perform the same operation on each item in the set (such as increment each variable in a set of integers), how would you avoid very repetitive code? This solution assumes that you know, when you write the program, how many items you will need, but how often is this the case? For example, if you are writing an application that reads and processes records from a database, how many records are in the database, and how likely is this number to change?

Arrays and collections provide mechanisms that help to solve the problems posed by these questions.

What Is an Array?

An *array* is an unordered sequence of elements. All the elements in an array have the same type (unlike the fields in a struct or class, which can have different types). The elements of an array live in a contiguous block of memory and are accessed by using an integer index (unlike fields in a struct or class, which are accessed by name).

Declaring Array Variables

You declare an array variable by specifying the name of the element type, followed by a pair of square brackets, followed by the variable name. The square brackets signify that the variable is an array. For example, to declare an array of *int* variables called *pins*, you would write:

```
int[] pins; // Personal Identification Numbers
```

Microsoft Visual Basic programmers should note that you use square brackets and not parentheses. C and C++ programmers should note that the size of the array is not part of the declaration. Java programmers should note that you must place the square brackets *before* the variable name.

> **Note**   You are not restricted to primitive types as array elements. You can also create arrays of structs, enums, and classes. For example, to create an array of *Time* structs you would use
> Time[] times;

> **Tip**   It is useful to give array variable plural names, such as *places* (where each element is a *Place*), *people* (where each element is a *Person*), or *times* (where each element is a *Time*).

Creating Array Instances

Arrays are reference types, regardless of the type of their elements. This means that an array variable *refers* to an array instance on the heap (just as a class variable refers to an object on the heap) and does not hold its array elements directly on the stack (as a struct does). (To review values and references and the differences between the stack and the heap, see Chapter 8, "Understanding Values and References.") Remember that when you declare a class variable, memory is not allocated for the object until you create the instance by using *new*. Arrays follow the same rules—when you declare an array variable, you do not declare its size. You specify the size of an array only when you actually create the array instance.

To create an array instance, you use the *new* keyword followed by the name of the element type, followed by the size of the array you're creating between square brackets. Creating an array also initializes its elements by using the now familiar default values (0, *null*, or *false* depending on the type). For example, to create and initialize a new array of four integers for the *pins* variable declared earlier, you write this:

```
pins = new int[4];
```

The following graphic illustrates the effects of this statement:

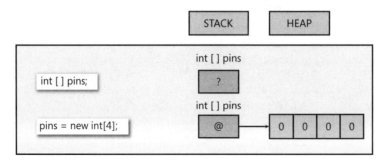

The size of an array instance does not have to be a constant; it can be calculated at run time, as shown in this example:

```
int size = int.Parse(Console.ReadLine());
int[] pins = new int[size];
```

You're allowed to create an array whose size is 0. This might sound bizarre, but it's useful in situations where the size of the array is determined dynamically and could be 0. An array of size 0 is not a *null* array.

It's also possible to create multidimensional arrays. For example, to create a two-dimensional array, you create an array that requires two integer indexes. Further discussion of multi-dimensional arrays is beyond the scope of this book, but here's an example:

```
int[,] table = new int[4,6];
```

Initializing Array Variables

When you create an array instance, all the elements of the array instance are initialized to a default value depending on their type. You can modify this behavior and initialize the elements of an array to specific values if you prefer. You achieve this by providing a comma-separated list of values between a pair of curly brackets. For example, to initialize *pins* to an array of 4 *int* variables whose values are 9, 3, 7, and 2, you would write this:

```
int[] pins = new int[4]{ 9, 3, 7, 2 };
```

The values between the curly brackets do not have to be constants. They can be values calculated at run time, as shown in this example:

```
Random r = new Random();
int[] pins = new int[4]{ r.Next() % 10, r.Next() % 10,

                         r.Next() % 10, r.Next() % 10 };
```

> **Note**   The *System.Random* class is a pseudo-random number generator. The *Next* method returns a nonnegative random number.

The number of values between the curly brackets must exactly match the size of the array instance being created:

```
int[] pins = new int[3]{ 9, 3, 7, 2 }; // compile time error
int[] pins = new int[4]{ 9, 3, 7 };    // compile time error
int[] pins = new int[4]{ 9, 3, 7, 2 }; // okay
```

When you're initializing an array variable, you can actually omit the *new* expression and the size of the array. The compiler calculates the size from the number of initializers, and generate codes to create the array. For example:

```
int[] pins = { 9, 3, 7, 2 };
```

If you create an array of structs, you can initialize each struct in the array by calling the struct constructor, as shown in this example:

```
Time[] schedule = { new Time(12,30), new Time(5,30) };
```

Accessing Individual Array Elements

To access an individual array element, you must provide an index indicating which element you require. For example, you can read the contents of element 2 of the *pins* array into an *int* variable by using the following code:

```
int myPin;
myPin = pins[2];
```

Similarly, you can change the contents of an array by assigning a value to an indexed element:

```
myPin = 1645;
pins[2] = myPin;
```

Array indexes are zero-based. The initial element of an array lives at index 0 and not index 1. An index value of 1 accesses the second element.

All array element access is bounds-checked. If you use an integer index that is less than 0 or greater than or equal to the length of the array, the compiler throws an *IndexOutOfRangeException*, as in this example:

```
try
{
    int[] pins = { 9, 3, 7, 2 };
    Console.WriteLine(pins[4]); // error, the 4th element is at index 3
}
catch (IndexOutOfRangeException ex)
{
    ...
}
```

Iterating Through an Array

Arrays have a number of useful built-in properties and methods (all arrays inherit methods and properties from the *System.Array* class in the Microsoft .NET Framework). You can use the *Length* property to find out how many elements an array contains. You can make use of the

Length property to iterate through all the elements of an array by using a *for* statement. The following sample code writes the array element values of the *pins* array to the console:

```
int[] pins = { 9, 3, 7, 2 };
for (int index = 0; index != pins.Length; index++)
{
    int pin = pins[index];
    Console.WriteLine(pin);
}
```

> **Note** *Length* is a property and not a method, which is why there are no brackets when you call it. You will learn about properties in Chapter 14, "Implementing Properties to Access Attributes."

It is common for new programmers to forget that arrays start at element zero, and that the last element is numbered *Length* − 1. C# provides the *foreach* statement to iterate through the elements of an array without worrying about these issues. For example, here's the previous *for* statement rewritten as an equivalent *foreach* statement:

```
int[] pins = { 9, 3, 7, 2 };
foreach (int pin in pins)
{
    Console.WriteLine(pin);
}
```

The *foreach* statement declares an iteration variable (in the example, *int pin*) that automatically acquires the value of each element in the array. This construct is much more declarative; it expresses the intention of the code much more directly and all of the *for* loop scaffolding drops away. The *foreach* statement is the preferred way to iterate through an array. However, in a few cases, you'll find you have to revert to a *for* statement:

- A *foreach* statement always iterates through the whole array. If you want only to iterate through a known portion of an array (for example, the first half), or to bypass certain elements (for example, every third element), it's easier to use a *for* statement.

- A *foreach* statement always iterates from index zero through index *Length* − 1. If you want to iterate backwards, it's easier to use a *for* statement.

- If the body of the loop needs to know the index of the element rather than just the value of the element, you'll have to use a *for* statement.

- If you need to modify the elements of the array, you'll have to use a *for* statement. This is because the iteration variable of the *foreach* statement is a read-only copy of each element of the array.

Copying Arrays

Arrays are reference types. An array variable contains a reference to an array instance. This means that when you copy an array variable, you end up with two references to the same array instance, for example:

```
int[] pins = { 9, 3, 7, 2 };
int[] alias = pins; //  alias and pins refer to the same array instance
```

In this example, if you modify the value at `pins[1]`, the change will also be visible by reading `alias[1]`.

If you want to make a copy of the array instance (the data on the heap) that an array variable refers to, you have to do two things. First, you need to create a new array instance of the same type and the same length as the array you are copying, as in this example:

```
int[] pins = { 9, 3, 7, 2 };
int[] copy = new int[4];
```

This works, but if you later modify the code to change the length of the original array, you must remember to also change the size of the copy. It's better to determine the length of an array by using its *Length* property, as shown in this example:

```
int[] pins = { 9, 3, 7, 2 };
int[] copy = new int[pins.Length];
```

The values inside *copy* are now all initialized to their default value of 0.

The second thing you need to do is set the values inside the new array to the same values as the original array. You could do this by using a *for* statement, as shown in this example:

```
int[] pins = { 9, 3, 7, 2 };
int[] copy = new int[pins.Length];
for (int i = 0; i != copy.Length; i++)
{
    copy[i] = pins[i];
}
```

Copying arrays is actually a fairly common requirement. So much so, that the *System.Array* class provides some useful methods that you can use to copy an array rather than writing your own code. For example, the *CopyTo*, method, which copies the contents of one array into another array given a specified starting index:

```
int[] pins = { 9, 3, 7, 2 };
int[] copy = new int[pins.Length];
pins.CopyTo(copy, 0);
```

Another way to copy the values is to use the *System.Array* static method called *Copy*. As with *CopyTo*, the target array must be initialized before the *Copy* call is made:

```
int[] pins = { 9, 3, 7, 2 };
int[] copy = new int[pins.Length];
Array.Copy(pins, copy, copy.Length);
```

Yet another alternative is to use the *System.Array* instance method called *Clone*, which can be used to create an entire array and copy it in one action:

```
int[] pins = { 9, 3, 7, 2 };
int[] copy = (int[])pins.Clone();
```

> **Note**   The *Clone* method actually returns an *object*, which is why you must cast it to an array of the appropriate type when you use it. Furthermore, all three methods create a *shallow* copy of an array—if the array being copied contains reference types, the methods simply copy the references, rather than the objects being referred to. After copying, both arrays refer to the same set of objects.

What Are Collection Classes?

Arrays are useful, but they have their limitations. However, arrays are only one way to collect elements of the same type. The .NET Framework provides several classes that also collect elements together in other specialized ways. These are the *Collection* classes, and they live in the *System.Collections* namespace and sub-namespaces.

The basic collection classes accept, hold, and return their elements as objects. That is, the element type of a collection class is an *object*. To understand the implications of this, it is helpful to contrast an array of *int* variables (*int* is a value type) with an array of objects (*object* is a reference type). Because *int* is a value type, an array of *int* variables holds its *int* values directly, as shown in the following graphic:

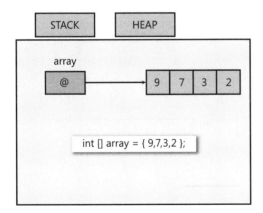

Now consider the effect when the array is an array of objects. You can still add integer values to this array (in fact, you can add values of any type to it). When you add an integer value, it is automatically boxed and the array element (an object reference) refers to the boxed copy of the integer value. (For a refresher on boxing, refer to Chapter 8.) This is illustrated in the following graphic:

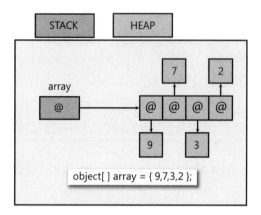

Remember that the element type of a collection class is an *object*. This means that when you insert a value into a collection, it is always boxed, and when you remove a value from a collection, you must unbox it by using a cast. The following sections provide a very quick overview of four of the most useful *Collection* classes. Refer to the .NET Framework documentation for more details on each class.

> **Note**   In fact, there are *Collection* classes that don't always use *object* as their element type and that can hold value types as well as references, but you need to know a bit more about C# before we can talk about them. You will meet these *Collection* classes in Chapter 17, "Introducing Generics."

The *ArrayList* Class

ArrayList is a useful class for shuffling elements around in an array. There are certain occasions when an ordinary array can be too restrictive:

■ If you want to resize an array, you have to create a new array, copy the elements (leaving out some if the new array is smaller), and then update the array references.

■ If you want to remove an element from an array, you have to make a copy of the element and then move all the trailing elements up by one place. Even this doesn't quite work because you end up with two copies of the last element.

■ If you want to insert an element into an array, you have to move elements down by one place to make a free slot. However, you lose the last element of the array!

Here's how you can overcome these restrictions by using the *ArrayList* class:

■ You can remove an element from an *ArrayList* by using its *Remove* method. The *ArrayList* automatically reorders its elements.

> **Note**   You cannot use the *Remove* method in a *foreach* loop that iterates through an *ArrayList*.

- You can add an element to the end of an *ArrayList* by using its *Add* method. You supply the element to be added. The *ArrayList* resizes itself if necessary.

- You can insert an element into the middle of an *ArrayList* by using its *Insert* method. Again, the *ArrayList* resizes itself if necessary.

Here's an example that shows how you can create, manipulate, and iterate through the contents of an *ArrayList*:

```
using System;
using System.Collections;
...
ArrayList numbers = new ArrayList();
...
// fill the ArrayList
foreach (int number in new int[12]{10,9,8,7,7,6,5,10,4,3,2,1})
{
    numbers.Add(number);
}
...
// remove first element whose value is 7 (the 4th element, index 3)
numbers.Remove(7);
// remove the element that's now the 7th element, index 6 (10)
numbers.RemoveAt(6);
...
// iterate remaining 10 elements using a for statement
for (int i = 0; i != numbers.Count; i++)
{
    int number = (int)numbers[i]; // Notice the cast
    Console.WriteLine(number);
}
...
// iterate remaining 10 using a foreach statement
foreach (int number in numbers)  // No cast needed
{
    Console.WriteLine(number);
}
```

The output of this code is shown below:

```
10
9
8
7
6
5
4
3
2
```

```
1
10
9
8
7
6
5
4
3
2
1
```

> **Note**   You use the *Count* property to find out how many elements are inside a collection. This is different from arrays, which use the *Length* property.

The *Queue* Class

The *Queue* class implements a first-in first-out (FIFO) mechanism. An element is inserted into the queue at the back (the enqueue operation) and is removed from the queue at the front (the dequeue operation).

Here's an example of a queue and its operations:

```
using System;
using System.Collections;
...
Queue numbers = new Queue();
...
// fill the queue
foreach (int number in new int[4]{9, 3, 7, 2})
{
    numbers.Enqueue(number);
    Console.WriteLine(number + " has joined the queue");
}
...
// iterate through the queue
foreach (int number in numbers)
{
    Console.WriteLine(number);
}
...
// empty the queue
while (numbers.Count != 0)
{
    int number = (int)numbers.Dequeue();
    Console.WriteLine(number + " has left the queue");
}
```

The output from this code is:

```
9 has joined the queue
3 has joined the queue
7 has joined the queue
2 has joined the queue
9
3
7
2
9 has left the queue
3 has left the queue
7 has left the queue
2 has left the queue
```

The *Stack* Class

The *Stack* class implements a last-in first-out (LIFO) mechanism. An element joins the stack at the top (the push operation) and leaves the stack at the top (the pop operation). To visualize this, think of a stack of dishes: new dishes are added to the top and dishes are removed from the top, making the last dish to be placed onto the stack the first one to be removed (the dish at the bottom is rarely used, and will inevitably require washing before you can put any food on it as it will be covered in grime!). Here's an example:

```csharp
using System;
using System.Collections;
...
Stack numbers = new Stack();
...
// fill the stack
foreach (int number in new int[4]{9, 3, 7, 2})
{
    numbers.Push(number);
    Console.WriteLine(number + " has been pushed on the stack");
}
...
// iterate through the stack
foreach (int number in numbers)
{
    Console.WriteLine(number);
}
...
// empty the stack
while (numbers.Count != 0)
{
    int number = (int)numbers.Pop();
    Console.WriteLine(number +  "has been popped off the stack");
}
```

The output from this program is:

```
9 has been pushed on the stack
3 has been pushed on the stack
7 has been pushed on the stack
2 has been pushed on the stack
2
7
3
9
2 has been popped off the stack
7 has been popped off the stack
3 has been popped off the stack
9 has been popped off the stack
```

The *Hashtable* Class

The array and *ArrayList* types provide a way to map an integer index to an element. You provide an integer index inside square brackets (for example, [4]), and you get back the element at index 4 (which is actually the fifth element). However, sometimes you might want to provide a mapping where the type you map from is not an *int* but rather some other type, such as *string*, *double*, or *Time*. In other languages, this is often called an *associative array*. The *Hashtable* class provides this functionality by internally maintaining two *object* arrays, one for the *keys* you're mapping from and one for the *values* you're mapping to. When you insert a key/value pair into a *Hashtable*, it automatically tracks which key belongs to which value, and enables you to retrieve the value that is associated with a specified key. There are some important consequences of the design of the *Hashtable* class:

- A *Hashtable* cannot contain duplicate keys. If you call the *Add* method to add a key that is already present in the keys array, you'll get an exception, unless you use the square bracket notation to add a key/value pair (see the following example). You can test whether a *Hashtable* already contains a particular key by using the *ContainsKey* method.

- When you use a *foreach* statement to iterate through a *Hashtable*, you get back a *DictionaryEntry*. The *DictionaryEntry* class provides access to the key and value elements in both arrays through the *Key* property and the *Value* properties.

Here is an example that associates the ages of members of my family with their names, and then prints them out (yes, I really am younger than my wife):

```
using System;
using System.Collections;
...
Hashtable ages = new Hashtable();
...
// fill the SortedList
ages["John"] = 41;
ages["Diana"] = 42;
ages["James"] = 13;
ages["Francesca"] = 11;
```

```
...
// iterate using a foreach statement
// the iterator generates a DictionaryEntry object containing a key/value pair
foreach (DictionaryEntry element in ages)
{
    string name = (string)element.Key;
    int age = (int)element.Value;
    Console.WriteLine("Name: {0}, Age: {1}", name, age);
}
```

The output from this program is:

```
Name: James, Age: 13
Name: John, Age: 41
Name: Francesca, Age: 11
Name: Diana, Age: 42
```

The *SortedList* Class

The *SortedList* class is very similar to the *Hashtable* class in that it allows you to associate keys with values. The main difference is that the keys array is always sorted (it is called a *SortedList*, after all).

When you insert a key/value pair into a *SortedList*, the key is inserted into the keys array at the correct index to keep the keys array sorted. The value is then inserted into the values array at the same index. The *SortedList* class automatically ensures that keys and values are aligned, even when you add and remove elements. This means you can insert key/value pairs into a *SortedList* in any order you like; they are always sorted based on the value of the keys.

Like the *Hashtable* class, a *SortedList* cannot contain duplicate keys. When you use a *foreach* statement to iterate through a *SortedList*, you get back a *DictionaryEntry*. However, the *DictionaryEntry* objects will be returned sorted by the *Key* property.

Here is the same example that associates the ages of members of my family with their names, and then prints them out, adjusted to use a *SortedList* rather than a *Hashtable*:

```
using System;
using System.Collections;
...
SortedList ages = new SortedList();
...
// fill the SortedList
ages["John"] = 39;
ages["Diana"] = 40;
ages["James"] = 12;
ages["Francesca"] = 10;
...
// iterate using a foreach statement
// the iterator generates a DictionaryEntry object containing a key/value pair
foreach (DictionaryEntry element in ages)
{
```

```
        string name = (string)element.Key;
        int age = (int)element.Value;
        Console.WriteLine("Name: {0}, Age: {1}", name, age);
    }
```

The output from this program is sorted by the names of my family members:

```
Name: Diana, Age: 40
Name: Francesca, Age: 10
Name: James, Age: 12
Name: John, Age: 39
```

Comparing Arrays and Collections

Here's a summary of the important differences between arrays and collections:

- An array declares the type of the element it holds, whereas a collection doesn't. This is because the collections store their elements as objects.

- An array instance has a fixed size and cannot grow or shrink. A collection can dynamically resize itself as required.

- An array is a read/write data structure—there is no way to create a read-only array. However, it is possible to use the collections in a read-only fashion by using the *ReadOnly* method provided by these classes. This method returns a read-only version of a collection.

Using Collection Classes to Play Cards

The following exercise presents a Microsoft Windows application that simulates dealing a pack of cards to four players. Cards will either be in the pack, or will be in one of four hands dealt to the players. The pack and hands of cards are implemented as *ArrayList* objects. You might think that these should be implemented as an array—after all, there are always 52 cards in a pack, and 13 cards in a hand. This is true, but it overlooks the fact that when you deal the cards to players' hands, they are no longer in the pack. If you use an array to implement a pack, you'll have to record how many slots in the array actually hold a *PlayingCard*. Similarly, when you return cards from a player's hand to the pack, you'll have to record which slots in the hand no longer contain a *PlayingCard*.

You will study the code and then write two methods: one to shuffle a pack of cards and one to return the cards in a hand to the pack.

Deal the cards

1. Start Microsoft Visual Studio 2005.

2. Open the *Cards* project, located in the \Microsoft Press\Visual CSharp Step by Step\Chapter 10\Cards folder in your My Documents folder.

3. On the Debug menu, click Start Without Debugging.

Visual Studio 2005 builds and runs the program. The Windows form displays the cards in the hands of the four players (North, South, East, and West). There are also two buttons: one to deal the cards and one to return the cards to the pack.

4.   On the Windows form, click Deal.

The 52 cards in the pack are dealt to the four hands, 13 cards per hand.

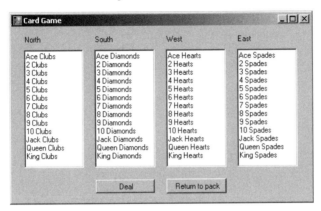

As you can see, the cards have not yet been shuffled. You will implement the *Shuffle* method in the next exercise.

5.   Click Return To Pack.

Nothing happens because the method to return the cards to the pack has also not yet been written.

6.   Click Deal.

This time the cards in each of the hands disappear, because before dealing the cards, each hand is reset. Because there are no cards in the pack (the method has not been written yet either), there is nothing to deal.

7.   Close the form to return to the Visual Studio 2005 programming environment.

Now that you know what parts are missing from this application, you will add them.

Shuffle the pack

1.   Open the Pack.cs source file in the Code and Text Editor window.

2.   Scroll through the code and examine it.

The *Pack* class represents a pack of cards. It contains a private *ArrayList* field called *cards*. Notice also that the *Pack* class has a constructor that creates and adds the 52 playing cards to the *ArrayList* by using the *Accept* method defined by this class. The remaining methods in this class constitute the typical operations that you would perform on a pack of cards (*Shuffle*, *Deal*, etc.).

Playing cards themselves are represented by the *PlayingCard* class (in PlayingCard.cs). A playing card exposes two fields of note: *suit* (which is an enumerated type and is one of Clubs, Diamonds, Hearts, or Spades), and *pips* (which indicates the numeric value of the card).

3. Locate the *Shuffle* method in the *Pack* class.

   The method is not currently implemented.

   There are a number of ways to simulate shuffling a pack of cards. Perhaps the simplest is to choose each card in sequence and swap it with another card selected at random. The .NET Framework contains a class called *Random* that you will now use to generate random integer numbers.

4. Declare a local variable of type *Random* called *random* and initialize it to a newly created *Random* object by using the default *Random* constructor.

   The *Shuffle* method should look like this:

   ```
   public void Shuffle()
   {
       Random random = new Random();
   }
   ```

5. Add a *for* statement with an empty body that iterates an *int i* from 0 up to the number of elements inside the cards *ArrayList*.

   The *Shuffle* method should now look like this:

   ```
   public void Shuffle()
   {
       Random random = new Random();
       for (int i = 0; i != cards.Count; i++)
       {
       }
   }
   ```

   The next step is to choose a random index between 0 and *cards.Count*. You will then swap the card at index *i* with the card at this random index. You can generate a positive random integer by calling the *Random.Next* instance method. The value of this positive random integer will almost certainly be greater than *cards.Count*. You must then convert this value into the range 0 to *cards.Count* – 1 inclusive. The easiest way to do this is to use the % operator to find the remainder when dividing by *cards.Count*.

6. Inside the *for* statement, declare a local variable called *cardToSwap* and initialize it to a random number between 0 and *cards.Count*.

   The *Shuffle* method should now look exactly like this:

   ```
   public void Shuffle()
   {
       Random random = new Random();
   ```

```
    for (int i = 0; i != cards.Count; i++)
    {
        int cardToSwap = random.Next() % cards.Count;
    }
}
```

The final step is to swap the card at index *i* with the card at index *cardToSwap*. To do this, you must use a temporary local variable. Remember that the elements inside a collection class (such as *ArrayList*) are of type *System.Object* (*object*).

7. Add three statements to swap the card at index *i* with the card at index *cardToSwap*.

    The *Shuffle* method should now look exactly like this:

```
public void Shuffle()
{
    Random random = new Random();
    for (int i = 0; i != cards.Count; i++)
    {
        int cardToSwap = random.Next() % cards.Count;
        object temp = cards[i];
        cards[i] = cards[cardToSwap];
        cards[cardToSwap] = temp;
    }
}
```

Notice that you have to use a *for* statement here. A *foreach* statement would not work because you need to modify each element in the *ArrayList* and a *foreach* loop provides read-only access.

8. On the Debug menu, click Start Without Debugging.

    Visual Studio 2005 builds and runs the program.

9. Click Deal.

    This time the pack is shuffled before dealing. (Your screen will differ slightly each time, because the card order is now random).

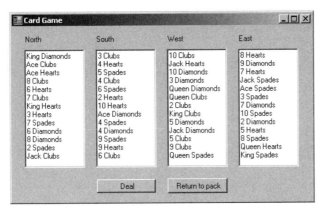

10.   Close the form.

The final step is to add the code to return cards to the pack.

Return the cards to the pack

1.   Display the Hand.cs source file in the Code and Text Editor window.

The *Hand* class, which also contains an *ArrayList* called *cards*, represents the cards held by a player. The idea is that at any one time, each card is either in the pack or in a hand.

2.   Locate the *ReturnCardsTo* method in the *Hand* class.

The *Pack* class has a method called *Accept* that takes a single parameter of type *Playing-Card*. You need to create a loop that goes through the cards in the hand and passes them back to the pack.

3.   Complete the *ReturnCardsTo* method as follows:

```
public void ReturnCardsTo(Pack pack)
{
    foreach (PlayingCard card in cards)
    {
        pack.Accept(card);
    }
    cards.Clear();
}
```

A *foreach* statement is convenient here because you do not need write access to the element and you do not need to know the index of the element. The *Clear* method removes all elements from a collection. It is important to call *cards.Clear* after returning the cards to the pack so that the cards aren't in both the pack and the hand.

4.   On the Debug menu, click Start Without Debugging.

5.   Click Deal.

The shuffled cards are dealt to the four hands as before.

6.   Click Return To Pack.

The hands are cleared. The cards are now back in the pack.

7.   Click Deal.

The shuffled cards are once again dealt to the four hands.

8.   Close the form.

> **Note**   If you click the Deal button twice without clicking Return to Pack, you lose all the cards. In the real world, you would disable the Deal button until the Return to Pack button was pressed. We will look more at using C# to write user-interface code like this in Part IV of this book.

In this chapter, you have learned how to create and use arrays to manipulate sets of data. You have also seen how to use some of the common collection classes to store and access data in memory in different ways.

■ **If you want to continue to the next chapter**

Keep Visual Studio 2005 running and turn to Chapter 11.

■ **If you want to exit Visual Studio 2005 now**

On the File menu, click Exit. If you see a Save dialog box, click Yes.

Chapter 10 Quick Reference

To	Do this
Declare an array variable	Write the name of the element type, followed by square brackets, followed by the name of the variable, followed by a semicolon. For example: `bool[] flags;`
Create an instance of an array	Write the keyword *new*, followed by the name of the element type, followed by the size of the array between square brackets. For example: `bool[] flags = new bool[10];`
Initialize the elements of an array instance to specific values	Write the specific values in a comma-separated list between curly brackets. For example: `bool[] flags = { true, false, true, false };`
Find the number of elements in an array	Use the *Length* property. For example: `int noOfElements = flags.Length;`
Access a single array element	Write the name of the array variable, followed by the integer index of the element between square brackets. Remember, array indexing starts at zero, not one. For example: `bool initialElement = flags[0 ];`

Iterate through the elements of an array or collection	Use a *for* statement or a *foreach* statement. For example:
	
	`bool[] flags = { true, false, true, false };`
	`for (int i = 0; i != flags.Length; i++)`
	`{`
	`    Console.WriteLine(flags[i ]);`
	`}`
	
	`foreach (bool flag in flags)`
	`{`
	`    Console.WriteLine(flag);`
	`}`

Find the number of elements in a collection	Use the *Count* property. For example: `int noOfElements = flags.Count;`

Chapter 11
Understanding Parameter Arrays

After completing this chapter, you will be able to:

- Write a method that can accept any number of arguments by using the *params* keyword.

- Write a method that can accept any number of arguments of any type by using the *params* keyword in combination with the object type.

Parameter arays are useful if you want to write methods that can take variable numbers of arguments, possibly of different types, as parameters. If you are familiar with object-oriented concepts, you might well be grinding your teeth in frustration at this sentence. After all, the object-oriented approach to solving this problem is to define overloaded methods.

Overloading is the technical term for declaring two or more methods with the same name in the same scope. Being able to overload a method is very useful in cases where you want to perform the same action on arguments of different types. The classic example of overloading in Microsoft Visual C# is *Console.WriteLine*. The *WriteLine* method is overloaded numerous times so that you can pass any primitive type argument:

```
class Console
{
    public static void WriteLine(int parameter)
    ...
    public static void WriteLine(double parameter)
    ...
    public static void WriteLine(decimal parameter)
    ...
}
```

As useful as overloading is, it doesn't cover every case. In particular, overloading doesn't easily handle a situation in which the type of parameters doesn't vary, but the number of parameters does. For example, what if you want to write many values to the console? Do you have to provide versions of *Console.WriteLine* that can take two parameters, other versions that can take three parameters, and so on? That would quickly get tedious. And doesn't the massive duplication of all these overloaded methods worry you? It should. Fortunately, there is a way to write one method that takes a variable number of arguments (a *variadic method*): You can use a parameter array (a parameter declared with a *params* keyword).

To understand how *params* arrays help to solve this problem, it helps to first understand the uses and shortcomings of plain arrays.

Using Array Arguments

Suppose you want to write a method to determine the minimum value in a set of parameters. One way would be to use an array. For example, to find the smallest of several *int* values, you could write a static method called *Min* with a single parameter representing an array of *int* values:

```
class Util
{
    public static int Min(int[] paramList)
    {
        if (paramList == null || paramList.Length == 0)
        {
            throw new ArgumentException("Util.Min");
        }
        int currentMin = paramList [0];
        foreach (int i in paramList)
        {
            if (i < currentMin)
            {
                currentMin = i;
            }
        }
        return currentMin;
    }
}
```

To use the *Min* method to find the minimum of two *int* values, you would write this:

```
int[] array = new int[2];
array[0] = first;
array[1] = second;
int min = Util.Min(array);
```

And to use the *Min* method to find the minimum of three *int* values, you would write this:

```
int[] array = new int[3];
array[0] = first;
array[1] = second;
array[2] = third;
int min = Util.Min(array);
```

You can see that this solution avoids the need for a large number of overloads, but it does so at a price: You have to write additional code to populate the array passed in. However, you can get the compiler to write some of this code for you by using the *params* keyword to declare a *params* array.

Declaring *params* Arrays

You use the *params* keyword as an array parameter modifier. For example, here's *Min* again, this time with its array parameter declared as a *params* array:

```
class Util
{
    public static int Min(params int[] paramList)
    {
        // code exactly as before
    }
}
```

The effect of the *params* keyword on the *Min* method is that it allows you to call it by using any number of integer arguments. For example, to find the minimum of two integer values, you would write this:

```
int min = Util.Min(first, second);
```

The compiler translates this call into code similar to this:

```
int[] array = new int[2];
array[0] = first;
array[1] = second;
int min = Util.Min(array);
```

To find the minimum of three integer values, you would write the code shown below, which is also converted by the compiler into the corresponding code that uses an array:

```
int min = Util.Min(first, second, third);
```

Both calls to *Min* (one call with two arguments and another with three arguments) resolve to the same *Min* method with the *params* keyword. And as you can probably guess, you can call this *Min* method with any number of *int* arguments. The compiler just counts the number of *int* arguments, creates an *int* array of that size, fills the array with the arguments, and then calls the method by passing the single array parameter.

> **Note** C and C++ programmers might recognize *params* as a type-safe equivalent of the *varargs* macros from the header file stdarg.h.

There are several points worth noting about *params* arrays:

■ You can use the *params* keyword on only one-dimensional arrays, as in this example:

```
// compile-time error
public static int Min(params int[,] table)
...
```

■ You can't overload a method based solely on the *params* keyword. The *params* keyword does not form part of a method's signature, as shown in this example:

```
// compile-time error: duplicate declaration
public static int Min(int[] paramList)
...
public static int Min(params int[] paramList)
...
```

■ You're not allowed *ref* or *out params* arrays, as shown in this example:

```
// compile-time errors
public static int Min(ref params int[] paramList)
...
public static int Min(out params int[] paramList)
...
```

■ A *params* array must be the last parameter. (This means you can have only one *params* array per method.) Consider this example:

```
// compile-time error
public static int Min(params int[] paramList, int i)
...
```

■ The compiler detects and rejects any potentially ambiguous overloads. For example, the following two *Min* methods are ambiguous; it's not clear which one should be called if you pass two *int* arguments:

```
// compile-time error
public static int Min(params int[] paramList)
...
public static int Min(int, params int[] paramList)
...
```

■ A non-*params* method always takes priority over a *params* method. This means if you want to, you can still create an overloaded version of a method for the common cases. For example:

```
public static int Min(int leftHandSide, int rightHandSide)
...
public static int Min(params int[] paramList)
...
```

The first version of the *Min* method is used when called using two *int* arguments. The second version is used if any other number of *int* arguments is supplied. This includes the case where the method is called with no arguments.

Adding the non-*params* array method might be a useful optimization technique because the compiler won't have to create and populate so many arrays.

Using *params object[ ]*

A *params int* array is very useful because it allows any number of *int* arguments in a method call. However, what if not only the number of arguments varies, but also the argument type? C# has a way to solve this problem, too. The technique is based on the facts that *System.Object* (*object*) is the root of all classes, and that the compiler can generate code that converts value types (things that aren't classes) into objects by using boxing, as described in Chapter 8, "Understanding Values and References." You can use a *params* object array to declare a method that accepts any number of arguments of *object*s, allowing the arguments passed in to be of any type. Look at this example:

```
class Black
{
    public static void Hole(params object [] paramList)
    ...
}
```

I've called this method *Black.Hole*, not because it swallows every argument, but because no argument can escape from it:

- You can pass it no arguments at all, in which case the compiler will pass an object array whose length is 0:

```
Black.Hole();
// converted into Black.Hole(new object[0]);
```

> **Tip** It's perfectly safe to iterate through a zero-length array by using a *foreach* statement.

- You can call it by passing *null* as the argument. An array is a reference type, so you're allowed to initialize an array with *null*:

```
Black.Hole(null);
```

- You can pass it an actual array. In other words, you can manually create the array normally created by the compiler:

```
object[] array = new object[2];
array[0] = "forty two";
array[1] = 42;
Black.Hole(array);
```

- You can pass it any other arguments of different types, and these arguments will automatically be wrapped inside an *object* array:

```
Black.Hole("forty two", 42);
//converted into Black.Hole(new object[]{"forty two", 42});
```

The *Console.WriteLine* Method

The *Console* class contains many overloads for the *WriteLine* method. One of these overloads looks like this:

```
public static void WriteLine(string format, params object[] arg);
```

Here's an example of a call to this method, that you met in Chapter 10, "Using Arrays and Collections":

```
Console.WriteLine("Name:{0}, Age:{1}", name, age);
```

The compiler resolves this call into the following:

```
Console.WriteLine("Name:{0}, Age:{1}", new object[2]{name, age});
```

Using *params* Arrays

In the following exercise, you will implement and test a *static* method called *Util.Sum*. The purpose of this method is to calculate the sum value of a variable number of *int* arguments passed to it, returning the result as an *int*. You will do this by writing *Util.Sum* to take a *params int[]* parameter. You will implement two checks on the *params* parameter to ensure the *Util.Sum* method is completely robust. You will then call the *Util.Sum* method with a variety of different arguments to test it.

Write a *params* array method

1. Start Visual Studio 2005.

2. Open the *ParamsArray* project, located in the \Microsoft Press\Visual CSharp Step by Step\Chapter 11\ ParamArrays folder in your My Documents folder.

3. Display the Util.cs source file in the Code and Text Editor window.

   The Util.cs file contains an empty class called *Util* in the *ParamsArray* namespace.

4. Add a public static method called *Sum* to the *Util* class.

   The *Util.Sum* method returns an *int* and accepts a *params* array of *int* values. *Util.Sum* should look like this:

   ```
   class Util
   {
       public static int Sum(params int[] paramList)
       {
       }
   }
   ```

   The first step in implementing *Util.Sum* is to check the *paramList* parameter. Apart from containing a valid set of integers, it could also be *null* or it could be an array of zero length. In both of these cases, it is difficult to calculate the sum, so the best option is to throw an *ArgumentException*. (You could argue that the sum of the integers in a zero-length array is zero, but we will treat this situation as an exception in this example.)

> **Note** The *ArgumentException* class is specifically designed to be thrown by a method if the arguments supplied do not meet the requirements of the method.

5. Add a statement to *Util.Sum* that throws an *ArgumentException* if *paramList* is *null*.

    Util.Sum should now look like this:

    ```
    public static int Sum(params int[] paramList)
    {
        if (paramList == null)
        {
            throw new ArgumentException("Util.Sum: null parameter list");
        }
    }
    ```

6. Add a statement to *Util.Sum* that throws an *ArgumentException* if the length of *array* is 0.

    Util.Sum should now look like this:

    ```
    public static int Sum(params int[] paramList)
    {
        if (paramList == null)
        {
            throw new ArgumentException("Util.Sum: null parameter list");
        }

        if (paramList.Length == 0)
        {
            throw new ArgumentException("Util.Sum: empty parameter list");
        }
    }
    ```

    If the array passes these two tests, the next step is to add all the elements inside the array together. You can use a *foreach* statement for this step. You will also need a local variable to hold the sum value.

7. Add a *foreach* statement to *Util.Sum* to add all the elements in the array together, and then return it from *Util.Sum* with a *return* statement.

    Util.Sum should now look like this:

    ```
    class Util
    {
        public static int Sum(params int[] paramList)
        {
            ...
            int sumTotal = 0;
    ```

```
        foreach (int i in paramList)
        {
            sumTotal += i;
        }
        return sumTotal;
    }
}
```

8. On the Build menu, click Build Solution. Confirm that there are no errors in your code.

Test the *Util.Sum* method

1. In the Code and Text Editor window, open the Program.cs source file.

2. In the Code and Text Editor window, locate the *Entrance* method in the *Program* class.

3. Add the following statement to the *Entrance* method:

```
Console.WriteLine(Util.Sum(null));
```

4. On the Debug menu, click Start Without Debugging.

    The program builds and runs, writing the following message to the console:

```
Exception: Util.Min: null parameter list
```

    This confirms that the first check in the method works.

5. Press the Enter key to finish the program return to Visual Studio 2005.

6. In the Code and Text Editor window, change the call to *Console.WriteLine* in *Entrance* to the following statement:

```
Console.WriteLine(Util.Sum());
```

    This time, the method is being called without any arguments. The compiler will translate the empty argument list into an empty array.

7. On the Debug menu, click Start Without Debugging.

    The program builds and runs, writing the following message to the console:

```
Exception: Util.Min: empty parameter list
```

    This confirms that the second check in the method works.

8. Press the Enter key to finish the program and return to Visual Studio 2005.

9. Change the call to *Console.WriteLine* in *Entrance* to the following:

```
Console.WriteLine(Util.Sum(10,9,8,7,6,5,4,3,2,1));
```

10. On the Debug menu, click Start Without Debugging.

    The program builds, runs, and writes 55 to the console.

11. Press Enter to close the application.

In this chapter, you have learned how to use a *params* array to define a method that can take variable numbers of arguments. You have also seen how to use a *params* array of *object* types to pass arguments of different types.

■ **If you want to continue to the next chapter**

Keep Visual Studio 2005 running and turn to Chapter 12.

■ **If you want to exit Visual Studio 2005 now**

On the File menu, click Exit. If you see a Save dialog box, click Yes.

Chapter 11 Quick Reference

To	Do this

Write a method that accepts any number of arguments of a given type	Write a method whose parameter is a *params* array of the given type. For example, a method that accepts any number of *bool* arguments would be:
	
	``
	someType Method(params bool[] flags)
	{
	    . . .
	}
	``

Write a method that accepts any number of arguments of any type	Write a method whose parameter is a *params* array of *object*. For example:
	
	``
	someType Method(params object[] paramList)
	{
	    . . .
	}
	``

Chapter 12
Working with Inheritance

After completing this chapter, you will be able to:

- Create a derived class that inherits features from a base class.

- Control method hiding and overriding by using the *new*, *virtual*, and *override* keywords.

- Limit accessibility within an inheritance hierarchy by using the *protected* keyword.

- Capture common implementation details in an abstract class.

- Declare that a class cannot be inherited by using the *sealed* keyword.

- Create an interface identifying the names of methods.

- Implement interfaces in a struct or class by writing the bodies of the methods.

Inheritance is a key concept in the world of object-orientation. You can use it as a tool to avoid repetition when defining different classes that have a number of features in common, and are quite clearly related to each other. Perhaps they are different classes of the same type, each with its own distinguishing feature; for example, *managers*, *manual workers*, and *all employees* of a factory. If you were writing an application to simulate the factory, how would you specify that managers and manual workers have a number of features that are the same, but also have other features that are diverse? For example, they all have an employee reference number, but managers have different responsibilities and perform different tasks than manual workers.

This is where inheritance proves useful.

What Is Inheritance?

There is generally a lot of confusion among programmers as to what inheritance is. Part of this trouble stems from the fact that the word "inheritance" itself has several subtly different meanings. If someone bequeaths something to you in a will, you are said to inherit it. Similarly, we say that you inherit half of your genes from your mother and half of your genes from your father. Both of these uses of the word inheritance have very little to do with inheritance in programming.

Inheritance in programming is all about classification—it's a relationship between classes. For example, when you were at school, you probably learned about mammals, and learned that horses and whales are examples of mammals. Each does everything that a mammal does (it breathes air, gives birth to live young, and so on), but also has its own special features (a horse has hooves, unlike a whale).

In Microsoft Visual C#, you could model this by creating two classes, one called *Mammal* and one called *Horse*, and declare that *Horse* inherits from *Mammal*. The inheritance would model that there is a relationship and would capture the fact that *all* horses are mammals. Similarly, you could also declare a class called *Whale* that also inherits from *Mammal*. Common functionality (such as breathing and giving birth) could be placed in the *Mammal* class; properties such as hooves or fins should be placed in the *Horse* or *Whale* class as appropriate.

Using Inheritance

This section covers the essential inheritance-related syntax that you need to understand in order to create classes that inherit from other classes.

Base Classes and Derived Classes

The syntax for declaring that a class inherits from another class is as follows:

```
class DerivedClass : BaseClass {
    ...
}
```

The derived class inherits from the base class. Unlike other languages such as C++, in C# a class is allowed to derive from, at most, one other class; a class is *not allowed* to derive from two or more classes. However, unless *DerivedClass* is declared as *sealed* (see the section titled "Sealed Classes" later in this chapter), you can create further derived classes that inherit from *DerivedClass* using the same syntax:

```
class DerivedSubClass : DerivedClass {
    ...
}
```

In this way, you can create inheritence hierarchies.

Suppose you are writing a syntax analyzer as part of a compiler. You need to define a class that represents each of the elements of a program according to the syntax rules of the language. Such elements are sometimes referred to as *tokens*. You could declare the *Token* class as shown below. The constructor builds a *Token* object from the string of characters passed in (which could be a keyword, an identifier, a piece of white space, or any other valid piece of syntax for the language being parsed):

```
class Token
{
    public Token(string name)
    {
        ...
```

```
    }
    ...
}
```

You could then define classes for each different classification (type) of token, based on the *Token* class, adding additional methods as necessary. For example:

```
class IdentifierToken : Token
{
    ...
}
```

> **Tip**   C++ programmers should note that you do not and cannot explicitly specify whether the inheritance is public, private, or protected. C# inheritance is always implicitly public. Java programmers should note the use of the colon, and that there is no *extends* keyword.

Remember that the *System.Object* class is the root class of all classes. All classes implicitly derive from the *System.Object* class. For example, if you implement the *Token* class like this:

```
class Token
{
    public Token(string name)
    {
        ...
    }
    ...
}
```

The compiler silently rewrites it as the following code (which you can write explicitly if you really want to):

```
class Token : System.Object
{
    public Token(string name)
    {
        ...
    }
    ...
}
```

What this means in practical terms is that all classes that you define automatically inherit all the features of the *System.Object* class. This includes methods such as *ToString* (first discussed in Chapter 2, "Working with Variables, Operators, and Expressions"), which is used to convert an object to a string.

Calling Base Class Constructors

All classes have at least one constructor. (Remember that if you don't provide one, the compiler generates a default constructor for you.) A derived class automatically contains all fields from the base class. These fields require initialization when an object is created. Therefore, the constructor for a derived class must call the constructor for its base class. You use the *base* keyword to call a base class constructor when the constructor is defined. Here's an example:

```
class IdentifierToken : Token
{
    public IdentifierToken(string name)
          : base(name) // calls Token(name)
    {
        ...
    }
    ...
}
```

If you don't explicitly call a base class constructor in a derived class constructor, the compiler attempts to silently insert a call to the base class's default constructor. Taking the earlier example, the compiler will rewrite this:

```
class Token
{
    public Token(string name)
    {
        ...
    }
    ...
}
```

As this:

```
class Token : System.Object
{
    public Token(string name)
        : base()
    {
        ...
    }
    ...
}
```

This works because *System.Object* has a public default constructor. However, not all classes have a public default constructor, in which case forgetting to call the base class constructor results in a compile-time error, because the compiler must insert a call to a constructor, but does not know which one to use. For example:

```
class IdentifierToken : Token
{
    public IdentifierToken(string name)
```

```
    // error, base class Token does not have
    // a public default constructor
    {
        ...
    }
    ...
}
```

Assigning Classes

In previous examples in this book, you have seen how to declare a variable using a class type, and then use the *new* keyword to create an object. You have also seen how the type-checking rules of C# prevent you from assigning a variable of one type to an object instantiated from a different type. For example, given the definitions of the *Token*, *IdentifierToken*, and *KeywordToken* classes, the following code is illegal:

```
class Token
{
    ...
}

class IdentifierToken : Token
{
    ...
}

class KeywordToken : Token
{
    ...
}

...
IdentifierToken it = new IdentifierToken();
KeywordToken kt = it;  // error – different types
```

However, it is possible to refer to an object from a variable of a different type as long as the type used is a class that is higher up the inheritance hierarchy. So the following statements are legal:

```
IdentierToken it = new IdentifierToken();
Token t = it; // legal as Token is a base class of IdentifierToken
```

The inheritance hierarchy means that you can think of an *IdentifierToken* as a special type of *Token* (it has everything that a *Token* has), with a few extra bits (defined by any methods and fields you add to the *IdentifierToken* class). You can also make a *Token* variable refer to a *KeywordToken* object as well. There is one significant limitation, however—when referring to a *KeywordToken* or *IdentifierToken* object using a *Token* variable, you can only access methods and fields that are defined by the *Token* class. Any additional methods defined by the *KeywordToken* or *IdentifierToken* classes are available only when using a *KeywordToken* or *IdentifierToken* variable.

> **Note**   This explains why you can assign almost anything to an *object* variable. Remember that *object* is an alias for *System.Object*, and all classes inherit from *System.Object* either directly or indirectly.

new Methods

One of the hardest problems in the realm of computer programming is the task of thinking up unique and meaningful names for identifiers. If you are defining a method for a class, and that class is part of an inheritance hierarchy, sooner or later you are going to try to reuse a name that is already in use by one of the classes higher up the hiererachy. If a base class and a derived class happen to declare two methods that have the same signature (the method signature is the name of the method and the number and types of its parameters), you will receive a warning when you compile the application. The method in the derived class masks (or hides) the method in the base class that has the same signature. For example, if you compile the following code, the compiler will generate a warning message telling you that *IdentifierToken.Name* hides the inherited method *Token.Name*:

```
class Token
{
    ...
    public string Name() { ... }
}

class IdentifierToken : Token
{
    ...
    public string Name() { ... }
}
```

Although your code will compile and run, you should take this warning seriously. If another class derives from *IdentifierToken* and calls the *Name* method, it might be expecting the method implemented in the *Token* class to be called. However, the *Name* method in the *IdentifierToken* class hides the *Name* method in the *Token* class, and it will be called instead. Most of the time, such a coincidence is at best a source of confusion, and you should consider renaming methods to avoid clashes. However, if you're sure that you want the two methods to have the same signature, you can silence the warning by using the *new* keyword as follows:

```
class Token
{
    ...
    public string Name() { ... }
}

class IdentifierToken : Token
{
    ...
    new public string Name() { ... }
}
```

Using the *new* keyword like this does not change the fact that the two methods are completely unrelated and that hiding still occurs. It just turns the warning off. In effect, the *new* keyword says, "I know what I'm doing, so stop showing me these warnings."

Virtual Methods

Sometimes you do want to hide the way in which a method is implemented in a base class. As an example, consider the *ToString* method in *System.Object*. The purpose of *ToString* is to convert an object to its string representation. Because this method is very useful, it is a member of *System.Object*, thereby automatically providing all classes with a *ToString* method. However, how does the version of *ToString* implemented by *System.Object* know how to convert a derived class into a string? A derived class might contain any number of fields with interesting values that should be part of the string. The answer is that the implementation of *ToString* in *System.Object* is actually a bit simplistic All it can do is convert an object into a string that represents its type, such as "Token" or "IdentifierToken". This is not too useful after all. So, why provide a method that is so useless? The answer to this second question requires a bit of detailed thought.

Obviously, *ToString* is a fine idea in concept (all classes should provide a method that can be used to convert objects into strings). It is only the implementation that is problematic. In fact, you are not expected to call the *ToString* method defined by *System.Object*—it is simply a placeholder. Instead, you should provide your own version of the *ToString* method in each class you define, overriding the default implementation in *System.Object*. The version in *System.Object* is only there as a safety net, in case a class does not implement its own *ToString* method. In this way, you can be confident that you can call *ToString* on any object, and the method will return its contents as a string, regardless of how it is implemented.

A method that is intended to be overridden is called a *virtual* method. You should be clear on the difference between overriding a method and hiding a method. Overriding a method is a mechanism for providing different implementations of the same method—the methods are all related because they are intended to perform the same task. Hiding a method is a means of replacing one method with another—the methods are usually unrelated and might perform totally different tasks. Overriding a method is a useful programming concept; hiding a method is probably an error.

You can mark a method as a virtual method by using the *virtual* keyword. For example, the *ToString* method in the *System.Object* class is defined like this:

```
namespace System
{
    class Object
    {
        public virtual string ToString()
        {
            ...
        }
```

```
        ...
    }
    ...
}
```

> **Note**   A C# method is not virtual by default. This is the same as in C++, but a major differ-
> ence from Java, in which all methods are virtual by default.

Virtual Methods and Polymorphism

Virtual methods allow you to call different versions of the same method, based on the
type of the object determined dynamically by the runtime. Consider the following example classes that define a variation on the Mammal hierarchy described earlier:

```
class Mammal
{
    ...
    public virtual string GetTypeName()
    {
        return "This is a mammal";
    }
}

class Horse : Mammal
{
    ...
    public override string GetTypeName()
    {
        return "This is a horse";
    }
}

class Whale : Mammal
{
    ...
    public override string GetTypeName ()
    {
        return "This is a whale";
    }
}

class Kangaroo : Mammal
{
    ...
}
```

Notice two things: First, the *override* keyword used by the *GetTypeName* method (which
will be described shortly) in the *Horse* and *Whale* classes, and second, that the *Kangaroo*
class does not have a *GetTypeName* method.

Now examine the following block of code:

```
Mammal m;
Horse h = new Horse();
Whale w = new Whale();
Kangaroo k = new Kangaroo();

m = h;
Console.WriteLine(m.GetTypeName()); // Horse
m = w;
Console.WriteLine(m.GetTypeName()); // Whale
m = k;
Console.WriteLine(m.GetTypeName()); // Kangaroo
```

What will be output by the three different *Console.WriteLine* statements? At first glance, you would expect them all to print "This is a mammal," because each statement calls the *GetTypeName* method on the *m* variable, which is a *mammal*. However, in the first case, you can see that *m* is actually a reference to a *Horse* (you are allowed to assign a *Horse* to a *Mammal* variable because the *Horse* class is derived from the *Mammal* class—all *Horses* are *Mammals*). Because the *GetTypeName* method is defined as virtual, the runtime works out that it should call the *Horse. GetTypeName* method, so the statement actually prints the message "This is a horse." The same logic applies to the second *Console.Write-Line* statement, which outputs the message "This is a whale." The third statement calls *Console.WriteLine* on a *Kangaroo* object. However, the *Kangaroo* class does not have a *GetTypeName* method, so the default method in the *Mammal* class is called, returning the string "This is a mammal."

This phenomenon of the same statement invoking multiple methods is called *polymorphism*, which literally means "many forms."

override Methods

If a base class declares that a method is virtual, a derived class can use the *override* keyword to declare another implementation of that method. For example:

```
class IdentifierToken : Token
{
    ...
    public override string Name() { ... }
}
```

There are some important rules you must follow when declaring polymorphic methods by using the *virtual* and *override* keywords:

■ You're not allowed to declare a private method by using the *virtual* or *override* keyword. If you try, you'll get a compile-time error. Private really is private.

- The two methods must be identical. That is, they must have the same name, the same parameter types, and the same return type.

- The two methods must have the same access. For example, if one of the two methods is public, the other must also be public. (C++ programmers should take note. In C++, the methods can have different accessibility.)

- You can only override a virtual method. If the base class method is not virtual and you try to override it, you'll get a compile-time error. This is sensible; it should be up to the base class to decide whether its methods can be overridden.

- If the derived class does not declare the method by using the *override* keyword, it does not override the base class method. In other words, it becomes an implementation of a completely different method that happens to have the same name. As before, this will cause a compile-time hiding warning, which you can silence by using the *new* keyword as previously described.

- An *override* method is implicitly virtual and can itself be overridden in a further derived class. However, you are not allowed to explicitly declare that an *override* method is virtual by using the *virtual* keyword.

protected Access

The *public* and *private* access keywords create two extremes of accessibility: public fields and methods of a class are accessible to everyone, whereas private fields and methods of a class are accessible to only the class itself.

These two extremes are sufficient when considering classes in isolation. However, as all experienced object-oriented programmers know, isolated classes cannot solve complex problems. Inheritance is a very powerful way of connecting classes, and there is clearly a very special and close relationship between a derived class and its base class. Frequently it is useful for a base class to allow derived classes to access some of its members, while hiding these same members from classes that are not part of the hierarchy. In this situation, you can use the *protected* keyword to tag members:

- A derived class can access a protected base class member. In other words, inside the derived class, a protected base class member is effectively public.

- If the class is not a derived class, it cannot access a protected class member. In other words, inside a class that is not a derived class, a protected class member is effectively private.

C# gives programmers complete freedom to declare both methods and fields as protected. However, most object-oriented guidelines recommend keeping your fields strictly private. Public fields violate encapsulation because all users of the class have direct, unrestricted access to the fields. Protected fields maintain encapsulation for users of a class, for whom the protected fields are inaccessible. However, protected fields still allow encapsulation to be violated by classes that inherit from the class.

> **Note**   You can access a protected base class member not only in a derived class, but also in classes derived from the derived class. A protected base class member retains its protected accessibility in a derived class and is accessible to further derived classes.

Creating Interfaces

Inheriting from a class is a powerful mechanism, but the real power of inheritance comes from inheriting from an interface. An interface allows you to completely separate the name of a method from its implementation.

For example, suppose you want to define a new collection class that allows you to store objects in a particular sequence. When you define the collection class, you do not want to restrict the types of object that it can hold, but you need to provide a way of sorting the objects into the specified sequence. The question is, how do you provide a method that sorts objects whose types you do not know when you write the collection class? At first glance, this problem seems similar to the *ToString* problem described earlier, and can be resolved by declaring a virtual method that other classes override. However, this is not the case. There is not necessarily any form of inheritance relationship between the collection class and the objects that it holds, so a virtual method would not be of much use. The solution is to specify that all objects in the collection must provide a method allowing them to be compared to each other, such as the *CompareTo* method shown below:

```
int CompareTo(object obj)
{
    // return 0 if this instance is equal to obj
    // return < 0 if this instance is less than obj
    // return > 0 if this instance is greater than obj
    ...
}
```

The collection class can then make use of this method to sort its contents.

You can define an interface that includes this method, and specify that the collection class will allow only classes that implement this interface as its contents. This mechanism guarantees that you will be able to call the *CompareTo* method on all objects in the collection and sort them.

Interfaces allow you to truly separate the "what" from the "how." The interface tells you only what the name, return type, and parameters of the method are. Exactly how the method is implemented is not a concern of the interface. The interface represents how you want an object to be used, rather than how it happens to be implemented at a particular moment in time.

Interface Syntax

To declare an interface, you use the *interface* keyword instead of the *class* or *struct* keyword. Inside the interface, you declare methods exactly as in a class or a struct, except that you never specify an access modifier (no public, private, or protected access), and you replace the method body with a semicolon. Here is an example:

```
interface IComparable
{
    int CompareTo(object obj);
}
```

> **Tip**   The Microsoft .NET Framework documentation recommends that you preface the name of your interfaces with a capital I. This convention is the last vestige of Hungarian Notation in C#. Incidentally, the *System* namespace already defines the *IComparable* interface as shown here.

Interface Restrictions

The essential idea to remember is that an interface never contains any implementation. The following restrictions are natural consequences of this:

■ You're not allowed any fields in an interface, not even static ones. A field is an implementation of an object attribute.

■ You're not allowed any constructors in an interface. A constructor contains the statements used to initialize the fields in an object, and an interface does not contain any fields!

■ You're not allowed a destructor in an interface. A destructor contains the statements used to destroy an object instance. (Destructors are described in Chapter 13, "Using Garbage Collection and Resource Management.")

■ You cannot supply an access modifier. All methods in an interface are implicitly public.

■ You cannot nest any types (enums, structs, classes, interfaces, or delegates) inside an interface.

■ You're not allowed to inherit an interface from a struct or a class. Structs and classes contain implementation; if an interface were allowed to inherit from either, it would be inheriting some implementation.

Implementing an Interface

To implement an interface, you declare a class or struct that inherits from the interface and implements *all* the interface methods. For example, suppose you are defining the *Token* hierarchy shown earlier, but need to specify that all classes in the hierarchy provide a method called *Name* that returns the name of the current token as a string. You could define the *IToken* interface that contains this method:

```
interface IToken
{
    string Name();
}
```

You could the implement this interface in the *Token* class:

```
class Token : IToken
{
    ...
    string IToken.Name()
    {
        ...
    }
}
```

When you implement an interface, you must ensure that each method matches its corresponding interface method exactly, according to the following guidelines:

- The method names and return types match exactly.

- Any parameters (including *ref* and *out* keyword modifiers, although not the *params* keyword modifier) match exactly.

- The method name is prefaced by the name of the interface. This is known as *explicit interface implementation*, and is a good habit to cultivate.

- If you are using explicit interface implementation, the method should not have an access qualifier. All methods implementing an interface are publicly accessible.

If there is any difference between the interface definition and its declared implementation, the class will not compile.

The Advantages of Explicit Interface Implementations

Implementing an interface explicitly can seem a little verbose, but it does offer a number of advantages that help you to write clearer, more maintainable, and more predictable code.

You can implement a method without explicitly specifying the interface name, but this can lead to some differences in the way the implementation behaves. Some of these differences can cause confusion. For example, a method defined by using explicit interface implementation cannot be declared as *virtual*, whereas omitting the interface name allows this behavior.

Explicit interface implementation disambiguates methods from different interfaces that have the same name, return type, and parameters. The methods that implement the interface are publicly accessible, but only through the interface. (We will look at how to do this in the section "Referencing a Class Through Its Interface" later in this chapter.) Without using explicit interface implementation it would not be possible to distinguish which method implements part of which interface if multiple interfaces contain methods with the same names, return types, and parameters.

In this book we recommend implementing an interface explicitly wherever possible.

A class can extend another class and implement an interface at the same time. In this case, C# does not distinguish between the base class and the interface by using keywords as, for example, Java does. Instead, C# uses a positional notation. The base class is named first, followed by a comma, followed by the interface. For example:

```
interface IToken
{
    ...
}

class DefaultTokenImpl
{
    ...
}

class IdentifierToken : DefaultTokenImpl , IToken
{
    ...
}
```

Referencing a Class Through Its Interface

In the same way that you can reference an object by using a variable defined as a class that is higher up the hierarchy, you can reference an object by using a variable defined as an interface that its class implements. Taking the previous example, you can reference an *IdentifierToken* object by using an *IToken* variable, as follows:

```
IdentifierToken it = new IdentifierToken();
IToken iTok = it; // legal
```

This technique is useful because it allows you to define methods that can take different types as parameters, as long as the types implement a specified interface. For example, the *Process* method shown below can take any argument that implements the *IToken* interface:

```
void Process(IToken iTok)
{
    ...
}
```

Note that you can invoke only methods that are visible through the interface when referencing an object in this way.

Working with Multiple Interfaces

A class can have at most one base class, but is allowed to implement an unlimited number of interfaces. A class must still implement all the methods it inherits from all its interfaces. An interface is not allowed to inherit from any kind of class, but an interface is allowed to inherit other interfaces.

If an interface, struct, or class inherits from more than one interface, you write the interfaces in a comma-separated list. If a class also has a base class, the interfaces are listed *after* the base class. For example:

```
class IdentifierToken : DefaultTokenImpl, IToken, IVisitable
{
    ...
}
```

Abstract Classes

The *IToken* interface could be implemented by many different classes, one for each type of token in a C# source file: *IdentifierToken*, *KeywordToken*, *LiteralToken*, *OperatorToken*, and *PunctuatorToken*. (You might also have classes for comments and white space.) In situations such as this, it's quite common for parts of the derived classes to share common implementations. For example, the duplication in the following two classes is obvious:

```csharp
class IdentifierToken : IToken
{
    public IdentifierToken(string name)
    {
        this.name = name;
    }

    public virtual string Name()
    {
        return name;
    }
    ...
    private string name;
}

class StringLiteralToken : IToken
{
    public StringLiteralToken(string name)
    {
        this.name = name;
    }

    public virtual string Name()
    {
        return name;
    }
    ...
    private string name;
}
```

Duplication in code is a warning sign. You should refactor the code to avoid the duplication and reduce any maintenance costs. However, there is a right way and a wrong way to do this. The wrong way is to push all the commonality up into the interface. This is wrong because you'd then have to change the interface to a class (because an interface can't contain any implementation). The right way to avoid the duplication is to refactor the common implementation into a new class created specifically for this purpose. For example:

```csharp
class DefaultTokenImpl
{
    public DefaultTokenImpl(string name)
    {
        this.name = name;
    }

    public string Name()
    {
        return name;
    }

    private string name;
```

```
}

class IdentifierToken : DefaultTokenImpl, IToken
{
    public IdentifierToken(string name)
        : base(name)
    {
    }
    ...
}

class StringLiteralToken : DefaultTokenImpl, IToken
{
    public StringLiteralToken(string name)
        : base(name)
    {
    }
    ...
}
```

This is a good solution, but there is one thing that is still not quite right: You can create instances of the *DefaultTokenImpl* class. This doesn't really make sense. The *DefaultTokenImpl* class exists to provide a common default implementation. Its sole purpose is to be inherited from. The *DefaultTokenImpl* class is an abstractration of common functionality rather than an entity in its own right.

> **Note**   If you find the situation with the *DefaultTokenImpl* class confusing, consider the *Mammal*, *Horse*, *Whale*, and *Kangaroo* example shown earlier. *Mammal* is a classic example of an abstract class. In the real world, you may see horses, whales, and kangaroos trotting, swimming, or bouncing around, but you will never see a "mammal" doing any of these things. Mammal is simply a convenient abstraction for classifying the actual animals.

To declare that you're not allowed to create instances of a class, you must explicitly declare that the class is abstract, by using the *abstract* keyword. For example:

```
abstract class DefaultTokenImpl                    .
{
    public DefaultTokenImpl(string name)
    {
        this.name = name;
    }

    public string Name()
    {
        return name;
    }
    private string name;
}
```

Notice that the new class *DefaultTokenImpl* does not implement the *IToken* interface. It could, but the *IToken* interface doesn't really fit with its purpose. An abstract class is all about common implementation, whereas an interface is all about usage. It's usually best to keep these two aspects separate, and to let the non-abstract classes (such as *StringLiteralToken*) determine how to implement their interfaces:

■ They can inherit from *DefaultTokenImpl* and *IToken*, in which case *DefaultToken-Impl.Name* becomes the implementation of *IToken.Name*. Notice that this means *Default-TokenImpl.Name* must be public. You could make the constructor for *DefaultTokenImpl* protected, but the *Name* method must remain public if it is to qualify as an implementation of *IToken.Name* in a derived class.

■ They can decide not to inherit from *DefaultTokenImpl*, in which case they'll have to implement *IToken.Name* themselves.

Sealed Classes

Using inheritance is not always easy and requires forethought. If you create an interface or an abstract class, you are knowingly writing something that will be inherited from in the future. The trouble is that predicting the future is a difficult business. It takes skill, effort, and knowledge of the problem you are trying to solve to craft a flexible, easy-to-use hierarchy of interfaces, abstract classes, and classes. To put it another way, unless you consciously design a class with the intention of using it as a base class, it's extremely unlikely that it will function very well as a base class. Fortunately, C# allows you to use the *sealed* keyword to prevent a class from being used as a base class if you decide that it should not be. For example:

```
sealed class LiteralToken : DefaultTokenImpl, IToken
{
    ...
}
```

If any class attempts to use *LiteralToken* as a base class, a compile-time error will be generated. A sealed class cannot declare any virtual methods. The sole purpose of the *virtual* keyword is to declare that this is the *first* implementation of a method that you intend to override in a derived class, but a sealed class cannot be derived from.

 Note   A struct is implicitly sealed. You can never derive from a struct.

Sealed Methods

You can also use the *sealed* keyword to declare that an individual method is sealed. This means that a derived class cannot then override the sealed method. You can only seal an *override* method (you declare the method as sealed override).You can think of the *interface*, *virtual*, *override*, and *sealed* keywords as follows:

- An interface introduces the *name* of a method.

- A virtual method is the *first implementation* of a method.

- An override method is *another implementation* of a method.

- A sealed method is the *last implementation* of a method.

Extending an Inheritance Hierarchy

In the following exercise, you will familiarize yourself with a small hierarchy of interfaces and classes that together implement a very simple framework. The framework is a Microsoft Windows application that simulates reading a C# source file and classifying its contents into tokens (identifiers, keywords, operators, and so on). The framework provides a mechanism for "visiting" each token in turn, performing various tasks. For example:

- A *displaying visitor class* that displays the source file in a rich text box.

- A *printing visitor class* that converts tabs to spaces and aligns braces correctly.

- A *spelling visitor class* that checks the spelling of each identifier.

- A *guideline visitor class* that checks that the public identifiers start with a capital letter and that interfaces start with a capital I.

- A *complexity visitor class* that monitors the depth of the brace nesting in the code.

- A *counting visitor class* that counts the number of lines in each method, the number of members in each class, and the number of lines in each source file.

Understand the inheritance hierarchy and its purpose

1. Start Microsoft Visual Studio 2005.

2. Open the *Tokenizer* project, located in the \Microsoft Press\Visual CSharp Step by Step\Chapter 12\Tokenizer folder in your My Documents folder.

3. Display the SourceFile.cs source file in the Code and Text Editor window.

   The *SourceFile* class contains a private array field called *tokens*:

   ```
   private IVisitableToken[] tokens =
   {
       new KeywordToken("using"),
       new WhitespaceToken(" "),
       new IdentifierToken("System"),
       new PunctuatorToken(";"),
       ...
   };
   ```

   The *tokens* array contains a sequence of objects that all implement the *IVisitableToken* interface. Together, these tokens simulate the tokens of a simple "hello, world" source file. (A complete version of this project would parse a named source file and construct these tokens dynamically.) The *SourceFile* class also contains a public method called *Accept*. The *Accept* method has a single parameter of type *ITokenVisitor*. The body of the *Accept* method iterates through the tokens, calling their *Accept* methods. The *Accept* method of each token will process the token in some way, according to the type of the token:

```
public void Accept(ITokenVisitor visitor)
{
    foreach (IVisitableToken token in tokens)
    {
        token.Accept(visitor);
    }
}
```

In this way, the visitor parameter *visits* each token in sequence.

4. Display the IVisitableToken.cs source file in the Code and Text Editor window.

   The *IVisitableToken* interface inherits from two other interfaces, the *IVisitable* interface and the *IToken* interface:

```
interface IVisitableToken : IVisitable, IToken
{
}
```

5. Display the IVisitable.cs source file in the Code and Text Editor window.

   The *IVisitable* interface declares a single *Accept* method:

```
interface IVisitable
{
    void Accept(ITokenVisitor visitor);
}
```

   Each object in the array of tokens inside the *SourceFile* class is accessed using the *IVisitableToken* interface. The *IVisitableToken* interface inherits the *Accept* method, and each token implements the *Accept* method.

6. Click the Class View tab underneath the Solution Explorer window. (If the Class View tab is not visible, click Class View in the View menu).

   This window displays the namespaces, classes, and interfaces defined by the project.

7. Expand the *Tokenizer* project, and then expand the *{} Tokenizer* namespace. The classes and interfaces in this namespace are listed. Notice the different icons used to distinguish interfaces from classes. Expand the *IVisitableToken* interface, and then expand the Base Types node. The interfaces that the *IVisitableToken* interface extends (*IToken* and *IVisitable*) are displayed:

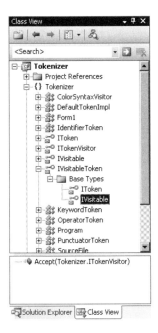

8. In the Class View window, right-click the *IdentifierToken* class and then click Go To Definition to display it in the Code and Text Editor window (it is actually located in Source-File.cs).

    The *IdentifierToken* class inherits from the *DefaultTokenImpl* abstract class and the *IVisitableToken* interface. It implements the *Accept* method as follows:

    ```
    void IVisitable.Accept(ITokenVisitor visitor)
    {
        visitor.VisitIdentifier(this.ToString());
    }
    ```

    The other token classes in this file follow a similar pattern.

9. In the Class View window, right-click the *ITokenVisitor* interface and then click Go To Definition. This action displays the ITokenVisitor.cs source file in the Code and Text Editor window.

    The *ITokenVisitor* interface contains one method for each type of token. The result of this hierarchy of interfaces, abstract classes, and classes is that you can create a class that implements the *ITokenVisitor* interface, create an instance of this class, and pass this instance as the parameter to the *Accept* method of a *SourceFile*. For example:

    ```
    class MyVisitor : ITokenVisitor
    {
        public void VisitIdentifier(string token)
        {
            ...
    ```

```
        }

        public void VisitKeyword(string token)
        {
            ...
        }
        ...
        static void Main()
        {
            SourceFile source = new SourceFile();
            MyVisitor visitor = new MyVisitor();
            source.Accept(visitor);
        }
    }
```

This will result in each token in the source file calling the matching method in the visitor object. You could create a number of different visitor classes to perform numerous different tasks as each token is visited.

In the following exercise, you will create a class that derives from the key framework interface and whose implementation displays the tokens of the source file in a rich text box in color syntax (for example, keywords in blue) by using the "visitor" mechanism.

Write the ColorSyntaxVisitor class

1. In the Solution Explorer (click the Solution Explorer tab underneath the Class View window), double-click Form1.cs to display the Color Syntax form in the Designer View window.

    This form contains an Open button for opening the file to be tokenized, and a rich text box for displaying the tokens. A rich text box is like an ordinary text box, except that it can display formatted content rather than simple, unformatted text.

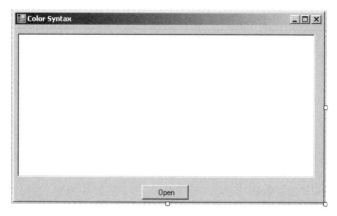

The rich text box in the middle of the form is called *codeText*, and the button is called *Open*.

2. Right-click the form and then click View Code to display the code in the Code and Text Editor window.

3. Locate the *Open_Click* method.

    This is the method that is called when the Open button is clicked. You must implement this method so that it displays the tokens defined in the *SourceFile* class in the rich text box, by using a *ColorSyntaxVisitor* object. Change the *Open_Click* method so that it looks exactly like this:

    ```
    private void Open_Click(object sender, EventArgs e)
    {
        SourceFile source = new SourceFile();
        ColorSyntaxVisitor visitor = new ColorSyntaxVisitor(codeText);
        source.Accept(visitor);
    }
    ```

    Remember that the *Accept* method of the *SourceFile* class iterates through all the tokens, processing each one by using the specified visitor. In this case, the visitor is the *ColorSyntaxVisitor* object, which renders each token in color.

4. Open the ColorSyntaxVisitor.cs source file in the Code and Text Editor window.

    The *ColorSyntaxVisitor* class has been partially implemented. It implements the *IToken-Visitor* interface and already contains two fields and a constructor to initialize a reference to a rich text box, called *target*, used to display tokens. Your task is to implement the methods inherited from the *ITokenVisitor* interface, and then write the tokens to the rich text box. In the *ColorSyntaxVisitor* class, the rich text box is referenced using a variable called *target*.

5. In the Code and Text Editor window, add a *Write* method to the *ColorSyntaxVisitor* class, exactly as follows:

    ```
    private void Write(string token, Color color)
    {
        target.AppendText(token);
        target.Select(this.index, this.index + token.Length);
        this.index += token.Length;
        target.SelectionColor = color;
    }
    ```

    This code appends each token to the rich text box using the specified color. The *Select* method of a rich text box selects a block of text indicated by start and end points; setting the *SelectionColor* property makes the selected block of text appear in the specified color. The *index* variable tracks the current end of the text in the rich text box, and is updated as new text is appended.

    Each of the various "visit" methods will call this *Write* method to display the results.

6. In the Code and Text Editor window, add the methods that implement the *ITokenVisitor* interface to the *ColorSyntaxVisitor* class. Use *Color.Blue* for keywords, *Color.Green* for *StringLiterals*, and *Color.Black* for all other methods (*Color* is a struct defined in the

System.Drawing namespace). Notice that this code implements the interface explicitly; it qualifies each method with the interface name:

```
void ITokenVisitor.VisitComment(string token)
{
    Write(token, Color.Black);
}

void ITokenVisitor.VisitIdentifier(string token)
{
    Write(token, Color.Black);
}

void ITokenVisitor.VisitKeyword(string token)
{
    Write(token, Color.Blue);
}

void ITokenVisitor.VisitOperator(string token)
{
    Write(token, Color.Black);
}

void ITokenVisitor.VisitPunctuator(string token)
{
    Write(token, Color.Black);
}

void ITokenVisitor.VisitStringLiteral(string token)
{
    Write(token, Color.Green);
}

void ITokenVisitor.VisitWhitespace(string token)
{
    Write(token, Color.Black);
}
```

> **Tip**   You can either type these methods into the Code and Text Editor window directly, or you can use a feature of Visual Studio 2005 to add default implementations for each one and then modify the method bodies with the appropriate code. To do this, right-click the *ITokenVisitor* identifier in the class definition: `sealed class ColorSyntaxVisitor : ITokenVisitor` In the context menu that appears, point to Implement Interface and then click the Implement Interface Explicitly option. Each method will contain a statement that throws an *Exception* with the message "This method or operation is not implemented." Replace this code with that shown above.

7. On the Build menu, click Build Solution. Correct any errors, and then rebuild if necessary.

8. On the Debug menu, click Start Without Debugging.

The Color Syntax form appears.

9. On the form, click Open.

   The dummy code is displayed in the rich text box, with keywords in blue and string literals in green.

   ```
   using System;

   class Greeting
   {
       static void Main()
       {
           Console.WriteLine("Hello, world");
       }
   }
   ```

10. Close the form to return to Visual Studio 2005.

Generating a Class Diagram

The Class View window is useful for displaying the hierarchy of classes and interfaces in a project. Visual Studio 2005 also enables you to generate class diagrams which depict this same information graphically (you can also use a class diagram to add new classes and interfaces, and define methods, properties, and other class members).

To generate a new class diagram, click the Project menu, and then click Add New Item. In the Add New Item window select the Class Diagram template and then click Add. This action will generate an empty diagram, and you can create new types by dragging items from the Class Designer category in the Toolbox. You can generate a diagram of all existing classes by clicking and dragging them individually from the Class View window, or by clicking and dragging the namespace to which they belong. The diagram shows the relationships between the classes and interfaces, and you can expand the definition of each class to show its contents. You can drag the classes and interfaces around to make the diagram more readable, as shown in the following image:

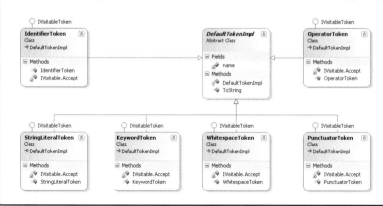

Summarizing Keyword Combinations

The following table summarizes the various valid (yes) and invalid (no) keyword combinations.

Keyword	Interface	Abstract class	Class	Sealed class	struct
Abstract	no	yes	no	no	no
New	yes[*]	yes	yes	yes	no[†]
override	no	yes	yes	yes	no[‡]
private	no	yes	yes	yes	yes
protected	no	yes	yes	yes	no[**]
public	no	yes	yes	yes	yes
sealed	no	yes	yes	yes	no
virtual	no	yes	yes	no	no

[*] An interface can extend another interface and introduce a new method with the same signautre.

[†] A struct implicitly derives from System.Object, which contains methods that the struct can hide.

[‡] A struct implicitly derives from System.Object, which contains no virtual methods.

[**] A struct is implicitly sealed and cannot be derived from.

■ **If you want to continue to the next chapter**

Keep Visual Studio 2005 running and turn to Chapter 13.

■ **If you want to exit Visual Studio 2005 now**

On the File menu, click Exit. If you see a Save dialog box, click Yes.

Chapter 12 Quick Reference

To	Do this
| Create a derived class from a base class | Declare the new class name followed by a colon and the name of the base class. For example:<br><br>```csharp
class Derived : Base
{
    ...
}
``` |
| Call a base class constructor | Supply a constructor parameter list before the body of the derived class constructor. For example:<br><br>```csharp
class Derived : Base
{
    ...
    public Derived(int x) : Base(x)
    {
        ...
    }
    ...
}
``` |
| Declare a virtual method | Use the *virtual* keyword when declaring the method. For example:<br><br>```csharp
class Mammal
{
    public virtual void Breathe()
    {
        ...
    }
    ...
}
``` |
| Declare an interface | Use the *interface* keyword. For example:<br><br>```csharp
interface IDemo
{
    string Name();
    string Description();
}
``` |
| Implement an interface | Declare a class using the same syntax as class inheritance, and then implement all the member functions of the interface. For example:<br><br>```csharp
class Test : IDemo
{
    public string IDemo.Name()
    {
        ...
    }

    public string IDemo.Description()
    {
        ...
    }
}
``` |
```

Chapter 13
Using Garbage Collection and Resource Management

After completing this chapter, you will be able to:

- Manage system resources by using garbage collection.
- Write code that runs when an object is finalized by using a destructor.
- Release a resource at a known point in time in an exception-safe manner by writing a *try/finally* statement.
- Release a resource at a known point in time in an exception-safe manner by writing a *using* statement.

You have seen in earlier chapters how to create variables and objects, and hopefully understand how memory is allocated when variables and objects are created (in case you cannot remember, value types are created on the stack, and reference types are given memory from the heap). Computers do not have infinite amounts of memory, so it must be reclaimed when a variable or object no longer needs it. Value types are destroyed and their memory reclaimed when the method in which they are created finishes. That's the easy bit. How about reference types? An object is created by using the *new* keyword, but how and when is an object destroyed? That's what this chapter is all about.

The Life and Times of an Object

First, let's recap what happens when you create and destroy an object.

You create an object like this:

```
TextBox message = new TextBox(); // TextBox is a reference type
```

From your point of view, the *new* operation is atomic, but underneath, object creation is really a two-phase process. First, the *new* operation has to allocate some raw memory from the heap. You have no control over this phase of an object's creation. Second, the *new* operation has to convert the raw memory into an object; it has to initialize the object. You can control this phase this by using a constructor.

> **Note**   C++ programmers should note that in C#, you cannot overload *new* to control allocation.

When you have created an object, you can then access its members by using the dot operator. For example:

```
message.Text = "People of Earth, your attention please";
```

You can make other reference variables refer to the same object:

```
TextBox ref = message;
```

How many references can you create to an object? As many as you want! The runtime has to keep track of all these references. If the variable *message* disappears (by going out of scope), other variables (such as *ref*) might still exist. Therefore, the lifetime of an object cannot be tied to a particular reference variable. An object can only be destroyed when *all* the references to it have disappeared.

> **Note**   C++ programmers should note that C# does not have a *delete* operator. The runtime controls when an object is destroyed.

Like object creation, object destruction is also a two-phase process. The two phases of destruction exactly mirror the two phases of creation. First, you have to perform some tidying up. You do this by writing a *destructor*. Second, the raw memory has to be given back to the heap; the memory that the object lived in has to be deallocated. Once again, you have no control over this phase. The process of destroying an object and returning memory back to the heap is known as *garbage collection*.

Writing Destructors

You can use a destructor to perform any tidying up required when an object is garbage collected. The syntax for writing a destructor is a tilde (~) followed by the name of the class. For example, here's a simple class that counts the number of live instances by incrementing a static count in the constructor and decrementing a static count in the destructor:

```
class Tally
{
    public Tally()
    {
        this.instanceCount++;
    }

    ~Tally()
    {
```

```
        this.instanceCount--;
    }

    public static int InstanceCount()
    {
        return this.instanceCount;
    }
    ...
    private static int instanceCount = 0;
}
```

There are some very important restrictions that apply to destructors:

- You cannot declare a destructor in a struct. A struct is a value type that lives on the stack and not the heap, so garbage collection does not apply.

```
struct Tally
{
    ~Tally() { ... } // compile-time error
}
```

- You cannot declare an access modifier (such as *public*) for a destructor. This is because you never call the destructor yourself—the garbage collector does.

```
public ~Tally() { ... } // compile-time error
```

- You never declare a destructor with parameters, and it cannot take any parameters. Again, this is because you never call the destructor yourself.

```
~Tally(int parameter) { ... } // compile-time error
```

- The compiler automatically translates a destructor into an override of the *Object.Finalize* method. The compiler translates the following destructor:

```
class Tally
{
    ~Tally() { ... }
}
```

Into this:

```
class Tally
{
    protected override void Finalize()
    {
        try { ... }
        finally { base.Finalize(); }
    }
}
```

The compiler-generated *Finalize* method contains the destructor body inside a *try* block, followed by a *finally* block that calls the base class *Finalize*. (The *try* and *finally* keywords were described in Chapter 6, "Managing Errors and Exceptions.") This ensures that a destructor always calls its base class destructor. It's important to realize that only the compiler can make this translation. You can't override *Finalize* yourself and you can't call *Finalize* yourself.

Why Use the Garbage Collector?

In C#, you can never destroy an object yourself. There just isn't any syntax to do it, and there are good reasons why the designers of C# decided to forbid you from doing it. If it was *your* responsibility to destroy objects, sooner or later one of the following situations would arise:

- You'd forget to destroy the object. This would mean that the object's destructor (if it had one) would not be run, tidying up would not occur, and memory would not be deallocated back to the heap. You could quite easily run out of memory.

- You'd try to destroy an active object. Remember, objects are accessed by reference. If a class held a reference to a destroyed object, it would be a dangling reference. The dangling reference would end up referring either to unused memory or possibly to a completely different object in the same piece of memory. Either way, the outcome of using dangling reference would be undefined. All bets would be off.

- You'd try and destroy the same object more than once. This might or might not be disastrous, depending on the code in the destructor.

These problems are unacceptable in a language like C#, which places robustness and security high on its list of design goals. Instead, the garbage collector is responsible for destroying objects for you. The garbage collector guarantees the following:

- Each object will be destroyed and its destructors run. When a program ends, all oustanding objects will be destroyed.

- Each object is destroyed exactly once.

- Each object is destroyed only when it becomes unreachable; that is, when no references refer to the object.

These guarantees are tremendously useful and free you, the programmer, from tedious housekeeping chores that are easy to get wrong. They allow you to concentrate on the logic of the program itself and be more productive.

When does garbage collection occur? This might seem like a strange question. After all, surely garbage collection occurs when an object is no longer needed. Well, it does, but not necessarily immediately. Garbage collection can be an expensive process, so the runtime collects garbage only when it needs to (when it thinks available memory is starting to run low), and then it collects as much as it can. Performing a few large sweeps of memory is more efficient than performing lots of little dustings!

> **Note**   You can invoke the garbage collector in a program by calling the static method *System.GC.Collect()*. However, except in a few cases, this is not recommended. The *System.GC.Collect* method starts the garbage collector, but the process runs asynchronously and when the method call finishes you still don't know whether your objects have been destroyed. Let the runtime decide when it is best to collect garbage!

One feature of the garbage collector is that you don't know, and should not rely upon, the order in which objects will be destroyed. The final point to understand is arguably the most important: Destructors do not run until objects are garbage collected. If you write a destructor, you know it will be executed, you just don't know when.

How Does the Garbage Collector Work?

The garbage collector runs in its own thread and can execute only at certain times (typically when your application reaches the end of a method). While it runs, other threads running in your application will temporarily halt. This is because the garbage collector may need to move objects around and update object references; it cannot do this while objects are in use. The steps that the garbage collector takes are as follows:

1. It builds a map of all reachable objects. It does this by repeatedly following reference fields inside objects. The garbage collector builds this map very carefully and makes sure that circular references do not cause an infinite recursion. Any object *not* in this map is deemed to be unreachable.

2. It checks whether any of the unreachable objects has a destructor that needs to be run (a process called *finalization*). Any unreachable object that requires finalization is placed in a special queue called the *freachable queue* (pronounced F-reachable).

3. It deallocates the remaining unreachable objects (those that don't require finalization) by moving the *reachable* objects down the heap, thus defragmenting the heap and freeing memory at the top of the heap. When the garbage collector moves a reachable object, it also updates any references to the object.

4. At this point, it allows other threads to resume.

5. It finalizes the unreachable objects that require finalization (now in the freachable queue) in a separate thread.

Recommendations

Writing classes that contain destructors adds complexity to your code and to the garbage collection process, and makes your program run more slowly. If your program does not contain any destructors, the garbage collector does not need to perform Steps 3 and 5 in the previous section. Clearly, not doing something is faster than doing it. Therefore, try to avoid using destructors except when you really need them. For example, consider a *using* statement instead (see the section titled "The *using* Statement" later in this chapter).

You need to write a destructor very carefully. In particular, you need to be aware that, if your destructor calls other objects, those other objects might have *already* had their destructor called by the garbage collector. Remember that the order of finalization is not guaranteed. Therefore, ensure that destructors do not depend on each other, or overlap with each other (don't have two destructors that try to release the same resource, for example).

Resource Management

Sometimes it's inadvisable to release a resource in a destructor; some resources are just too valuable and too scarce to lie around unreleased for arbitrary lengths of time. Scarce resources need to be released, and they need to be released as soon as possible. In these situations, your only option is to release the resource yourself. A *disposal* method is a method that disposes of a resource. If a class has a disposal method, you can call it explicitly and thereby control when the resource is released.

Disposal Methods

An example of a class that implements a disposal method is the *TextReader* class from the *System.IO* namespace. This class provides mechanisms to read characters from a sequential stream of input. *TextReader* contains a virtual method called *Close*, which closes the stream. The *StreamReader* class (which reads characters from a stream, such as an open file) and the *StringReader* class (which reads characters from a string) both derive from *TextReader,* and both override the *Close* method. Here's an example that reads lines of text from a file by using the *StreamReader* class, and then displays them on the screen:

```
TextReader reader = new StreamReader(filename);
string line;
while ((line = reader.ReadLine()) != null)
{
    Console.WriteLine(line);
}
reader.Close();
```

The *ReadLine* method reads the next line of text from the stream into a string. The *ReadLine* method returns null if there is nothing left in the stream. It's important to call *Close* when you have finished with *reader* to release the file handle and associated resources. However, there is a problem with this example; it's not exception-safe. If the call to *ReadLine* (or *WriteLine*) throws an exception, the call to *Close* will not happen; it will be bypassed. If this happens often enough, you will run out of file handles and be unable to open any more files.

Exception-Safe Disposal

One way to ensure that a disposal method (such as *Close*) is always called, regardless of whether there is an exception, is to call the disposal method inside a *finally* block. Here's the previous example coded by using this technique:

```
TextReader reader = new StreamReader(filename);
try
{
    string line;
    while ((line = reader.ReadLine()) != null)
    {
        Console.WriteLine(line);
```

```
    }
}
finally
{
    reader.Close();
}
```

Using a *finally* block like this works, but it has several drawbacks that make it a less than ideal solution:

- ■ It quickly gets unwieldy if you have to dispose of more than one resource (you end up with nested *try* and *finally* blocks).

- ■ In some cases, you might have to modify the code (for example, reorder the declaration of the resource reference, remember to initialize the reference to *null*, and remember to check that the reference isn't *null* in the *finally* block).

- ■ It fails to create an abstraction of the solution. This means the solution is hard to understand and you must repeat the code everywhere you need this functionality.

- ■ The reference to the resource remains in scope after the *finally* block. This means that you can accidentally try to use the resource after it has been released.

The *using* statement is designed to solve all these problems.

The *using* Statement

The *using* statement provides a clean mechanism for controlling the lifetimes of resources. You can create an object, and this object will be destroyed when the *using* statement block finishes.

Important   Do not confuse the *using* statement shown in this section with the *using* directive that brings a namespace into scope. It is unfortunate that the same keyword has two different meanings.

The syntax for a *using* statement is as follows:

```
using ( type variable = initialization ) embeddedStatement
```

Here is the best way to ensure that your code always calls *Close* on a *TextReader*:

```
using (TextReader reader = new StreamReader(filename))
{
    string line;
    while ((line = reader.ReadLine()) != null)
    {
        Console.WriteLine(line);
    }
}
```

This *using* statement is precisely equivalent to the following translation:

```
{
    TextReader reader = new StreamReader(filename);
    try
    {
        string line;
        while ((line = reader.ReadLine()) != null)
        {
            Console.WriteLine(line);
        }
    }
    finally
    {
        if (reader != null)
        {
            ((IDisposable)reader).Dispose();
        }
    }
}
```

Note   Note the outer block scope. This arrangement means that the variable you declare in a *using* statement goes out of scope at the end of the embedded statement.

The variable you declare in a *using* statement must be of a type that implements the *IDisposable* interface. The *IDisposable* interface lives in the *System* namespace and contains just one method called *Dispose*:

```
namespace System
{
    interface IDisposable
    {
        void Dispose();
    }
}
```

It just so happens that the *StreamReader* class implements the *IDisposable* interface, and its *Dispose* method calls *Close* to close the stream. You can use a *using* statement as a clean, exception-safe, robust way to ensure that a resource is always automatically released. This solves all of the problems that existed in the manual *try/finally* solution. You now have a solution that:

- Scales well if you need to dispose of multiple resources.
- Doesn't distort the logic of the program code.
- Abstracts away the problem and avoids repetition.
- Is robust. You can't use the variable declared inside the *using* statement, (in this case, *reader*) after the *using* statement has ended because it's not in scope anymore—you'll get a compile-time error.

Calling the *Dispose* Method from a Destructor

When writing a class, should you write a destructor, or implement the *IDisposable* interface? A call to a destructor *will* happen but you just don't know when. On the other hand you know exactly when a call to the *Dispose* method happens, but you just can't be sure that it will actually happen, because it relies on the programmer remembering to write a *using* statement. However, it is possible to ensure that the *Dispose* method always runs by calling it from the destructor. This acts as a useful backup. You might forget to call the *Dispose* method, but at least you can be sure that it will be called, even if it's only when the program shuts down. Here's an example of how to do this:

```
class Example : IDisposable
{
    ...
    ~Example()
    {
        Dispose();
    }

    public virtual void Dispose()
    {
        if (!this.disposed)
        {
            try {
                // release scarce resource here
            }
            finally {
                this.disposed = true;
                GC.SuppressFinalize(this);
            }
        }
    }

    public void SomeBehavior() // example method
    {
        checkIfDisposed();
        ...
    }
    ...
    private void checkIfDisposed()
    {
        if (this.disposed)
        {
            throw new ObjectDisposedException("Example");
        }
    }

    private Resource scarce;
    private bool disposed = false;
}
```

Notice the following:

- The class implements *IDisposable*.

- The destructor calls *Dispose*.

- The *Dispose* method is public and can be called at any time.

- The *Dispose* method can safely be called multiple times. The variable *disposed* indicates whether the method has aleady been run before. The scarce resource is released only the first time the method runs.

- The *Dispose* method calls the static *GC.SuppressFinalize* method. This method stops the garbage collector from calling the destructor on this object, because the object has now been finalized.

- All the regular methods of the class (such as *SomeBehavior*) check to see whether the object has already been disposed. If it has, they throw an exception.

Making Code Exception-Safe

In the following exercise, you will rewrite a small piece of code to make it exception-safe. The code opens a text file, reads its contents one line at a time, writes these lines to a rich text box on a Windows form, and then closes the text file. However, if an exception arises as the file is read or as the lines are written to the rich text box, the call to close the text file will be by-passed. You will rewrite the code to use a *using* statement instead, thus ensuring that the code is exception-safe.

Write a *using* statement

1. Start Microsoft Visual Studio 2005.

2. Open the *UsingStatement* project, located in the \Microsoft Press\Visual CSharp Step by Step\Chapter 13\UsingStatement folder in your My Documents folder.

3. On the Debug menu, click Start Without Debugging.

   The Windows form appears.

4. On the form, click Open File.

5. In the Open dialog box, navigate to the \Microsoft Press\Visual CSharp Step by Step\Chapter 13\UsingStatement\UsingStatement folder in your My Documents folder and select the Form1.cs source file.

   This is the source file for the application itself.

6. Click Open.

   The contents of the file are loaded into the Windows form.

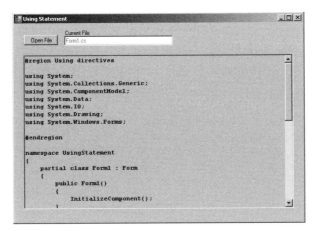

7. Close the form to return to Visual Studio 2005.

8. Open the Form1.cs source file in the Code and Text Editor window, and then locate the *openFileDialog_FileOk* method.

    This method should look like this:

```
private void openFileDialog_FileOk(object sender,
    System.ComponentModel.CancelEventArgs e)
{
    string fullPathname = openFileDialog.FileName;
    FileInfo src = new FileInfo(fullPathname);
    filename.Text = src.Name;
    source.Text = "";
    TextReader reader = new StreamReader(fullPathname);
    string line;
    while ((line = reader.ReadLine()) != null)
    {
        source.Text += line + "\n";
    }
    reader.Close();
}
```

    The variables *filename*, *openFileDialog*, and *source* are three private fields of the *Form1* class. The problem with this code is that the call to *reader.Close* is not guaranteed to happen. If an exception occurs after opening the file, the method will terminate with an exception, but the file will remain open until the application finishes.

9. Rewrite the *openFileDialog_FileOk* method with a *using* statement, exactly as follows:

```
private void openFileDialog_FileOk(object sender,
    System.ComponentModel.CancelEventArgs e)
{
    string fullPathname = openFileDialog.FileName;
    FileInfo src = new FileInfo(fullPathname);
    filename.Text = src.Name;
    source.Text = "";
```

```
using (TextReader reader = new StreamReader(fullPathname))
{
    string line;
    while ((line = reader.ReadLine()) != null)
    {
        source.Text += line + "\n";
    }
}
}
```

Notice that you no longer need to call *reader.Close* as it will be invoked by the *Dispose* method of the *StreamReader* class when the *using* statement finishes. This applies whether the *using* statement finishes naturally or terminates because of an exception.

10.   Rebuild and re-run the application to verify that it still works.

■ **If you want to continue to the next chapter**

Keep Visual Studio 2005 running and turn to Chapter 14.

■ **If you want to exit Visual Studio 2005 now**

On the File menu, click Exit. If you see a Save dialog box, click Yes.

Chapter 13 Quick Reference

To	Do this
| Write a destructor | Write a method whose name is the same as the name of the class and is prefixed with a tilde (~). The method must not have an access modifier (such as *public*) and cannot have any parameters or return a value. For example:<br><br>```csharp
class Example
{
    ~Example()
    {
        ...
    }
}
``` |
| Call a destructor | You can't call a destructor. Only the garbage collector can call a destructor. |
| Force garbage collection | Call *System.GC.Collect*. |
| Release a resource at a known point in time | Write a disposal method (a method that disposes of a resource) and call it explicitly from the program. For example:<br><br>```csharp
class TextReader
{
    ...
    public virtual void Close()
    {
        ...
    }
}

class Example
{
    void Use()
    {
        TextReader reader = ...;
        // use reader
        reader.Close();
    }
}
``` |

To	Do this
Release a resource at a known point in time in an exception-safe manner	Release the resource with a *using* statement. For example:

```
class TextReader : IDisposable
{
    ...
    public virtual void Dispose()
    {
        // calls Close
    }
    public virtual void Close()
    {
        ...
    }
}

class Example
{
    void Use()
    {
        using (TextReader reader = ...)
        {
            // use reader
        }
    }
}
```

Part III
Creating Components

Chapter 14

Implementing Properties to Access Attributes

After completing this chapter, you will be able to:

- Encapsulate logical fields by using properties.
- Control read access to properties by declaring *get* accessors.
- Control write access to properties by declaring *set* accessors.
- Create interfaces that declare properties.
- Implement interfaces containing properties, by using structs and classes.

The first two parts of this book have introduced the core syntax of the C# language, and shown you how to use C# to build new types, such as structs, enums, and classes. You have also seen how the runtime manages the memory used by variables and objects when a program runs, and you should now understand the lifecycle of C# objects. The chapters in Part III, "Creating Components," build on this information, showing you how to use C# to create reusable components—functional classes that you can reuse in many different applications.

This chapter looks at how to define and use properties to hide fields in a class. Previous chapters have emphasized that you should make the fields in a class private, and provide methods to store values in them, or retrieve their values. While this provides safe and controlled access to fields, the syntax for accessing a field in this way is unnatural. When you want to read or write a variable you normally use an assignment statement, so calling a method to achieve the same effect on a field (which is, after all, just a variable) feels a little clumsy. Properties are designed to alleviate this awkwardness.

Comparing Fields and Methods

First, let's recap the original motivation for using methods to hide fields.

Consider the following *struct* that represents a position on a screen as an *(X, Y)* coordinate pair:

```
struct ScreenPosition
{
    public ScreenPosition(int x, int y)
    {
        this.X = rangeCheckedX(x);
```

```
        this.Y = rangeCheckedY(y);
    }

    public int X;
    public int Y;

    private static int rangeCheckedX(int x)
    {
        if (x < 0 || x > 1280)
        {
            throw new ArgumentOutOfRangeException("X");
        }
        return x;
    }
    private static int rangeCheckedY(int y)
    {
        if (y < 0 || y > 1024)
        {
            throw new ArgumentOutOfRangeException("Y");
        }
        return y;
    }
}
```

The problem with this *struct* is that it does not follow the golden rule of encapsulation; it does not keep its data private. Public data is a bad idea because its use cannot be checked and controlled. For example, the *ScreenPosition* constructor range checks its parameters, but no such check can be done on the "raw" access to the public fields. Sooner or later (probably sooner), either *X* or *Y* will stray out of its range, possibly as the result of a programming error:

```
ScreenPosition origin = new ScreenPosition(0, 0);
...
int xpos = origin.X;
origin.Y = -100; // Oops
```

The common way to solve this problem is to make the fields private and add an accessor method and a modifier method to respectively read and write the value of each private field. The modifier methods can then range-check the new field values because the constructor already checks the initial field values. For example, here's an accessor (*GetX*) and a modifier (*SetX*) for the *X* field. Notice how *SetX* checks its parameter value:

```
struct ScreenPosition
{
    ...
    public int GetX()
    {
        return this.x;
    }

    public void SetX(int newX)
    {
        this.x = rangeCheckedX(newX);
    }
}
```

```
    ...
    private static int rangeCheckedX(int x) { ... }
    private static int rangeCheckedY(int y) { ... }
    private int x, y;
}
```

The code now successfully enforces the range constraints, which is good. However, there is a price to pay for this valuable guarantee—*ScreenPosition* no longer has a natural field-like syntax; it uses awkward method-based syntax instead. The following example increases the value of *X* by 10. To do so, it has to read the value of *X* by using the *GetX* accessor method, and then write the value of *X* by using the *SetX* modifier method:

```
int xpos = origin.GetX();
origin.SetX(xpos + 10);
```

Compare this with the equivalent code if the *X* field were public:

```
origin.X += 10;
```

There is no doubt that, in this case, using fields is cleaner, shorter, and easier. Unfortunately, using fields breaks encapsulation. Properties allow you to combine the best of both examples: to retain encapsulation while allowing a field-like syntax.

What Are Properties?

A *property* is a cross between a logical field and a physical method. You use a property in exactly the same way that you use a field. Logically, a property looks like a field. However, the compiler automatically translates this field-like syntax into calls to special method-like accessors. A property declaration looks like this:

```
AccessModifier Type PropertyName
{
    get
    {
        // read accessor code
    }

    set
    {
        // write accessor code
    }
}
```

A property can contain two blocks of code, starting with the *get* and *set* keywords. The *get* block contains statements that execute when the property is read, and the *set* block contains statements that run when the property is written to. The type of the property specifies the type of data read and written to by the *get* and *set* accessors.

The next code segment shows the *ScreenPosition* struct rewritten by using properties. When reading this code, notice the following:

- Lowercase *x* and *y* are *private* fields.

- Uppercase *X* and *Y* are *public* properties.

- All *set* accessors are passed the data to be written, by using a hidden parameter called *value*.

> **Tip**   The fields and properties follow the standard Microsoft Visual C# *public/private* naming convention. Public fields and properties should start with an uppercase letter but private fields and properties should start with a lowercase letter.

```
struct ScreenPosition
{
    public ScreenPosition(int X, int Y)
    {
        this.x = rangeCheckedX(X);
        this.y = rangeCheckedY(Y);
    }

    public int X
    {
        get { return this.x; }
        set { this.x = rangeCheckedX(value); }
    }

    public int Y
    {
        get { return this.y; }
        set { this.y = rangeCheckedY(value); }
    }

    private static int rangeCheckedX(int x) { ... }
    private static int rangeCheckedY(int y) { ... }
    private int x, y;
}
```

In this example, a private field directly implements each property. This is only one way to implement a property. All that is required is that a *get* accessor returns a value of the specified type. Such a value could easily be calculated, in which case there would be no need for a physical field.

> **Note**   Although the examples in this chapter show how to define properties for a struct, they are equally applicable to classes; the syntax is the same.

Using Properties

When you use a property in an expression, you use it either in a read context (when you are not modifying its value) or in a write context (when you are modifying its value). The following example shows how to read values from the *X* and *Y* properties of a *ScreenPosition* struct:

```
ScreenPosition origin = new ScreenPosition(0, 0);
int xpos = origin.X;
int ypos = origin.Y;
```

Notice that you access properties and fields by using the same syntax. When you use a property in a read context, the compiler automatically translates your field-like code into a call to the *get* accessor of that property. Similarly, if you use a property in a write context, the compiler automatically translates your field-like code into a call to the *set* accessor of that property:

```
origin.X = 40;
origin.Y = 100;
```

The values being assigned are passed in to the *set* accessors by using the *value* variable, as described earlier. The runtime does this automatically.

It's also possible to use a property in a read/write context. In this case, both the *get* accessor and the *set* accessor are used. For example, the compiler automatically translates statements such as the following into calls to the *get* and *set* accessors:

```
origin.X += 10;
```

> **Tip** You can declare *static* properties, in the same way that you can declare *static* fields and methods. Static properties are accessed by using the name of the class or struct rather than an instance of the class or struct.

Read-Only Properties

You're allowed to declare a property that contains only a *get* accessor. In this case, you can use the property only in a read context. For example, here's the *X* property of the *ScreenPosition* struct declared as a read-only property:

```
struct ScreenPosition
{
    ...
    public int X
    {
        get { return this.x; }
    }
}
```

The *X* property does not contain a *set* accessor; therefore, any attempt to use *X* in a write context will fail. For example:

```
origin.X = 140; // compile-time error
```

Write-Only Properties

Similarly, you're allowed to declare a property that contains only a *set* accessor. In this case, you can use the property only in a write context. For example, here's the *X* property of the *ScreenPosition* struct declared as a write-only property:

```
struct ScreenPosition
{
    ...
    public int X
    {
        set { this.x = rangeCheckedX(value); }
    }
}
```

The *X* property does not contain a *get* accessor; any attempt to use *X* in a read context will fail. For example:

```
Console.WriteLine(origin.X); // compile-time error
origin.X = 200;              // compiles ok
origin.X += 10;             // compile-time error
```

> **Note** Write-only properties are useful for secure data such as passwords. Ideally, an application that implements security should allow you to set your password but should never allow you to read it back. A login method should only compare a user-supplied string with the stored password, and return an indication of whether they match.

Property Accessibility

The accessibility of a property (*public*, *private*, or *protected*) is specified when you declare the property. However, it is possible to specify different accessibilities for *get* and *set* accessors. For example, the version of the *ScreenPosition* struct shown below defines the *set* accessors of the *X* and *Y* properties as *private* (the *get* accessors remain *public*):

```
struct ScreenPosition
{
    ...
    public int X
    {
        get { return this.x; }
        private set { this.x = rangeCheckedX(value); }
    }
```

```
    public int Y
    {
        get { return this.y; }
        private set { this.y = rangeCheckedY(value); }
    }
    ...
    private int x, y;
}
```

You must observe some rules when defining accessors with different accessibility from each other:

- You can change the accessibility of only one of the accessors when you define it. It wouldn't make much sense to define a property as *public* only to change the accessibility of both accessors to *private* anyway!

- The modifier must not specify an accessibility that is less restrictive than that of the property. For example, if the property is declared as *private*, you cannot specify the read accessor as *public* (in this example, you would make the property *public*, and make the read accessor *private*).

Understanding the Property Restrictions

Properties look, act, and feel like fields. However, they are not true fields, and certain restrictions apply to them:

- You can't initialize a property of a struct or class by using a *set* accessor. The code in the following example is illegal as the location variable has not been initialized (by using *new*):

```
ScreenPosition location;
location.X = 40; // compile-time error, location not assigned
```

> **Note** This may seem trivial, but if *X* was a field rather than a property, the code would be legal. What this really means is that there are some differences between fields and properties. You should define structs and classes by using properties from the start, rather than by using fields that you later migrate to properties—code that uses your classes and structs might no longer work if you change fields into properties.

- You can't use a property as a *ref* or *out* argument (whereas you can use a writeable field as a *ref* or *out* argument). For example:

```
MyMethod(ref location.X); // compile-time error
```

- A property can contain at most one *get* accessor and one *set* accessor. A property cannot contain other methods, fields, or properties.

■ The *get* and *set* accessors cannot take any parameters. The data being assigned is passed to the *set* accessor automatically, by using the *value* variable.

■ You can't declare *const* or *readonly* properties. For example:

```
const int X { get { ... } set { ... } } // compile-time error
```

> **Note**   To make a property read-only, simply omit the *set* accessor.

Using Properties Appropriately

Properties are a powerful feature with a clean, field-like syntax. Used in the correct manner properties help to make code easier to understand and maintain. However, they are no substitute for careful object-oriented design that focuses on the behavior of objects rather than their properties. Accessing private fields through regular methods or through properties does not, by itself, make your code well-designed. For example, a bank account holds a balance. You might therefore be tempted to create a *Balance* property on a *BankAccount* class, like this:

```
class BankAccount
{
    ...
    public money Balance
    {
        get { ... }
        set { ... }
    }

    private money balance;
}
```

This would be a poor design. It fails to represent the functionality required when withdrawing money from and depositing money into an account. (If you know of a bank that allows you to set the balance directly, please let me know.) When you're programming, try not to lose the expression of the problem in a mass of low-level syntax; try to express the problem you are solving in the solution:

```
class BankAccount
{
    ...
    public money Balance { get { ... } }
    public void Deposit(money amount) { ... }
    public bool Withdraw(money amount) { ... }
    private money balance;
}
```

Declaring Interface Properties

You met interfaces in Chapter 12, "Working with Inheritance." Interfaces can also specify properties. To do this, you declare the *get* or *set* keyword, or both, but replace the body of the *get* or *set* accessor with a semicolon. For example:

```
interface IScreenPosition
{
    int X { get; set; }
    int Y { get; set; }
}
```

Any class or struct that implements this interface must implement the accessors. For example:

```
struct ScreenPosition : IScreenPosition
{
    ...
    public int X
    {
        get { ... }
        set { ... }
    }

    public int Y
    {
        get { ... }
        set { ... }
    }
    ...
}
```

If you implement the interface properties in a class, you can declare the property implementations as *virtual*, which allows further derived classes to override the implementations. For example:

```
class ScreenPosition : IScreenPosition
{
    ...
    public virtual int X
    {
        get { ... }
        set { ... }
    }

    public virtual int Y
    {
        get { ... }
        set { ... }
    }
    ...
}
```

> **Note**   The example shows a class. Remember that the *virtual* keyword is not valid in structs because you can't derive from structs; structs are implicitly sealed.

You can also choose to implement a property by using the explicit interface implementation syntax covered in Chapter 12. An explicit implementation of a property is non-public and non-virtual (and cannot be overridden). For example:

```
struct ScreenPosition : IScreenPosition
{
    ...
    int IScreenPosition.X
    {
        get { ... }
        set { ... }
    }

    int IScreenPosition.Y
    {
        get { ... }
        set { ... }
    }
    ...
    private int x, y;
}
```

Using Properties in a Windows Application

When you use the Properties window in Microsoft Visual Studio 2005, you are actually generating code that sets and retrieves the values of properties of various application components—items such as *TextBox* controls, *Forms*, and *Button* controls. Some components have a large number of properties, although some properties are more commonly used than others. You can modify many of these properties at runtime by using the same syntax you have seen throughout this chapter.

In the following exercise, you will use some predefined properties of the *TextBox* controls and the *Form* class to create a simple application that continually displays the size of its main window, even when the window is resized. You will also display the current form size in this form's caption.

Use properties

1. Start Visual Studio 2005.

2. Open the *Properties* project, located in the \Microsoft Press\Visual CSharp Step by Step\Chapter 14\Properties folder in your My Documents folder.

3. On the Debug menu, click Start Without Debugging.

The project builds and runs. A Windows form displays two empty text boxes labeled Width and Height.

In the program, the *TextBox* controls are called *width* and *height. TextBox* controls have many properties. In this exercise, you will make use of the *Text* property, which specifies the text displayed in the text box.

4. Close the form and return to the Visual Studio 2005 programming environment.

5. Display the Form1.cs source file in the Code and Text Editor window. Locate the first *resize* method containing the comment // to do.

This method is called by the *Form1* constructor. You will use it to display the current size of the form in the *width* and *height* text boxes. The initial width of the form is 232 pixels, and its height is 96 pixels.

6. Add two statements to the *resize* method to display the size of the form. The first statement should assign the string "232" to the *Text* property of the Width text box. The second statement should assign the string "96" to the *Text* property of the Height text box.

The *resize* method should look exactly like this:

```
private void resize()
{
    width.Text = "232";
    height.Text = "96";
}
```

7. On the Debug menu, click Start Without Debugging to build and run the project.

The Windows form displays the two text boxes containing the values 232 and 103. The *set* accessor of the *TextBox.Text* property causes the specified string to be displayed.

8. Resize the form. Notice that the text in the text boxes remains unchanged.

The next step is to ensure that the text in the *TextBox.Text* properties always displays the current size of the form.

9. Close the form.

10. Display Form1 in the Designer View window.

11. Click Properties to display the properties of the form, and then locate the *Size* property.

Notice that the *Size* property actually contains two values—the width and the height of the form. At runtime, you can read and write the *Size* property of a form. The type of the *Size* property is a *struct* that contains these two values. If you look up the *Size* property of the *Form* class in the MSDN Library for Visual Studio 2005, you will see that the type of this property is rather confusingly also called *Size:*

```
struct Size
    {
        public int Height
```

```
        {
            get { ... }
            set { ... }
        }
        public int width
        {
            get { ... }
            set { ... }
        }
    }
}
```

You can see that the *Size* struct itself exposes *Width* and *Height* as further properties. You read the *Size.Width* property to retrieve the current width of the form and *Size.Height* to retrieve the current height of the form.

12. Display the source file Form1.cs in the Code and Text Editor window and return to the *resize* method you modified earlier.

13. Modify the two statements so that the value *Size.Width* for the form is assigned to the *width.Text* property and *Size.Height* is assigned to the *height.Text* property. You will need to convert from an *int* to a string. The easiest way to do this is to use the *ToString* method.

The *resize* method should now look like this:

```
private void resize()
{
    int w = this.Size.width;
    width.Text = w.ToString();
    int h = this.Size.Height;
    height.Text = h.ToString();
}
```

14. On the Debug menu, click Start Without Debugging to build and run the project.

15. Resize the Windows form.

As you resize, the text boxes change to display the changing size. (The *resize* method is called whenever the form changes its size by using the form's Resize event. Events are explained in Chapter 16, "Delegates and Events.")

16. Close the form.

Your final task is to display the size of the form in the form caption.

17. Return to the *resize* method you edited earlier in the Form1.cs source file.

18. Add two more statements to the *resize* method. The first statement should use the *string.Format* method to create a single string containing the width and height of the form. The second statement should write this string to the public *Text* property of the form.

The *Text* property represents the title in the caption of the form.

> **Note**   The *string.Format* static method is useful for building and formatting strings from other data types, such as numbers. It operates in a similar manner to the *Console.WriteLine* method, which formats strings for output to the screen.

Your *resize* method should now look exactly like this:

```
private void resize()
{
    int w = this.Size.Width;
    width.Text = w.ToString();
    int h = this.Size.Height;
    height.Text = h.ToString();
    string s = string.Format("({0}, {1})", w, h);
    this.Text = s;
}
```

19. On the Debug menu, click Start Without Debugging.

The project builds and runs. The caption now displays the size of the form and also changes as you resize the form.

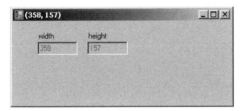

20. Close the form and return to the Visual Studio 2005 programming environment.

■ **If you want to continue to the next chapter**

Keep Visual Studio 2005 running and turn to Chapter 15.

■ **If you want to exit Visual Studio.NET now**

On the File menu, click Exit. If you see a Save dialog box, click Yes.

Chapter 14 Quick Reference

To	Do this
Declare a read/write property for a struct or class.	Declare the type of the property, its name, a *get* accessor, and a *set* accessor. For example:

```
struct ScreenPosition
{
    ...
    public int X
    {
        get { ... }
        set { ... }
    }
    ...
}
```

To	Do this
Declare a read-only property for a struct or class.	Declare a property with only a *get* accessor. For example:

```
struct ScreenPosition
{
    ...
    public int X
    {
        get { ... }
    }
    ...
}
```

To	Do this
Declare a write-only property for a struct or class.	Declare a property with only a *set* accessor. For example:

```
struct ScreenPosition
{
    ...
    public int X
    {
        set { ... }
    }
    ...
}
```

To	Do this
Declare a property in an interface	Declare a property with just the *get* or *set* keyword, or both. For example:

```
interface IScreenPosition
{
    int X { get; set; } //  no body
    int Y { get; set; } //  no body
}
```

To	Do this
Implement an interface property in a struct or class.	In the class or struct that implements the interface, declare the property and implement the accessors. For example:

```
struct ScreenPosition : IScreenPosition
{
    public int X
    {
        get { ... }
        set { ... }
    }
    public int Y
    {
        get { ... }
        set { ... }
    }
}
```

Chapter 15
Using Indexers

After completing this chapter, you will be able to:

- Encapsulate logical array-like declarations by using indexers.
- Control read access to indexers by declaring *get* accessors.
- Control write access to indexers by declaring *set* accessors.
- Create interfaces that declare indexers.
- Implement indexers in structs and classes that inherit from interfaces.

The previous chapter described how to use and implement properties as a means of providing controlled access to the fields in a class. Properties are useful for mirroring fields that contain a single value. However, indexers are invaluable if you want to provide access to items that contain multiple values, by using a natural and familiar syntax.

What Is an Indexer?

An *indexer* is a smart array in exactly the same way that a property is a smart field. The syntax that you use for an indexer is exactly the same as the syntax you use for an array. Let's work through an example. First, we'll examine a problem and see a weak solution that doesn't use indexers. Then we'll work through the same problem and look at a better solution that does use indexers. The problem concerns integers, or more precisely, the *int* type.

An Example That Doesn't Use Indexers

You normally use an *int* to hold an integer value. Internally an *int* stores its value as a sequence of 32 bits, where each bit can be either 0 or 1. Most of the time you don't care about this internal binary representation; you just use an *int* type as a bucket to hold an integer value. However, sometimes programmers use the *int* type for other purposes; some programs manipulate the individual bits within an *int*. (If you are an old C programmer you should feel at home with what follows!) In other words, occasionally a program might use an *int* because it holds 32 bits and not because it can represent an integer.

> **Note** Some older programs might use *int* types to try to save memory. A single *int* holds 32 bits, each of which can be 1 or 0. In some cases, programmers assigned 1 to indicate a value of *true* and 0 to indicate *false*, and then employed an *int* as a set of Boolean values.

For example, the following expression uses the << and & bit manipulation operators to find out whether the bit at index 6 of the *int* called *bits* is set to 0 or to 1:

```
(bits & (1 << 6)) != 0
```

If the bit at index 6 is 0, this expression evaluates to *false*; if the bit at index 6 is 1, this expression evaluates to *true*. This is a fairly complicated expression, but it's trivial in comparison to the following expression that sets the bit at index 6 to 0:

```
bits &= ~(1 << 6)
```

It's also trivial compared with this expression that sets the bit at index 6 to 1:

```
bits |= (1 << 6)
```

The trouble with these examples is that although they work, it's not clear why or how they work. They're complicated and the solution is a very low-level one. It fails to create an abstraction of the problem it solves.

The Bitwise and Shift Operators

You might have noticed some unfamiliar symbols in the expressions shown in these examples. In particular, ~, <<, |, and &. These are some of the bitwise and shift operators, and they are used to manipulate the individual bits held in the *int* and *long* data types.

The ~ operator is a unary operator that performs a bitwise complement. For example, if you take the 8-bit value 11001100 (204 decimal) and apply the ~ operator to it, you obtain the result 00110011 (51 decimal).

The << operator is a binary operator that performs a left-shift. The expression 204 << 2 returns the value 48 (in binary, 204 decimal is 11001100, and left-shifting it by two places yields 00110000, or 48 decimal). The far-left bits are discarded, and zeroes are introduced from the right. There is a corresponding right-shift operator >>.

The | operator is a binary operator that performs a bitwise OR operation, returning a value containing a 1 in each position in which either of the operands has a 1. For example, the expression 204 | 24 has the value 220 (204 is 11001100, 24 is 00011000, and 220 is 11011100).

The & operator performs a bitwise AND operation. AND is similar to the bitwise OR operator, except that it returns a value containing a 1 in each position where both of the operands have a 1. So 204 & 20 is 8 (204 is 11001100, 24 is 00011000, and 8 is 00001000).

> The ^ operator performs a bitwise XOR (exclusive or) operation, returning a 1 in each bit where there is a 1 in one operand or the other, but not both. (Two 1s yield a 0—this is the "exclusive" part of the operator.) So 204 ^ 24 is 212 (11001100 ^ 00011000 is 11010100).

The Same Example Using Indexers

Let's pull back from the previous low-level solution for a moment and stop to remind ourselves what the problem is. We'd like to use an *int* not as an *int* but as an array of 32 bits. Therefore, the best way to solve this problem is to use an *int* as if it were an array of 32 bits! In other words, if *bits* is an *int*, what we'd like to be able to write to access the bit at index 6 is:

```
bits[6]
```

And, for example, set the bit at index 6 to *true*, we'd like to be able to write:

```
bits[6] = true
```

Unfortunately, you can't use the square bracket notation on an *int*. It only works on an array or on a type that behaves like an array; that is, on a type that declares an indexer. So the solution to the problem is to create a new type that acts like, feels like, and is used like an array of *bool* variables but is implemented by using an *int*. Let's call this new type *IntBits*. *IntBits* will contain an *int* value (initialized in its constructor), but the idea is that we'll use *IntBits* as an array of *bool* variables.

> **Tip** Because *IntBits* is small and lightweight, it makes sense to create it as a struct rather than as a class.

```
struct IntBits
{
    public IntBits(int initialBitValue)
    {
        bits = initialBitValue;
    }

    // indexer to be written here

    private int bits;
}
```

To define the indexer, you use a notation that is a cross between a property an an array. The indexer for the *IntBits* struct looks like this:

```
struct IntBits
{
    ...
```

```
public bool this [ int index ]
{
    get
    {
        return (bits & (1 << index)) != 0;
    }

    set
    {
        if (value)  // Turn the bit on if value is true, otherwise turn it off
            bits |=  (1 << index);
        else
            bits &= ~(1 << index);
    }
}
...
}
```

Notice the following:

- An indexer is not a method; there are no parentheses, but there are square brackets.

- An indexer always takes a single argument, supplied between the square brackets. This argument is used to specify which element is being accessed.

- All indexers use the *this* keyword in place of the method name. A class or struct is allowed to define one indexer only, and it is always named *this*.

- Indexers contain *get* and *set* accessors just like properties. The *get* and *set* accessors contain the complicated bitwise expressions previously discussed.

- The argument specified in the indexer declaration is populated with the index value specified when the indexer is called. The *get* and *set* accessor methods can read this argument to determine which element should be accessed.

> **Note**   You should perform a range check on the index value in the indexer to prevent any unexpected exceptions from occurring in your indexer code.

After the indexer has been declared, we can use a variable of type *IntBits* instead of an *int* and apply the square bracket notation as desired:

```
int adapted = 63;
IntBits bits = new IntBits(adapted);
bool peek = bits[6];  // retrieve bool at index 6
bits[0] = true;       // set the bit at index 0 to true
bits[31] = false;     // set the bit at index 31 to false
```

This syntax is certainly much easier to understand. It directly and succinctly captures the essence of the problem.

> **Note** Indexers and properties are similar in that both use *get* and *set* accessors. An indexer is like a property with multiple values. However, although you're allowed to declare *static* properties, *static* indexers are illegal.

Understanding Indexer Accessors

When you read an indexer, the compiler automatically translates your array-like code into a call to the *get* accessor of that indexer. For example, consider the following example:

```
bool peek = bits[6];
```

This statement is converted into a call to the *get* accessor for *bits*, and the value of the *index* argument is set to 6.

Similarly, if you write to an indexer, the compiler automatically translates your array-like code into a call to the *set* accessor of that indexer, setting the *index* argument to the specified value. For example, consider the following statement:

```
bits[6] = true;
```

This statement is converted into a call to the *set* accessor for *bits* where the value of *index* is 6. As with ordinary properties, the value you are writing to the indexer (in this case, *true*) is made available inside the *set* accessor by using the *value* keyword. The type of value is the same as the type of indexer itself (in this case, *bool*).

It's also possible to use an indexer in a combined read/write context. In this case, the *get* and *set* accessors are used. For example, consider the following statement:

```
bits[6] ^= true;
```

This is automatically translated into:

```
bits[6] = bits[6] ^ true;
```

This code works because the indexer declares both a *get* and a *set* accessor.

> **Note** You're also allowed to declare an indexer that contains only a *get* accessor (a read-only indexer), or a *set* accessor (a write-only accessor).

Comparing Indexers and Arrays

When you use an indexer, the syntax is deliberately very array-like. However, there are some important differences between indexers and arrays:

- Indexers can use non-numeric subscripts, whereas arrays can use only integer subscripts:

```
public int this [ string name ] { ... } // okay
```

> **Tip**   Many collection classes, such as *Hashtable*, that implement an associative lookup based on key/value pairs implement indexers as a convenient alternative to using the *Add* method to add a new value, and iterating through the *Values* property to locate a value in your code. For example, instead of this:
>
> ```
> Hashtable ages = new Hashtable();
> ages.Add("John", 41);
> ```
>
> you can use this:
>
> ```
> Hashtable ages = new Hashtable();
> ages["John"] = 41;
> ```

- Indexers can be overloaded (just like methods), whereas arrays can't:

```
public Name        this [ PhoneNumber number ] { ... }
public PhoneNumber this [ Name name ] { ... }
```

- Indexers can't be used as *ref* or *out* parameters, whereas array elements can:

```
IntBits bits;        // bits contains an indexer
Method(ref bits[1]); // compile-time error
```

Properties, Arrays, and Indexers

It is possible for a property to return an array, but remember that arrays are reference types, so exposing an array as a property makes it possible to accidentally overwrite a lot of data. Look at the following struct that exposes an array property called *Data*:

```
struct Wrapper
{
    int[] data;
    ...
    public int[] Data
    {
        get { return this.data; }
        set { this.data = value; }
    }
}
```

Now consider the following code that uses this property:

```
Wrapper wrap = new Wrapper();
...
int[] myData = wrap.Data;
myData[0]++;
myData[1]++;
```

This looks pretty innocuous. However, because arrays are reference types, the variable *myData* refers to the same object as the private *data* variable in the *Wrapper* struct. Any changes you make to elements in *myData* are made to the *data* array; the statement myData[0]++ has exactly the same effect as data[0]++. If this is not the intention, it is possible to use the *Clone* method in the *get* accessor of the *Data* property to return a copy of the data array, but this can become very messy and expensive in terms of memory use. Indexers provide a natural solution to this problem—don't expose the entire array as a property, just make its individual elements available through an indexer:

```
struct Wrapper
{
    int[] data;
    ...
    public int this [int i]
    {
        get { return this.data[i]; }
        set { this.data[i] = value; }
    }
}
```

The following code uses the indexer in a similar manner to the property shown earlier:

```
Wrapper wrap = new Wrapper();
...
int[] myData = new int[2];
myData[0] = wrap[0];
myData[1] = wrap[1];
myData[0]++;
myData[1]++;
```

This time, incrementing the values in the *MyData* array has no effect on the original array in the *Wrapper* object. If you really want to modify the data in the *Wrapper* object, you must write statements such as this:

```
wrap[0]++;
```

This is much clearer, and safer!

Indexers in Interfaces

You can declare indexers in an interface. To do this, specify the *get* and/or *set* keyword, but replace the body of the *get* or *set* accessor with a semicolon. Any class or struct that implements the interface must implement the *indexer* accessors declared in the interface. For example:

```
interface IRawInt
{
    bool this [ int index ] { get; set; }
}

struct RawInt : IRawInt
{
    ...
    public bool this [ int index ]
    {
        get { ... }
        set { ... }
    }
    ...
}
```

If you implement the interface indexer in a class, you can declare the indexer implementations as virtual. This allows further derived classes to override the *get* and *set* accessors. For example:

```
class RawInt : IRawInt
{
    ...
    public virtual bool this [ int index ]
    {
        get { ... }
        set { ... }
    }
    ...
}
```

You can also choose to implement an indexer by using the explicit interface implementation syntax covered in Chapter 12, "Working with Inheritance." An explicit implementation of an indexer is non-public and non-virtual (and so cannot be overridden). For example:

```
struct RawInt : IRawInt
{
    ...
    bool IRawInt.this [ int index ]
    {
        get { ... }
        set { ... }
    }
    ...
}
```

Using Indexers in a Windows Application

In the following exercise, you will examine a simple phone book application and complete its implementation. Your task will be to write two indexers in the *PhoneBook* class: one that accepts a *Name* parameter and returns a *PhoneNumber*, and another that accepts a *PhoneNumber* parameter and returns a *Name*. (The *Name* and *PhoneNumber* structs have already been written.) You will also need to call these indexers from the correct places in the program.

Familiarize yourself with the application

1. Start Microsoft Visual Studio 2005.

2. Open the *Indexers* project, located in the \Microsoft Press\Visual CSharp Step by Step\Chapter 15\Indexers folder in your My Documents folder.

   This is a Microsoft Windows Forms application.

3. On the Debug menu, click Start Without Debugging.

   The project builds and runs. A form displays two empty text boxes labeled Name and Phone Number. The form also contains three buttons—one to add a name/phone number pair to a list of names and phone numbers held by the application, one to find a phone number when given a name, and one to find a name when given a phone number. These buttons currently do nothing. Your task is to finish the application so that these buttons work.

4. Close the form and return to Visual Studio 2005.

5. Display the Name.cs source file in the Code and Text Editor window. Examine the *Name* struct. Its purpose is to act as a holder for names.

   The name is provided as a string to the constructor. The name can be retrieved by using the read-only string property called *Text*. (The *Equals* and *GetHashCode* methods are used for comparing *Name*s when searching through an array of *Name* values—you can ignore them for the time being.)

6. Display the PhoneNumber.cs source file in the Code and Text Editor window and examine the *PhoneNumber* struct. It is very similar to the *Name* struct.

7. Display the PhoneBook.cs source file in the Code and Text Editor window and examine the *PhoneBook* class.

   This class contains two private arrays: an array of *Name* values called *names*, and an array of *PhoneNumber* values called *phoneNumbers*. The *PhoneBook* class also contains an *Add* method which adds a phone number and name to the phone book. This method is called when the Add button on the form is clicked. The *enlargeIfFull* method is called by *Add* to check whether the arrays are full when the user adds another entry. This method creates two new bigger arrays, copies the contents of the existing arrays to them, and then discards the old arrays.

Write the indexers

1. In the PhoneBook.cs source file, add a *public* read-only indexer that returns a *Name* and accepts a single *PhoneNumber* parameter to the *PhoneBook* class. Leave the body of the *get* accessor blank.

    The indexer should look like this:

    ```
    sealed class PhoneBook
    {
        ...
        public Name this [PhoneNumber number]
        {
            get
            {
            }
        }
        ...
    }
    ```

2. Implement the *get* accessor.

    The purpose of the accessor is to find the name that matches the specifed phone number. To do this, you will need to call the static *IndexOf* method of the *Array* class. The *IndexOf* method performs a search through an array, returning the index of the first item in the array that matches. The first argument to *IndexOf* is the array to search through (*phoneNumbers*). The second argument to *IndexOf* is the item you are searching for. *IndexOf* returns the integer index of the element if it finds it, otherwise *IndexOf* will return –1. If the indexer finds the phone number, it should return it, otherwise it should return an empty *Name* value. (Note that *Name* is a struct and will always have a default constructor that sets its *private* field to *null*.)

    The indexer with its completed *get* accessor should look like this:

    ```
    sealed class PhoneBook
    {
        ...
        public Name this [PhoneNumber number]
        {
            get
            {
                int i = Array.IndexOf(this.phoneNumbers, number);
                if (i != -1)
                    return this.names[i];
                else
                    return new Name();
            }
        }
        ...
    }
    ```

3. Add a second *public* read-only indexer to the *PhoneBook* class that returns a *PhoneNumber* and accepts a single *Name* parameter. Implement this indexer in the same way as the first one (again note that *PhoneNumber* is a struct and therefore always has a default constructor).

    The second indexer should look like this:

    ```
    sealed class PhoneBook
    {
        ...
        public PhoneNumber this [Name name]
        {
            get
            {
                int i = Array.IndexOf(this.names, name);
                if (i != -1)
                    return this.phoneNumbers[i];
                else
                    return new PhoneNumber();
            }
        }
        ...
    }
    ```

    Notice that these overloaded indexers can co-exist because their signatures are different. If the *Name* and *PhoneNumber* structs were replaced by simple strings (which they wrap), the overloads would have the same signature and the class would not compile.

4. On the Build menu, click Build Solution. Correct any syntax errors and then rebuild if necessary.

Call the indexers

1. Display the Form1.cs source file in the Code and Text Editor window, and then locate the *findPhone_Click* method.

    This method is called when the first Search button is clicked. (This method is called by using events and delegates, which you will learn about in Chapter 16, "Delegates and Events.") This method is currently empty. It should perform the following tasks:

    a. Read the *Text* string from the Name text box.

    b. If the string is not empty, then search for the phone number corresponding to that name in the *PhoneBook* by using the indexer (notice that *Form1* contains a private *PhoneBook* field called *phoneBook*); construct a *Name* object from the string, and pass it as the parameter to the *PhoneBook* indexer.

    c. Write the *PhoneNumber* returned by the indexer to the *phoneNumber* text box.

2. Implement the *findPhone_Click* method now.

It should look like this:

```
partial class Form1 : System.Windows.Forms.Form
{
    ...
    private void findPhone_Click(object sender, System.EventArgs e)
    {
        string text = name.Text;
        if (text != "")
        {
            phoneNumber.Text = phoneBook[new Name(text)].Text;
        }
    }
    ...
    private PhoneBook phoneBook = new PhoneBook();
}
```

3. Locate the *findName_Click* method in the Form1.cs source file. It is below the *findPhone_Click* method.

   The *findName_Click* method is called when the second search button is clicked. This method should be similar to *findPhoneClick*:

   a. Read the *Text* string from the Phone Number text box.

   b. If the string is not empty, then search for the name corresponding to that phone number in the *PhoneBook*, by using the indexer.

   c. Write the *Name* returned by the indexer to the Name text box.

4. Implement this method.

   It should look like this:

```
partial class Form1 : System.Windows.Forms.Form
{
    ...
    private void findName_Click(object sender, System.EventArgs e)
    {
        string text = phoneNumber.Text;
        if (text != "")
        {
            name.Text = phoneBook[new PhoneNumber(text)].Text;
        }
    }
    ...
}
```

5. On the Build menu, click Build Solution.

Run the application

1. On the Debug menu, click Start Without Debugging.

2. Type your name and phone number into the text boxes, and then click the Add button.

   When you click the Add button, the *Add* method puts the entries into the phone book and clears the text boxes so that they are ready to perform a search.

3. Repeat Step 2 a few times with some different names and telehone numbers so that the phone book contains a number of entries.

4. Type a name you used in Step 2 into the Name text box, and then click the Search -> button.

   The phone number you added in Step 2 is retrieved from the phone book and is displayed in the Phone Number text box.

5. Clear the name from the Name text box, and then click the <- Search button.

   The name is retrieved from the phone book and is displayed in the Name text box.

6. Type a name that you did not enter in the phone book into the Name text box, and then click the Search -> button.

   This time the Phone Number text box is empty, indicating that the name could not be found in the phone book.

7. Close the form.

■ **If you want to continue to the next chapter**

   Keep Visual Studio 2005 running and turn to Chapter 16.

■ **If you want to exit Visual Studio 2005 now**

   On the File menu, click Exit. If you see a Save dialog box, click Yes.

Chapter 15 Quick Reference

To	Do this
Create an indexer for a class or struct	Declare the type of the indexer, followed by the keyword *this*, and then the indexer arguments between square brackets. The body of the indexer can contain a *get* and/or *set* accessor. For example: ```\nstruct RawInt\n{\n ...\n public bool this [int index]\n {\n get { ... }\n set { ... }\n }\n ...\n}\n```
Define an indexer in an interface	Define an indexer with the *get* and/or *set* keywords. For example: ```\ninterface IRawInt\n{\n bool this [int index] get; set; }\n}\n```
Implement an interface indexer in a class or struct	In the class or struct that implements the interface, define the indexer and implement the accessors. For example: ```\nstruct RawInt : IRawInt\n{\n ...\n public bool this [int index]\n {\n get { ... }\n set { ... }\n }\n ...\n}\n```
Implement an interface indexer by using explicit interface implementation in a class or struct	In the class or struct that implements the interface, explicitly name the interface, but do not specify the indexer accessibility. For example: ```\nstruct RawInt : IRawInt\n{\n ...\n bool IRawInt.this [int index]\n {\n get { ... }\n set { ... }\n }\n ...\n}\n```

Chapter 16
Delegates and Events

After completing this chapter, you will be able to:

■ Declare a delegate type to create an abstraction of a method signature.

■ Create an instance of a delegate to refer to a specific method and to an anonymous method.

■ Call a method through a delegate.

■ Declare an event field.

■ Handle an event by using a delegate.

■ Raise an event.

Much of the code you have written in the various exercises in this book has assumed that statements execute sequentially. While this is a common scenario, you will find that it is sometimes necessary to interrupt the current flow of execution and perform another more important task. When the task has completed, the program can continue where it left off. The classic example of this style of program is the Windows Form. A form displays controls such as buttons and text boxes. When you click a button or type text in a text box, you expect the form to respond immediately. The application has to temporarily stop what it is doing, and go and handle your input. This style of operation applies not just to graphical user interfaces, but to any application where an operation must be performed urgently—shutting down the reactor in a nuclear power plant if it is getting too hot, for example.

In order to handle this type of application, the runtime has to provide two things: a means of indicating that something urgent has happened, and a way of indicating a method that should be run when it happens. This is the purpose of events and delegates. We will start by looking at delegates.

Declaring and Using Delegates

A delegate is a pointer to a method. A delegate looks and behaves much like an ordinary method when it is called. However, when you call a delegate, the runtime actually executes the method the delegate refers to. You can dynamically change the method that a delegate references, so code that calls a delegate might actually run a different method each time it executes. The best way to understand delegates is to see them in action, so let's work through an example.

> **Note**   If you are familiar with C++, a delegate is very similar to a function pointer. However, unlike function pointers, delegates are type-safe; you can only make a delegate refer to a method that matches the signature of the delegate, and you cannot call a delegate that does not refer to a valid method.

The Automated Factory Scenario

Suppose you are writing the control systems for an automated factory. The factory contains a large number of different machines, each performing distinct tasks in the production of the articles manufactured by the factory—shaping and folding metal sheets, welding sheets together, painting sheets, and so on. Each machine was built and installed by a specialist vendor. The machines are all computer-controlled, and each vendor has provided a set of APIs that you can use to control their machine. Your task is to integrate the different systems used by the machines into a single control program. One aspect that you have decided to concentrate on is to provide a means of shutting all the machines down, quickly if needed!

> **Note**   The term API means Application Programming Interface. It is a method, or set of methods, exposed by a piece of software allowing you to control that software. You can think of the .NET Framework as a set of APIs, as it provides methods allowing you to control the .NET common language runtime and the Microsoft Windows operating system.

Each machine has its own unique computer-controlled process (and API) for shutting down safely. These are summarized below:

```
StopFolding();    // Folding and shaping machine
FinishWelding();  // Welding machine
PaintOff();       // Painting machine
```

Implementing the Factory Without Using Delegates

A simple approach to implementing the shutdown functionality in the control program is shown below:

```
class Controller
{
    ...
    public void ShutDown()
    {
        folder.StopFolding();
        welder.FinishWelding();
        painter.PaintOff();
    }
    ...
    // Fields representing the different machines
    private FoldingMachine folder;
```

```
    private WeldingMachine welder;
    private PaintingMachine painter;
}
```

Although this approach works, it is not very extensible or flexible. If the factory buys a new machine, you must modify this code; the *Controller* class and the machines are tightly coupled.

Implementing the Factory by Using a Delegate

However, although the names of each method are different, they all have the same "shape"; they take no parameters, and they do not return a value (we will consider what happens if this isn't the case later, so bear with me!). The general format of each method is, therefore:

```
void methodName();
```

This is where a delegate is useful. A delegate that matches this shape can be used to refer to any of the machinery shutdown methods. You declare a delegate like this:

```
delegate void stopMachineryDelegate();
```

Note the following points:

- Use the delegate keyword when declaring a delegate.

- A delegate defines the shape of the methods it can refer to. You specify the return type (void), a name for the delegate (stopMachineryDelegate), and any parameters (there are none in this case).

After you have defined the delegate, you can create an instance and make it refer to a matching method by using the += operator. You can do this in the constructor of the controller class like this:

```
class Controller
{
    delegate void stopMachineryDelegate();
    ...
    public Controller()
    {
        this.stopMachinery += folder.StopFolding;
    }
    ...
    private stopMachineryDelegate stopMachinery; // Create an instance of the delegate
}
```

This syntax takes a bit of getting used to. You *add* the method to the delegate; you are not actually calling the method at this point. The + operator is overloaded to have this new meaning when used with delegates (we will talk more about operator overloading in Chapter 19, "Operator Overloading"). Notice that you simply specify the method name, and should not include any parentheses or parameters.

It is safe to use the += operator on an uninitialized delegate. It will be initialized automatically. You can also use the *new* keyword to explicitly initialize a delegate with a specific method, like this:

```
this.stopMachinery = new stopMachineryDelegate(folder.stopFolding);
```

You can call the method by invoking the delegate, like this:

```
public void ShutDown()
{
    this.stopMachinery();
    ...
}
```

Invoking a delegate uses exactly the same syntax as making a method call. If the method that the delegate refers to takes any parameters, you should specify them at this time.

> **Note**   If you attempt to invoke a delegate that is uninitialized, you will get a *NullReference-Exception*.

The principal advantage of using a delegate is that it can refer to more than one method; you simply use the += operator to add them to the delegate, like this:

```
public Controller()
{
    this.stopMachinery += folder.StopFolding;
    this.stopMachinery += welder.FinishWelding;
    this.stopMachinery += painter.PaintOff;
}
```

Invoking this.stopMachinery() in the *Shutdown* method of the *Controller* class will automatically call each of the methods in turn. The *Shutdown* method does not need to know how many machines there are, or what the method names are. You can remove a method from a delegate by using the −= operator:

```
this.stopMachinery -= folder.StopFolding;
```

The current scheme adds the machine methods to the delegate in the *Controller* constructor. To make the *Controller* class totally independent of the various machines, you need to supply a means of allowing classes outside of *Controller* to add methods to the delegate. You have several options:

- Make the delegate variable, stopMachinery, public:

    ```
    public stopMachineryDelegate stopMachinery;
    ```

- Keep the stopMachinery delegate variable private, but provide a read/write property to provide access to it. You also need to make the stopMachineryDelegate type public as well:

```
public delegate void stopMachineryDelegate();
...
public stopMachineryDelegate StopMachinery
{
    get
    {
        return this.stopMachinery;
    }

    set
    {
        this.stopMachinery = value;
    }
}
```

- Provide complete encapsulation by implementing separate Add and Remove methods. The Add method takes a method as a parameter and adds it to the delegate, while the Remove method removes the specified method from the delegate. (Notice that you specify a method as a parameter by using a delegate type):

```
public void Add(stopMachineryDelegate stopMethod)
{
    this.stopMachinery += stopMethod;
}

public void Remove(stopMachineryDelegate stopMethod)
{
    this.stopMachinery -= stopMethod;
}
```

If you are an object-oriented purist you will probably opt for the Add/Remove approach. However, the others are viable alternatives which are frequently used, which is why we have shown them.

Whichever technique you choose, you should remove the code that adds the machine methods to the delegate from the *Controller* constructor. You can then instantiate a *Controller* and objects representing the other machines like this (this example uses the Add/Remove approach):

```
Controller control = new Controller();
FoldingMachine folder = new FoldingMachine();
WeldingMachine welder = new WeldingMachine();
PaintingMachine painter = new PaintingMachine();
...
control.Add(folder.StopFolding);
control.Add(welder.FinishWelding);
control.Add(painter.PaintOff);
...
control.ShutDown();
...
```

Using Delegates

In the following exercise, you will create a delegate to encapsulate a method that displays the time in a Microsoft Windows text box. You will attach the delegate object to a class called *Ticker* that invokes the delegate every second. In this way, you will create a Windows application that acts as a simple digital clock.

Finish the digital clock application

1. Start Microsoft Visual Studio 2005.

2. Open the *Delegates* project, located in the \Microsoft Press\Visual CSharp Step by Step\Chapter 16\Delegates folder in your My Documents folder.

3. On the Debug menu, click Start Without Debugging.

   The project builds and runs. A Windows form displays a digital clock. The clock displays the wrong time.

4. Click Start, and then click Stop.

   Nothing happens. The *Start* and *Stop* methods have not been implemented yet. Your task is to implement these methods.

5. Close the window to return to the Visual Studio 2005 environment.

6. Open the Ticker.cs source file and display it in the Code and Text Editor window. This file contains a class called *Ticker*, that models the inner workings of a clock. It uses a *System.Timers.Timer* object, called *ticking*, to arrange for a pulse to be sent every second. This class catches the pulse by using an event (events will be described shortly), and then arranges for the display to be updated by invoking a delegate.

7. In the Code and Text Editor window, locate the declaration of the *Tick* delegate. It is located near the top of the file and looks like this:

   ```
   public delegate void Tick(int hh, int mm, int ss);
   ```

   The *Tick* delegate can be used to refer to a method that takes three integer parameters, but does not return a value. There is a delegate variable called *tickers* at the end of the class that is based on this type. The *Add* and *Remove* methods in this class allow matching methods to add and remove themselves from the *tickers* delegate variable:

   ```
   class Ticker
   {
       ...
       public void Add(Tick newMethod)
       {
           this.tickers += newMethod;
       }

       public void Remove(Tick oldMethod)
       {
   ```

```
            this.tickers -= oldMethod;
    }
    ...
    private Tick tickers;
}
```

8. Open the Clock.cs source file and display it in the Code and Text Editor window. The *Clock* class models the clock display. It has methods called *Start* and *Stop* which will be used to start and stop the clock running (when they are implemented), and a method called *RefreshTime* that formats a string to depict the time specified by its three parameters (hours, minutes, and seconds), and then displays it in the *TextBox* field called *display*. This *TextBox* field is initialized in the constructor. The class also contains a private *Ticker* field called *pulsed*, which tells the clock when to update its display:

```
class Clock
{
    ...

    public Clock(TextBox displayBox)
    {
        this.display = displayBox;
    }
    ...
    private void RefreshTime(int hh, int mm, int ss )
    {
        this.display.Text =  string.Format("{0:D2}:{1:D2}:{2:D2}", hh, mm, ss);
    }

    private Ticker pulsed = new Ticker();
    private TextBox display;
}
```

9. Display the code for the Form1.cs source file in the Code and Text Editor window. Notice that the constructor creates a new instance of the *Clock* class passing in the *TextBox* field called *digital* as its parameter:

```
public Form1()
{
    ...
    clock = new Clock(digital);
}
```

The *digital* field is the *TextBox* control displayed on the form. The clock will display its output in this *TextBox*.

10. Return to the Clock.cs source file. Implement the *Clock.Start* method so that it adds the *Clock.RefreshTime* method to the delegate in the pulsed object by using the *Ticker.Add* method.

The *Start* method should look like this:

```
public void Start()
{
    pulsed.Add(this.RefreshTime);
}
```

11. Implement the *Clock.Stop* method so that it removes the *Clock.RefreshTime* method from the delegate in the pulsed object by using the *Ticker.Remove* method.

    The *Stop* method should look like this:

```
public void Stop()
{
    pulsed.Remove(this.RefreshTime);
}
```

12. On the Debug menu, click Start Without Debugging. The project builds and runs.

13. Click the Start button.

    The Windows form now displays the correct time and updates every second.

14. Click Stop.

    The display stops responding or "freezes." This is because the Stop button calls the *Clock.Stop* method, which removes the *RefreshTime* method from the *Ticker* delegate; *RefreshTime* is no longer being called every second.

15. Click Start.

    The display resumes processing and updates the time every second. This is because the Start button calls the *Clock.Start* method, which attaches the *RefreshTime* method to the *Ticker* delegate again.

16. Close the form.

Anonymous Methods and Delegates

All the examples of adding a method to a delegate that you have seen so far use the method's name. For example, returning to the automated factory scenario shown earlier, to add the *StopFolding* method of the folder object to the *stopMachinery* delegate, we did this:

```
this.stopMachinery += folder.StopFolding;
```

This approach is very useful if there is a convenient method that matches the signature of the delegate, but what if this is not the case? Suppose that the *StopFolding* method actually had the following signature:

```
void StopFolding(int shutDownTime); // Shut down within the specified number of seconds
```

This is now different from the *FinishWelding* and *PaintOff* methods, therefore we cannot use the same delegate to handle all three methods.

Creating a Method Adapter

The way around this problem is to create another method that calls *StopFolding*, but that takes no parameters itself, like this:

```
void FinishFolding()
{
    folder.StopFolding(0); // Shutdown immediately
}
```

> **Note**   The *FinishFolding* method is a classic example of an Adapter; a method that converts (or adapts) a method to give it a different signature. This pattern is very common, and is one of the set of patterns documented in the book *Design Patterns: Elements of Reusable Object-Oriented Architecture* by Gamma, Helm, Johnson, and Vlissides (Addison-Wesley Professional; 1994).

In many cases, adapter methods such as this are small, and it is easy to lose them in a sea of methods, especially in a large class. Furthermore, apart from using it to adapt the *StopFolding* method for use by the delegate, it is unlikely to be called elsewhere. C# provides anonymous methods for situations such as this.

Using an Anonymous Method as an Adapter

An anonymous method is a method that does not have a name. This sounds very strange, but anonymous methods are actually quite useful.

There might well be occasions when you have a block of code that you are never going to call directly, but you would like to be able to invoke using a delegate. The *FinishFolding* method discussed just now is an example; its sole purpose is to provide an adapter for the *StopFolding* method. Thinking up a name for the method is really just an overhead for the developer (albeit a small one), but consider what happens if there are a number of these adapter methods in an application—they start to clutter up the classes. You can use an anonymous method anywhere that you can use a delegate. You simply provide the code, enclosed in curly braces, and prefixed with the *delegate* keyword. To use an anonymous method as an adapter for the *StopFolding* method and add it to the *stopMachinery* delegate, you can write this:

```
this.stopMachinery += delegate { folder.StopFolding(0); };
```

You no longer need to create the *FinishFolding* method.

You can also pass an anonymous method as a parameter in place of a delegate, like this:

```
control.Add(delegate { folder.StopFolding(0);  } );
```

Features of Anonymous Methods

Anonymous methods have several idiosyncracies that you should be aware of. They include the following:

- Any parameters needed are specified in braces following the delegate keyword. For example:

```
control.Add(delegate(int param1, string param2) { /* code that uses param1 and param2 */
... });
```

- Anonymous methods can return values, but the return type must match that of the delegate they are being added to.

- You can use the -= operator to remove a method from a delegate variable. However, it does not make much sense to do so as it will not remove anything. Anonymous methods that happen to contain the same code are actually different instances of the code.

- The code in an anonymous method is ordinary C# code. It can comprise multiple state-ments, method calls, variable definitions, and so on.

- Variables defined in an anonymous method go out of scope when the method finishes.

- An anonymous method can access and modify variables in scope when the anonymous method is defined. Variables manipulated in this way are known as captured outer vari-ables. Be very careful with this feature!

Enabling Notifications with Events

In the previous section, you saw how to declare a delegate type, call a delegate, and create del-egate instances. However, this is only half the story. Although delegates allow you to invoke any number of methods indirectly, you still have to invoke the delegate explicitly. In many cases, it would be useful to have the delegate run automatically when something significant happens. For example, in the automated factory scenario, it could be vital to be able to invoke the *stopMachinery* delegate and halt the equipment if a machine overheats. In the .NET Frame-work, events allow you to define and trap significant actions, and arrange for a delegate to be called to handle the situation. Many classes in the .NET Framework expose events. Most of the controls that you can place on a Windows form, and the Windows Form class itself, use events to allow you to run code when, for example, the user clicks a button or types some-thing in to a field. You can also define your own events.

Declaring an Event

You declare an event in a class intended to act as an event source. An event source is usually a class that monitors its environment, and raises an event when something significant happens. In the automated factory, an event source could be a class that monitors the temperature of each machine. The temperature monitor class would raise a "machine overheating" event if it detects that a machine has exceeded its thermal radiation boundary (i.e. it has become too hot). An event maintains a list of methods to call when it is raised. These methods are sometimes referred to as subscribers. These methods should be prepared to handle the "machine overheating" event and take the necessary corrective action: shut the machines down.

You declare an event in a way similar to declaring a field. However, because events are intended be used with delegates, the type of an event must be a delegate, and you must prefix the declaration with the *event* keyword. For example, here's the *StopMachineryDelegate* delegate from the automated factory. I have relocated it to a new class called *TemperatureMonitor*, which provides an interface to the various electonic probes monitoring the temperature of the equipment (this is a more logical place for the event than the *Controller* class):

```
class TemperatureMonitor
{
    public delegate void StopMachineryDelegate();
    ...
}
```

You can define the *MachineOverheating* event, which will invoke the *stopMachineryDelegate*, like this:

```
class TemperatureMonitor
{
    public delegate void StopMachineryDelegate();
    public event StopMachineryDelegate MachineOverheating;
    ...
}
```

The logic (not shown) in the *TemperatureMonitor* class automatically raises the *MachineOverheating* event as necessary. An event maintains its own internal collection of attached delegates, so there is no need to manually maintain your delegate variable.

Subscribing to an Event

Like delegates, events come ready-made with a += operator. You subscribe to an event by using this += operator. In the automated factory, the software controlling each machine can arrange for the shutdown methods to be called when the *MachineOverheating* event is raised like this:

```
TemperatureMonitor tempMonitor = new TemperatureMonitor();
...
tempMonitor.MachineOverheating += delegate { folder.StopFolding(0) };
tempMonitor.MachineOverheating += welder.FinishWelding;
tempMonitor.MachineOverheating += painter.PaintOff;
```

Notice that the syntax is the same as for adding a method to a delegate. You can even subscribe by using an anonymous method. When the *tempMonitor.MachineOverheating* event runs, it will call all the subscribing methods and shut the machines down.

Unsubscribing from an Event

Knowing that you use the += operator to attach a delegate to an event, you can probably guess that you use the -= operator to detach a delegate from an event. Calling the -= operator removes the method from the event's internal delegate collection. This action is often referred to as unsubscribing from the event.

Raising an Event

An event can be raised, just like a delegate, by calling it like a method. When you raise an event, all the attached delegates are called in sequence. For example, here's the *Temperature-Monitor* class with a private *Notify* method that raises the *MachineryOverheating* event:

```
class TemperatureMonitor
{
    public delegate void StopMachinerDelegate;
    public event StopMachineryDelegate MachineOverheating;
    ...
    private void Notify()
    {
        if (this.MachineOverheating != null)
        {
            this.MachineOverheating();
        }
    }
    ...
}
```

This is a common idiom. The *null* check is necessary because an event field is implicitly *null* and only becomes non-*null* when a method subscribes to it by using the += operator. If you try and raise a *null* event, you will get a *NullReferenceException*. If the delegate defining the event expects any parameters, the appropriate arguments must be provided when you raise the event. You will see some examples of this later.

> **Important**   Events have a very useful built-in security feature. A public event (such as *MachineOverheating*) can only be raised by methods within the class that define it (the *TemperatureMonitor* class). Any attempt to raise the method outside of the class will result in a compiler error.

Understanding GUI Events

As mentioned earlier, the .NET Framework classes and controls used for building GUIs employ events extensively. You'll see and use GUI events on many occasions in the second half of this book. For example, the *Button* class derives from the *Control* class, inheriting a public event called *Click* of type *EventHandler*. Let's see this in code. The *EventHandler* delegate expects two parameters; a reference to the object that caused the event to be raised, and an *EventArgs* object that contains additional information about the event:

```
namespace System
{
    public delegate void EventHandler(object sender, EventArgs args) ;

    public class EventArgs
    {
        ...
    }
}

namespace System.Windows.Forms
{
    public class Control :
    {
        public event EventHandler Click;
        ...
    }

    public class Button : Control
    {
        ...
    }
}
```

The *Button* class automatically raises the *Click* event when you click the button on-screen (how this actually happens is beyond the scope of this book). This arrangement makes it easy to create a delegate for a chosen method and attach that delegate to the required event. The following example shows a Windows form that contains a button called *okay*, a method called *okay_Click*, and the code to connect the *Click* event in the *okay* button to the *okay_Click* method:

```
class Example : System.Windows.Forms.Form
{
    private System.Windows.Forms.Button okay;
    ...
    public Example()
    {
        this.okay = new System.Windows.Forms.Button();
        this.okay.Click += new System.EventHandler(this.okay_Click);
        ...
    }

    private void okay_Click(object sender, System.EventsArgs args)
    {
        // Your code to handle the Click event
    }
}
```

When you use the Designer View in Visual Studio 2005, the IDE generates the code that subscribes methods to events automatically. All you have to do is write the logic in the event handling method.

> **Note**   It is possible to add a method to an event without creating an instance of a delegate. You could replace the following statement:
>
> ```
> this.okay.Click += new System.EventHandler(this.okay_Click);
> ```
>
> with this:
>
> ```
> this.okay.Click += this.okay_Click;
> ```
>
> However, the Windows Forms designer in Visual Studio 2005 always generates the first version.

The events that the GUI classes generate always follow the same pattern. The events are of a delegate type whose signature has a *void* return type and two arguments. The first argument is always the sender of the event and the second argument is always an *EventArgs* argument (or a class derived from *EventArgs*).

The *sender* argument allows you to reuse a single method for multiple events. The delegated method can examine the *sender* argument and respond accordingly. For example, you can use the same method to subscribe to the *Click* event fo two buttons (you add the same method to two different events). When the event is raised, the code in the method can examine the *sender* argument to ascertain which button was clicked.

Using Events

In the following exercise, you will use events to simplify the program you completed in the first exercise. You will add an event field to the *Ticker* class and delete its *Add* and *Remove* methods. You will then modify the *Clock.Start* and *Clock.Stop* methods to subscribe to the event. You will also examine the *Timer* object, used by the *Ticker* class to obtain a pulse once each second.

Rework the digital clock application

1. Return to Visual Studio 2005 displaying the Delegates project. In the Code and Text Editor window, display the Ticker.cs source file.

    This file contains the declaration of the *Tick* delegate type in the *Ticker* class:

    ```
    public delegate void Tick(int hh, int mm, int ss);
    ```

2. Add a public event called tick of type Tick to the Ticker class.

    The *Ticker* class should now look like this:

    ```
    class Ticker
    {
        public delegate void Tick(int hh, int mm, int ss);
    ```

```
    public event Tick tick;
    ...
}
```

3. Comment out the following delegate variable *tickers* from end of *Ticker* class as it is now obsolete:

```
// private Tick tickers;
```

4. Comment out the *Add* and *Remove* methods from the *Ticker* class.

   The add and remove functionality is automatically provided by the += and -= operators of the event.

5. In the Code and Text Editor window, locate the *Ticker.Notify* method. This method previously invoked an instance of the *Tick* delegate. Modify it so that it calls the *tick* event instead. Don't forget to check whether *tick* is *null* before calling the event.

   The *Notify* method should look like this:

```
class Ticker
{
    ...
    private void Notify(int hours, int minutes, int seconds)
    {
        if (this.tick != null)
        {
            this.tick(hours, minutes, seconds);
        }
    }
    ...
}
```

   Notice that the *Tick* delegate specifies parameters, so the statement that raises the *tick* event must specify arguments for each of these parameters.

6. Examine the ticking variable at the end of the class:

```
private System.Timers.Timer ticking = new System.Timers.Timer();
```

   The *Timer* class is part of the .NET Framework. It can be programmed to repeatedly raise an event at a specified interval. Examine the constructor for the *Ticker* class:

```
public Ticker()
{
    this.ticking.Elapsed += new ElapsedEventHandler(this.OnTimedEvent);
    this.ticking.Interval = 1000; // 1 second
    this.Enabled = true;
}
```

   The *Timer* class exposes the *Elapsed* event, which can be raised at regular intervals according to the *Interval* property. Setting *Interval* to 1000 causes the *Elapsed* event to be raised once a second (the value is specified in milliseconds). The timer starts when you set the *Enabled* property to *true*. The *Timer* class also provides the *ElapsedEventHandler* delegate, which specifies the signature of methods that can subscribe to the *Elapsed* event. The constructor creates an instance of this delegate referring to the *OnTimedEvent* method and subscribes to the *Elapsed* event. The *OnTimedEvent* method in the *Ticker* class extracts the information about the current time, which is passed in by using the *ElapsedEventArgs* parameter, and uses this information in turn to raise the *tick* event through the *Notify* method:

```
private void OnTimedEvent(object source, ElapsedEventArgs args)
{
    int hh = args.SignalTime.Hour;
    int mm = args.SignalTime.Minutes;
    int ss = args.SignalTime.Seconds;
    Notify(hh, mm, ss);
}
```

> **Note**   For more information about the *Timer* class and the *ElapsedEventArgs* class, see the Microsoft Visual Studio 2005 Documentation provided with Visual Studio 2005.

7. In the Code and Text Editor window, display the Clock.cs source file.

8. Change the *Clock.Start* method so that the delegate is attached to the *tick* event of the *pulsed* field by using the += operator.

    The *Clock.Start* method should look like this:

```
public void Start()
{
    pulsed.tick += this.RefreshTime;
}
```

9. In the Code and Text Editor window, change the *Clock.Stop* method so that the delegate is detached from the *tick* event of the *pulsed* field by using the -= operator.

    The *Clock.Stop* method should look like this:

```
public void Stop()
{
    pulsed.tick -= this.RefreshTime;
}
```

10. On the Debug menu, click Start Without Debugging. The project builds and runs.

11. Click Start.

    The digital clock form displays the correct time and updates the display every second.

12. Click the Stop button to verify that the clock stops.

13. Close the form.

■ **If you want to continue to the next chapter**

Keep Visual Studio 2005 running and turn to Chapter 17.

■ **If you want to exit Visual Studio 2005 now**

On the File menu, click Exit. If you see a Save dialog box, click Yes.

Chapter 16 Quick Reference

To	Do this
Declare a delegate type.	Write the keyword delegate, followed by the return type, followed by the name of the delegate type, followed by any parameter types. For example: ```\ndelegate void Tick();\n```
Invoke a delegate.	Use the same syntax as a method call. For example: ```\nTick m;\n...\nm();\n```
Create an instance of a delegate.	Use the same syntax you use for a class or struct: write the keyword new, followed by the name of the type (the name of the delegate), followed by the argument between parentheses. The argument must be a method whose signature exactly matches the signature of the delegate. For example: ```\ndelegate void Tick();\nprivate void Method() { ... }\n...\nTick m = new Tick(this.Method);\n```
Declare an event.	Write the keyword event, followed by the name of the type (the type must be a delegate type), followed by the name of the event. For example: ```\ndelegate void TickHandler();\n\nclass Ticker\n{\n public event TickHandler Tick;\n}\n```

To	Do this
Subscibe to an event.	Create a delegate instance (of the same type as the event), and attach the delegate instance to the event by using the += operator. For example:

```
class Clock
{
    ...
    public void Start()
    {
        ticker.Tick += new TickHandler
            (this.RefreshTime);
    }

    private void RefreshTime()
    {
        ...
    }

    private Ticker ticker = new Ticker();
}
```

You can also get the compiler to automatically generate the new delegate by just specifying the subscribing method:

```
public void Start()
{
    ticker.Tick += this.RefreshTime;
}
```

To	Do this
Unsubscribe from an event.	Create a delegate instance (of the same type as the event), and detach the delegate instance from the event by using the −= operator. For example:

```
class Clock
{
    ...
    public void Stop()
    {
        ticker.Tick - = new TickHandler
            (this.RefreshTime);
    }

    private void RefreshTime()
    {
        ...
    }
    private Ticker ticker = new Ticker();
}
```

Or:

```
public void Stop()
{
    ticker.Tick -= this.RefreshTime;
}
```

To	Do this
Raise an event.	Use parentheses exactly as if the event were a method. You must supply arguments to match the type of the event. Don't forget to check whether the event is null. For example:

```
class Ticker
{
    public event TickHandler Tick;
    ...
    private void Notify()
    {
        if (this.Tick != null)
        {
            this.Tick();
        }
    }
    ...
}
```

Chapter 17
Introducing Generics

After completing this chapter, you will be able to:

- Define a type-safe class by using Generics.

- Create instances of a generic class based on types specified as type-parameter.

- Implement a generic interface.

- Define a generic method that implements an algorithm independent of the type of data that it operates on.

In Chapter 8, "Understanding Values and References," you learned how to use the *object* type to refer to an instance of any class. You can use the *object* type to store a value of any type, and you can define parameters by using the *object* type when you need to pass values of any type into a method. A method can also return values of any type by specifying *object* as the return type. Although this practice is very flexible, it puts the onus on the programmer to remember what sort of data is actually being used and can lead to run-time errors if the programmer makes a mistake. In this chapter, you will learn about Generics, a feature that has been added to C# 2.0 to help you prevent these kinds of mistakes.

The Problem with *Objects*

In order to understand Generics, it is worth looking in detail at the problems they are designed to solve, specifically when using the *object* type.

You can use the *object* type as a reference to any type of value or variable. All reference types automatically inherit (either directly or indirectly) from the *System.Object* class in the .NET Framework. You can use this information to create highly generalized classes and methods. For example, many of the classes in the *System.Collections* namespace exploit this fact to allow you to create collections of any type. You will also notice in the *System.Collections.Queue* class that you can create queues containing almost anything (you have already been introduced to the collection classes in Chapter 10, "Using Arrays and Collections"). The following fragment shows how to create and manipulate a queue of *Circle* objects:

```
using System.Collections;
...
Queue myQueue = new Queue();
Circle myCircle = new Circle();
myQueue.Enqueue(myCircle);
...
myCircle = (Circle)myQueue.Dequeue();
```

The *Enqueue* method adds an *object* to the head of a queue, and the *Dequeue* method removes the *object* at the other end of the queue. These methods are defined like this:

```
public void Enqueue( object item );
public object Dequeue();
```

Because the *Enqueue* and *Dequeue* methods manipulate *object*s, you can operate on queues of *Circles*, *PhoneBooks*, *Clocks*, or any of the other classes you have seen in earlier exercises in this book. However, it is important to notice that you have to cast the value returned by the *Dequeue* method to the appropriate type because the compiler will not perform the conversion from the object type automatically. If you don't cast the returned value, you will get the compiler error "Cannot implicitly convert type 'object' to 'Circle'" as shown in the following code fragment:

```
Circle myCircle = new Circle();
myQueue.Enqueue(myCircle);
...
myCircle = (Circle)myQueue.Dequeue();   // Cast is mandatory
```

This need to perform an explicit cast denigrates much of the flexibility afforded by the *object* type. It is very easy to write code such as this:

```
Queue myQueue = new Queue();
Circle myCircle = new Circle();
myQueue.Enqueue(myCircle);
...
Clock myClock = (Clock)myQueue.Dequeue();
```

Although this code will compile, it is not valid and throws a *System.InvalidCastException* at runtime. The error is caused by trying to store a reference to a *Circle* in a *Clock* variable, and the two types are not compatible. This error is not spotted until runtime because the compiler does not have enough information. It can only determine the real type of the object being dequeued at runtime.

Another disadvantage of using the *object* approach to create generalized classes and methods is that it can use additional memory and processor time if the runtime needs to convert an *object* into a value type and back again. Consider the following piece of code that manipulates a queue of *int*s:

```
Queue myQueue = new Queue();
int myInt = 99;
myQueue.Enqueue(myInt);          // box the int to an object
...
myInt = (int)myQueue.Dequeue(); // unbox the object to an int
```

The *Queue* data type expects the items it holds to be reference types. Enqueueing a value type, such as an *int*, requires that it is boxed to convert it into a reference type. Similarly, dequeueing into an *int* requires that the item is unboxed to convert it back to a value type. See the sections

"Boxing" and "Unboxing" in Chapter 8 for more details. Although boxing and unboxing happen transparently, they add a performance overhead as they involve dynamic memory allocations. While this overhead is small for each item, it adds up when a program creates queues of large numbers of value types.

The Generics Solution

Generics was added to C# 2.0 to remove the need for casting, improve type safety, reduce the amount of boxing required, and to make it easier to create generalized classes and methods. Generic classes and methods accept *type parameters*, which specify the type of objects that they operate on. Version 2.0 of the .NET Framework Class Library includes generic versions of many of the collection classes and interfaces in the *System.Collections.Generic* namespace. The following code fragment shows how to use the generic *Queue* class found in this namespace to create a queue of *Circle* objects:

```
using System.Collections.Generic;
...
Queue<Circle> myQueue = new Queue<Circle>();
Circle myCircle = new Circle();
myQueue.Enqueue(myCircle);
...
myCircle = myQueue.Dequeue();
```

There are two new things to note about the code in the above sample:

- The use of the type parameter between the angle brackets, <Circle>, when declaring the myQueue variable.

- The lack of a cast when executing the Dequeue method.

The type parameter specifies the type of objects accepted by the queue. All references to methods in this queue will automatically expect to use this type rather than *object*, rendering the cast to the *Circle* type when invoking the *Dequeue* method unnecessary. The compiler will check to ensure that types are not accidentally mixed, generating an error at compile time rather than runtime if you try to dequeue an item from *circleQueue* into a *Clock* object, for example.

If you examine the description of the generic *Queue* class in the Visual Studio 2005 Documentation, you will notice that it is defined as:

```
public class Queue<T> : …
```

The *T* identifies the type parameter and acts as a placeholder for a real type at compile time. When you write code to instantiate a generic *Queue*, you provide the type that should be substituted for *T*, as shown in the previous example which specifies *Circle*. Furthermore, if you then look at the methods of the *Queue<T>* class you will observe that some of them, such as *Enqueue* and *Dequeue*, specify *T* as a parameter type or return value:

```
public void Enqueue( T item );
public T Dequeue();
```

The type parameter, *T*, will be replaced with the type you specified when you declared the queue. What is more, the compiler now has enough information to perform strict type-checking when you build the application and can trap any type mismatch errors early.

You should also be aware that this substitution of *T* for a specified type is not simply a textual replacement mechanism. Instead, the compiler performs a complete semantic substitution allowing you to specify any valid type for *T*. Here are more examples:

```
struct Person
{
    ...
}
...
Queue<int> intQueue = new Queue<int>();
Queue<Person> personQueue = new Queue<Person>();
Queue<Queue<int>> queueQueue = new Queue<Queue<int>>();
```

The first two examples create queues of value types, while the third creates a queue of queues (of *ints*). If we take the *intQueue* variable as an example, the compiler will also generate the following versions of the *Enqueue* and *Dequeue* methods:

```
public void Enqueue( int item );
public int Dequeue();
```

Contrast these definitions with those of the non-generic *Queue* class shown in the previous section. In the methods derived from the generic class, the *item* parameter to *Enqueue* is passed as a value type that does not require boxing. Similarly, the value returned by *Dequeue* is also a value type that does not need to be unboxed.

It is also possible for a generic class to have multiple type parameters. For example, the generic *System.Collecions.Generic.Dictionary* class expects two type parameters: one type for keys, and another for the values. The following definition shows how to specify multiple type parameters:

```
public class Dictionary<T, U>
```

A dictionary provides a collection of key/value pairs. You store values (type *U*) with an associated key (type *T*), and then retrieve them by specifying the key to look up. The *Dictionary* class provides an indexer that allows you to access items by using array notation. It is defined like this:

```
public virtual U this[ T key ] { get; set; }
```

Notice that the indexer accesses values of type *U* by using a key of type *T*. To create and use a dictionary, called *directory*, containing *Person* values identified by *string* keys, you could use the following code:

```
struct Person
{
    ...
}
...
Dictionary<string, Person> directory = new Dictionary<string, Person>();
Person john = new Person();
directory["John"] = john;
...
john = directory["John"];
```

As with the generic *Queue* class, the compiler will detect attempts to store values other than *Person* structures, as well as ensuring that the key is always a *string* value. For more information about the *Dictionary* class, you should read the Visual Studio 2005 documentation.

 Note   You can also define generic structs and interfaces by using the same syntax as generic classes.

Generics vs. Generalized Classes

It is important to be aware that a generic class that uses type parameters is different from a *generalized* class designed to take parameters that can be cast to different types. For example, the *System.Collections.Queue* class is a generalized class. There is a *single* implementation of this class, and its methods take *object* parameters and return *object* types. You can use this class with *ints*, *strings*, and many other types, but these are all instances of the same class.

Contrast this with the *System.Collections.Generic.Queue<T>* class. Each time you use this class with a type parameter (such as *Queue<int>* or *Queue<string>*) you actually cause the compiler to generate an entirely new class that happens to have functionality defined by the generic class. You can think of a generic class as one that defines a template that is then used by the compiler to generate new type-specific classes on demand. The type-specific versions of a generic class (*Queue<int>*, *Queue<string>*, and so on) are referred to as *constructed types*.

Generics and Constraints

Sometimes there will be occasions when you want to ensure that the type parameter used by a generic class identifies a type that provides certain methods. For example, if you are defining a *PrintableCollection* class, you might want to ensure that all objects stored in the class have a *Print* method. You can specify this condition by using a *constraint*.

Using a constraint enables you to limit the type parameters of a generic class to those that implement a particular set of interfaces, and therefore provide the methods defined by those interfaces. For example, if the *IPrintable* interface contained the *Print* method, you could define the *PrintableCollection* class like this:

```
public class PrintableCollection<T> where T : IPrintable
```

When the class is compiled, the compiler will check to ensure that the type used for *T* actually implements the *IPrintable* interface and will stop with a compilation error if it doesn't.

Creating a Generic Class

The .NET Framework Class Library contains a number of generic classes readily available for you. You can also define your own generic classes, which is what you will do in this section. Before we do this, I will provide a bit of background theory.

The Theory of Binary Trees

In the following exercises, you will define and use a class that represents a binary tree. This is a very practical exercise because this class happens to be one that is missing from the *System.Collections.Generic* namespace. A binary tree is a very useful data structure used for a variety of operations, including sorting and searching through data very quickly. There are volumes written on the minutiae of binary trees, but it is not the purpose of this book to cover binary trees in detail. Instead, we will just look at the pertinent details. If you are interested you should consult a book such as *The Art of Computer Programming, Volume 3: Sorting and Searching* by Donald E. Knuth (Addison-Wesley Professional; 2nd edition 1998).

A binary tree is a recursive (self-referencing) data structure that can either be empty or comprise three elements: some data that is typically referred to as the *node* and two sub-trees, which are themselves binary trees. The two sub-trees are conventionally called the *left sub-tree* and the *right sub-tree* because they are typically depicted to the left and right of the node respectively. Each left sub-tree or right sub-tree is either empty, or contains a node and other sub-trees. In theory, the whole structure can continue ad infinitum. Figure 17-1 shows the structure of a small binary tree.

The real power of binary trees becomes evident when you use them for sorting data. If you start with an unordered sequence of objects of the same type, you can use them to construct an ordered binary tree and then walk through the tree to visit each node in an ordered sequence. The algorithm for inserting an item into an ordered binary tree is shown below:

```
If the tree, T, is empty
Then
  Construct a new tree T with the new item I as the node, and empty left and
  right sub-trees
Else
  Examine the value of the node, N, of the tree, T
```

```
If the value of N is greater than that of the new item, I
Then
  If the left sub-tree of T is empty
  Then
    Construct a new left sub-tree of T with the item I as the node, and
    empty left and right sub-trees
  Else
    Insert I into the left sub-tree of T
  End If
Else
  If the right sub-tree of T is empty
  Then
    Construct a new right sub-tree of T with the item I as the node, and
    empty left and right sub-trees
  Else
    Insert I into the right sub-tree of T
  End If
End If
End If
```

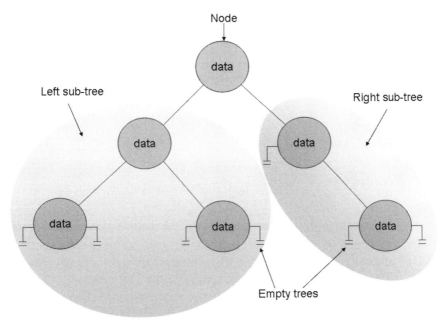

Figure 17-1   A binary tree.

Notice that this algorithm is recursive, calling itself to insert the item into the left or right sub-tree depending on the value of the item and the current node in the tree.

> **Note**   The definition of the expression *greater than* depends on the type of data in the item and node. For numeric data, greater than can be a simple arithmetic comparison, for text data it can be a string comparison, but other forms of data must be given their own means of comparing values. This is discussed in more detail when we implement a binary tree in the section "Building a Binary Tree Class Using Generics" later in this chapter.

If you start with an empty binary tree and an unordered sequence of objects, you can iterate through the unordered sequence inserting each one into the binary tree by using this algorithm, resulting in an ordered tree. Figure 17-2 shows the steps in the process for constructing a tree from a set of 5 integers.

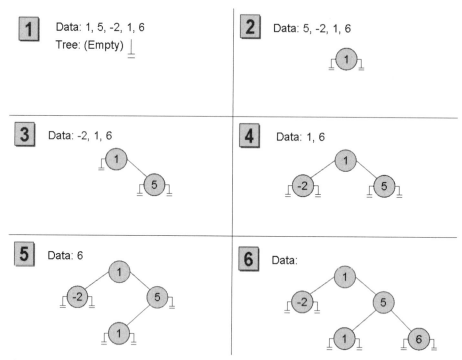

Figure 17-2   Constructing an ordered binary tree.

Once you have built an ordered binary tree, you can display its contents in sequence by visiting each node in turn and printing the value found. The algorithm for achieving this task is also recursive:

```
If the left sub-tree is not empty
Then
   Display the contents of the left sub-tree
End If
Display the value of the node
If the right sub-tree is not empty
Then
   Display the contents of the right sub-tree
End If
```

Figure 17-3 shows the steps in the process for outputting the tree constructed earlier. Notice that the integers are now displayed in ascending order.

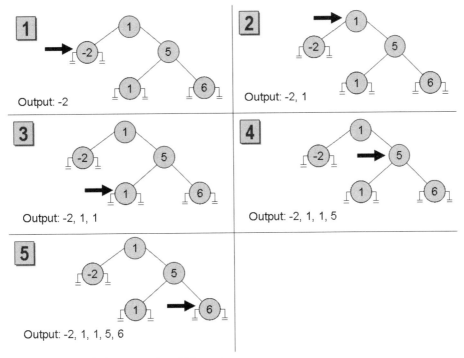

Figure 17-3   Printing an ordered binary tree.

Building a Binary Tree Class Using Generics

In the following exercise, you will use generics to define a binary tree class capable of holding almost any type of data. The only restriction is that the data type must provide a means of comparing values between different instances.

The binary tree class is a class that you might find useful in many different applications. Therefore, you will implement it as a class library rather than an application in its own right. You can then reuse this class elsewhere without needing to copy the source code and recompile it. A class library is a set of compiled classes (and other types such as structs and delegates) stored in an assembly. An assembly is a file that usually has the ".dll" suffix. Other projects and applications can make use of the items in a class library by adding a reference to its assembly, and then bringing its namespaces into scope with *using* statements. You will do this when you test the binary tree class.

The *System.IComparable* and *System.IComparable<T>* Interfaces

If you need to create a class that requires you to be able to compare values according to some natural (or possibly unnatural) ordering, you should implement the *IComparable* interface. This interface contains a method called *CompareTo*, which takes a single parameter specifying the object to be compared to the current instance and returns an integer that indicates the result of the comparison as shown in the following table.

Value	Meaning
Less than zero	The current instance is less than the value of the parameter
Zero	The current instance is equal to the value of the parameter.
Greater than zero	The current instance is greater than the value of the parameter

As an example, consider the *Circle* class that was described in Chapter 7, "Creating and Managing Classes and Objects," and is reproduced below:

```
class Circle
{
    public Circle(double initialRadius)
    {
        radius = initialRadius;
    }

    public double Area()
    {
        return 3.141593 * radius * radius;
    }

    private double radius;
}
```

You can make the Circle class comparable by implementing the System.IComparable interface and providing the CompareTo method. In the example shown, the CompareTo method compares Circle objects based on their areas. The area of a circle with a larger area is greater than a circle with a smaller area.

```
class Circle : System.IComparable
{
    ...
    public int CompareTo(object obj)
    {
        Circle circObj = (Circle)obj;  // cast the parameter to its real type
        if (this.Area() == circObj.Area())
            return 0;

        if (this.Area() > circObj.Area())
            return 1;

        return -1;
    }
}
```

If you examine the *System.IComparable* interface, you will see that its parameter is defined as an *object*. However, this approach is not typesafe. To understand why this is so, consider what happens if you try to pass something that is not a *Circle* to the *CompareTo* method. The *System.IComparable* interface requires the use of a cast in order to be able to access the *Area* method. If the parameter is not a *Circle* but some other type of object then this cast will fail. However, the *System* namespace also defines the generic *IComparable<T>* interface, which contains the following methods:

```
int CompareTo(T other);
bool Equals(T other);
```

Notice there is an additional method in this interface, called *Equals*, which should return *true* if both instances are equals, *false* if they are not equals.

Also notice that these methods take a type parameter (T) rather than an object, and as such, are much safer than the non-generic version of the interface. The following code shows how you can implement this interface in the Circle class:

```
class Circle : System.IComparable<Circle>
{
    ...
    public int CompareTo(Circle other)
    {
        if (this.Area() == other.Area())
            return 0;

        if (this.Area() > other.Area())
            return 1;

        return -1;
    }

    public bool Equals(Circle other)
    {
        return (this.CompareTo(other) == 0);
    }
}
```

The parameters for the *CompareTo* and *Equals* method must match the type specified in the interface, *IComparable<Circle>*. In general, it is preferable to implement the *System.IComparable<T>* interface rather than *System.IComparable*. You can also implement both, as many of the types in the .NET Framework do.

Create the Tree<T> class

1. Start Visual Studio 2005.

2. Create a new Visual C# project using the Class Library template (on the File menu, point to New, and then click Project). Name the project **BinaryTree** and set the Location to **\Microsoft Press\Visual CSharp Step By Step\Chapter 17**.

3. In the Solution Explorer change the name of the file Class1.cs to Tree.cs.

4. In the Code and Text Editor window, change the definition of the *Class1* class to *Tree<T>*.

   The definition of the *Tree<T>* class should look like this:

```
public class Tree<T>
{
    ...
}
```

> **Note**   It is conventional to use a single letter (often T) to indicate a type parameter, although any C# legal identifier is allowed. If a generic class uses multiple type parameters, you must use a different identifier for each type. For example, the generic *Dictionary* class in the .NET Framework is defined as *Dictionary<K, V>*. The K type indicates the type used for dictionary keys, and the V type indicates the type used for dictionary values.

5. In the Code and Text Editor window, modify the definition of the *Tree<T>* class to specify that the type parameter *T* must denote a type that implements the generic *IComparable<T>* interface.

   The modified definition of the *Tree<T>* class should look like this:

```
public class Tree<T> where T : IComparable<T>
{
    ...
}
```

6. Add three private variables to the *Tree<T>* class; a *T* variable called *data*, and two *Tree<T>* variables called *left* and *right*:

```
private T data;
private Tree<T> left;
private Tree<T> right;
```

7. Add a constructor to the *Tree<T>* class that takes a single *T* parameter called *nodeValue*. In the constructor, set the *data* variable to *nodeValue*, and initialize the *left* and *right* variables to *null*, as shown below:

```
public Tree(T nodeValue)
{
    this.data = nodeValue;
    this.left = null;
    this.right = null;
}
```

8.   Add a public property of type *T* called *NodeData* to the *Tree<T>* class. This property should provide *get* and *set* accessors allowing the user to read and modify the *data* variable:

The *NodeData* property should look like this:

```
public T NodeData
{
    get { return this.data; }
    set { this.data = value; }
}
```

9.   Add two more properties to the *Tree<T>* class called *LeftTree* and *RightTree*. These properties are very similar to each other, and provide *get* and *set* access to the *left* and *right* *Tree<T>* variables respectively.

The *LeftTree* property should look like this (the *RightTree* property is the same except that it uses the *right* variable):

```
public Tree<T> LeftTree
{
    get { return this.left; }
    set { this.left = value; }
}
```

10. Add a public method called *Insert* to the *Tree<T>* class. This method will insert a *T* value into the tree.

The method definition should look like this:

```
public void Insert (T newItem)
{
}
```

The *Insert* method will follow the algorithm described earlier. The programmer will have used the constructor to insert the initial node into the tree, so the *Insert* method can assume that the tree is not empty. The next part of the algorithm is reproduced below to help you understand the code you will write in the following steps:

```
...
Examine the value of the node, N, of the tree, T
If the value of N is greater than that of the new item, I
Then
  If the left sub-tree of T is empty
  Then
    Construct a new left sub-tree of T with the item I as the node, and empty
    left and right sub-trees
  Else
    Insert I into the left sub-tree of T End If
...
```

11.   In the *Insert* method, add a statement that declares a local variable of type *T*, called *currentNodeValue*. Initialize this variable to the value of the *NodeData* property of the tree, as shown below:

```
public void Insert(T newItem)
{
    T currentNodeValue = this.NodeData;
}
```

12.   Add the following *if-else* statement to the *Insert* method, after the definition of the *currentNodeValue* variable. This statement uses the *CompareTo* method of the *IComparable<T>* interface to determine whether the value of the current node is greater then the new item:

```
if (currentNodeValue.CompareTo(newItem) > 0)
{
    //Insert the new item into the left sub-tree
}
else
{
    // Insert the new item into the right sub-tree
}
```

13.   Replace the //Insert the new item into the left sub-tree comment with the following block of code:

```
if (this.LeftTree == null)
{
    this.LeftTree = new Tree<T>(newItem);
}
else
{
    this.LeftTree.Insert(newItem);
}
```

These statements check whether the left sub-tree is empty. If so, a new left sub-tree is created using the new item; otherwise the new item is inserted into the existing left sub-tree by calling the *Insert* method recursively.

14.   Replace the //Insert the new item into the right sub-tree comment with the equivalent code that inserts the new node into the right sub-tree:

```
if (this.RightTree == null)
{
    this.RightTree = new Tree<T>(newItem);
}
else
{
    this.RightTree.Insert(newItem);
}
```

15. Add another public method called *WalkTree* to the *Tree<T>* class. This method will walk through the tree, visiting each node in sequence and printing out its value.

The method definition should look like this:

```
public void walkTree()
{
}
```

16. Add the following statements to the *WalkTree* method. These statements implement the algorithm described earlier for printing the contents of a binary tree:

```
if (this.LeftTree != null)
{
    this.LeftTree.walkTree();
}

Console.WriteLine(this.NodeData.ToString());

if (this.RightTree != null)
{
    this.RightTree.walkTree();
}
```

17. On the Build menu, click Build Solution. The class should compile cleanly, so correct any errors that are reported and rebuild the solution if necessary.

In the next exercise, you will test the Tree<T> class by creating binary trees of integers and strings.

Test the Tree<T> class

1. On the File menu, point to Add and then click New Project. Add a new project using the Console Application template. Name the project **BinaryTreeTest** and set the Location to **\Microsoft Press\Visual CSharp Step By Step\Chapter 17**.

> **Note**   Remember that a Visual Studio 2005 solution can contain more than one project. You are using this feature to add a second project to the BinaryTree solution for testing the *Tree<T>* class. This is the recommended way of testing class libraries.

2. Ensure the BinaryTreeTest project is selected in the Solution Explorer. On the Project menu, click Set as Startup Project. The BinaryTreeTest project will be highlighted in the Solution Explorer.

When you run the application, this is the project that will actually be executed.

3. On the Project menu, click Add Reference. In the Add Reference dialog box, click the Projects tab. Click the BinaryTree project and then click OK.

The BinaryTree assembly will appear in the list of references for the BinaryTreeTest project in the Solution Explorer. You will now be able to create *Tree<T>* objects in the BinaryTreeTest project.

> **Note**   If the class library project is not part of the same solution as the project that uses it, you must add a reference to the assembly (the ".dll" file) and not to the class library project. You do this by selecting the assembly from the Browse tab in the Add Reference dialog box. You will use this technique in the final set of exercises in this chapter.

4. In the Code and Text Editor window displaying the Program class, add the following *using* directive to the list at the top of the class:

    ```
    using BinaryTree;
    ```

5. Add the following statements to the Main method:

    ```
    Tree<int> tree1 = new Tree<int>(10);
    tree1.Insert(5);
    tree1.Insert(11);
    tree1.Insert(5);
    tree1.Insert(-12);
    tree1.Insert(15);
    tree1.Insert(0);
    tree1.Insert(14);
    tree1.Insert(-8);
    tree1.Insert(10);
    tree1.Insert(8);
    tree1.Insert(8);
    tree1.WalkTree();
    ```

    These statements create a new binary tree for holding *ints*. The constructor creates an initial node containing the value 10. The *Insert* statements add nodes to the tree, and the *WalkTree* method prints out the contents of the tree, which should be sorted in ascending order.

> **Note**   Remember that the *int* keyword in C# is actually just an alias for the *System.Int32* type; whenever you declare an *int* variable, you are actually declaring a *struct* variable of type *System.Int32*. The *System.Int32* type implements the *IComparable* and *IComparable<T>* interfaces, which is why you can create *Tree<int>* variables. Similarly, the *string* keyword is an alias for *System.String*, which also implements *IComparable* and *IComparable<T>*.

6. On the Build menu, click Build Solution. Verify that the solution compiles, correcting any errors if necessary.

7. On the Debug menu, click Start Without Debugging.

When the program runs, the values should be displayed in the following sequence:

–12, –8, 0, 5, 5, 8, 8, 10, 10, 11, 14, 15

Press the Enter key to return to Visual Studio 2005.

8. Add the following statements to the end of the Main method, after the existing code:

```
Tree<string> tree2 = new Tree<string>("Hello");
tree2.Insert("World");
tree2.Insert("How");
tree2.Insert("Are");
tree2.Insert("You");
tree2.Insert("Today");
tree2.Insert("I");
tree2.Insert("Hope");
tree2.Insert("You");
tree2.Insert("Are");
tree2.Insert("Feeling");
tree2.Insert("Well");
tree2.walkTree();
```

These statements create another binary tree for holding *strings*, populate it with some test data, and then print the tree. This time, the data will be sorted alphabetically.

9. On the Build menu, click Build Solution. Verify that the solution compiles, correcting any errors if necessary.

10. On the Debug menu, click Start Without Debugging.

When the program runs, the integer values will be displayed as before followed by the strings in the following sequence:

Are, Are, Feeling, Hello, Hope, How, I, Today, Well, World, You, You

11. Press the Enter key to return to Visual Studio 2005.

Creating a Generic Method

As well as defining generic classes, you can also use the .NET Framework to create generic methods.

A generic method allows you to specify parameters and return type by using a type parameter in a manner similar to that used when defining a generic class. In this way, you can define generalized methods that are typesafe, and avoid the overhead of casting (and boxing in some cases). Generic methods are frequently used in conjunction with generic classes—you need them for methods that take a generic class as a parameter, or that have a return type that is a generic class.

You define generic methods by using the same type parameter syntax that you use when creating generic classes (you can also specify constraints). For example, the generic *Swap<T>* method shown below can be used to swap the values in its parameters. As this functionality is useful regardless of the type of data being swapped, it is helpful to define it as a generic method:

```
static void Swap<T>( ref T first, ref T second)
{
    T temp = first;
    first = second;
    second = temp;
}
```

You invoke the method by specifying the appropriate type for its type parameter. The following examples show how to use the *Swap<T>* method to swap over two *ints*, and two *strings*:

```
int a = 1, b = 2;
Swap<int>(ref a, ref b);
...
string s1 = "Hello", s2 = "World";
Swap<string>(ref s1, ref s2);
```

> **Note**   Just as instantiating a generic class with different type parameters causes the compiler to generate different types, each distinct use of the *Swap<T>* method causes the compiler to generate a different version of the method. *Swap<int>* is not the same method as *Swap<string>*; both methods just happen to have been generated from the same generic method and so exhibit the same behavior, albeit over different types.

Defining a Generic Method to Build a Binary Tree

The previous exercise showed you how to create a generic class for implementing a binary tree. The *Tree<T>* class provides the *Insert* method for adding data items to the tree. However, if you want to add a large number of items, repeated calls to the *Insert* method are not very convenient. In the following exercise, you will define a generic method called *BuildTree* that allows you to create a new binary tree from a list of data items. You will test this method by using it to construct a tree of characters.

Write the BuildTree method

1.   Using Visual Studio 2005, create a new project by using the Console Application template. In the New Project dialog box, name the project **BuildTree** and set the Location to **\Microsoft Press\Visual CSharp Step By Step\Chapter 17**. Select Create a new Solution from the Solution dropdown.

2.   On the Project menu, click Add Reference. In the Add Reference dialog box click the Browse tab. Navigate to the folder **\Microsoft Press\Visual CSharp Step By Step\Chapter 17\BinaryTree\bin\Debug**, click BinaryTree.dll, and then click OK.

   The BinaryTree assembly will be added to the list of references shown in the Solution Explorer.

3. In the Code and Text Editor window, add the following *using* directive to the top of the Program.cs file:

```
using BinaryTree;
```

This namespace contains the *Tree<T>* class.

4. Add a method called *BuildTree* method to the *Program* class. This should be a *static* method that takes a *params* array of *T* elements called *data*, and returns a *Tree<T>* object.

The method definition should look like this:

```
static Tree<T> BuildTree<T>(params T[] data)
{
}
```

> **Note** The *params* keyword was described in detail in Chapter 11, "Understanding Parameter Arrays."

5. The *T* type used for building the binary tree must implement the *IComparable<T>* interface. Modify the definition of the *BuildTree* method and add the appropriate *where* clause.

The updated definition of the method should look like this:

```
static Tree<T> BuildTree<T>(params T[] data) where T : IComparable<T>
{
}
```

6. Add the statements shown below to the *BuildTree* method. These statements instantiate a new *Tree* object by using the appropriate type parameter, and then iterate through the *params* list, adding each item to the tree by using the *Insert* method.

The tree is passed back as the return value:

```
static Tree<T> BuildTree<T>(params T[] data) where T : IComparable<T>
{
    Tree<T> sortTree = new Tree<T> (data[0]);
    for (int i = 1; i < data.Length; i++)
    {
        sortTree.Insert(data[i]);
    }
    return sortTree;
}
```

Test the BuildTree method

1. In the *Main* method of the *Program* class, add the following statements that create a new *Tree* for holding character data, populates it with some sample data by using the *BuildTree* method, and then displays it by using the *WalkTree* method of the *Tree*:

```
Tree<char> charTree = BuildTree<char>('Z', 'X', 'A', 'M', 'Z', 'M', 'N');
charTree.WalkTree();
```

2. On the Build menu, click Build Solution. Verify that the solution compiles, correcting any errors if necessary.

3. On the Debug menu, click Start Without Debugging.

   When the program runs, the character values will be displayed, in order:

   A, M, M, N, X, Z, Z

4. Press the Enter key to return to Visual Studio 2005.

■ **If you want to continue to the next chapter**

   Keep Visual Studio 2005 running and turn to Chapter 18.

■ **If you want to exit Visual Studio 2005 now**

   On the File menu, click Exit. If you see a Save dialog box, click Yes.

Chapter 17 Quick Reference

To	Do this	Example
Instantiate an object by using a generic type.	Specify the appropriate type parameter.	```Queue<int> myQueue = new Queue<int>();```
Create a new generic type.	Define the class by using a type parameter.	```public class Tree<T> { ... }```
Restrict the type that can be substituted for the type parameter.	Specify a constraint by using a where clause when defining the class.	```public class Tree<T> where T : IComparable<T> { ... }```
Define a generic method.	Define the method by using type parameters.	```static Tree<T> BuildTree<T> (params T[] data) { ... }```
Invoke a generic method.	Provide types for each of the type parameters.	```Tree<char> charTree = BuildTree<char>('Z', 'X');```

Chapter 18
Enumerating Collections

After completing this chapter, you will be able to:

■ Manually define an enumerator that can be used to iterate over the elements in a collection.

■ Implement an enumerator automatically by creating an iterator.

■ Provide additional iterators that can step through the elements of a collection in different sequences.

In Chapter 10, "Using Arrays and Collections," you learned about arrays and collection classes for holding sequences or sets of data. Chapter 10 also introduced the *foreach* statement which you can use for stepping through, or iterating over, the elements in a collection. At the time, you just used the *foreach* statement as a quick and convenient way of accessing the contents of a collection, but now it is time to learn a little more about how this statement actually works. This topic becomes important when you start defining your own collection classes, especially since Iterators have been added to C# 2.0 to help you automate much of the process.

Enumerating the Elements in Collection

In Chapter 10, you saw an example of using the *foreach* statement to list the items in a simple array. The code looked like this:

```
int[] pins = { 9, 3, 7, 2 };
foreach (int pin in pins)
{
    Console.WriteLine(pin);
}
```

The *foreach* construct provides an elegant mechanism that greatly simplifies the code that you need to write, but it can only be exercised under certain circumstances—you can only use *foreach* to step through an *enumerable* collection. So, what exactly is an enumerable collection? The quick answer is that it is a collection that implements the *System.Collections.IEnumerable* interface.

 Note   Remember that all arrays in C# are actually instances of the *System.Array* class. The *System.Array* class is a collection class that implements the *IEnumerable* interface.

The *IEnumerable* interface contains a single method called *GetEnumerator*:

```
IEnumerator GetEnumerator();
```

The *GetEnumerator* method returns an enumerator object that implements the *System.Collections.IEnumerator* interface. The enumerator object is used for stepping through (enumerating) the elements of the collection. The *IEnumerator* interface itself specifies the following property and methods:

```
object Current {get;}
bool MoveNext();
void Reset();
```

Think of an enumerator as a pointer pointing to elements in a list. Initially the pointer points *before* the first element. You call the *MoveNext* method to move the pointer down to the next (first) item in the list; the *MoveNext* method should return *true* if there actually is another item, and *false* if there isn't. You use the *Current* property to access the item currently pointed to, and the *Reset* method to return the pointer back to *before* the first item in the list. By creating an enumerator by using the *GetEnumerator* method of a collection, and repeatedly calling the *MoveNext* method and retrieving the value of the *Current* property by using the enumerator, you can move forward through the elements of a collection one item at a time. This is exactly what the *foreach* statement does. So, if you want to create your own enumerable collection class, you must implement the *IEnumerable* interface in your collection class, and also provide an implementation of the *IEnumerator* interface to be returned by the *GetEnumerator* method of the collection class.

If you are observant, you will have noticed that the *Current* property of the *IEnumerator* interface exhibits non-typesafe behavior inasmuch that it returns an *object* rather than a specific type. However, you should be pleased to know that the .NET Framework class library also provides the generic *IEnumerator<T>* interface, providing a *Current* property that returns a *T* instead. Likewise, there is also an *IEnumerable<T>* interface containing a *GetEnumerator* method that returns an *Enumerator<T>* object. If you are building applications for the .NET Framework version 2.0, you should make use of these generic interfaces when defining enumerable collections rather than using the non-generic definitions.

> **Note**   The *IEnumerator<T>* interface has some further differences from the *IEnumerator* interface; it does not contain a *Reset* method, but extends the *IDisposable* interface.

Manually Implementing an Enumerator

In the next exercise you will define a class that implements the generic *IEnumerator<T>* interface and create an enumerator for the binary tree class that you built in Chapter 17, "Introducing Generics." In Chapter 17 you saw how easy it was to traverse a binary tree and display its contents. You would therefore be inclined to think that defining an enumerator that retrieves each element in a binary tree in the same order would be a simple matter. Sadly, you would be mistaken. The main problem is that when defining an enumerator you need to remember where you are in the structure so that subsequent calls to the *MoveNext* method can update the position appropriately. Recursive algorithms, such as that used when walking a binary tree, do not lend themselves to maintaining state information between method calls in an easily accessible manner. For this reason, you will first pre-process the data in the binary tree into a more amenable data structure (a queue) and actually enumerate this data structure instead. Of course, this deviousness will be hidden from the user iterating through the elements of the binary tree!

Create the TreeEnumerator class

1. Start Visual Studio 2005 if it is not already running.

2. Open the Visual C# solution **\Microsoft Press\Visual CSharp Step By Step \Chapter 18\BinaryTree\BinaryTree.sln**. This solution contains a working copy of the BinaryTree project you created in Chapter 17.

3. Add a new class to the project: click Add Class on the Project menu, select the Class template, and type **TreeEnumerator.cs** for the Name, and then click Add.

4. The *TreeEnumerator* class will generate an enumerator for a *Tree<T>* object. To ensure that the class is typesafe, it is necessary to provide a type parameter and implement the *IEnumerator<T>* interface. Also, the type parameter must be a valid type for the *Tree<T>* object that the class enumerates, so it must be constrained to implement the *IComparable<T>* interface.

   Modify the class definition to satisfy these requirements. It should look like this:

   ```
   public class TreeEnumerator<T> : IEnumerator<T> where T : IComparable<T>
   {

   }
   ```

5. Add the following three private variables to the *TreeEnumerator<T>* class:

   ```
   private Tree<T> currentData = null;
   private T currentItem = default(T);
   private Queue<T> enumData = null;
   ```

   The *currentData* variable will be used to hold a reference to the tree being enumerated, and the *currentItem* variable will hold the value returned by the Current property. You will populate the *enumData* queue with the values extracted from the nodes in the tree, and the *MoveNext* method will return each item from this queue in turn.

6. Add a *TreeEnumerator* constructor that take a single *Tree<T>* parameter called *data*. In the body of the constructor, add a statement that initializes the *currentData* variable to *data*:

   ```
   public TreeEnumerator(Tree<T> data)
   {
   ```

```
        this.currentData = data;
    }
```

7. Add the following private method, called *populate*, to the *TreeEnumerator<T>* class, after the constructor:

```
private void populate(Queue<T> enumQueue, Tree<T> tree)
{
    if (tree.LeftTree != null)
    {
        populate(enumQueue, tree.LeftTree);
    }

    enumQueue.Enqueue(tree.NodeData);

    if (tree.RightTree != null)
    {
        populate(enumQueue, tree.RightTree);
    }
}
```

This method walks a binary tree, adding the data it contains to the queue. The algorithm used is very similar to that used by the *WalkTree* method in the *Tree<T>* class, and which was described in Chapter 17. The main difference is that rather than outputting *NodeData* values to the screen, they are stored in the queue.

8. Return to the definition of the *TreeEnumerator<T>* class. Right-click anywhere in the *IEnumerator<T>* interface in the class declaration, point to Implement Interface, and then click Implement Interface Explicitly.

This action generates stubs for the methods of the *IEnumerator<T>* interface and the *IEnumerator* interface, and adds them to the end of the class. It also generates the *Dispose* method for the *IDisposable* interface.

> **Note** The *IEnumerator<T>* interface inherits from the *IEnumerator* and *IDisposable* interfaces, which is why their methods also appear. In fact, the only item that belongs to the *IEnumerator<T>* interface is the generic *Current* property. The *MoveNext* and *Reset* methods belong to the non-generic *IEnumerator* interface. The *IDisposable* interface was described in Chapter 13, "Using Garbage Collection and Resource Management."

9. Examine the code that has been generated. The bodies of the properties and methods contain a default implementation that simply throws an *Exception* with the message "The method or operation is not implemented." You will replace this code with a real implementation in the following steps.

10. Replace the body of the *MoveNext* method with the code shown below:

```
bool System.Collections.IEnumerator.MoveNext()
{
```

```
    if (this.enumData == null)
    {
        this.enumData = new Queue<T>();
        populate(this.enumData, this.currentData);
    }

    if (this.enumData.Count > 0)
    {
        this.currentItem = this.enumData.Dequeue();
        return true;
    }

    return false;
}
```

The purpose of the *MoveNext* method of an enumerator is actually twofold. The first time it is called it should initialize the data used by the enumerator and advance to the first piece of data to be returned. (Remember that prior to calling *MoveNext* for the first time, the value returned by the *Current* property is undefined and should result in an exception). In this case, the initialization process consists of instantiating the queue, and calling the *populate* method to extract the data from the tree and using it to fill the queue.

Subsequent calls to the *MoveNext* method should just move through data items until there are no more left, dequeuing items from the queue until it is empty in this example. It is important to bear in mind that *MoveNext* does not actually return data items—that is the purpose of the *Current* property. All *MoveNext* does is update internal state in the enumerator (the value of the *currentItem* variable is set to the data item extracted from the queue) for use by the *Current* property, returning *true* if there is a next value, *false* otherwise.

11. Modify the definition of the *get* accessor of the *Current* property as follows:

```
T IEnumerator<T>.Current
{
    get
    {
        if (this.enumData == null)
            throw new InvalidOperationException("Use MoveNext before calling Current");

        return this.currentItem;
    }
}
```

The *Current* property examines the *enumData* variable to ensure that *MoveNext* has been called (this variable will be null prior to the first call to *MoveNext*). If this is not the case, the property throws an *InvalidOperationException*—this is the conventional mechanism used by .NET Framework applications to indicate that an operation cannot be per-formed in the current state. If *MoveNext* has been called beforehand, it will have updated the *currentItem* variable, so all the *Current* property needs to do is return the value in this variable.

12. Locate the *IDisposable.Dispose* method. Comment out the `throw new Exception` statement. The enumerator does not use any resources that require explicit disposal, so this method does not need to do anything. It must still be present, however. For more information about the *Dispose* method, refer to Chapter 13.

13. Build the solution and fix any errors that are reported.

Initializing a Variable Defined with a Type Parameter

You should have noticed that the statement that defines and initializes the *currentItem* variable uses the *default* keyword. This keyword is a new feature in C# 2.0.

The *currentItem* variable is defined by using the type parameter T. When the program is written and compiled, the actual type that will be substituted for T might not be known—this issue is only resolved when the code is executed. This makes it difficult to specify how the variable should be initialized. The temptation would be to set it to *null*. However, if the type substituted for T is a value type, then this is an illegal assignment (you cannot set value types to null, only reference types). Similarly, if you set it to 0 in the expectation that the type will be numeric, then this will be illegal if the type used is actually a reference type. There are other possibilities as well—T could be a *boolean* for example. The *default* keyword solves this problem. The value used to initialize the variable will be determined when the statement is executed; if T is a reference type *default(T)* returns null, if T is numeric, *default(T)* returns 0, and if T is a *boolean*, *default(T)* returns *false*. If T is a *struct*, the individual fields in the *struct* are initialized in the same way (reference fields are set to *null*, numeric fields are set to 0, and *boolean* fields are set to *false*.)

Implementing the IEnumerable Interface

In the following exercise, you will modify the binary tree class to implement the *IEnumerable* interface. The *GetEnumerator* method will return a *TreeEnumerator<T>* object.

Implement the IEnumerable<T> interface in the Tree<T> class

1. In the Solution Explorer, double click the file Tree.cs to display the *Tree<T>* class in the Code and Text Editor window.

2. Modify the definition of the *Tree<T>* class so that it implements the *IEnumerable<T>* interface, as shown below:

```
public class Tree<T> : IEnumerable<T> where T : IComparable<T>
```

Notice that constraints are always placed at the end of the class definition.

3. Right-click the *IEnumerable<T>* interface in the class definition, point to Implement Interface, and then click Implement Interface Explicitly.

    This action generates implementations of the *IEnumerable<T>.GetEnumerator* and the *IEnumerable.GetEnumerator* methods and adds them to the close. The IEnumerable interface method is implemented because the *IEnumerable<T>* interface inherits from *IEnumerable.*

4. Locate the *IEnumerable<T>.GetEnumerator* method near the end of the class. Modify the body of the *GetEnumerator()* method, replacing the existing *throw* statement as follows:

    ```
    IEnumerator<T> IEnumerable<T>.GetEnumerator()
    {
        return new TreeEnumerator<T>(this);
    }
    ```

    The purpose of the *GetEnumerator* method is to construct an enumerator object for iterating through the collection. In this case, all we need to do is build a new *TreeEnumerator<T>* object by using the data in the tree.

5. Build the solution.

    The project should compile cleanly, so correct any errors that are reported and rebuild the solution if necessary.

You will now test the modified *Tree<T>* class by using a *foreach* statement to display the contents of a binary tree.

Test the enumerator

1. On the File menu, point to Add and then click New Project. Add a new project by using the Console Application template. Name the project **EnumeratorTest** and set the Location to **\Microsoft Press\Visual CSharp Step By Step\Chapter 18\BinaryTree**, and then click OK.

2. Right-click the EnumeratorTest project in the Solution Explorer, and then click Set as Startup Project.

3. On the Project menu, click Add Reference. In the Add Reference dialog box, click the Projects tab. Click the BinaryTree project and then click OK.

    The BinaryTree assembly will appear in the list of references for the EnumeratorTest project in the Solution Explorer.

4. In the Code and Text Editor window displaying the Program class, add the following *using* directive to the list at the top of the file:

    ```
    using BinaryTree;
    ```

5. Add the following statements that create and populate a binary tree of integers to the *Main* method:

```
Tree<int> tree1 = new Tree<int>(10);
tree1.Insert(5);
tree1.Insert(11);
tree1.Insert(5);
tree1.Insert(-12);
tree1.Insert(15);
tree1.Insert(0);
tree1.Insert(14);
tree1.Insert(-8);
tree1.Insert(10);
```

6. Add a *foreach* statement that enumerates the contents of the tree and displays the results:

```
foreach (int data in tree1)
    Console.WriteLine(data);
```

7. Build the solution, correcting any errors if necessary.

8. On the Debug menu, click Start Without Debugging.

    When the program runs, the values should be displayed in the following sequence:

    −12, −8, 0, 5, 5, 10, 10, 11, 14, 15

    Press Enter to return to Visual Studio 2005.

Implementing an Enumerator by Using an Iterator

As you can see, the process of making a collection enumerable can become complex and potentially error-prone. To make life easier, C# 2.0 includes iterators which can automate much of this process.

According to the C# 2.0 specification, an iterator is a block of code that *yields* an ordered sequence of values. Additionally, an iterator is not actually a member of an enumerable class. Rather, it specifies the sequence that an enumerator should use for returning its values. In other words, an iterator is just a description of the enumeration sequence that the C# compiler can use for creating its own enumerator. This concept requires a little thought to understand it properly, so let's consider a basic example before returning to binary trees and recursion.

A Simple Iterator

The *BasicCollection<T>* class shown below illustrates the basic principles of implementing an iterator. The class uses a *List<T>* for holding data, and provides the *FillList* method for populating this list. Notice also that the *BasicCollection<T>* class implements the *IEnumerable<T>* interface. The *GetEnumerator* method is implemented by using an iterator:

```
class BasicCollection<T> : IEnumerable<T>
{
    private List<T> data = new List<T>();

    public void FillList(params T [] items)
    {
        for (int i = 0; i < items.Length; i++)
            data.Add(items[i]);
    }

    IEnumerator<T> IEnumerable<T>.GetEnumerator()
    {
        for (int i = 0; i < data.Count; i++)
            yield return data[i];
    }

    IEnumerator IEnumerable.GetEnumerator()
    {
        // Not implemented in this example
    }
}
```

The *GetEnumerator* method appears to be straightforward, but bears closer examination. The first thing you should notice is that it doesn't appear to return an *IEnumerator<T>* type. Instead, it loops through the items in the *data* array, returning each item in turn. The key point is the use of the *yield* keyword. The *yield* keyword indicates the value that should be returned by each iteration. If it helps, you can think of the *yield* statement as calling a temporary halt to the method, passing back a value to the caller. When the caller needs the next value, the *GetEnumerator* method continues at the point it left off, looping round and then yielding the next value. Eventually, the data will be exhausted, the loop will finish, and the *GetEnumerator* method will terminate. At this point the iteration is complete.

Remember that this is not a normal method in the usual sense. The code in the *GetEnumerator* method defines an *iterator*. The compiler uses this code to generate an implementation of the *IEnumerator<T>* class containing a *Current* and a *MoveNext* method. This implementation will exactly match the functionality specified by the *GetEnumerator* method. You don't actually get to see this generated code (unless you decompile the assembly containing the compiled code), but that is a small price to pay for the convenience and reduction in code that you need to write. You can invoke the enumerator generated by the iterator in the usual manner, as shown in this block of code:

```
BasicCollection<string> bc = new BasicCollection<string>();
bc.FillList("Twas", "brillig", "and", "the", slithy", "toves");
foreach (string word in bc)
    Console.WriteLine(word);
```

This code simply outputs the contents of the *bc* object in this order:

Twas, brillig, and, the, slithy, toves

If you want to provide alternative iteration mechanisms presenting the data in a different sequence, you can implement additional properties that implement the *IEnumerable* interface and that use an iterator for returning data. For example, the *Reverse* property of the *BasicCollection<T>* class, shown below, emits the data in the list in reverse order:

```
public IEnumerable<T> Reverse
{
    get
    {
        for (int i = data.Count - 1; i >= 0; i--)
            yield return data[i];
    }
}
```

You can invoke this property as follows:

```
BasicCollection<string> bc = new BasicCollection<string>();
bc.FillList("Twas", "brillig", "and", "the", slithy", "toves");
...
foreach (string word in bc.Reverse)
    Console.WriteLine(word);
```

This code outputs the contents of the *bc* object in reverse order:

toves, slithy, the, and, brillig, Twas

Defining an Enumerator for the Tree<T> Class by Using an Iterator

In the next exercise, you will implement the enumerator for the *Tree<T>* class by using an iterator. Unlike the previous set of exercises which required the data in the tree to be preprocessed into a queue by the *MoveNext* method, you can define an iterator that traverses the tree by using the more natural recursive mechanism, similar to the *WalkTree* method discussed in Chapter 17.

Add an enumerator to the Tree<T> class

1. Start Visual Studio 2005 if it is not already running.

2. Open the Visual C# solution **\Microsoft Press\Visual CSharp Step By Step\Chapter 18\IteratorBinaryTree\BinaryTree.sln**. This solution contains another working copy of the BinaryTree project you created in Chapter 17.

3. Display the file Tree.cs in the Code and Text Editor window. Modify the definition of the *Tree<T>* class so that it implements the *IEnumerable<T>* interface:

```
public class Tree<T> : IEnumerable<T> where T : IComparable<T>
{
    ...
}
```

4. Right-click the *IEnumerable<T>* interface in the class definition, point to Implement Interface, and then click Implement Interface Explicitly.

    The *IEnumerable<T>.GetEnumerator* and *IEnumerable.GetEnumerator* methods are added to the class.

5. Locate the *IEnumerable<T>.GetEnumerator* method. Replace the contents of the *GetEnumerator* method as shown below:

```
IEnumerator<T> IEnumerable<T>.GetEnumerator()
{
    if (this.LeftTree != null)
    {
        foreach (T item in this.LeftTree)
        {
            yield return item;
        }
    }

    yield return this.NodeData;

    if (this.RightTree != null)
    {
        foreach (T item in this.RightTree)
        {
            yield return item;
        }
    }
}
```

It might not look like it at first glance, but this code is recursive. If the *LeftTree* is not empty, the first *foreach* statement implicitly calls the *GetEnumerator* method (which you are currently defining) over it. This process continues until a node is found that has no left sub-tree. At this point, the value in the *NodeData* property is yielded, and the right sub-tree is examined in the same way. When the right sub-tree is exhausted, the process unwinds to parent node, outputting its *NodeData* property and examining its right sub-tree. This course of action continues until the entire tree has been enumerated and all the nodes have been output.

Test the new enumerator

1. On the File menu, point to Add and then click Existing Project. Move to the folder **\Microsoft Press\Visual CSharp Step By Step\Chapter 18\BinaryTree\EnumeratorTest** and click the EnumeratorTest.csproj file. This is the project that you created to test the enumerator you developed manually, earlier in this chapter. Click Open.

2. Right-click the EnumeratorTest project in the Solution Explorer, and then click Set as Startup Project.

3. Expand the References folder for the EnumeratorTest project in the Solution Explorer. Right-click the BinaryTree assembly and then click Remove.

   This action removes the reference to the BinaryTree assembly from the project.

4. On the Project menu, click Add Reference. In the Add Reference dialog box, click the Projects tab. Click the BinaryTree project and then click OK.

   The BinaryTree assembly appears in the list of references for the EnumeratorTest project in the Solution Explorer.

> **Note** These two steps ensure that the EnumeratorTest project references the version of the BinaryTree assembly that uses the iterator to create its enumerator, rather than the earlier version.

5. Review the *Main* method in the Program.cs file. Recall that this method instantiates a *Tree<int>* object, fills it with some data, and then uses a *foreach* statement to display its contents.

6. Build the solution, correcting any errors if necessary.

7. On the Debug menu, click Start Without Debugging.

   When the program runs, the values should be displayed in the same sequence as before:

   −12, −8, 0, 5, 5, 10, 10, 11, 14, 15

8. Press Enter and return to Visual Studio 2005.

- **If you want to continue to the next chapter**

  Keep Visual Studio 2005 running and turn to Chapter 19.

- **If you want to exit Visual Studio 2005 now**

  On the File menu, click Exit. If you see a Save dialog box, click Yes.

Chapter 18 Quick Reference

To	Do this	Example
| Make a class enumerable, allowing it to support the *foreach* construct. | Implement the *IEnumerable* interface and provide a *GetEnumerator* method that returns an *IEnumerator* object. | ```csharp
public class Tree<T>:IEnumerable<T>
{
    ...
    IEnumerator<T> GetEnumerator()
    {
        ...
    }
}
``` |
| Implement an enumerator not by using an iterator. | Define an enumerator class that implements the *IEnumerator* interface and that provides the *Current* property and the *MoveNext* (and *Reset*) methods. | ```csharp
public class TreeEnumerator<T> :
IEnumerator<T>
{
    ...
    T Current
    {
        get
        {
            ...
        }
    }

    bool MoveNext()
    {
        ...
    }
}
``` |
| Define an enumerator by using an iterator. | Implement the enumerator by using the *yield* statement indicating which items should be returned and in which order. | ```csharp
IEnumerator<T> GetEnumerator()
{
    for (...)
        yield return ...
}
``` |
```

Chapter 19
Operator Overloading

After completing this chapter, you will be able to:

- Implement binary operators for your own types.

- Implement unary operators for your own types.

- Write increment and decrement operators for your own types.

- Understand the need to implement some operators as pairs.

- Implement implicit conversion operators for your own types.

- Implement explicit conversion operators for your own types.

You have made a great deal of use of the standard operator symbols (such as + and –) to perform standard operations (such as addition and subtraction) on types (such as *int* and *double*). Many of the built-in types come with their own predefined behaviors for each operator. You can also define operators for your own structs and classes, which is the subject of this chapter.

Understanding Operators

You use operators to combine operands together into expressions. Each operator has its own semantics dependent on the type it works with. For example, the + operator means "add" when used with numeric types, or "concatenate" when used with strings.

Each operator symbol has a precedence. For example, the * operator has a higher precedence than the + operator. This means that the expression a + b * c is the same as a + (b * c).

Each operator symbol also has an associativity to define whether the operator evaluates from left to right or from right to left. For example, the = operator is right-associative (it evaluates from right to left), so a = b = c is the same as a = (b = c).

> **Note** The right-associativity of the = operator allows you to perform multiple assignments in the same statement. For example, you can initialize several variables to the same value like this:
>
> ```
> int a, b, c, d, e;
> a = b = c = d = e = 99;
> ```
>
> The expression e = 99 is evaluated first. The result of the expression is the value that was assigned (99), which is then assigned to *d, c, b,* and finally *a* in that order.

A *unary* operator is an operator that has just one operand. For example, the increment operator (++) is a unary operator.

A *binary* operator is an operator that has two operands. For example, the multiplication operator (*) is a binary operator.

Operator Constraints

C# allows you to overload most of the existing operator symbols for your own types. When you do this, the operators you implement automatically fall into a well-defined framework with the following rules:

- You cannot change the precedence and associativity of an operator. The precedence and associativity are based on the operator symbol (for example, +) and not on the type (for example, *int*) on which the operator symbol is being used. Hence, the expression a + b * c is *always* the same as a + (b * c), regardless of the type of *a*, *b*, and *c*.

- You cannot change the multiplicity of an operator (the number of operands). For example, * (the symbol for multiplication), is a binary operator. If you declare a * operator for your own type, it must be a binary operator.

- You cannot invent new operator symbols. For example, you can't create a new operator symbol, such as ** for raising one number to the power of another number. You'd have to create a method for that.

- You can't change the meaning of operators when applied to built-in types. For example, the expression 1 + 2 has a predefined meaning and you're not allowed to override this meaning. If you could do this, things would be too complicated!

- There are some operator symbols that you can't overload. For example, you can't overload the dot operator (member access). Again, if you could do this, it would lead to unnecessary complexity.

> **Tip** You can use indexers to simulate *[ ]* as an operator. Similarly, you can use properties to simulate = (assignment) as an operator, and you can use delegates to simulate a function call as an operator.

Overloaded Operators

To define your own operator behavior, you must overload a selected operator. You use method-like syntax with a return type and parameters, but the name of the method is the keyword *operator* together with the operator symbol you are declaring. For example, here's a user-defined struct called *Hour* that defines a binary + operator to add together two instances of *Hour*:

```
struct Hour
{
    public Hour(int initialValue)
    {
        this.value = initialValue;
    }

    public static Hour operator+ (Hour lhs, Hour rhs)
    {
        return new Hour(lhs.value + rhs.value);
    }
    ...
    private int value;
}
```

Notice the following:

■ The operator is public. All operators *must* be public.

■ The operator is static. All operators *must* be static. Operators are never polymorphic, and cannot use the *virtual*, *abstract*, *override*, or *sealed* modifiers.

■ A binary operator (such as + shown above) has two explicit arguments and a unary operator has one explicit argument (C++ programmers should note that operators never have a hidden *this* parameter).

> **Tip**   When declaring highly stylized functionality (such as operators), it is useful to adopt a naming convention for the parameters. For example, developers often use *lhs* and *rhs* (acronyms for left-hand side and right-hand side, respectively) for binary operators.

When you use the + operator on two expressions of type *Hour*, the C# compiler automatically converts your code into a call to the user-defined operator. The C# compiler converts this:

```
Hour Example(Hour a, Hour b)
{
    return a + b;
}
```

Into this:

```
Hour Example(Hour a, Hour b)
{
    return Hour.operator+(a,b); // pseudocode
}
```

Note, however, that this syntax is pseudocode and not valid C#. You can use a binary operator only in its standard infix notation (with the symbol between the operands).

There is one final rule you must follow when declaring an operator otherwise your code will not compile: At least one of the parameters should always be of the containing type. In the previous *operator+* example for the *Hour* class, one of the parameters, *a* or *b*, must be an *Hour* object. In this example, both parameters are *Hour* objects. However, there could be times when you want to define additional implementations of *operator+* that add an integer (a number of hours) to an *Hour* object–the first parameter could be *Hour*, and the second parameter could be the integer. This rule makes it easier for the compiler to know where to look when trying to resolve an operator invocation, and it also ensures that you can't change the meaning of the built-in operators.

Creating Symmetric Operators

In the previous section, you saw how to declare a binary + operator to add together two instances of type *Hour*. The *Hour* struct also has a constructor that creates an *Hour* from an *int*. This means that you can add together an *Hour* and an *int*–you just have to first use the *Hour* constructor to convert the *int* into an *Hour*. For example:

```
Hour a = ...;
int b = ...;
Hour sum = a + new Hour(b);
```

This is certainly valid code, but it is not as clear or as concise as adding together an *Hour* and an *int* directly, like this:

```
Hour a = ...;
int b = ...;
Hour sum = a + b;
```

To make the expression (a + b) valid, you must specify what it means to add together an *Hour* (*a*, on the left) and an *int* (*b*, on the right). In other words, you must declare a binary + operator whose first parameter is an *Hour* and whose second parameter is an *int*. The following code shows the recommended approach:

```
struct Hour
{
    public Hour(int initialValue)
    {
        this.value = initialValue;
    }
    ...
    public static Hour operator+ (Hour lhs, Hour rhs)
    {
        return new Hour(lhs.value + rhs.value);
    }

    public static Hour operator+ (Hour lhs, int rhs)
    {
        return lhs + new Hour(rhs);
    }
```

```
    ...
    private int value;
}
```

Notice that all the second version of the operator does is construct an *Hour* from its *int* argument, and then call the first version. In this way, the real logic behind the operator is held in a single place. The point is that the extra *operator+* simply makes existing functionality easier to use. Also, notice that you should not provide many different versions of this operator, each with a different second parameter type—only cater for the common and meaningful cases, and let the user of the class take any additional steps if an unusual case is required.

This *operator+* declares how to add together an *Hour* as the left-hand operand and an *int* as the right-hand operator. It does not declare how to add together an *int* as the left-hand operand and an *Hour* as the right-hand operand:

```
int a = ...;
Hour b = ...;
Hour sum = a + b; // compile-time error
```

This is counter-intuitive. If you can write the expression a + b, you expect to also be able to write b + a. Therefore, you should provide another overload of *operator+*:

```
struct Hour
{
    public Hour(int initialValue)
    {
        this.value = initialValue;
    }
    ...
    public static Hour operator+ (Hour lhs, int rhs)
    {
        return lhs + new Hour(rhs);
    }

    public static Hour operator+ (int lhs, Hour rhs)
    {
        return new Hour(lhs) + rhs;
    }
    ...
    private int value;
}
```

> **Note**   C++ programmers should notice that you must provide the overload yourself. The compiler won't write it for you or silently swap the sequence of the two operands to find a matching operator.

> ## Operators and the Common Language Specification
>
> Not all languages that execute use the common language runtime (CLR) support or understand operator overloading. For this reason, the Common Language Specification (CLS) requires that if you overload an operator, you should provide an alternative mechanism that supports the same functionality as the CLR. For example, suppose you implement *operator+* for the *Hour* struct:
>
> ```
> public static Hour operator+ (Hour lhs, int rhs)
> {
>     ...
> }
> ```
>
> You should also provide an *Add* method that achieves the same thing:
>
> ```
> public static Hour Add(Hour lhs, int rhs)
> {
>     ...
> }
> ```

Understanding Compound Assignment

C# does not allow you to declare any user-defined assignment operators. However, a compound assignment operator (such as +=) is always evaluated in terms of its associated operator (such as +). In other words, this:

```
a += b;
```

Is automatically evaluated as this:

```
a = a + b;
```

In general, the expression a @= b (where @ represents any valid operator) is always evaluated as a = a @ b. If you have declared the appropriate simple operator, it is automatically called when you use its associated compound assignment operator. For example:

```
Hour a = ...;
int b = ...;
a += a; // same as a = a + a
a += b; // same as a = a + b
```

The first compound assignment expression (a += a) is valid because *a* is of type *Hour*, and the *Hour* type declares a binary *operator+* whose parameters are both *Hour*. Similarly, the second compound assignment expression (a += b) is also valid because *a* is of type *Hour* and *b* is of type *int*. The *Hour* type also declares a binary *operator+* whose first parameter is an *Hour* and whose second parameter is an *int*. Note, however, that you cannot write the expression b += a because that's the same as b = b + a. Although the addition is valid, the assignment is not because there is no way to assign an *Hour* to the built-in *int* type.

Declaring Increment and Decrement Operators

C# allows you to declare your own version of the increment (++) and decrement (−−) operators. The usual rules apply when declaring these operators; they must be public, they must be
static, and they must be unary. Here is the increment operator for the *Hour* struct:

```
struct Hour
{
    ...
    public static Hour operator++ (Hour arg)
    {
        arg.value++;
        return arg;
    }
    ...
    private int value;
}
```

The increment and decrement operators are unique in that they can be used in prefix and
postfix forms. C# cleverly uses the same single operator for both the prefix and postfix versions. The result of a postfix expression is the value of the operand *before* the expression takes
place. In other words, the compiler effectively converts this:

```
Hour now = new Hour(9);
Hour postfix = now++;
```

Into this:

```
Hour now = new Hour(9);
Hour postfix = now;
now = Hour.operator++(now); // pseudocode, not valid C#
```

The result of a prefix expression is the return value of the operator. The C# compiler effectively converts this:

```
Hour now = new Hour(9);
Hour prefix = ++now;
```

Into this:

```
Hour now = new Hour(9);
now = Hour.operator++(now); // pseudocode, not valid C#
Hour prefix = now;
```

This equivalence means that the return type of the increment and decrement operators must
be the same as the parameter type.

Operators in Structs and Classes

It is important to realize that the implementation of the increment operator in the *Hour* struct works only because *Hour* is a struct. If you change *Hour* into a class but leave the implementation of its increment operator unchanged, you will find that the postfix translation won't give the correct answer. If you remember that a class is a reference type and revisit the compiler translations explained previously, you can see why this occurs:

```
Hour now = new Hour(9);
Hour postfix = now;
now = Hour.operator++(now); // pseudocode, not valid C#
```

If *Hour* is a class, the assignment statement postfix = now makes the variable *postfix* refer to the same object as *now*. Updating *now* automatically updates *postfix*! If *Hour* is a struct, the assignment statement makes a copy of *now* in *postfix*, and any changes to *now* leave *postfix* unchanged, which is what we want.

The correct implementation of the increment operator when *Hour* is a class is as follows:

```
class Hour
{
    public Hour(int initialValue)
    {
        this.value = initialValue;
    }
    ...
    public static Hour operator++(Hour arg)
    {
        return new Hour(arg.value + 1);
    }
    ...
    private int value;
}
```

Notice that *operator++* now creates a new object based on the data in the original. The data in the new object is incremented but the data in the original is left unchanged. Although this works, the compiler translation of the increment operator results in a new object being created each time it is used. This can be expensive in terms of memory use and garbage collection overhead. Therefore, it is recommended that you limit operator overloads when you define classes.

Defining Operator Pairs

Some operators naturally come in pairs. For example, if you can compare two *Hour* values by using the *!=* operator, you would expect to be able to also compare two *Hour* values by using the *==* operator. The C# compiler enforces this very reasonable expectation by insisting that if you define either *operator==* or *operator!=*, you must define them both. This neither-or-both rule also applies to the < and > operators and the <= and >= operators. The C# compiler does not write any of these operator partners for you. You must write them all explicitly yourself, regardless of how obvious they might seem. Here are the == and != operators for the *Hour* struct:

```
struct Hour
{
    public Hour(int initialValue)
    {
        this.value = initialValue;
    }
    ...
    public static bool operator==(Hour lhs, Hour rhs)
    {
        return lhs.value == rhs.value;
    }

    public static bool operator!=(Hour lhs, Hour rhs)
    {
        return lhs.value != rhs.value;
    }
    ...
    private int value;
}
```

The return type from these operators does not actually have to be Boolean. However, you would have to have a very good reason for using some other type or these operators could become very confusing!

> **Note**   If you define *operator==* and *operator!=*, you should also override the *Equals* and *GetHashCode* methods inherited from *System.Object*. The *Equals* method should exhibit *exactly* the same behavior as *operator==* (define one in terms of the other). The *GetHashCode* method is used by other classes in the .NET Framework. (When you use an object as a key in a hash table for example, the *GetHashCode* method is called on the object to help calculate a hash value. For more information, see the .NET Framework Reference documentation supplied with Visual Studio 2005). All this method needs to do is return a distinguishing integer value (don't return the same integer from the *GetHashCode* method of all your objects though as this will reduce the effectiveness of the hashing algorithms).

Implementing an Operator

In the following exercise, you will complete another Microsoft Windows digital clock application. This version of the code is similar to the exercise in Chapter 16, "Delegates and Events." However, in this version, the *delegate* method (which is called every second) does not receive the current *hour*, *minute*, and *second* values when the event is raised. Instead, the *delegate* method keeps track of the time itself by updating three fields, one each for the *hour*, *minute*, and *second* values. The type of these three fields is *Hour*, *Minute*, and *Second*, respectively, and they are all structs. However, the application will not yet compile because the *Minute* struct is not finished. In the first exercise, you will finish the *Minute* struct by implementing its missing addition operators.

Write the operator+ overloads

1. Start Microsoft Visual Studio 2005 if it is not already running.

2. Open the *Operators* project, located in the \Microsoft Press\Visual CSharp Step by Step\Chapter 19\Operators folder in your My Documents folder.

3. In the Code and Text Editor window, open the Clock.cs source file and locate the declarations of the *hour*, *minute*, and *second* fields at the end of the class.

   These fields hold the clock's current time:

   ```
   class Clock
   {
       ...
       private Hour hour;
       private Minute minute;
       private Second second;
   }
   ```

4. Locate the tock method of the Clock class. This method is called every second to update the hour, minute, and seconds variables.

   The *tock* method looks like this:

   ```
   private void tock()
   {
       this.second++;
       if (this.second == 0)
       {
           this.minute++;
           if (this.minute == 0)
           {
               this.hour++;
           }
       }
   }
   ```

   The constructors for the *Clock* class contain the following statement that arranges for this method to be called whenever the *tick* event of the *pulsed* field is raised (the *pulsed* field is a *Ticker*, that uses a *Timer* object to generate an event every second, as described in the exercises in Chapter 16.

   ```
   this.pulsed.tick += tock;
   ```

5. On the Build menu, click Build Solution.

   The project builds but displays the following error message in the Output pane:

   ```
   Operator '==' cannot be applied to operands of type 'Operators.Minute' and 'int'.
   ```

The problem is that the *tock* method contains the following *if* statement, but the appropriate *operator==* is not declared in the *Minute* struct:

```
if (minute == 0)
{
    hour++;
}
```

Your next task is to implement this operator for the *Minute* struct.

6. In the Code and Text Editor window, open the Minute.cs file.

7. In the Code and Text Editor window, implement a version of *operator==* that accepts a *Minute* as its left-hand operand and an *int* as its right-hand operand. Don't forget that the return type of this operator should be a bool.

The completed operator should look exactly as shown in the following class:

```
struct Minute
{
    ...
    public static bool operator== (Minute lhs, int rhs)
    {
        return lhs.value == rhs;
    }
    ...
    private int value;
}
```

8. On the Build menu, click Build Solution.

The project builds but displays the following error message in the Output pane:

```
The operator 'Operators.Minute.operator ==(Operators.Minute, int)' requires a matching
    operator "!=" to also be defined.
```

There is a still an error. The problem is that you have implemented a version of *operator==* but have not implemented its required *operator!=* partner.

9. Implement a version of operator!= that accepts a Minute as its left-hand operand and an int as its right-hand operand.

The completed operator should look exactly like this:

```
struct Minute
{
    ...
    public static bool operator!= (Minute lhs, int rhs)
    {
        return lhs.value != rhs;
    }
    ...
    private int value;
}
```

10. On the Build menu, click Build Solution.

    This time, the application builds without errors.

11. On the Debug menu, click Start Without Debugging.

    The application runs and displays a digital clock that updates itself every second.

12. Close the application and return to the Visual Studio 2005 programming environment.

Understanding Conversion Operators

Sometimes it is necessary to convert an expression of one type into another. For example, the following method is declared with a single *double* parameter:

```
class Example
{
    public static void MyDoubleMethod(double parameter)
    {
        ...
    }
}
```

You might reasonably expect that only values of type *double* could be used as arguments when calling *MyDoubleMethod*, but this is not so. The C# compiler also allows *MyDoubleMethod* to be called with an argument whose type is not *double*, but only as long as that value can be converted to a *double*. The compiler will generate code that performs this conversion when the method is called.

Providing Built-In Conversions

The built-in types have some built-in conversions. For example, an *int* can be implicitly converted to a *double*. An implicit conversion requires no special syntax and never throws an exception:

```
Example.MyDoubleMethod(42); // implicit int to double conversion
```

An implicit conversion is sometimes called a *widening conversion*, as the result is wider than the original value—it contains at least as much information as the original value, and nothing is lost.

On the other hand, a *double* cannot be implicitly converted to an *int*:

```
class Example
{
    public static void MyIntMethod(int parameter)
    {
        ...
    }
}
```

```
...
Example.MyIntMethod(42.0); // compile-time error
```

Converting from a *double* to an *int* runs the risk of losing information, so it will not be done automatically (consider what would happen if the argument to *MyIntMethod* was 42.5—how should this be converted?) A *double* can be converted to an *int*, but the conversion requires an explicit notation (a cast):

```
Example.MyIntMethod((int)42.0);
```

An explicit conversion is sometimes called a *narrowing conversion* as the result is narrower than the original value (it can contain less information), and can throw an *OverflowException*. C# allows you to provide conversion operators for your own user-defined types to control whether they can be implicitly or explicitly converted to other types.

Implementing User-Defined Conversion Operators

The syntax for declaring a user-defined conversion operator is similar to an overloaded operator. A conversion operator must be *public* and must also be *static*. Here's a conversion operator that allows an *Hour* object to be implicitly converted into an *int*:

```
struct Hour
{
    ...
    public static implicit operator int (Hour from)
    {
        return this.value;
    }

    private int value;
}
```

The type you are converting from is declared as the single parameter (in this case, *Hour*), and the type you are converting to is declared as the type name after the keyword *operator* (in this case, *int*). There is no return type specified before the keyword *operator*.

When declaring your own conversion operators, you must specify whether they are implicit conversion operators or explicit conversion operators. You do this by using the *implicit* and *explicit* keywords. For example, the *Hour* to *int* conversion operator mentioned previously is implicit, meaning that the C# compiler can use it implicitly (without a cast):

```
class Example
{
    public static void Method(int parameter) { ... }
    public static void Main()
    {
        Hour lunch = new Hour(12);
        Example.MyOtherMethod(lunch); // implicit Hour to int conversion
    }
}
```

If the conversion operator had been declared *explicit*, the previous example would not have compiled because an explicit conversion operator requires an explicit cast:

```
Example.MyOtherMethod((int)lunch); // explicit Hour to int conversion
```

When should you declare a conversion operator as explicit or implicit? If a conversion is always safe, does not run the risk of losing information, and cannot throw an exception, then it can be defined as an *implicit* conversion. Otherwise, it should be declared as an *explicit* conversion. Converting from an *Hour* to an *int* is always safe—every *Hour* has a corresponding *int* value—so it makes sense for it to be implicit. An operator that converted a *string* to an *Hour* should be explicit, as not all strings represent valid *Hours*. (While the string "7" is fine, how would you convert the string "Hello, World" into an *Hour*?)

Creating Symmetric Operators Revisited

Conversion operators provide you with an alternate way to resolve the problem of providing symmetric operators. For example, instead of providing three versions of *operator+* (*Hour + Hour, Hour + int*, and *int + Hour*) for the *Hour* struct as shown earlier, you can provide a single version of *operator+* (that takes two *Hour* parameters) and an implicit *int* to *Hour* conversion, like this:

```
struct Hour
{
    public Hour(int initialValue)
    {
        this.value = initialValue;
    }

    public static Hour operator+(Hour lhs, Hour rhs)
    {
        return new Hour(lhs.value + rhs.value);
    }

    public static implicit operator Hour (int from)
    {
        return new Hour (from);
    }
    ...
    private int value;
}
```

If you add an *Hour* and an *int* (in either order), the C# compiler automatically converts the *int* to an *Hour* and then calls *operator+* with two *Hour* arguments:

```
void Example(Hour a, int b)
{
    Hour eg1 = a + b; // b converted to an Hour     Hour eg2 = b + a; //
    b converted to an Hour
}
```

Adding an Implicit Conversion Operator

In the following exercise, you will modify the digital clock application from the previous exercise. You will add an implicit conversion operator to the *Second* struct and remove the operators that it replaces.

Write the conversion operator

1. Return to Visual Studio 2005 displaying the Operators project. Display the Clock.cs file in the Code and Text Editor window and examine the tock method again:

```
private void tock()
{
    this.second++;
    if (this.second == 0)
    {
        this.minute++;
        if (this.minute == 0)
        {
            this.hour++;
        }
    }
}
```

Notice the statement if (this.second == 0). This fragment of code compares a *Second* to an *int* using the == operator.

2. In the Code pane, open the Second.cs source file.

The *Second* struct currently contains three overloaded implementations of *operator==* and three overloaded implementations of *operator!=*. Each operator is overloaded for the parameter type pairs (*Second*, *Second*), (*Second*, *int*), and (*int*, *Second*).

3. In the Code and Text Editor window, delete the versions of *operator==* and operator!= that take one *Second* and one *int* parameter (do not delete the operators that take two *Second* parameters). The following three operators should be the only versions of operator== and operator!= in the *Second* struct:

```
struct Second
{
    ...
    public static bool operator==(Second lhs, Second rhs)
    {
        return lhs.value == rhs.value;
    }

    public static bool operator!=(Second lhs, Second rhs)
    {
        return lhs.value != rhs.value;
    }

    public static bool operator++(Second lhs, Second rhs)
    {
        return lhs.value ++ rhs.value;
    }
    ...
}
```

4. On the Build menu, click Build Solution.

    The build fails with the message:

    ```
    Operator '==' cannot be applied to the operands of type 'Operators.Second' and 'int'
    ```

    Removing the operators that compare a *Second* and an *int* cause the statement highlighted earlier to fail to compile.

5. In the Code and Text Editor window, add an implicit conversion operator to the *Second* struct that converts from an *int* to a *Second*.

    The conversion operator should look like this:

    ```
    struct Second
    {
        ...
        public static implicit operator Second (int arg)
        {
            return new Second(arg);
        }
        ...
    }
    ```

6. On the Build menu, click Build Solution and correct any errors.

    The program successfully builds this time because the conversion operator and the remaining two operators together provide the same functionality as the four deleted operator overloads. The only difference is that using an implicit conversion operator is potentially a little slower than not using an implicit conversion operator.

7. On the Debug menu, click Start Without Debugging.

    Verify that the application still runs.

8. Close the application and return to the Visual Studio 2005 programming environment.

■ **If you want to continue to the next chapter**

    Keep Visual Studio 2005 running and turn to Chapter 20.

■ **If you want to exit Visual Studio 2005 now**

    On the File menu, click Exit. If you see a Save dialog box, click Yes.

Chapter 19 Quick Reference

To	Do this
Implement an operator.	Write the keywords public and static, followed by the return type, followed by the operator keyword, followed by the operator symbol being declared, followed by the appropriate parameters between parentheses. For example:

```
struct Hour
{
    ...
    public static bool operator==(Hour lhs,
        Hour rhs)s
    {
        ...
    }
    ...
}
```

| Declare a conversion operator. | Write the keywords public and static, followed by the keyword implicit or explicit, followed by the operator keyword, followed by the type being converted to, followed by the type being converted from as a single parameter between parentheses. For example: |

```
struct Hour
{
    ...
    public static implicit operator Hour(int arg)
    {
        ...
    }
    ...
}
```

Part IV
Working with Windows Applications

Introducing Windows Forms

After completing this chapter, you will be able to:

- Create Windows Forms applications.

- Use common Windows Forms controls such as labels, text boxes, and buttons.

- Change the properties of Windows Forms and controls at design time and programmatically at run time.

- Subscribe to and process events exposed by Windows Forms and controls.

Now that you have completed the exercises and examined the examples in the first three parts of this book, you should be well-versed in the Microsoft Visual C# language. You have learned how to write programs and create components by using C#, and you should understand many of the finer points of the language, such as the differences between value types and reference types. Because you now have the essential language skills, Part IV will show you how to expand upon them and use C# to take advantage of the graphical user interface (GUI) libraries provided as part of the Microsoft .NET Framework. In particular, you will see how to use the objects in the *System.Windows.Forms* namespace to create Windows Forms applications.

In this chapter, you will learn how to build a basic Windows Forms application using the common components that are a feature of most GUI applications. You will see how to set the properties of Windows Forms and components by using the Visual Designer and the Properties windows. You'll also learn how to change or examine the values of these properties dynamically by using C# code. Finally, you will learn how to intercept and handle some of the common events that Windows Forms and components expose.

Creating Your Application

As an example, you are going to create an application that allows a user to input and display details for members of the Middleshire Bell Ringers Association, an esteemed collection of the finest campanologists. Initially you will keep the application very simple, concentrating on laying out the form and making sure that it all works. In later chapters, you will provide menus and learn how to implement validation to ensure that the data that is entered makes sense. The following graphic shows what the application will look like after you have completed it. (You can see the completed version by running *BellRingers.exe*, located in the \Microsoft Press\Visual CSharp Step by Step\Chapter 20\BellRingers Complete\ BellRingers\bin\Debug folder in your My Documents folder.)

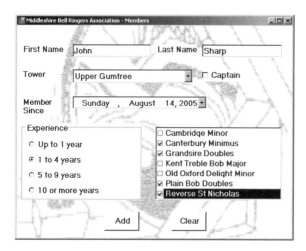

Creating a Windows Forms Application

In this exercise, you'll start building the Middleshire Bell Ringers Association application by creating a new project, laying out the form, and adding Windows Forms controls to the form. Because you have been using existing Windows Forms applications in Microsoft Visual Studio 2005 in previous chapters, much of the first couple of exercises will be a review for you.

Create the Middleshire Bell Ringers Association project

1. Start Visual Studio 2005.

2. On the File menu, point to New, and then click Project.

3. In the Project Types pane, select Visual C#.

4. In the Templates pane, select Windows Application.

5. In the Name text box, type **BellRingers**.

6. In the Location list box, navigate to the Microsoft Press\Visual CSharp Step by Step\Chapter 20 folder in your My Documents folder. .

7. Click OK.

   The new project is created and contains a blank form called *Form1*.

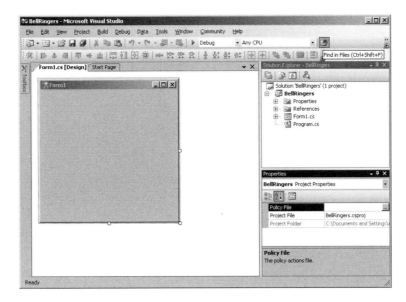

Set the properties of the form

1. Select the form in the Designer View window. In the Properties window, click the *(Name)* property, and then type **MemberForm** in the (Name) text box to change the name of the form. (If the Properties window is not displayed, click Properties Window on the View menu, or press F4.)

2. In the Properties window, click the *Text* property, and then type **Middleshire Bell Ringers Association – Members**, to change the text in the title bar of the form.

3. In the Properties window, click the *BackgroundImage* property, and then click the Ellipses button in the adjacent text box.

    The Select Resource dialog box opens.

4. In the Select Resource dialog box, click Local resource and then click Import.

    The Open dialog box opens.

5. In the Open dialog box, navigate to the \Microsoft Press\Visual CSharp Step by Step\Chapter 20 folder in your My Documents folder, select the Bell.gif file, and then click Open.

    Part of the image will be displayed in the Select Resource dialog box.

6. In the Select Resource dialog box, click OK.

    The *BackgroundImage* property is now set to the bell image.

7. In the Properties window, click the *BackColor* property, and then click the down-arrow button in the adjacent text box.

    A dialog box opens.

8. On the System tab of the dialog box, click Window. This value sets the background color of all the controls that you drop onto the form to the same color as the window itself.

9. Select the *Font* property. This is a composite property that has many attributes. In the Properties window, click the plus sign (+) to expand the *Font* property and display the attributes. Type **12** for the *Size* attribute of the font, and set the *Bold* attribute to *True*.

> **Tip** You can also change some composite properties, such as *Font*, by clicking the ellipses button that appears when you select the property. When you click the ellipses button in the *Font* property, the standard Font dialog box opens and allows you to select the font and effects that you want.

10. Change the form's *Size* property, which is also a composite property. In the Properties window, click the plus sign (+) to expand the *Size* property and display the attributes. Set the Width attribute to 600 and the Height attribute to 470.

The form should look like the image in the following graphic.

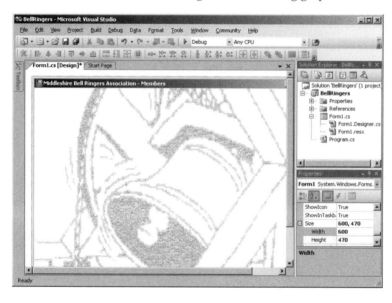

11. On the Build menu, click Build Solution.

The form should build successfully.

12. On the Debug menu, click Start Without Debugging.

The application will start running and will display the main form containing the image. The form does not do anything useful yet, so close it and return to Visual Studio.

How a Windows Forms Application Runs

A Windows Forms application can comprise any number of forms—you can add additional forms to an application by using the Add Windows Form command on the Project menu in Visual Studio 2005. How does an application know which form to display when an application starts?

If you look in the Solution Explorer, you will see another file called Program.cs. You can right-click this file and select View Code to display its contents in the Code And Text Editor window. This file contains the *Main* method, defining the entry point for the application. The key statement in this method is:

```
Application.Run(new MemberForm());
```

This statement creates a new instance of *MemberForm* and displays it. When the form closes, the *Application.Run* statement terminates, and as this is the final statement in *Main*, the program exits.

> **Tip**   If you have previously developed applications using Visual Basic 6, you will know that in that application, you can designate a form as the default form; this form is displayed automatically when the application starts. There is no such option in Visual Studio 2005. If you want to change the form that a .NET Framework application runs when an application starts, edit the *Application.Run* statement in the *Main* method.

You should only use the *Application.Run* statement for displaying the initial form for an application. If you have defined additional forms, you can display them from your own code, typically in an event handler, using the *Show* method inherited by all Windows Forms objects. For example, if you have added another form called *AnotherForm* to your application, you can display it like this:

```
AnotherForm aForm =  new AnotherForm();
aForm.Show();
```

What Are the Common Windows Forms Properties?

If you look closely at the Properties window when a form is selected, you can see that there are over fifty properties available. Some of them are fairly obvious; for example, the Text property that corresponds to the text displayed in the form's title bar. Some properties are useful under certain circumstances; for example, you can remove the Minimize, Maximize, and Close buttons, or remove the System menu from the title bar of a form by setting the *ControlBox* property to *False*–useful if you want to ensure users cannot close the form unless they execute some code that closes it explicitly. Other properties apply to very specific circumstances; for example, the *Opacity* property can be used to control the level of transparency of the form. The following table describes some of the common form properties that you can change at design time. You should also be aware that there are additional properties not listed in the Properties window that you can use only programmatically at run time. For example, the *ActiveControl* property shows which control in the form currently has the focus.

Property	Description
(Name)	The name of the form. Two forms in the same project cannot have the same name.
BackColor	The default background color of any text and graphics in the form.
BackgroundImage	A bitmap, icon, or other graphic file to be used as a backdrop to the form. If the image is smaller than the form, it can be tiled to fill the form, stretched, centered, or zoomed by using the *BackgroundImageLayout* property.
Font	The default font used by the controls embedded on the form that display text. This is a compound property—you can set many attributes of the font including the font name, size, and whether the font appears italic, bold, or underlined.
ForeColor	The default foreground color of any text and graphics in the form.
FormBorderStyle	This controls the appearance and type of border of the form. The default setting is Sizable. Other options specify borders that are not resizable or do not have the various System menu buttons.
Icon	This specifies the icon that appears in the form's System menu and on the Microsoft Windows taskbar. You can create your own icons by using Visual Studio 2005.
Location	This is another compound property that specifies the coordinates of the top left corner of the form with respect to its container, which might be another form or the screen.
MaximizeBox	This property specifies whether the Maximize command on the System menu and caption bar is enabled or disabled. By default, it is enabled.
MaximumSize	This specifies the maximum size of the form. The default value (0, 0) indicates that there is no maximum size and the user can resize the form to any size.
MinimizeBox	This property is similar to the *MaximizeBox* property. It specifies whether the Minimize command on the System menu and title bar is enabled or disabled. By default, it is enabled.
MinimumSize	This property specifies the minimum size of the form.

Property	Description
Size	This is the default size of the form when it is first displayed.
Text	This property contains the text that appears on the title bar of the form.
WindowState	This property determines the initial state of the form when it is first displayed. The default state (Normal) positions the form according to the *Location* and *Size* properties. The other options are Minimized and Maximized.

> **Tip** You can view a summary of a property by selecting the property in the Properties window, right-clicking it, and then clicking Description. A pane displaying a description of any selected property appears at the bottom of the Properties window. Clicking Description again hides the description of the property.

Changing Properties Programmatically

In addition to setting properties statically at design time, you can write code that changes properties dynamically at run time. For example, you can change the *Size* property of a form in your program to make it shrink or grow without the user dragging the border to resize it. In actual fact, if you look at the code behind the form, you will see that Visual Studio 2005 generates code to change the properties of a form at run time according to the values you specify at design time. If you click the + sign adjacent to Form1.cs in the Solution Explorer you will see the file Form1.Designer.cs (you will also see Form1.resx which contains information about resources, such as bitmaps, used by your application). Right-click the file Form1.Designer.cs and click View Code to display the generated code. You already saw this code in Chapter 1, "Welcome to C#," but now you can start to appreciate what it actually does.

In this code, you will notice that the form is simply a class that contains a private *System.ComponentModel.IContainer* variable, called *components*, and a *Dispose* method. *IContainer* is an interface that includes a collection for holding references to the components belonging to the form. The *Dispose* method implements the disposal pattern described in Chapter 13, "Using Garbage Collection and Resource Management," to quickly release any unmanaged resources used by the form when it is closed.

Expanding the Windows Forms Designer generated code region reveals another method called *InitializeComponent*. If you expand this method, you can see how the property values you specified in the Properties window are translated into code. Later, when you add additional controls to the form, code will be inserted into this method to create them and set their properties as well. If you change the values in the Properties window, Visual Studio 2005 will keep the code in this method synchronized with your changes.

> **Important** You should not modify the code in the *InitializeComponent* method, or anywhere else in the Windows Forms Designer-generated code region. If you do, the changes you make will likely be lost the next time any property values are amended in Design View.

You should notice that the code in Form1.Designer.cs is actually a partial class, used to separate the statements and methods generated by Visual Studio from your own code. In the Solution Explorer, right-click Form1.cs and then click View Code to display the file that you add your own methods and fields to. You will see that this file already contains a default constructor that simply calls the *InitializeComponent* method to create and layout the form at runtime.

Adding Controls to the Form

So far you have created a form, set some of its properties, and examined the code that Visual Studio 2005 generates. To make the form useful, you need to add controls and write some code of your own. The Windows Forms library contains a varied collection of controls. The purposes of some are fairly obvious—for example, *TextBox*, *ListBox*, *CheckBox*, and *ComboBox*—whereas other, more powerful controls (such as the *DateTimePicker*) might not be so familiar.

Using Windows Forms Controls

In the next exercise, you will add controls to the form that allow a user to input member details. You will use a variety of different controls, each suited to a particular type of data entry.

You will use *TextBox* controls for entering the first name and last name of the member. Each member belongs to a "tower" (where bells hang). The Middleshire district has several towers, but the list is static—new towers are not built very often and hopefully, old towers do not to fall down with any great frequency. The ideal control for handling this type of data is a *ComboBox*. The form also records whether the member is the tower "captain" (the person in charge of the tower who conducts the other ringers). A *CheckBox* is the best sort of control for this; it can either be selected (*True*) or cleared (*False*).

> **Tip**   *CheckBox* controls can actually have three states if the *ThreeState* property is set to *True*. The states are *True*, *False*, and *Indeterminate*. These states are useful if you are displaying information that has been retrieved from a relational database. Some columns in a table in a database allow *null* values, indicating that the value held is not defined or is unknown. If you want to display this data in a *CheckBox*, you can use the *Indeterminate* state to handle *null* values.

The application also gathers statistical information about when members joined the association and how much bell ringing experience they have (up to one year, between one and four years, between five and nine years, and ten or more years). A *DateTimePicker* control is very suitable for selecting and displaying dates, and a group of options, or radio buttons, is useful for indicating the member's experience—radio buttons provide a mutually exclusive set of values.

Finally, the application records the tunes the member can ring—rather confusingly, these tunes are referred to as "methods" by the bell-ringing fraternity. Although a bell ringer only rings one bell at a time, a group of bell ringers under the direction of the tower captain can ring their bells in different sequences and generally play simple music. There are a variety of bell ringing methods, and they have names like Canterbury Minimus, Plain Bob Doubles, and Old Oxford Delight Minor. New methods are being written with alarming regularity, so the list of methods can vary over time. In a real-world application, you would store this list in a database. In this application, you will use a small selection of methods that you will hard-wire into the form. (You will see how to use databases in the next part of the book.) A good control for displaying this information and indicating whether a member can ring a method is the *CheckedListBox*.

When the user has entered the member's details, the Add button will validate and store the data. The user can click Clear to reset the controls on the form and cancel any data entered.

Add Windows Forms controls

1. Ensure that Form1 is displayed in the Designer View window. Using the Toolbox, verify that the Common Controls category is expanded, and then drag a *Label* control onto *MemberForm*. (If the Toolbox is not displayed, click Toolbox from the View menu, or click the Toolbox tab in the left-hand border of Visual Studio.)

2. In the Properties window, click the *Location* property, and then type **10,40** to set the *Location* property of the label.

3. From the Toolbox, drag a *TextBox* control onto *MemberForm*, to the right of the label. Do not worry about aligning the *TextBox* exactly because you will set the *Location* property for this and the following controls later.

> **Tip**   You can use the guide lines displayed by the Designer to help align controls.

4. Add a second *Label* to the form. Place it to the right of the *TextBox*.

5. Add another *TextBox* to *MemberForm* and position it to the right of the second *Label*.

6. From the Toolbox, drag a third *Label* onto the form. Place it directly under the first *Label*.

7. From the Toolbox, drag a *ComboBox* control onto the form. Place it on *MemberForm* under the first *TextBox* and to the right of the third *Label*.

8. From the Toolbox, drag a *CheckBox* control onto the form and place it under the second *TextBox*.

9. Add a fourth *Label* to *MemberForm* and place it under the third *Label*.

10. From the Toolbox, drag a *DateTimePicker* control and place it under the *ComboBox*.

11. In the Toolbox, expand the Containers category. Drag a *GroupBox* control from the Toolbox and place it under the fourth *Label* control.

12. From the Common Controls category in the Toolbox, drag the *RadioButton* control and place it inside the *GroupBox* control you just added.

13. Add three more *RadioButton* controls, vertically aligned with each other, to the *GroupBox*. You might need to make the *GroupBox* bigger to accommodate them.

14. From the Toolbox, drag a *CheckedListBox* control and place it under the second *Label* and to the right of the *GroupBox* control.

15. From the Toolbox, drag a *Button* control and place it near the bottom on the lower-left side of *MemberForm*.

16. Add another *Button* control to the bottom of the form, just to the right of the first.

Setting Control Properties

You now need to set the properties of the controls you just added to the form. To change the value of a control's property, click the control on the form to select it, and then enter the correct value in the Properties window. You will start with the basic properties. The following table lists the properties and values you need to assign to each of the controls.

Control	Property	Value
label1	Text	First Name
	Location	10, 40
textBox1	(Name)	firstName
	Location	120, 40
	Size	170, 26
label2	Text	Last Name
	Location	300, 40
textbox2	(Name)	lastName
	Location	400, 40
	Size	170, 26
label3	Text	Tower
	Location	10, 92
comboBox1	(Name)	towerNames
	DropDownStyle	DropDownList (This setting forces users to pick one of the items in the list; users cannot type in a value of their own.)
	Location	120, 92
	Size	260, 28
checkBox1	(Name)	isCaptain

Control	Property	Value
	Location	400, 92
	Text	**Captain**
	CheckAlign	**MiddleLeft** (This property specifies the location of the checkbox relative to the text in the control. When you click the drop-down arrow for this property, an interesting graphic containing a grid appears. Click the left square in the middle row.)
label4	Text	**Member**
		Since (This text should be split over two lines. You can click the drop-down arrow in this property to display a simple text editor that also allows you to enter multi-line text values)
	Location	**10, 148**
DateTimePicker	(Name)	**memberSince**
	Location	**120, 148**
	Size	**290, 26**
groupBox1	(Name)	**yearsExperience**
	Location	**10, 204**
	Size	**260, 160**
	Text	**Experience**
radioButton1	(Name)	**novice**
	Location	**16, 32** (Note that this location is relative to the radio button's container, the *experience GroupBox*.)
	Text	**Up to 1 year**
radioButton2	(Name)	**intermediate**
	Location	**16, 64**
	Text	**1 to 4 years**
radioButton3	(Name)	**experienced**
	Location	**16, 96**
	Text	**5 to 9 years**
radioButton4	(Name)	**accomplished**
	Location	**16, 128**

Control	Property	Value
	Text	10 or more years
checkedListBox1	(Name)	methods
	Location	300, 212
	Size	270, 165
	Sorted	True
button1	(Name)	Add
	Location	190, 388
	Size	75, 40
	Text	Add
button2	(Name)	Clear
	Location	335, 388
	Size	75, 40
	Text	Clear

It is a good idea to save your project at this point.

Control Properties

As you have just seen, like forms, controls have many properties that you can set. Each different type of control has different properties. Also, like forms, you can set and query control properties dynamically in your own programs, and there are a number of properties that are available only at run time. If you want to learn more about the different properties available for each type of control, you can find a list of them in the MSDN Library for Visual Studio 2005 supplied with Visual Studio 2005.

Changing Properties Dynamically

You have been using the Design View to set properties statically. When the form runs, it would be useful to reset the value of each control to an initial default value. To do this, you will need to write some code (at last). In the following exercises, you will create a *private* method called *Reset*. Later, you will invoke the *Reset* method when the form first starts, and when the user clicks the Clear button.

Rather than coding the method from scratch, you will use the Class Diagram editor to generate the method. The Class Diagram editor provides a schematic way to view and amend classes.

Create the *Reset* method

1. In the Solution Explorer, right-click Form1.cs. A menu appears.

2. On the menu, click View Class Diagram.

    A new class diagram appears displaying the MemberForm class.

3. Right-click the MemberForm class in the diagram, point to Add, and then click Method. The MemberForm class expands to display a list of all defined methods (*Dispose*, *InitializeComponent*, and the *MemberForm* constructor). A new method, simply called *Method*, is added. Change the name of this method to Reset by overtyping the name and pressing the Enter key.

4. In the Class Details pane that appears underneath the class diagram, verify that the Type of the Reset method is *void*, and that the Modifier is *public*. If they are wrong, you can click these fields in the Class Details pane and modify them.

> **Tip**   The Class Details pane sometimes shares the same window as the Error List pane. If the Class Details pane is not visible, click the Class Details tab below the Error List pane to display it.

The following graphic shows the class diagram with the new method added:

5. In the Class Details pane that appears underneath In the Class Diagram, right-click the Reset method and then click View Code.

   You are placed in the Code and Text Editor window displaying the MemberForm class. The *Reset* method has been added with a default implementation that throws a *NotImplementedException*:

   ```
   public void Reset()
   {
       throw new System.NotImplementedException();
   }
   ```

6. In the Code And Text Editor window, replace the *throw* statement in the *Reset* method with the following lines of code:

   ```
   firstName.Text = "";
   lastName.Text = "";
   ```

   These two statements ensure that the *firstName* and *lastName* text boxes are blank by assigning an empty string to their *Text* property.

Programming the User Interface

You now need to configure the properties of the remaining controls on the form. You will do this programmatically.

Populating the *ComboBox*   If you recall, the *towerName ComboBox* will contain a list of all the bell towers in the Middleshire district. This information would usually be held in a database and you would write code to retrieve the list of towers and populate the *ComboBox*. Because you have not been shown how to access a database yet, the application will use a hard-coded collection.

A *ComboBox* has a property called *Items* that contains a list of the data to be displayed. In the *Reset* method, after the code you have already written, add the following statements to clear this list (this is important because otherwise you would end up with many duplicate values in the list) and create four items in the *ComboBox*:

```
towerNames.Items.Clear();
towerNames.Items.Add("Great Shevington");
towerNames.Items.Add("Little Mudford");
towerNames.Items.Add("Upper Gumtree");
towerNames.Items.Add("Downley Hatch");
```

Set the current date   The next step is to initialize the *memberSince DateTimePicker* control to the current date. The date can be set by using the *Value* property. You can obtain the current date by using the static property *Today* of the *DateTime* class. Add the following statement to the *Reset* method:

```
memberSince.Value = DateTime.Today;
```

Initialize the *CheckBox*   The *isCaptain CheckBox* should default to *False*. To do this, you need to set the *Checked* property. Add the following statement to the *Reset* method:

```
isCaptain.Checked = false;
```

Initialize the radio button group   The form contains four radio buttons that indicate the number of years of bell ringing experience the member has. A radio button is similar to a *CheckBox* in that it can contain a *True* or *False* value. However, the power of radio buttons increases when you put them together in a *GroupBox*. In this case, the radio buttons form a mutually exclusive collection—at most, only one radio button in a group can be selected (set to *true*), and all the others will automatically be cleared (set to *false*). By default, none of the buttons will be selected. You should rectify this by setting the *Checked* property of the *novice* radio button. Add the following statement to the *Reset* method:

```
novice.Checked = true;
```

Fill the *ListBox*   Like the Tower *ComboBox*, the *CheckedListBox* containing the list of bell ringing methods has a property called *Items* that contains a collection of values to be displayed. Also, like the *ComboBox*, it could be populated from a database. However, as before, you will supply some hard-coded values for now. Complete the *Reset* method by adding the following code:

```
methods.Items.Clear();
methods.Items.Add("Canterbury Minimus");
methods.Items.Add("Reverse St Nicholas");
methods.Items.Add("Plain Bob Doubles");
methods.Items.Add("Grandsire Doubles");
methods.Items.Add("Cambridge Minor");
methods.Items.Add("Old Oxford Delight Minor");
methods.Items.Add("Kent Treble Bob Major");
```

Call the *Reset* method   You need to arrange for the *Reset* method to be called when the form is first displayed. A good place to do this is in the *MemberForm* constructor. In the Code And Text Editor window, scroll to the beginning of the *MemberForm* class in the file Form1.cs, and find the constructor (it is called *MemberForm*, just like the class). Insert a call to the *Reset* method after the statement that calls the *InitializeComponent* method:

```
this.Reset();
```

Compile and test the application

1.   It is a good practice to name the file containing a form after the form itself. In the Solution Explorer, right-click Form1.cs, click Rename, and then type **MemberForm.cs**.

2.   On the Debug menu, click Start Without Debugging to verify that the project compiles and runs.

3.   When the form runs, click the Tower *ComboBox*.

     You will see the list of bell towers, and you can select one of them.

4. Click the drop-down arrow on the right side of the Member Since date/time picker.

   You will be presented with a calendar of dates. The default value will be the current date. You can click a date, and use the arrows to select a month. You can also click the month name to display the months as a drop-down list, and click the year to allow you to select a year using a numeric up-down control.

5. Click each of the radio buttons in the Experience group.

   Notice that you cannot select more than one at a time.

6. In the Methods list box, click some of the methods and select the corresponding check box. You will have to click once to select a method and a second time to select or clear the checkbox.

7. Close the form and return to Visual Studio 2005.

Publishing Events in Windows Forms

If you are familiar with Microsoft Visual Basic, Microsoft Foundation Classes (MFC), or any of the other tools available for building GUI applications for Windows, you are aware that Windows uses an event-driven model to determine when to execute code. In Chapter 16, "Delegates and Events," you saw how to publish your own events and subscribe to them. Windows Forms and controls have their own predefined events that you can subscribe to, and these events should be sufficient to handle most eventualities.

Processing Events in Windows Forms

Your task as a developer is to capture the events that you feel are relevant to your application and write the code that responds to these events. A familiar example is the *Button* control, which raises a "Somebody clicked the button" event when a user clicks it with the mouse or presses Enter when the button has the focus. If you want the button to do something, you write code that responds to this event. This is what you will do in the final exercise in this chapter.

Handle the *Click* event for the Clear button

1. In Design View (on the View menu, click Designer), select the Clear button on *Member-Form*.

   When the user clicks the Clear button, you want the form to be reset to its default values.

2. In the Properties window, click the Events button.

Event button

List of events

The list of properties is replaced with a list of events that you can intercept.

3. Select the *Click* event.

4. Type **clearClick** in the text box and press Enter.

A new event method called *clearClick* is created and displayed in the Code And Text Editor window. Notice that the event method conforms to the convention in that it takes two parameters: the sender (an *object*) and additional arguments (an *EventArgs*). The Windows Forms runtime will populate these parameters with information about the source of the event and any additional information that might be useful when handling the event. You will not use these parameters in this exercise.

5. In the body of the *clearClick* method, call the *Reset* method.

The body of the method now should look exactly like this:

```
private void clearClick(object sender, System.EventArgs e)
{
    this.Reset();
}
```

Handle the *Click* event for the Add button

The users will click the Add button when they have filled in all the data for a member and want to store the information. The *Click* event should validate the information entered to ensure it makes sense (for example, should you allow a tower captain to have less than one year of experience?) and, if it is okay, arrange for the data to be sent to a database or other persistent store. You will learn more about validation and storing data in later chapters. For now, the code for the *Click* event of the Add button will display a message box echoing the data input.

1. Return to Design View and select the Add button.

2. In the Properties window, ensure that you are displaying events rather than properties, type **addClick** in the *Click* event, and then press Enter.

   Another event method called *addClick* is created.

3. Add the following code to the *addClick* method:

```
string details;
details = "Member name " + firstName.Text + " "
    + lastName.Text + " from the tower at " + towerNames.Text;
MessageBox.Show(details, "Member Information");
```

This block of code creates a string variable called *details* that it fills with the name of the member and the tower that the member belongs to. Notice how the code accesses the *Text* property of the *TextBox* and *ComboBox* to read the current values of those controls. The *MessageBox* class provides static methods for displaying dialog boxes on the screen. The *Show* method used here will display the contents of the *details* string in the body of the message box and will put the text "Member Information" in the title bar. *Show* is an overloaded method, and there are other variants that allow you to specify icons and buttons to display in the message box.

Handle the *Closing* event for the form

As an example of an event that can take a different set of parameters, you will also trap the *FormClosing* event for a form. The *FormClosing* event is raised when the user attempts to close the form but before the form actually closes. You can use this event to prompt the user to save any unsaved data or even ask the user whether she really wants to close the form—you can cancel the event in the event handler and prevent the form from closing.

1. Return to Design View and select the form (click anywhere on the background of the form rather than selecting a control).

2. In the Properties window, ensure that you are displaying events, type **memberForm-Closing** in the *FormClosing* event, and then press Enter.

   An event method called *memberFormClosing* is created.

   You should observe that the second parameter for this method has the type *FormClosingEventArgs*. The *FormClosingEventArgs* class has a Boolean property called *Cancel*. If you set *Cancel* to *true* in the event handler, the form will not close. If you set *Cancel* to *false* (the default value), the form will close when the event handler finishes.

3. Add the following statements to the *memberFormClosing* method:

```
DialogResult key = MessageBox.Show(
    "Are you sure you want to quit",
    "Confirm",
    MessageBoxButtons.YesNo,
    MessageBoxIcon.Question);
e.Cancel = (key == DialogResult.No);
```

These statements display a message box asking the user to confirm whether to quit the application. The message box will contain Yes and No buttons and a question mark icon. When the user clicks either the Yes or No button, the message box will close and the button clicked will be returned as the value of the method (as a *DialogResult*–an enumeration identifying which button was clicked). If the user clicks No, the second statement will set the *Cancel* property of the *CancelEventArgs* parameter (*e*) to *true*, preventing the form from closing.

Delegates for Windows Forms Events

When you use the Properties window to define an event method (see Chapter 16), Visual Studio 2005 generates code that creates a delegate that references the method and subscribes to the event. If you look at the block of code that defines the Clear button in the *InitializeComponent* method in the MemberForm.Designer.cs file, you will see the following statement:

```
//
// clear
//
...
this.clear.Click += new System.EventHandler(this.clearClick);
```

The statement creates an *EventHandler* delegate pointing to the *clearClick* method. It then adds the delegate to the *Click* event for the Clear button. As you create additional event methods, Visual Studio 2005 will generate the required delegates and subscribe to the events for you.

Run the Application

1. On the Debug menu, click Start Without Debugging to run the application.

2. Type in a first name and a last name, and then select a tower from the list. Click Add. In the message box that appears displaying the member data you entered, click OK.

3. Try and close the form. In the message box that appears, click No.

    The form should continue running.

4. Try and close the form again. In the message box, click Yes.

    This time the form closes and the application finishes.

- **If you want to continue to the next chapter**

    Keep Visual Studio 2005 running and turn to Chapter 21.

- **If you want to exit Visual Studio 2005 for now**

    On the File menu, click Exit. If you see a Save dialog box, click Yes.

Chapter 20 Quick Reference

To	Do this
Create a Windows Forms project.	Use the Windows Application template.
Change the properties of a form.	Click the form in Design View. In the Properties window, select the property you want to change and enter the new value.
View the code behind a form.	On the View menu, click Code.
Add controls to a form.	Drag the control from the Toolbox onto the form.
Change the properties of a control.	While in Design View, click the control. In the Properties window, select the property you want to change and enter the new value.

Dynamically populate a ComboBox or a ListBox.	Use the Add method of the Items property. For example:
	
	`towerNames.Items.Add("Upper Gumtree");`
	
	You might need to clear the Items property first, depending on whether you want to retain the existing contents of the list. For example:
	
	`towerNames.Items.Clear();`

Initialize a CheckBox or radio button.	Set the Checked property to true or false. For example: `novice.Checked = true;`
Handle an event for a control or form.	Select the control or form in Design View. In the Properties window, click the Events button. Find the event you want to handle and type the name of an event method. Write the code that handles the event in the event method.

Chapter 21

Working with Menus and Dialog Boxes

After completing this chapter, you will be able to:

- Create and edit menus for Windows Forms applications.

- Use the *MenuStrip* and *ContextMenuStrip* controls.

- Respond to menu events for performing processing when a user clicks a menu command.

- Manipulate menus programmatically and create dynamic menus.

- Create context-sensitive pop-up menus.

- Use common dialog boxes in your applications to prompt the user for the names of files and printers.

- Send documents to a printer.

In Chapter 20, "Introducing Windows Forms," you saw how to create a simple Windows Forms application that used a selection of controls and events. Many professional Microsoft Windows applications also provide menus containing commands and options, giving the user the ability to perform various tasks related to the application. In this chapter, you will learn how to create menus and add them to forms by using the *MenuStrip* control. You will see how to respond when the user clicks a command on a menu. You'll learn how to create pop-up menus whose contents vary according to the current context. Finally, you will find out about the common dialog controls supplied as part of the Windows Forms library. These dialog controls allow you to prompt the user for frequently used items, such as files and printers, in a quick, easy, and familiar manner.

Menu Guidelines and Style

If you look at most Windows applications, you'll notice that some items on the menu strip tend to appear repeatedly in the same place, and the contents of these items are often predictable. For example, the File menu is typically the first item on the menu strip, and on this menu, you typically find commands for creating a new document, opening an existing document, saving the document, printing the document, and exiting the application. The term *document* means the data that the application manipulates. In Microsoft Excel, it would be a spreadsheet; in the Bell Ringers application that you created in Chapter 20, it could be a new member.

The order in which these commands appear tends to be the same across applications; for example, the Exit command is invariably the last command on the File menu. There might be other application-specific commands on the File menu as well.

An application often has an Edit menu containing commands such as Cut, Paste, Clear, and Find. There are usually some additional application-specific menus on the menu strip, but again, convention dictates that the final menu is the Help menu, which contains access to help as well as "about" information, which contains copyright and licensing details for the application. In a well-designed application, most menus are predictable and help ensure the application becomes easy to learn and use.

> **Tip** Microsoft publishes a full set of guidelines for user interfaces, including menu design, on the Microsoft Web site at *http://msdn.microsoft.com/ui*.

Adding Menus and Processing Menu Events

Microsoft Visual Studio 2005 lets you add menus and menu items to a form in two ways. You can use the Visual Studio 2005 integrated development environment (IDE) and the menu editor to create a menu graphically. You can also write code that creates a *MenuStrip* object (*MenuStrip* is a class defined in the Windows Forms library), and then add *ToolStripMenuItem* objects to it (*ToolStripMenuItem* is another class in the Windows Forms library).

Laying out a menu is only half of the story. When a user clicks a command on a menu, the user expects something to happen! You activate the commands by trapping menu events and executing code in much the same way as you do for handling control events.

Creating a Menu

In the following exercise, you will use the graphical approach to create menus for the Middleshire Bell Ringers Association application. We will cover how to manipulate and create menus programmatically later in this chapter.

Create the File menu

1. Start Visual Studio 2005.

2. Open the *BellRingers* project, located in the \Microsoft Press\Visual CSharp Step by Step\Chapter 21\BellRingers folder in your My Documents folder. This is the Middleshire Bell Ringers application. It should be the same as the version that you completed in Chapter 20.

3. Display *MemberForm* in the Design View window. (Click MemberForm.cs in the Solution Explorer, and then click Designer on the View menu, or double-click Member-Form.cs in the Solution Explorer).

    MemberForm appears.

4. In the Toolbox, expand the Menus & Toolbars category. Drag a *MenuStrip* control anywhere onto *MemberForm*.

> **Important**   Be sure to drop the *MenuStrip* control onto the form, and not onto a control on the form. Some controls, such as *GroupBox*, can have their own menus, and dropping a menu on such a control will create a menu for that control only.

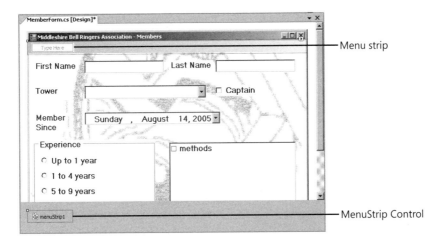

The control, by default called *menuStrip1*, appears at the bottom of the form, and a menu strip containing the caption, Type Here, is added to the top of the form.

5. Click the Type Here caption on the menu strip, type **&File**, and then press Enter. (If the Type Here caption on the menu strip disappears, click the *mainStrip1* control at the bottom of the form and the menu reappear.)

    When you click the Type Here caption, a second Type Here caption appears to the right of the current item, and a third Type Here caption appears under the File menu item.

> **Tip**   The & character in front of a letter provides fast access to that menu item when the user presses the Alt key and the letter following the & (in this case, Alt+F). This is another common convention. When you press the Alt key, the F at the start of File appears with an underscore. Do not use the same access key more than once on any menu because you will confuse the user (and probably the application).

6. Click the Type Here caption that appears under the File menu item, type **&New**, and then press Enter.

    Another Type Here caption appears under the New menu item.

7. Click the Type Here caption under the New menu item, type **&Open**, and then press Enter.

> **Tip**   If you mistype the text for a menu item, you can easily correct it. Click the menu item, and then use the Properties window to change the Text property of the item to the correct value.

8. Click the Type Here caption under the Open menu item, type **&Save Member**, and then press Enter.

9. Click the Type Here caption under the Save Member menu item, type a minus sign (–), and then press Enter.

    The minus sign appears as a menu separator bar used to group related menu items together.

10. Click the Type Here caption under the separator bar, type **&Print**, and then press Enter.

11. Click the Type Here caption under the Print menu item, type a minus sign (–), and then press Enter.

    Another separator bar appears.

12. Click the Type Here caption under the second separator bar, type **E&xit**, and then press Enter.

    Notice that the conventional access key for exit is "x." When you have finished, the menu should look like this:

Menu Strip Item Types

You have been using MenuItem controls, which are the default item type for MenuStrip objects. However, you can also add combo boxes and text boxes to menus in Visual Studio 2005 applications. You might have noticed that a drop-down arrow appears when hovering the mouse over the Type Here caption in a MenuStrip control. If you click this drop down, you will see three items: MenuItem, ComboBox, and TextBox, as shown in the following graphic:

The combo box and text box controls in a MenuStrip behave in a similar manner to ComboBox and TextBox controls on a form, and you can set their properties in the same way that you saw in Chapter 20. However, strictly speaking they are different from the versions of the controls that you drop onto forms. They are ToolStripComboBox and ToolStripTextBox controls, and are designed and optimized specifically for use in MenuStrip controls, and other related "strip" controls, such as the ContextMenuStrip and ToolStrip controls.

Setting Menu Item Properties

In the following exercise, you will set the properties of the *MainMenu* control and the menu items. You will use the Properties window to perform these tasks.

Set the menu item properties

1. Click the *menuStrip1* control under the form. In the Properties window, change its name to *mainMenu*. (If the Properties window is not displayed, click Properties Window on the View menu, or press F4.)

2. Right-click the File menu item on the menu strip of *MemberForm*. On the menu that appears, click Edit DropDownItems.

    The Items Collection Editor displays the names of the menu items as well as their properties.

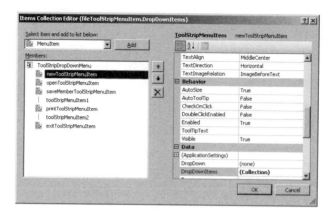

> **Tip**   You can use the Items Collection Editor to delete menu items, add new menu items, reorder the items in a drop-down menu, and set the properties of menu items.

3.   Notice the names generated for each menu item. They should be the same as those listed in the following table. If not, click the menu item and then change the (Name) property using the properties displayed on the right-hand side of the Items Collection Editor.

Item	New name
New	newToolStripMenuItem
Open	openToolStripMenuItem
Save Member	saveMemberToolStripMenuItem
Print	printToolStripMenuItem
Exit	exitToolStripMenuItem

The access keys for menu items (such as Alt+X for the Exit command) are available only when the menu is actually displayed. Commonly accessed menu items should also have shortcut keys that the user can press at any time to invoke the corresponding command. For example, the New command can usually be executed by pressing Ctrl+N in many Windows applications. You can add a shortcut key to a menu item by setting the *ShortcutKeys* property.

4.   Select the *newToolStripMenuItem* from the list of members, and then click ShortcutKeys in the list of properties. Check the Ctrl Modifier, and select N for the key, then press Enter.

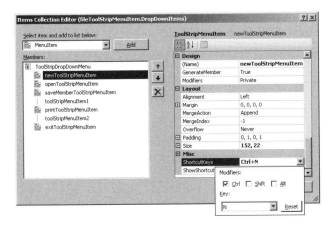

5.   There is another property called *ShowShortcutKeys* under the *ShortcutKeys* property. This property determines whether the shortcut key is displayed on the menu when the application runs. Verify that this property is set to *True*.

6.   Change the shortcut keys for the other menu items using the values in the following table. Ensure that the *ShowShortcut* property for each menu item remains set to True.

Item	Shortcut
openToolStripMenuItem	Ctrl+O
saveMemberToolStripMenuItem	Ctrl+S
printToolStripMenuItem	Ctrl+P
exitToolStripMenuItem	Alt+F4

Menu items can be enabled and disabled (disabled items are unavailable and their text appears dimmed) depending on the current actions and context. For example, in the Middleshire Bell Ringers Association application, it would not make sense to allow the user to use the Save Member or Print commands if there is no data to save or print.

7.   Select the *printToolStripMenuItem* item, and then click *Enabled* in the list of properties. Select the *False* option from the drop-down list. You will write some code later to update this property to *True* after data has displayed.

Repeat this task for the *saveMemberToolStripMenuItem* item.

8.   Click OK to close the Items Collection Editor.

Test the menu

1.   On the Debug menu, click Start Without Debugging to compile and run the application.

2.   When the form appears, click the File menu.

The new menu appears.

Notice that the Print and Save commands are disabled. You can click any of the other commands (although they won't do anything yet).

3. Close the form. You can't use the Exit command on the File menu yet; click the Close button (the 'X' button in the top right-hand corner of the form) instead.

Other Menu Item Properties

Menu items have a number of other properties. The following table describes the most common ones. If you want more information about the other properties, consult the documentation in the MSDN Library for Visual Studio 2005.

> **Tip**   You can set menu item properties using the Items Collection Editor as described in the previous exercises, or by clicking a menu item in the Designer View window and then using the Properties window.

Property	Description
(Name)	This property is the name of the menu item.
Checked	Menu items can act like check boxes and cause a check mark to appear when they are clicked. Setting the *Checked* property to *True* displays a check mark, and setting it to *False* hides the check mark.
CheckOnClick	Setting the *CheckOnClick* property to *True* causes the menu item to be checked and unchecked automatically when the user clicks it.
DisplayStyle	Menu items can display images as well as text names. If you set the *DisplayStyle* property to the value *Image* or *ImageAndText*, the image specified by the *Image* property will appear on the menu.
Enabled	This property specifies whether the menu item is enabled or disabled. If a menu item is not enabled, it appears dimmed and the user will not be able to select it.
Shortcut	This property specifies the shortcut key that a user can press to execute the corresponding menu command.
ShowShortcut	If this property is *True*, the shortcut key is displayed on the menu alongside the text of the menu item.
Text	This is the text that is displayed on the menu for the menu item. You can use the & character to specify an access key.
ToolTipText	This property specifies the text to display as a tool tip when the user hovers the mouse over the menu item.
Visible	This property determines whether the item should be displayed on the menu. It is more common to use the *Enabled* property to show that a menu item is present but unavailable.

Menu Events

There are several different events that can occur when a user gains access to a menu item. Some are more useful than others. The most frequently used event is the *Click* event, which occurs when the user clicks the menu item. You typically trap this event to perform the tasks associated with the menu item.

In the following exercise, you will learn more about menu events and how to process them. You will create *Click* events for the New and Exit menu items. The purpose of the New command is to allow the user to enter the details of a new member. Therefore, until the user clicks New, all fields on the form should be disabled. When the user clicks the New command on the File menu, you want to enable all the fields, reset the contents of *MemberForm* so that the user can start adding information about a new member, and enable the Print command.

Handle menu item events

1. In the *MemberForm* in the Design View window, click the *firstName* text box. In the Properties window, set the *Enabled* property to *False*. Repeat this process for the *lastName*, *towerNames*, *isCaptain*, *memberSince*, *yearsExperience*, *methods*, *add*, and *clear* controls.

> **Tip** If you press the Shift key and click several controls they will all be selected. You can then set properties, such as *Enabled*, to the same value for all the controls at once.

2. Click the File menu, and then click New.

3. In the Properties window, click the Events button. Select the *Click* event, type **newClick**, and then press Enter.

   A new event method is created and the source code displayed in the Code And Text Editor window.

4. In the body of the *newClick* event method, type the following statement:

   ```
   this.Reset();
   ```

   This calls the *Reset* method. If you remember in Chapter 20, the *Reset* method resets the controls on the form to their default values. (If you don't recall how the *Reset* method works, scroll the Code And Text Editor window to display the method and refresh your memory.)

5. You now need to enable the Save Member and Print menu items to allow the user to save and print the current member's information. You can do this by setting the *Enabled* property of the *saveMemberToolStripMenuItem* and *printToolStripMenuItem* items to *true*.

After the call to the *Reset* method in the *newClick* event method, add the following statements:

```
saveMemberToolStripMenuItem.Enabled = true;
printToolStripMenuItem.Enabled = true;
```

6. You must also enable the controls on the form. Append the following statements to the *newClick* method:

```
firstName.Enabled = true;
lastName.Enabled = true;
towerNames.Enabled = true;
isCaptain.Enabled = true;
memberSince.Enabled = true;
yearsExperience.Enabled = true;
methods.Enabled = true;
add.Enabled = true;
clear.Enabled = true;
```

7. Next, you need to create a Click event method for the Exit command. This method should cause the form to close. Return to the Design View displaying *MemberForm*, and then on the File menu, click Exit.

8. In the Properties window, verify that the events are displayed and select the *Click* event. Type **exitClick**, and press Enter.

The *exitClick* event method is created and the source code displayed in the Code And Text Editor window.

9. In the body of the *exitClick* method, type the following statement:

```
this.Close();
```

The *Close* method of a form attempts to close the form. Notice the use of *attempts* in that sentence—remember that a form might intercept the *Closing* event and prevent the form from closing. The Middleshire Bell Ringers Association application does precisely this, and asks the user if he or she wants to quit. If the user says no, the form does not close and the application continues to run.

Test the menu events

1. On the Debug menu, click Start Without Debugging to compile and run the application.

Notice that all the fields on the form are disabled.

2. Click the File menu.

The Print and Save commands are disabled.

3. Click New. Click the File menu again.

The Print and Save commands are now enabled, as are all the fields on the form.

4. Click Exit. The form tries to close. You are asked if you are sure you want to close the form. If you click No, the form remains open; if you click Yes, the form closes and the application finishes.

5. Click Yes to close the form.

Pop-Up Menus

Many Windows applications make use of *pop-up* menus that appear when you right-click a form or control. These menus are usually context-sensitive and display commands that are applicable only to the control or form that currently has the focus. They are sometimes referred to as *context* menus.

Creating Pop-Up Menus

In the following exercises, you will create two pop-up menus. The first pop-up menu is attached to the *firstName* and *lastName* text box controls and allows the user to clear these controls. The second pop-up menu is attached to the form and contains commands for saving the currently displayed member's information and for clearing the form. To do this, you will make a copy of an existing menu item as well as create a new one.

Create the *firstName* and *lastName* pop-up menus

1. In the Design View window displaying *MemberForm*, drag a *ContextMenuStrip* control from the Menus & Toolbars category in the Toolbox and drop it on the form.

    A *ContextMenuStrip* object called *contextMenuStrip1* appears at the bottom of the form and another menu strip appears at the top of the form. Note that this is only a temporary location for this new menu strip; it is just placed there by Visual Studio 2005 to allow you to edit it and add menu items. At runtime its location will actually be determined by the position of the mouse when the user clicks the right mouse button.

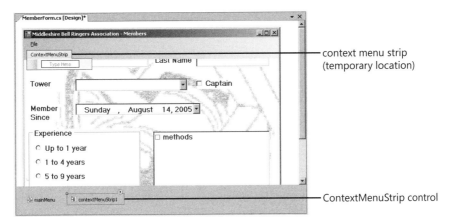

2. Select the *contextMenuStrip1* control, type **textBoxMenu** in the *(Name)* text box in the Properties window, and then press Enter.

3. Click the Type Here caption that appears under the ContextMenuStrip menu strip at the top of the form (not the control). Type **Clear Text**, and then press Enter

> **Tip** If the ContextMenuStrip menu strip has disappeared from the form, click the text-BoxMenu control underneath the form to display it again.

4. Click the *firstName* text box control (next to the First Name label). In the Properties window, change the *ContextMenuStrip* property to *textBoxMenu*. The *ContextMenu* property determines which menu (if any) will be displayed when the user right-clicks the control.

5. Click the *lastName* text box control. In the Properties window, change the *ContextMenuStrip* property to *textBoxMenu*.

   Notice that multiple controls are allowed to share the same context menu.

6. Click the *textBoxMenu* context menu control. Click the Events button, type **textBoxContextMenuPopup** in the *Opening* event text box, and then press Enter.

   A new event method called *textBoxContextMenuPopup* is created and displayed in the Code And Text Editor. This event is raised whenever the context menu appears.

7. Add the following statements to the *textBoxContextMenuPopup* event method:

   ```
   this.Tag = ((ContextMenuStrip)sender).SourceControl;
   ```

   The *sender* parameter to this event method will be the *textBoxMenu* object. This object contains a useful property called *SourceControl* that references the control the user is visiting when invoking the context menu. This statement stores a reference to the current text box control in the *Tag* property of the form.

   The *Tag* property of a form is a general-purpose item that can be use to hold any useful piece of data.

8. Return to the Design View window. Click the *textBoxMenu* control at the bottom of the form to display the ContextMenuStrip again. Click the Clear Text item.

9. In the Properties window, click the Events button, type **textBoxClearClick** in the *Click* event text box, and then press Enter.

   A new event method called *textBoxClearClick* is created and displayed in the Code And Text Editor.

10. Add the following statements to the *textBoxClearClick* event method:

    ```
    if (this.Tag.Equals(firstName))
    {
        firstName.Clear();
    ```

```
        firstName.Focus();
}
else
{
    lastName.Clear();
    lastName.Focus();
}
```

The *if* statement determines which of the two text boxes was clicked and clears it. The *Focus* method for a control places the cursor in that control; right-clicking a control does not automatically give it the focus.

> **Tip**   This use of the *Opening* event to cache a reference to the current text box control in the *Tag* property property of a form is a workaround for a minor bug in Visual Studio 2005. A context menu item also has a *SourceControl* property that identifies which control the user was in when invoking the menu item. However, in Beta 2 of Visual Studio 2005, this property currently returns the value *null*.

11.   On the Debug menu, click Start Without Debugging.

      The project compiles and runs.

12.   When the form appears, click File and then click New. Type a name into the First Name and Last Name text boxes.

13.   Right-click the First Name text box.

      The pop-up menu appears containing only the Clear Text command.

14.   Click the Clear Text command.

      The First Name text box is cleared.

15.   Type a name into the First Name text box, and then move to the Last Name text box. Right-click the Last Name text box to display the pop-up menu. Click the Clear Text command.

      This time, the Last Name text box is cleared (the first name information should still be there).

16.   Right-click anywhere on the form.

      Because only the First Name and Last Name text boxes have pop-up menus, no pop-up menu appears.

17.   Close the form.

Before tackling the second pop-up menu, you need to add some functionality to the Save Member menu item. Currently, it doesn't do anything. When it is clicked, the data on the form should be saved to a file. For the time being, you will save the information to an ordinary text file called Members.txt in the current folder. Later, you will modify the code to allow the user to select an alternative filename and location.

Write the *saveMemberClick* event method

1. Display *MemberForm* in the Design View window. Click the File menu, and then click Save Member.

2. In the Properties window, click the Events button. Select the *Click* event, type **saveMemberClick**, and then press Enter.

3. In the Code And Text Editor window, scroll to the top of the MemberForm.cs file and add the following using statement to the list:

```
using System.IO;
```

4. Return to the *saveMemberClick* event method at the end of the MemberForm.cs file. Add the following statements to the body of the method:

```
StreamWriter writer = new StreamWriter("Members.txt");
writer.WriteLine("First Name: " + firstName.Text);
writer.WriteLine("Last Name: " + lastName.Text);
writer.WriteLine("Tower: " + towerNames.Text);
writer.WriteLine("Captain: " + isCaptain.Checked);
writer.WriteLine("Member Since: " + memberSince.Text);
writer.WriteLine("Methods: ");
foreach(object methodChecked in methods.CheckedItems) {
    writer.WriteLine(methodChecked.ToString());
}
writer.Close();

MessageBox.Show("Member details saved", "Saved");
```

This block of code creates a *StreamWriter* object that is used for writing text to the Member.txt file. Using the *StreamWriter* class is very similar to displaying text in a console application by using the *Console* object—you can simply use the *WriteLine* method.

The most complex part of this code is the *foreach* statement that iterates through the *methods* control. The *CheckedListBox* class provides a property called *CheckedItems* that contains all of the items that have been checked. The foreach statement sends each checked item to the *StreamWriter* for output.

> **Tip**   When the user runs the form, they currently have to click each method in the *CheckedListBox* twice; once to select the method, and the second time to check it. The *CheckedListBox* control has another property called *CheckOnClick*. When you set this property to *true*, clicking a row in the *CheckedListBox* control selects and checks it with a single click.

When the details have all been written out, the *StreamWriter* is closed and a message box is displayed giving the user some feedback (always a good idea).

5.   On the Debug menu, click Start Without Debugging to build and run the application.

6.   Add a new member and type some details. Click File, and then click Save Member. After a short delay, you will see the message "Member details saved". Click OK, and then close the form.

7.   Using Windows Explorer, navigate to the \Microsoft Press\Visual CSharp Step by Step\Chapter 21\BellRingers\bin\Debug folder in your My Documents folder.

     You will see a file called Members.txt in this folder.

8.   Double-click Members.txt to display its contents using Notepad. You should see the details of the new member.

9.   Close Notepad, and return to Visual Studio 2005.

Now you can add the second pop-up menu.

To provide a bit of variation, and to show you how easy it is to create pop-up menus, in the following exercise you will create the *MemberForm* pop-up menu by using code. The best place to put this code is in the constructor of the form.

Create the *MemberForm* context menu

1.   Switch to the Code View for *MemberForm*. (On the View menu, click Code.)

2.   Locate the constructor for *MemberForm*. This is actually the first method in the class and is called *MemberForm*.

     A menu contains an array of menu items. In this example, the pop-up menu for the form will contain two menu items (Save Member and Clear).

3.   In the constructor, after the call to the *Reset* method, add the following statement:

```
ToolStripMenuItem[] formMenuItemList = new ToolStripMenuItem[2];
```

This line of code creates an array big enough to hold two menu items.

4.   The first item on the menu is a copy of the existing *saveMemberToolStripItem* menu item you created earlier. Add it to the *formMenuItemList* array:

```
formMenuItemList[0] = new ToolStripMenuItem("Save Member", null,
    new System.EventHandler(saveMemberClick));
```

The constructor specifies the text that appears for the menu item, an image to use (*null* in this case), and a delegate referring to the event method to be called when the *Click* event occurs. This is the same method that you created in the previous exercise.

You might be tempted simply to reference the existing *saveMemberToolStripItem* object created earlier rather than creating another, identical menu item. You should avoid doing so for two reasons. First, you might want to change the properties of this instance of the item without affecting the main menu of the form. Second, if you don't copy the Save Member menu item, it disappears from the form's main menu when you reference it in the context menu. (Try it and you will see!)

5.   You can create the second item (Clear) in the same way. In Chapter 20, you created a button (also called Clear) that did the same thing. You can take the event method of that button and recycle it for this menu item. Add the following statements:

```
formMenuItemList[1] = new ToolStripMenuItem("Clear", null
    new System.EventHandler(clearClick));
```

6.   Add the following statements:

```
ContextMenuStrip formMenu = new ContextMenuStrip();
formMenu.Items.AddRange(formMenuItemList);
```

This code creates a new *ContextMenuStrip* and adds the array containing the Save Member and Clear menu items.

7.   Associate the pop-up menu with the form by adding the following statements:

```
this.ContextMenuStrip = formMenu;
```

```
this.ContextMenuStrip.Enabled = false;
```

The context menu should be disabled initially as the user cannot input any member data until she clicks New on the File menu.

8.   Locate the *newClick* method. Add the following statement that enables the *formMenu* to the end of the method:

```
this.ContextMenuStrip.Enabled = true;
```

9.   Compile and run the project. Create a new member and input some values. If you right-click anywhere on the form (apart from the First Name and Last Name text boxes), the pop-up menu appears. If you click Clear, the form resets back to its default values. If you click Save Member, the details you have entered are saved to the file Members.txt.

10.   Close the form when you have finished.

Using Common Dialog Controls

The Bell Ringers application now allows you to save information, but it always saves data to the same file, overwriting anything that is already there. Also, the print functionality is still missing. Now is the time to address these issues.

There are a number of everyday tasks that require the user to specify some sort of information. For example, if the user wants to print a file, the user is usually asked which printer to use, and the user can set additional properties such as the number of copies. You might have noticed that the same Print dialog box is used by many different applications. This is not due to lack of imagination by applications developers; it is just that the requirement is so common that Microsoft has standardized it and made it available as a "common dialog"—a component supplied with the Microsoft Windows operating system that you can use in your own applications.

There are a number of other common dialog boxes available as well, including dialog boxes for opening and saving files, selecting colors and fonts, specifying page formats, and performing print previews. You can use any of these common dialog boxes in Visual Studio 2005 through the common dialog controls.

Using the *SaveFileDialog* Control

In the following exercise, you will use the *SaveFileDialog* control. In the BellRingers application, when the user saves details to a file you will prompt the user for the name and location of the file by using a *SaveFileDialog* control.

Use a *SaveFileDialog* control

1. Display *MemberForm* in the Design View window.

2. In the Toolbox, expand the Dialogs category.

3. Drag a SaveFileDialog control onto the form.

    The control appears under the form and is given the name *saveFileDialog1*.

4. Click the *saveFileDialog1* control. In the Properties window, set its properties by using the values specified in the following table.

Property	Value	Description
(Name)	saveFileDialog	The name of the control.
AddExtension	True	Setting this property to *True* allows the dialog box to add the file extension indicated by the *DefaultExt* property to the name of the file specified by the user if the user omits the file extension.
DefaultExt	txt	The default file extension to use if the user does not specify the extension when providing the filename.
FileName	Leave blank	The name of the currently selected file. Delete the value if you don't want a file to be selected by default.
InitialDirectory	C:\	The default directory to be used by the dialog box.

Property	Value	Description
OverwritePrompt	True	If this property is *True*, the user is warned when an attempt is made to overwrite an existing file with the same name. For this to work, the *ValidateNames* property must also be set to *True*.
Title	Bell Ringers	A string that is displayed on the title bar of the dialog box.
ValidateNames	True	This property indicates whether filenames are validated. It is used by some other properties, such as OverwritePrompt. If this property is set to True, the dialog box also checks to verify that any filename typed in by the user contains only valid characters.

5. In the Code And Text Editor window displaying MemberForm.cs, locate the saveMemberClick method at the end of the file.

6. Type the following statements at the start of this method, surrounding the code that creates and uses the *StreamWriter* object:

```
DialogResult buttonClicked = saveFileDialog.ShowDialog();
if (buttonClicked.Equals(DialogResult.OK))
{
    StreamWriter writer = new StreamWriter("Members.txt"); // existing code
    ...
    MessageBox.Show("Member details saved", "Saved"); // existing code
}
```

7. The first statement displays the Save File dialog box by using the *ShowDialog* method. The Save File dialog box is modal, which means that the user cannot continue using any other forms in the application until she has closed this dialog box by clicking one of its buttons. Modal dialog boxes also have a *DialogResult* property that indicates which button the user clicked (the Save dialog has a Save button and a Cancel button). The *ShowDialog* method returns the value of this *DialogResult* property; if the user clicks Save, the *DialogResult* property will be OK (not Save because there is no such *DialogResult* value).

> **Important**   The *SaveFileDialog* control prompts the user for the name of a file to save to, but does not actually do any saving—you still have to supply that code yourself.

8. Modify the statement that creates the *StreamWriter* object:

```
StreamWriter writer = new StreamWriter(saveFileDialog.FileName);
```

The method will now write to the file specified by the user rather than Members.txt.

9. Build and run the application. Create a new member. On the File menu, click Save Member. The Bell Ringers dialog box opens and you are asked for the name of the file you

want to save. If you omit the file extension, ".txt" is added automatically when the file is saved. If you pick an existing file, the dialog box warns you before it closes.

10.   When you have finished, close the application.

You can use a similar technique for opening a file; add an *OpenFileDialog* control to the form, invoke it by using the *ShowDialog* method, and retrieve the *FileName* property when the method returns if the user has clicked the Open button. You can then open the file, read its contents, and populate the fields on the screen.

For more details on using the *OpenFileDialog* control, consulting the MSDN Library for Visual Studio 2005.

Using a Printer

Printing is another common requirement of professional Windows applications. Visual Studio provides controls that can help you send data to a printer very quickly and easily. One of these controls is another Common Dialog that allows the user to specify the printer to use. Additionally, the *PrintDocument* control allows the programmer to manipulate the data being sent to the printer.

In the final exercise in this chapter, you will implement the Print menu command, making use of the *PrintDialog* and *PrintDocument* controls.

Use a *PrintDialog* control

1.   Display *MemberForm* in the Design View window.

2.   In the Toolbox, expand the Printing category.

3.   Drag a *PrintDialog* control onto the form.

   The control appears under the form and is given the name *printDialog1*.

4.   Click the *printDialog1* control. In the Properties window, change the (Name) property to printDialog.

5.   On *MemberForm*, click the File menu, and then click Print.

6.   Click the Events button in the Properties window. Select the *Click* event, type **print-Click**, and then press Enter.

7.   In the Code And Text Editor window, add the following statements to the *printClick* method:

```
DialogResult buttonClicked = printDialog.ShowDialog();
if (buttonClicked.Equals(DialogResult.OK))
{
    // You will write this code shortly
}
```

This is the same idiom that you saw earlier, when using the *SaveFileDialog* control.

Use a *PrintDocument* control

1. Return to the Design View window.

2. Click and drag a *PrintDocument* control from the Printing category in the Toolbox onto *MemberForm*.

    Another control appears under the form, called *printDocument1*.

3. Using the Properties window, change the name of this control to *printDocument*. Clear the *DocumentName* property.

4. Click the *printDialog* control. In the Properties window, set the *Document* property of this control to *printDocument*. This is necessary as the *printDialog* control uses the *print-Document* control to obtain printer settings.

5. Switch back to the Code And Text Editor displaying MemberForm.cs, and return to the *printClick* method.

6. Replace the comment in the middle of this method with the following statement:

    ```
    printDocument.Print();
    ```

    This statement starts the printing process on the selected printer. However, you still need to do some work; you must format the data to be printed by using the *PrintPage* event of the *printDocument* control.

7. In the Design View window, click the *printDocument* control. Click the Events button in the Properties window. Select the *PrintPage* event, type **printPage**, and then press Enter.

8. In the Code And Text Editor window, add the following statements to the *printPage* method:

    ```
    StringBuilder data = new StringBuilder();

    StringWriter writer = new StringWriter(data);
    writer.WriteLine("First Name: " + firstName.Text);
    writer.WriteLine("Last Name: " + lastName.Text);
    writer.WriteLine("Tower: " + towerNames.Text);
    writer.WriteLine("Captain: " + isCaptain.Checked);
    writer.WriteLine("Member Since: " + memberSince.Text);
    writer.WriteLine("Methods: ");
    foreach (object methodChecked in methods.CheckedItems)
    {
        writer.WriteLine(methodChecked.ToString());
    }
    writer.Close();
    ```

    You should recognize much of this code as it is very similar to the logic used when saving a member's data to a file.

The *StringWriter* class is another stream-oriented class, much like *StreamWriter* that you saw earlier in this chapter. It supports many of the same methods and properties. The only real difference is that it sends its data to a *StringBuilder* object rather than a file.

The *StringBuilder* class provides a very efficient way for creating and manipulating strings. It has many of the same features as the *string* type, but also allows you to easily add and remove characters in a string.

By the end of this block of code, the *data* variable contains the information ready to be sent to the printer.

> **Note**   In the .NET Framework and C#, the *string* data type is immutable; when you modify the value in a string, the runtime actually creates a new string containing the modified value, and then discards the old string. Repeatedly modifying a string can cause your code to become inefficient as a new string has to be created in memory at each change (the old string will eventually be garbage collected). The *StringBuilder* class, in the *System.Text* namespace, is designed to avoid this inefficiency. You can add and remove characters from a *StringBuilder* object using the *Append*, *Insert*, and *Remove* methods without creating a new object each time.

9. Append the following statements to the end of the *printPage* method:

```
float leftMargin = e.MarginBounds.Left;
float topMargin = e.MarginBounds.Top;
float yPos = 0;
Font printFont = null;

printFont = new Font("Arial", 12);
yPos = topMargin + printFont.GetHeight(e.Graphics);
e.HasMorePages = false;
e.Graphics.DrawString(data.ToString(), printFont, Brushes.Black,
                      leftMargin, yPos, new StringFormat());
```

This block of code sends the contents of the *data* variable to the printer. The page is printed using the Arial font (you can specify any font and size that is installed on your computer). The margins of the document are determined by using the bounds specified by the *PrintPageEventArgs* parameter passed to the method.

The line that actually sends the data to the printer is the *DrawString* statement. You can experiment with different values for the parameters. The code shown above outputs a simple page of text. If you are feeling adventurous, you can add a page header and footer, and graphics to the output.

10. Build and run the application. Create a new member.

11. On the File menu, click Print. The Print dialog box appears. Select a printer and then click Print.

A message box appears while the data is formatted and printed.

12.   When you have finished, close the application.

■   **If you want to continue to the next chapter**

Keep Visual Studio 2005 running and turn to Chapter 22.

■   **If you want to exit Visual Studio 2005 for now**

On the File menu, click Exit. If you see a Save dialog box, click Yes.

Chapter 21 Quick Reference

To	Do this
Create a menu for a form.	Add a *MenuStrip* control to the form.
Add menu items to a menu.	Click the *MenuStrip* control at the bottom of the form. Click the Type Here caption on the menu strip of the form and type the name of the menu item. To add additional items, replace the other Type Here captions that appear. You can add an access key to a menu item by prefixing the corresponding letter with a & character.
Create a separator bar in a menu.	Create a menu item by replacing the Type Here caption with a minus sign (–).
Add a shortcut key to a menu item.	Select the menu item, and then set the *ShortcutKeys* property to the required key combination in the Properties window.
Enable or disable a menu item.	At design time, set the *Enabled* property to True or False in the Properties window. At run time, assign the value true or false to the *Enabled* property of the menu item. For example: `printToolStripmenuItem.Enabled = true;`
Perform an action when the user clicks a menu item.	Select the menu item. In the Properties window, click Events. In the Click event, type the name of an event method. Add your code to the event method.
Create a pop-up menu.	Add a *ContextMenuStrip* control to the form. Add items to the pop-up menu just as you add items to a main menu.
Associate a pop- up menu with a form or control.	Set the *ContextMenuStrip* property of the form or control to refer to the pop-up menu itself.
Create a pop-up menu dynamically.	Create an array of menu items. Populate the array. Create the pop-up menu by using the array. Set the *ContextMenuStrip* property of the form or control to refer to the pop-up menu.
Prompt the user for the name of a file to save.	Use a *SaveFileDialog* control. Display the dialog box by using the *ShowDialog* method. When the dialog box closes, the *FileName* property contains the name of the file selected by the user, and you can use the *OpenFile* method of the dialog box to read and write the file.
Send a document to a printer.	Use a *PrintDialog* control to prompt the user for the printer to use. Use the *PrintPage* event of a *PrintDocument* control to actually send the document to the printer.

Chapter 22

Performing Validation

After completing this chapter, you will be able to:

- Examine the information entered by a user to ensure that it does not violate any application or business rules.

- Use the *CausesValidation* property and understand the limitations of the validation events of forms and controls.

- Perform validation effectively but unobtrusively.

- Use the *ErrorProvider* control for reporting error messages.

- Use the *StatusStrip* control to implement a status bar for a form.

In the previous two chapters, you saw how to create a Windows Forms application that uses a variety of controls for data entry. You created menus to make the application easier to use. You have learned how to trap events raised by menus, forms, and controls so that your application can actually do something besides just look pretty. While careful design of a form and the appropriate use of controls can help to ensure that the information entered by a user makes sense, there are often additional checks that you need to perform. In this chapter, you will learn how to validate the data entered by a user running an application to ensure that it matches any business rules specified by the application's requirements.

Validating Data

The concept of input validation is simple enough, but it is not always easy to implement, especially if validation involves cross-checking data the user has entered into two or more controls. The underlying business rule might be relatively straightforward, but all too often, the validation is performed at an inappropriate time making the form difficult (and often infuriating) to use.

The *CausesValidation* Property

Windows forms and controls have a Boolean property called *CausesValidation* that indicates whether the form or control raises validation events. If the property is set to *true* (which is the default) for a control, when that control receives the focus, the previous control (the one losing the focus) will be validated. If the validation fails, the focus will return to the previous control. It is important to realize that the *CausesValidation* property does not apply to the control itself but instead affects all the other controls on the form. If you are feeling a little confused by this statement, don't panic—you will see an example in a moment.

Validation Events

To validate data in a control, you can use two events: *Validating* and *Validated*. The *Validating* event occurs when focus leaves a control and attempts to switch to a control that has its *CausesValidation* property set to *true*. You can use the *Validating* event to examine the value of the control losing the focus. If you don't like what you see, you can set the Cancel property of the *CancelEventArgs* parameter to prevent the focus from changing. It would probably also help to report the reason why the validation failed.

The *Validated* event occurs after the *Validating* event (as long as it was not canceled) but before the control loses focus. You cannot cancel this event, so it is not as useful as the *Validating* event for checking the user's input.

> **Tip**   The *Validating* event fires only if you move to a control that has *CausesValidation* set to *true*. For this reason, it is unusual to have a form where some of the controls have this property set to *false* and others have it set to *true*—validation might occur depending on where the user clicks next. Don't do this unless you have a very good reason because it will confuse the user and could lead to inconsistent data.

An Example—Customer Maintenance

As an example, consider a simple scenario. You have been asked to build a Customer Maintenance application. Part of the application needs to record the essential details of a customer, including title, name, and gender. You decide to create a form like the one shown in the following graphic.

You need to ensure that the user's input is consistent; the title (Mr, Mrs, Miss, or Ms) must match the selected gender (Male or Female), and vice versa.

A First Attempt at Performing Validation

In the following exercises, you will examine the Customer Maintenance application and run it to see how easily you can get validation wrong.

Examine the program

1. Open the *CustomerDetails* project, located in the \Microsoft Press\Visual CSharp Step By Step\ Chapter 22\CustomerDetails folder in your My Documents folder.

2. In the Solution Explorer, double-click CustomerForm.cs to display the Customer Details form in Design View.

3. Click the Title combo box on the form, and then click the *Items* property in the Properties window. It should appear as (Collection). Click the Ellipses button to display the strings in the collection.

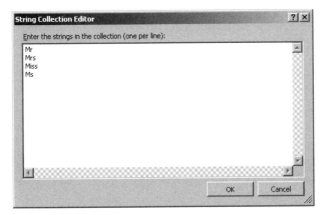

You can see from this collection that the list box contains four titles: Mr, Mrs, Miss, and Ms. Click Cancel to close the String Collection Editor window.

4. Examine the Gender group box and radio buttons. The group box contains two radio buttons called Male and Female.

The application enforces the business rule that the gender and the title must match. If the title is Mr, the gender must be male, and if the title is Mrs, Miss, or Ms, the gender must be female.

5. On the View menu, click Code to switch to the Code And Text Editor window displaying CustomerForm.cs. Look at the *checkTitleAndGender* method situated immediately below the *CustomerForm* constructor:

```
// Cross check the gender and the title to make sure they correspond
private bool checkTitleAndGender()
{
    if (title.Text == "Mr")
    {
        // Check that gender is Male
        if (!male.Checked)
        {
```

```
                   MessageBox.Show("If the title is Mr the gender must be male", "Error",
         MessageBoxButtons.OK, MessageBoxIcon.Error);
                   return false;
               }
         }
         else
         {
             // Check that the gender is Female
             if (!female.Checked)
             {
                   MessageBox.Show("If the title is Mrs, Miss, or Ms
        the gender must be female", "Error", MessageBoxButtons.OK, MessageBoxIcon.Error);
                   return false;
             }
         }

         // Title and gender match
         return true;
     }
```

This method performs a simple cross-check between the contents of the Title combo box and the radio buttons in the Gender group box. If the title is "Mr," the business rule states that the gender must be male, and the method checks to ensure that the Male radio button is selected. If this option is not selected, the method displays an error message and returns *false*. Likewise, if the title is one of the other values (Mrs, Miss, or Ms), the business rule states that the gender must be female, and the method looks at the Female radio button to ensure it is selected. Again, if this is not the case, a different error message is displayed and the method returns *false*. If the title and the gender match, the method returns *true*.

6. Look at the *titleValidating* and *genderValidating* methods at the end of the file. These are implementations of the *Validating* event handler for the Title combo box and the Gender group box. They both call the *checkTitleAndGender* method, and then set the *Cancel* property of the *CancelEventArgs* parameter to *true* if the *checkTitleAndGender* method returns *false*:

```
private void titleValidating(object sender, CancelEventArgs e)
{
    if (!checkTitleAndGender())
    {
        e.Cancel = true;
    }
}

private void genderValidating(object sender, CancelEventArgs e)
{
    if (!checkTitleAndGender())
    {
        e.Cancel = true;
    }
}
```

7. Examine the remaining methods, *exitClick* and *saveClick*. The form has a menu strip with a File menu, containing Save and Exit items. These two methods are called when the user clicks either of these two menu items. The *exitClick* method closes the form and exits the application. The *saveClick* method displays the message "Customer Saved" (this is just a prototype form—the production version would actually save the information somewhere).

Now you'll run the application and see what happens when it tries to validate the user's input.

Run the application

1. On the Debug menu, click Start Without Debugging to run the application.

    The Customer Details form appears. Notice that the default gender is Male.

2. Select Mrs from the Title combo box and tab to or click the first Name text box.

    Notice that the *checkTitleAndGender* method generates and displays an error message because the title and the gender don't agree.

3. Click OK in the Error dialog box to close it, and then try to click the Female radio button in the group box.

    You will fail, as the *CausesValidation* property of the group box makes the *Validating* event run again, causing the error message to be displayed once more.

4. Click OK in the Error dialog box. Set the title to Mr and click the Female radio button.

    Remember that the *Validating* event fires just before the focus is passed to the Female radio button. When the *checkTitleAndGender* method is called, the title (Mr) and the gender (male) will agree. You are successfully able to set the gender to female.

5. Now that you have now set the gender to female, try to save the customer's details by clicking Save in the File menu. This action works without error and the message Customer Saved appears in a message box. Confused? Click OK.

6. Correct the (non-reported) error by trying to set the title to Mrs.

    The *Validating* event (this time for the Gender group box) runs, spots that the gender and title don't match, and then displays an error. You will not be able to escape until you set the Gender to Male again (but then you are back to square one).

7. Exit the application.

The validation strategy failed because the *Validating* event fires only when you move to another control on the same form (and not to a control in a toolbar or a menu bar, for example). Developers often put much effort into getting it all to work. The next sections explain how to get it to work by using the tools properly.

> **Tip**   Use the *Validating* event to validate controls in isolation only; don't use it to check the contents of one control against another.

Being Unobtrusive

The issue with the Customer Maintenance application is that the validation is performed at the wrong time, is inconsistently applied, and interferes too much. The actual logic is fine though. We just need an alternative approach to handling the validation.

A better solution would be to check the user's input when the user saves the data. This way you can ensure that the user has finished entering all the data and that it is consistent. If there are any problems, an error message will appear and prevent the data from being saved until the data is corrected. In the following exercise, you will change the Customer Maintenance application to postpone validation until the customer information is saved.

Change the point where data is validated

1. Return to the Design View window displaying *CustomerForm*. Click the Title combo box.

2. In the Properties window, click the Events button. Scroll down to the *Validating* event, and then delete the *titleValidating* method.

   This unsubscribes the Title combo box from the *Validating* event.

3. On the *CustomerForm*, select the Gender group box.

4. In the Properties window, click the Events button. Find the *Validating* event, and then delete the *genderValidating* method.

> **Important**   Unsubscribing from an event in this way detaches the event method from the event itself but does not delete the event method—if you no longer need the method, you can remove it manually in the Code And Text Editor window.

5. Display the file CustomerForm.cs in the Code And Text Editor window. Delete the *title-Validating* and *genderValidating* methods. You are going to call the *checkTitleAndGender* method when the Save menu item is clicked.

6. Locate the *saveClick* method. This is where you are going to place the validation code. Modify this method as shown below:

```
private void saveClick(object sender, EventArgs e)
{
    if (checkTitleAndGender())
    {
        // Save the current customer's details
        MessageBox.Show("Customer saved", "Saved");
    }
    else
    {
        MessageBox.Show("Customer title and gender are inconsistent" +
                    " - please correct and save again", "Error",
                    MessageBoxButtons.OK, MessageBoxIcon.Error);
    }
}
```

The *if* statement calls the *checkTitleAndGender* method. If the method returns *true*, the *saveCustomerForm* method displays the "Customer Saved" message box. If the *checkTitle-AndGender* method returns false, an error message box is displayed and the customer's details are not saved.

Test the application again

1. Build and run the application. When the Customer Details form appears, set the Title combo box to Mrs, and then click in the first Name text box. This should work without error because the *Validating* event is no longer trapped by the Title combo box.

2. Verify that the Male radio button is selected, and then click the Save item in the File menu. At this point, the *checkTitleAndGender* method is called and the inconsistency is reported. Click OK.

3. Notice that another message box occurs—this is the message reported by the *saveClick* method. Click OK again.

4. Select the Female radio button, and then click the Save Customer button on the toolbar.

   This time no errors are reported and Customer Saved message box is displayed.

5. Click OK, and exit the application.

Using an *ErrorProvider* Control

Postponing validation is good and makes the form less frustrating to use. But what happens if there are several validation errors reported when the data is saved? If you use message boxes to present error information, you might end up displaying several of them in succession if there are multiple errors. Additionally, the user will have to remember each error so that it can be corrected. This can get tedious for a user after more than two or three errors are reported. A much better technique is to use an *ErrorProvider* control as shown in the following exercise.

Add an *ErrorProvider* control

1. Return to *CustomerForm* in the Design View window.

2. In the Toolbox, expand the Components category. Click the *ErrorProvider* control and drop it anywhere on the form.

   It appears under the form.

3. Click the *errorProvider1* control, and select the Properties window. Change the *(Name)* property to *errorProvider* and verify that the *BlinkStyle* property is set to *BlinkIfDifferentError*.

    When an error is reported by a control, an error icon (which you can select by setting the *Icon* property) appears by the control in error and blinks for a short while and then remains static. You can change the *BlinkRate* property if you want to make it blink faster or slower—the default rate is 250 milliseconds (four times a second). If a subsequent error is reported, the icon blinks only if the error is different from the current one. If you want the icon to blink every time, you can set its *BlinkStyle* to *AlwaysBlink*.

    On the *CustomerForm*, select the Title combo box. If you look at the Properties window, you will discover a new property called *Error on errorProvider*. This property only appears when an *ErrorProvider* control has been added to a form, and is titled according to the name of the *ErrorProvider* control. If you type a message here (such as "Testing"), an error icon appears next to the Title combo box. If you hold the mouse pointer over the error icon, a ToolTip appears displaying the error message.

    If you leave this property set as it is, the error icon is always displayed, which is not what you want. The icon should be displayed (with a meaningful error message) only in the event of an error, so delete the text "Testing" from the *Error on errorProvider* property. You will write some code to dynamically use the *errorProvider* control shortly.

4. Switch to the Code And Text Editor window for *CustomerForm*. Locate the *checkTitleAnd-Gender* method and replace the statements that call *MessageBox.Show* with invocations of the *errorProvider.SetError* method, as shown here:

```
// Cross check the gender and the title to make sure they correspond
private bool checkTitleAndGender()
{
```

```
if (title.Text == "Mr")
{
    // Check that gender is Male
    if (!male.Checked)
    {
        errorProvider.SetError(gender, "If the title is Mr " +
            "the gender must be male");
        errorProvider.SetError(title, "If the gender is " +
            "female the title must be Mrs, Miss, or Ms");
        return false;
    }
}
else
{
    // Check that the gender is Female
    if (!female.Checked)
    {
        errorProvider.SetError(gender, "If the title is Mrs, " +
            "Miss, or Ms the gender must be female");
        errorProvider.SetError(title, "If the gender is male " +
            "the title must be Mr");
        return false;
    }
}

// Title and gender match - clear any errors
errorProvider.SetError(gender, "");
errorProvider.SetError(title, "");
return true;
}
```

The *SetError* method of the *ErrorProvider* control specifies which control to mark with an error icon and the message to be displayed as a ToolTip. If you provide an empty string as the second parameter, as the code does at the end of the method, the error icon is removed.

Test the *ErrorProvider* control

1. Build and run the application.

2. Select Mrs in the Title combo box, and then verify that the Male radio button is selected.

3. On the File menu, click Save. A message box appears indicating that the save failed, and error icons are displayed next to the controls that are in error. Click OK. If you hover the mouse pointer over each of the error icons, you see the error message, as shown in the graphic on the next page.

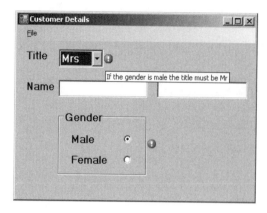

This is a much less intrusive but more reliable and consistent type of validation than the original application contained.

4. Select the Female gender radio button and click the Save item on the File menu.

   As the data is now consistent, you will see the Customer Saved message box and the error icons will disappear.

5. Exit the application.

Adding a Status Bar

Although some of the message boxes have disappeared, some still remain—a message box appears when customer information is successfully saved or if an error occurs. This is feedback that the user needs to be able to see, but it is annoying to the user to have to click the OK button to acknowledge the messages. A better way to inform the user of these situations is to display the messages in a status bar at the bottom of the form; the user can still see them, but does not have to click anything to move them out of the way.

In the final exercise in this chapter, you will implement a status bar in the *CustomerForm* form by using a *StatusStrip* control.

Add a *StatusStrip* control

1. Return to *CustomerForm* in the Design View window.

2. In the Toolbar, expand the Menus & Toolbars category. Drag a *StatusStrip* control from the Toolbar onto the form.

   The control appears underneath the form, and a status bar is added to the base of the form.

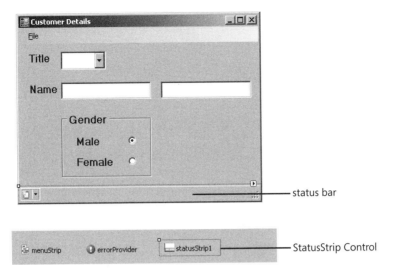

status bar

StatusStrip Control

3. Click the *statusStrip1* control, and select the Properties window. Change the *(Name)* property to *statusStrip*.

4. In the status bar on the form, click the drop-down arrow as shown in the following graphic, and click StatusLabel.

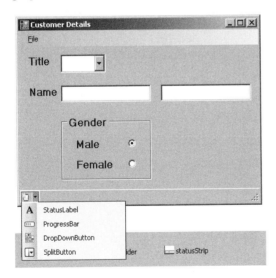

This action adds a *ToolStripStatusLabel* control to the status bar. This is a version of the *Label* control that is intended for use in tool strips and status bars.

5. Click the *toolStripStatusLabel1* control in the status bar. Using the Properties window, change its name to *statusMessages*. Clear the *Text* property.

The control shrinks in size, but is still present in the status bar.

6. Switch to the Code And Text Editor window for *CustomerForm*. Find the *saveClick* method. This method contains the *MessageBox* statements that you need to convert into status bar messages.

7. Change the first *MessageBox* statement (in the *if* statement) to display a message in the status bar instead, as follows:

```
statusMessages.ForeColor = Color.Black;
statusMessages.Text = "Customer Saved";
```

You will see why you need to set the text color to black in the next step.

8. Change the second *MessageBox* statement (in the *else* statement) to display the following error message in the status bar:

```
statusMessages.ForeColor = Color.Red;
statusMessages.Text = "Customer title and gender are inconsistent. Changes not saved";
```

The error message is displayed in red to make it stand out. When an ordinary information message (such as "Customer Saved") is displayed, the color should be reset back to black.

Test the status bar

1. Build and run the application. (A finished version is available in the \Microsoft Press\Visual CSharp Step By Step\Chapter 22\CustomerDetails Complete folder in your My Documents folder, if you need it.)

2. Select Mrs in the Title combo box, and then verify that the Male radio button is selected.

3. On the File menu, click Save.

   A red error message appears in the status bar indicating that the save failed. The error icons are displayed next to the controls that are in error, as before.

4. Select the Female gender radio button and click the Save item on the File menu.

   You will see the Customer Saved message in the status bar (in black) and the error icons will disappear.

5. Exit the application.

■ **If you want to continue to the next chapter**

Keep Microsoft Visual Studio 2005 running and turn to Chapter 23.

■ **If you want to exit Visual Studio 2005 for now**

On the File menu, click Exit. If you see a Save dialog box, click Yes.

Chapter 22 Quick Reference

To	Do this
| Validate the contents of a single control. | Use the *Validating* event method. For example:<br><br>```csharp
private void titleValidating(
object sender, CancelEventArgs e)
{
    if (!checkTitleAndGender() )
    {
        e.Cancel = true;
    }
}
``` |
Allow the *Validating* event to be raised.	Set the *CausesValidation* property of all controls on the form to *true*.
Validate the contents of multiple controls or an entire form.	Use form-level validation. Create a method that validates all the data on the form. Call it when the user indicates that data input is complete, such as when the user clicks the Save Customer button.
Indicate which values are in error and display error information in a non-intrusive manner.	Use an *ErrorProvider* control. Call the *SetError* method of the *ErrorProvider* control to display an error icon and record an error message that can be displayed as a ToolTip when the user holds the mouse over the error icon.
Display messages in a status bar at the base of a form.	Add a *StatusStrip* control to the form. Add a *ToolStripStatusLabel* control to the StatusStrip. Set the *Text* property of the *ToolStripStatusLabel* control to the message you want to display at runtime.
```

Part V
Managing Data

Chapter 23
Using a Database

After completing this chapter, you will be able to:

- Create a connection to a database by using the Data Source Configuration Wizard.

- Retrieve data from a database and browse it graphically in Microsoft Visual Studio 2005.

- Fetch data from an SQL Server database by using ADO.NET.

In Part IV of this book, you learned how to use Microsoft Visual C# to build user interfaces and present information. In Part V, you will learn about managing data by using the data access functionality available in Visual Studio 2005 and the Microsoft .NET Framework. The chapters in this part of the book describe ADO.NET, a family of objects specifically designed to make it easy to write applications that use databases. If you have previously used Microsoft Visual Basic 6 or Microsoft Access for building applications, you will see that ADO.NET is an updated version of ActiveX Data Objects (ADO) designed and optimized for the .NET Framework common language runtime.

Important To perform the exercises in this chapter, you must have installed Microsoft SQL Server 2005 Express Edition. SQL Server 2005 Express Edition is provided with Visual Studio 2005, and can also be downloaded free of charge from the Microsoft Web site at *http://www.microsoft.com/sql/2005/default.asp*.

Using ADO.NET Databases

With the advent of the .NET Framework, Microsoft decided to update its model for accessing databases, ActiveX Data Objects (ADO), and created ADO.NET. ADO.NET contains several enhancements over the original ADO architecture, providing improved interoperability and performance. If you are already familiar with ADO, you will notice that the object model of ADO.NET is a little different. For one thing, the RecordSet type no longer exists—Microsoft has created the TableAdapter and DataSet classes that support disconnected data access and operations, allowing greater scalability because you no longer have to be connected to the database all the time. (To be fair, ADO provided disconnected RecordSets, but they were the exception rather than the rule when used by programmers.) Therefore, your applications can consume fewer resources. With the connection pooling mechanisms of ADO.NET, database connections can be reused by different applications, thereby reducing the need to continually connect to and disconnect from the database, which can be a time-consuming operation.

ADO.NET is designed to be easy to use, and Visual Studio 2005 provides several wizards and other features that you can use to generate data access code.

The Northwind Traders Database

Northwind Traders is a fictitious company that sells edible goods with exotic names. The Northwind database contains several tables with information about the goods that Northwind Traders sells, the customers they sell to, orders placed by customers, suppliers that Northwind Traders obtains goods from to re-sell, shippers that they can use to send goods to customers, and employees who work for Northwind Traders. Figure 23-1 shows all the tables in the Northwind Traders database and how they are related to each other. The tables that you will be using in this chapter are Orders and Products.

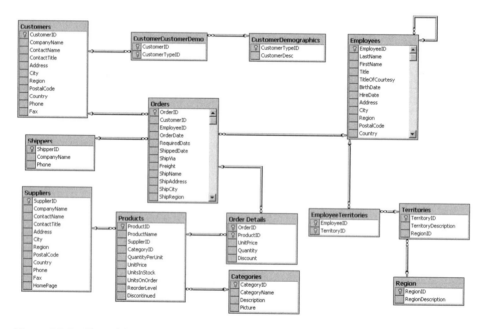

Figure 23-1   The tables in the Northwind Traders database.

Creating the Database

Before proceeding further, you need to create the Northwind Traders database.

Create the database

1. On the Windows Start menu, click All Programs, click Accessories, and then click Command Prompt to open a command prompt window. In the command prompt window, go to the \Microsoft Press\Visual CSharp Step by Step\Chapter 23 folder in your My Documents folder.

2. In the command prompt window, type the following command:

```
sqlcmd -S YourServer\SQLExpress -E -iinstnwnd.sql
```

Replace YourServer with the name of your computer.

> **Tip**   You can find the name of your computer by running the *hostname* command in the command prompt window, before running the *sqlcmd* command.

This command uses the sqlcmd utility to connect to your local instance of SQL Server 2005 Express and run the instnwnd.sql script. This script contains the SQL commands that create the Northwind Traders database and the tables in the database, and fills them with some sample data.

> **Tip**   Ensure SQL Server 2005 Express is running before you attempt to create the Northwind Traders database. You can check the status of SQL Server 2005 Express, and start it running if necessary, by using the SQL Configuration Manager available in the Configuration Tools folder of the Microsoft SQL Server 2005 CTP program group.

3. When the script finishes running, close the command prompt window.

Accessing the Database

In this set of exercises, you will write a program that connects to the database, retrieves the contents of the Products and Suppliers tables, and displays their contents. In the Northwind Traders database, each product is supplied by a single supplier, but an individual supplier can supply more than one product.

In the first exercise, you will create a data source that connects to the Northwind Traders database and retrieves the contents of these tables, by using the wizards provided with Visual Studio 2005.

Create a data source

1. Using Visual Studio 2005, create a new project by using the Windows Application template. Name the project **DisplayProducts** and save it in the \Microsoft Press\Visual CSharp Step by Step\Chapter 23 folder in your My Documents folder.

> **Tip**   If you cannot remember how to create a new Windows Application, refer to the first exercise, "Create the Middleshire Bell Ringers Association project," in Chapter 20, "Introducing Windows Forms."

2. On the Data menu, click Add New Data Source.

    The Data Source Configuration Wizard starts. You use this wizard to create a connection to a data source. A data source can be a database, an object, or a Web service. Using an object or a Web service as a data source is beyond the scope of this book, but we will describe how to create and use Web services in Chapter 28, "Creating and Using a Web Service."

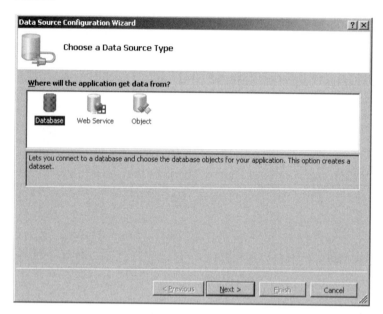

3. Ensure the Database icon is selected, and then click Next. The next page of the wizard prompts you to provide information about the connection to the database you want to use. You have not created any data connections yet, so click the New Connection button.

    The Choose Data Source dialog box appears, allowing you to select the data source and data provider to use. The data source specifies the type of database you want to use, and the data provider specifies how you will connect to the database. Some data sources can be accessed by using more than one data provider. For example, you can connect to SQL Server by using the .NET Framework Data Provider for SQL Server, or the .NET Framework Data Provider for OLE DB. The .NET Data Provider for SQL Server is optimized for connecting to SQL Server databases, whereas the .NET Framework Data Provider for OLE DB is a more generic provider that can be used to connect to a variety of data sources, not just SQL Server.

4. For this application, click the Microsoft SQL Server data source, and make sure the .NET Framework Data Provider for SQL Server is selected as the data provider.

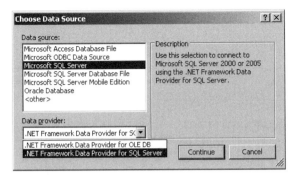

5. Click Continue to proceed to the next step.

    The Add Connection dialog box appears next. You use this dialog box to specify which SQL Server you want to connect to, the authentication mechanism to use, and the database you want to access.

6. Type *YourServer*\SQLExpress in the Server name box, where YourServer is the name of your computer. Select the Use Windows Authentication option to log on to the server. This option uses your Windows account name to connect to the database, and is the recommended way to log on to SQL Server. Select the Northwind database, and then click OK.

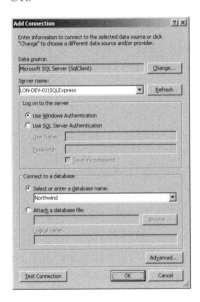

    You are returned to the Data Source Configuration Wizard. The new data connection is given the name *YourServer*\SQLExpress.Northwind.dbo.

7.   Click the + sign by the Connection String label.

You will see a string that contains the connection details you have just specified. This information is held in a format that can be used by the SQL Server provider to connect to the server.

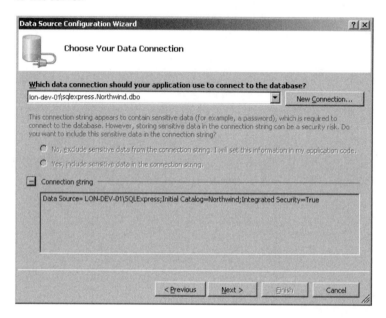

8.   Click Next.

The connection information you have specified can also be saved in an application configuration file. This feature allows you to modify the connection string without needing to rebuild the application; you simply edit the application configuration file. It is useful if you envisage ever needing to use a different database from the one you built the application with.

Save the connection information with the default name.

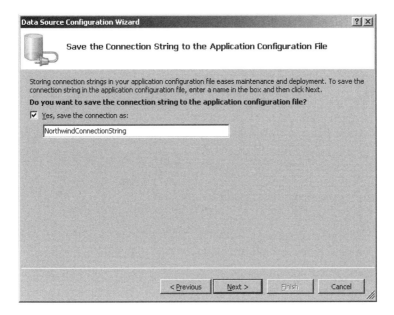

9. Click Next.

   The next page of the wizard allows you to select the data you want to use. You can retrieve data from tables or views in the database, or access the results of stored procedures and functions in SQL Server.

10. Expand the Tables folder and select the Products and Suppliers tables.

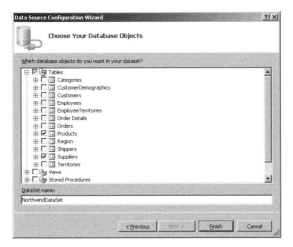

   The wizard generates a *DataSet* object called NorthwindDataSet that you can use to manipulate the data returned. A *DataSet* object represents an in-memory copy of tables and rows retrieved from a database.

11. Click Finish to complete the wizard.

Using an Application Configuration File

An application configuration file provides a very useful mechanism allowing the user to modify some of the resources used by the application without actually needing to rebuild the application itself. The connection string is an example of such a resource.

When you save the connection string generated by the Data Source Configuration Wizard, a new file is added to your project–app.config. This is the source of the application configuration file, and it appears in the Solution Explorer. You can examine the contents of this file by double-clicking it. You will see that it is an XML file, as shown below:

```xml
<?xml version="1.0" encoding="utf-8" ?>
<configuration>
    <configSections>
        <sectionGroup name="userSettings" ... >
            <section name="DisplayProducts.Properties.Settings" ... />
        </sectionGroup>
        <sectionGroup name="applicationSettings" ... >
            <section name="DisplayProducts.Properties.Settings" ... />
        </sectionGroup>
    </configSections>
    <connectionStrings>
        <add name="DisplayProducts.Properties.Settings.NorthwindConnectionString"
            connectionString="Data Source=LON-DEV-01\SQLExpress;Initial
Catalog=Northwind;Integrated Security=True"
providerName="System.Data.SqlClient" />
    </connectionStrings>
    <userSettings>
        <DisplayProducts.Properties.Settings />
    </userSettings>
    <applicationSettings>
        <DisplayProducts.Properties.Settings />
    </applicationSettings>
</configuration>
```

The connection string is held in the <connectionStrings> element of the file. When the application is built, this file is used to generate another file called DisplayProducts.exe.config, which holds exactly the same information in the same format, and is placed in the same folder as the executable program. This is the application configuration file. You should deploy this file with the executable (the .exe file). If the user needs to connect to a different database, she can edit the configuration file by using a text editor and modifying the <connectionString> attribute of the *<connectionStrings>* element. When the application runs, it will use the new value automatically.

Understanding DataSets, DataTables, and TableAdapters

The ADO.NET object model uses DataSets to cache data retrieved from a database. An application that defines DataSet objects can execute queries that populate them, and then display and update the data that they contain. Internally, a DataSet object contains one or more DataTable objects; each DataTable corresponds to a table specified when the DataSet is defined. In the following exercise you will see that NorthwindDataSet contains two DataTable objects called Products and Suppliers.

In the Northwind database, the Products and Suppliers tables have a many-to-one relationship; each product is supplied by a single supplier, but each supplier can supply many products. The Northwind database implements this relationship by using primary and foreign keys. The Data Source Configuration Wizard uses this information to create a DataRelation object as part of NorthwindDataSet. A DataRelation object ensures that the same relationship that exists in the database is maintained between the Products and Suppliers DataTable objects in memory.

At runtime, how does an application actually populate a DataSet? The answer lies in another object called the TableAdapter. A TableAdapter contains methods that you can use to build a DataSet. The two most common methods are called Fill and GetData. The Fill method fills an existing DataSet and returns an integer specifying how many rows were retrieved. The Get-Data method creates a new, populated DataSet.

That's enough theory for now. Let's see what this all means in practice.

Browse product and supplier information

1. In the Data menu, click Preview Data.

   The Preview Data dialog box appears, enabling you to view the data returned by the data source you have just created.

> **Tip** If the Preview Data menu item does not appear, double-click Form1.cs in the Solution Explorer to display Form1 in the Design View window.

2. Click the drop-down list labelled Select an object to preview.

   You will see a tree-view containing the contents of NorthwindDataSet. The DataSet contains two DataTable objects called Products and Suppliers described earlier. Underneath each DataTable you will see a node marked Fill, GetData(). (You might need to expand the Suppliers DataTable to view its child node.) This node corresponds to the TableAdapter object for each TableAdapter.

3. Click the Fill, GetData() node under Products, and then click the Preview button.

The Results window displays the rows from the Products table in the database.

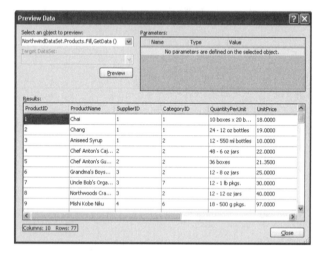

4. In the Select an object to preview drop-down list, click the Fill, GetData() node under Suppliers. Click Preview.

This time, the data from the Suppliers table is displayed.

5. Click Close to close the Preview Data dialog box.

Displaying Data in an Application

Now that you have seen how to define DataSets, let's see how you can use them in an application.

Display product data in the Windows Forms application

1. In the Solution Explorer, right-click Form1.cs and rename the form as DataForm.cs. A dialog box appears asking whether you would like Visual Studio 2005 to modify all the references in this project to use the new name. Click Yes.

2. Display DataForm in the Designer View window. Using the Properties window, change its Text property to Suppliers and Products, and change its Size property to 800, 410.

3. On the Data menu, click Show Data Sources. The Data Sources window appears, displaying NorthwindDataSet with the Products and Suppliers DataTable objects. Expand the Products and Suppliers DataTable objects.

    The columns in each table appear, together with an icon indicating how each column will be displayed on the form. Most columns will be displayed as textbox controls, although the Discontinued column in the Products DataTable will appear as a checkbox; this is because the corresponding column in the database is a bit column that can only contain True/False values. Also notice that Products appears twice: once as a DataTable object in its own right, and once as a column in the Suppliers DataTable. You will shortly see how this feature allows the relationship between a supplier and the products it supplies to be coordinated.

4. Click the Suppliers DataTable. A drop-down menu appears by the name. Click the drop-down menu, and select Details.

    This action will change the display layout for suppliers to a set of fields rather than the default grid layout. The Details layout is useful for displaying the data in the "one" side of a many-to-one relationship, while the Grid view is more suited to the "many" side.

    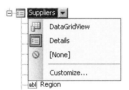

5. Click the SupplierID column in the Suppliers DataTable. Another drop-down menu appears. Click this drop-down menu. You will see the different ways that the data in this column can be presented. The SupplierID column is actually the primary key for this table in the database, and so it should not be changed. For this reason, click the Label control.

6. Click the Suppliers DataTable and drag it to the top left corner of the Suppliers and Products form.

Notice that a number of components appear underneath the form. The table below summarizes these components. Also notice the tool strip that appears at the top of the form. This tool strip contains items for navigating through the list of suppliers, as well as for adding, modifying, and deleting rows, and for saving changes back to the database.

Component	Description
northwindDataSet	This is the data source used by the form. It is a NorthwindDataSet object. It provides methods for updating data in the database.
suppliersBindingSource	This component acts as an intermediary between the controls on the form, and the data source. A BindingSource component keeps track of the currently selected row in the DataSet, and ensures that the controls on the form display the data for that row. A BindingSource provides methods for navigating through a DataSet, adding, removing, and updating rows
suppliersTableAdapter	This is the TableAdapter object for the Suppliers table, providing methods for retrieving rows from the Suppliers table in the database and populating the data source.
suppliersBindingNavigator	This is a BindingNavigator control that provides a standardized mechanism for navigating through the rows in a DataSet. It is the visible tool strip that appears at the top of the form containing the tool strip items for most of the common data-related actions.

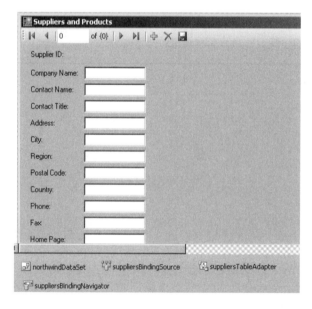

> **Tip**   If the fields are displayed too high up on the form and encroach on the tool strip, while they are still selected, simply drag the Supplier ID field to the appropriate location. The remaining fields will also move.

7. Click the Products DataTable that is nested inside the Suppliers DataTable and drag it onto the form, to the right of the Supplier fields.

   A DataGridView control appears on the form. Also notice that two more components appear underneath the form: productsBindingSource which is a BindingSource control that coordinates the rows in the DataGridView with northwindDataSet, and products-TableAdapter which is used to retrieve rows from the database into the Products Data-Table.

> **Tip**   Be sure to drag the Products DataTable that is nested inside the Suppliers DataTable rather than the top-level Products DataTable in the NorthwindDataSet. If you use the top-level Products DataTable, the display will not be coordinated properly at runtime; all products will always be displayed rather than those supplied by the displayed supplier.

8. Click the DataGridView control on the form and expand it to fill the right-hand side of the form.

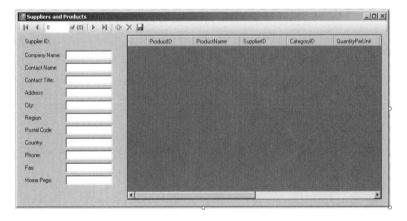

9. While the DataGridView control is still selected (click it if it is not), click the Smart Tag handle that appears at the top right-hand corner of the control.

The DataGridView Tasks dialog box appears. You can use this dialog box to quickly modify the commonly used properties of the DataViewGrid control, and perform tasks such as changing the properties of the columns displayed, and changing the actions supported by the control. To keep the application straightforward, clear the Enable Adding, Enable Editing, Enable Deleting, and Enable Column Reordering checkboxes. You will learn more about using the DataGridView control in Chapter 24, "Working with Data Binding and DataSets."

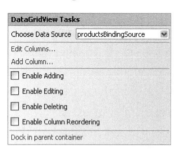

10. Start the application running without debugging. When the form appears, the first supplier (Exotic Liquids) is displayed together with the three products it supplies. Click the Move next button in the tool strip.

    The supplier New Orleans Cajun Delights appears, together with the four products it supplies. You can overtype any of the supplier's details to change them, although the changes will not be saved to the database until you click the Save button in the tool strip.

11. Click the Add new button in the toolstrip.

    The form clears, and you can enter the details of the new supplier. Notice how a new supplier ID is automatically generated. As before, the details of the new supplier will not be saved to the database unless you click the Save button in the tool strip.

12. Click the Delete button in the tool strip to remove this new supplier.

    Existing supplier number 29 automatically appears.

13. Close the form without saving any changes to the data and return to the Visual Studio 2005 programming environment.

Using ADO.NET Programmatically

In the next set of exercises, you will write your own code to access the database rather than dragging tables from the Data Sources window. The aim of the exercise is to help you learn more about ADO.NET and understand the object model implemented by ADO.NET by programming it manually. In many cases, this is what you will have to do in real life—the drag-and-drop approach is fine for creating prototypes, but on many occasions you will want more control over how data is retrieved and manipulated.

The application you are going to create will generate a simple report displaying information about customers' orders. The program will prompt the user for a CustomerID and then display the orders for that customer.

Connect to the database

1. Create a new project called ReportOrders by using the Console Application template. Save it in the \Microsoft Press\Visual CSharp Step By Step\Chapter 23 folder in your My Documents folder. Click OK.

2. In the Solution Explorer, change the name of Program.cs to Report.cs.

   Notice that the name of the Program class in the Code and Text Editor window changes to Report automatically.

3. In the Code And Text Editor window add the following statement under the using Sys-tem.Text; statement:

   ```
   using System.Data.SqlClient;
   ```

   The System.Data.SqlClient namespace contains the specialized ADO.NET classes used to gain access to SQL Server.

4. Locate the Main method of the Report class. Add the following statement that declares a *SqlConnection* object: SqlConnection dataConnection = new SqlConnection(); Sql-Connection is a subclass of the ADO.NET Connection class. It is designed to handle connections to SQL Server databases only.

5. After the variable declaration, add a try/catch block to the Main method. All the code that you will write for gaining access to the database goes inside the try part of this block—remember that you must be prepared to handle exceptions whenever you use a database.

   ```
   try
   {
       // You will add your code here in a moment
   }
   catch(Exception e)
   {
       Console.WriteLine("Error accessing the database: " + e.Message);
   }
   ```

6. Replace the comment in the try block with the following code that connects to the database:

   ```
   dataConnection.ConnectionString = "Integrated Security=true;" +
                                     "Initial Catalog=Northwind;" +
                                     "Data Source=YourServer\\SQLExpress";
   dataConnection.Open();
   ```

> **Important** In the ConnectionString property, replace *YourServer* with the name of your computer or the computer running SQL Server.

The contents of the ConnectionString property of the *SqlConnection* object are the same as those generated by the Data Source Configuration Wizard that you saw in step 7 of the earlier exercise, "Create a data source." This string specifies that the connection will use Windows Authentication to connect to the Northwind database on your local instance of SQL Server 2005 Express Edition. This is the preferred method of access because you do not have to prompt the user for any form of user name or password, and you are not tempted to hard-code user names and passwords into your application. Notice that a semicolon separates all the elements in the ConnectionString.

There are also many other parameters that you can encode in the ConnectionString. See the MSDN Library for Visual Studio 2005 for details.

Using SQL Server Authentication

Windows Authentication is useful for authenticating users that are all members of a Windows domain. However, there might be occasions when the user accessing the database does not have a Windows account; for example, if you are building an application designed to be accessed by remote users over the Internet. In these cases, you can use the User ID and Password parameters instead, like this:

```
string userName = ...;
string password = ...;
// Prompt the user for their name and password, and fill these variables

myConnection.ConnectionString = "User ID=" + userName + ";Password=" + password +
";Initial Catalog=Northwind;Data Source=YourServer\SQLExpress";
```

At this point, I should offer a sentence of advice: Never hard code user names and passwords into your applications. Anyone who obtains a copy of the source code (or who reverse-engineers the compiled code) can see this information, and this renders the whole purpose of security meaningless.

The next step is to prompt the user for a CustomerID and then query the database to find all of the orders for that customer.

Query the Orders table

1. Add the following statements after the `dataConnection.Open();` statement:

```
Console.Write("Please enter a customer ID (5 characters): ");
string customerId = Console.ReadLine();
```

These statements prompt the user for a CustomerID and get the user's response in the string variable customerId.

2. Type the following statements after the code you just entered:

```
SqlCommand dataCommand = new SqlCommand();
dataCommand.Connection = dataConnection;
dataCommand.CommandText =
    "SELECT OrderID, OrderDate, " +
    "ShippedDate, ShipName, ShipAddress, ShipCity, " +
    "ShipCountry ";
dataCommand.CommandText +=
    "FROM Orders WHERE CustomerID='" +
    customerId + "'";
Console.WriteLine("About to execute: {0}\n\n", dataCommand.CommandText);
```

The first statement creates an SqlCommand object. Like SqlConnection, this is a special-ized version of an ADO.NET class, Command, that has been designed for gaining access to SQL Server. A Command object is used to execute a command against a data source. In the case of a relational database, the text of the command is an SQL statement.

The second line of code sets the Connection property of the SqlCommand object to the database connection you opened in the previous exercise. The next two statements pop-ulate the CommandText property with an SQL SELECT statement that retrieves infor-mation from the Orders table for all orders that have a CustomerID that matches the value in the customerId variable (you could do this in a single statement, but it has been split over two lines to make it easier to read). The Console.WriteLine statement just repeats the command about to be executed to the screen.

3. Add the following statement after the code you just entered:

```
SqlDataReader dataReader = dataCommand.ExecuteReader();
```

The fastest way to get data from an SQL Server database is to use the SqlDataReader class. This class extracts rows from the database as fast as your network allows and deposits them in your application.

The next task is to iterate through all the orders (if there are any) and display them.

Fetch data and display orders

1. Add the while loop shown below after the statement that creates the SqlDataReader object:

```
while (dataReader.Read())
{
    // Code to display the current row
}
```

The Read method of the SqlDataReader class fetches the next row from the database. It returns true if another row was retrieved successfully; otherwise, it returns false, usually because there are no more rows. The while loop you have just entered keeps reading rows from the dataReader variable and finishes when there are no more rows.

2. Add the following statements to the body of the while loop you created in the previous step:

```
int orderId = dataReader.GetInt32(0);
DateTime orderDate = dataReader.GetDateTime(1);
DateTime shipDate = dataReader.GetDateTime(2);
string shipName = dataReader.GetString(3);
string shipAddress = dataReader.GetString(4);
string shipCity = dataReader.GetString(5);
string shipCountry = dataReader.GetString(6);
Console.WriteLine(
    "Order {0}\nPlaced {1}\nShipped {2}\n" +
    "To Address {3}\n{4}\n{5}\n{6}\n\n", orderId, orderDate,
    shipDate, shipName, shipAddress, shipCity, shipCountry);
```

This process is how you read the data from an SqlDataReader object. An SqlDataReader object contains the most recent row retrieved from the database. You can use the GetXXX methods to extract the information from each column in the row—there is a GetXXX method for each common type of data. For example, to read an int value, you use the GetInt32 method; to read a string, you use the GetString method; and you can probably guess how to read a DateTime value. The GetXXX methods take a parameter indicating which column to read: 0 is the first column, 1 is the second column, and so on. The previous code reads the various columns from the current Orders row, stores the values in a set of variables, and then prints out the values of these variables.

Firehose Cursors

One of the major drawbacks in a multi-user database application is locked data. Unfortunately, it is common to see applications retrieve rows from a database and keep those rows locked to prevent another user from changing the data while the application is using them. In some extreme circumstances, an application can even prevent other users from reading data that it has locked. If the application retrieves a large number of rows, it locks a large proportion of the table. If there are many users running the same application at the same time, they can end up waiting for each other to release locks and it all leads to a slow-running and frustrating mess.

The SqlDataReader class has been designed to remove this drawback. It fetches rows one at a time and does not retain any locks on a row after it has been retrieved. It is wonderful for improving concurrency in your applications. The SqlDataReader class is sometimes referred to as a "firehose cursor." (The term *cursor* is an acronym that stands for "current set of rows.")

The SqlDataReader class also offers higher performance than using a DataSet if you are simply retrieving data. DataSets use XML to represent the data that they hold internally. This approach offers flexibility, and any component that can read the XML format used by the DataSet class can process data. The SqlDataReader class uses the native SQL Server data-transfer format to retrieve data directly from the database, rather than requiring that data is converted into an intermediate format such as XML. However, this gain in performance comes at the expense of the flexibility offered by DataSets.

When you have finished using a database, it's good practice to release any resources you have been using.

Disconnect from the database

1. In the Code pane, add the following statements after the while loop:

```
dataReader.Close();
```

This statement closes the SqlDataReader object. You should always close an SqlData-Reader when you have finished with it because you are not able to use the current Sql-Connection object to run any more commands until you do. It is also considered good practice to do it even if all you are going to do next is close the SqlConnection.

2. After the catch block, add the following finally block:

```
finally
{
    dataConnection.Close();
}
```

Database connections are scarce resources. You need to ensure that they are closed when you have finished with them. Putting this statement in a *finally* block guarantees that the *SqlConnection* will be closed, even if an exception occurs; remember that the code in the *finally* block will be executed when the *catch* handler has finished.

3. On the Debug menu, click Starting Without Debugging to build and run the application.

By default, the Start Without Debugging command runs the application and then prompts you before it closes the Console window so that you get a chance to read the output. If you click the Start Debugging command instead, the Console window closes as soon as the application finishes without giving you the same opportunity.

4. At the customer ID prompt, type VINET and press Enter. The SQL SELECT statement appears, followed by the orders for this customer. You can scroll back through the Console window to view all the data. Press the Enter key to close the Console window when you have finished.

5. Run the application again, and then type BONAP when prompted for the customer ID.

Some rows appear, but then an error message is displayed: "Error accessing the database. Data is Null." The problem is that relational databases allow some columns to contain null values. A null value is a bit like a null variable in C#: it doesn't have a value and, if you try to use it, you get an error. In the Orders table, the ShippedDate column can contain null if the order has not yet been shipped.

6. Press Enter to close the Console window.

Closing Connections

In many older applications, you might notice a tendency to open a connection when the application starts and not close the connection until the application terminates. The rationale behind this strategy was that opening and closing database connections was an expensive and time-consuming operation. This strategy had an impact on the scalability of applications because each user running the application had a connection to the database open while the application was running, even if the user went to lunch for a couple of hours. Most databases have a limit on the number of concurrent connections that they allow. (Sometimes this is because of licensing reasons, but more often it's because each connection consumes a certain amount of resources on the database server and these resources are not infinite.) Eventually the database would hit a limit on the number of users that could operate concurrently.

Most .NET Framework data providers (including the SQL Server provider) implement *connection pooling*. Database connections are created and held in a pool. When an application requires a connection, the data access provider extracts the next available connection from the pool. When the application closes the connection, it is returned to the pool and made available for the next application that wants a connection. This means that opening and closing a database connection is no longer an expensive operation. Closing a connection does not disconnect from the database; it just returns the connection to the pool. Opening a connection is simply a matter of obtaining an already-open connection from the pool. Therefore, you should not hold on to connections longer than you need to— open a connection when you need it and close it as soon as you have finished with it.

You should note that the ExecuteReader method of the SqlCommand class, which creates an SqlDataReader, is overloaded. You can specify a System.Data.CommandBehavior parameter that automatically closes the connection used by the SqlDataReader when the SqlDataReader is closed. For example:

```
SqlDataReader dataReader =
    dataCommand.ExecuteReader(System.Data.CommandBehavior.CloseConnection);
```

When you read the data from the SqlDataReader object, you should check that the data you are reading is not null. In the final exercise, you will add statements to the ReportOrders application that check for null values.

Handle null database values

1. In the Code And Text Editor window, locate the while loop that iterates through the rows retrieved by using the dataReader variable. Change the body of the while loop as shown here:

```
while (dataReader.Read())
{
    int orderId = dataReader.GetInt32(0);
    if (dataReader.IsDBNull(2))
    {
        Console.WriteLine("Order {0} not yet shipped\n\n", orderId);
    }
    else
    {
        DateTime orderDate = dataReader.GetDateTime(1);
        DateTime shipDate = dataReader.GetDateTime(2);
        string shipName = dataReader.GetString(3);
        string shipAddress = dataReader.GetString(4);
        string shipCity = dataReader.GetString(5);
        string shipCountry = dataReader.GetString(6);
        Console.WriteLine(
            "Order {0}\nPlaced {1}\nShipped{2}\n" +
            "To Address {3}\n{4}\n{5}\n{6}\n\n", orderId, orderDate,
            shipDate, shipName, shipAddress, shipCity, shipCountry);
    }
}
```

The if statement uses the IsDBNull method to determine whether the ShippedDate column (column 2 in the table) is null. If it is null, no attempt is made to fetch it (or any of the other columns, which should also be null if there is no ShippedDate value); otherwise, the columns are read and printed as before.

2. Compile and run the application again. Type BONAP for the CustomerID when prompted.

This time you do not get any errors, but you receive a list of orders that have not yet been shipped.

■ **If you want to continue to the next chapter**

Keep Visual Studio 2005 running and turn to Chapter 24.

■ **If you want to exit Visual Studio 2005 for now**

On the File menu, click Exit. If you see a Save dialog box, click Yes.

Chapter 23 Quick Reference

To	Do this
Create a connection to a database graphically in Visual Studio 2005.	Use the Data Source Configuration Wizard. The wizard prompts you for the details of the connection to create and the database objects to use.
Browse data in Visual Studio 2005.	In the Data menu, click Preview Data. The Preview Data dialog box allows you to select a DataSet and DataTable object. Click the Preview button to view the data.
Change the way in which a DataTable will be presented on a form.	In the Data Sources window (click Show Data Sources on the Data menu if this window is not displayed) click the DataTable. Select the style (DataGridView, Details, or None) from the drop-down menu that appears.
Modify the way in which fields in a data source will be displayed on a form.	In the Data Sources window, expand the DataTable containing the fields to be modified. Click the field, and select the presentation style from the drop-down menu that appears.
Add a DataTable to a form.	Click and drag a DataTable object from the Data Sources window onto the form. Either a collection of fields or a DataGridView is added to the form. Visual Studio 2005 also generates a DataSet, a BindingSource, a TableAdapter, and a BindingNavigator object for connecting the form fields or DataGridView to the database and moving through the data.
Programmatically connect to a database.	Create an *SqlConnection* object, set its *ConnectionString* property with details specifying the database to use, and call the *Open* method.
Create and execute a database query in code.	Create an *SqlCommand* object. Set its *Connection* property to a valid *SqlConnection* object. Set its *CommandText* property to a valid SQL *SELECT* statement. Call the *ExecuteReader* method to run the query and create an *SqlDataReader* object.
Fetch data by using a *SqlData-Reader* object.	Ensure the data is not null by using the *IsDBNull* method. If the data is not null, use the appropriate *GetXXX* method (such as *GetString* or *GetInt32*) to retrieve the data.

Chapter 24

Working with Data Binding and DataSets

After completing this chapter, you will be able to:

- Bind a property of a control to a data source at design time or run time by using simple binding.

- Bind a control to a list of values from a data source by using complex binding.

- Design a DataSet class containing TableAdapter and DataTable classes.

- Write code to instantiate and populate a DataSet object.

- Use a DataGridView to modify the data held in a DataSet object.

- Validate the changes the user has made to the data in a DataGridView control

- Update a database with the changes made to a DataSet object using a TableAdapter object.

In Chapter 23, "Using a Database," you learned the essentials of using Microsoft ADO.NET for executing queries and updating databases. You used a *DataSet* to retrieve data from the Suppliers and Products tables and display it in a master/details form. You achieved this simply by using the Data Source Configuration Wizard, configuring *DataTable* classes, and dragging and dropping *DataTable* classes onto a form to generate *DataSet*, *BindingSource*, *TableAdapter*, and *BindingNavigator* controls. You actually wrote very little code to do all of this. In this chapter, you will write C# statements that perform many of these tasks—this will help you to understand what Microsoft Visual Studio 2005 is doing for you, and enable you to write more complex applications that can achieve more functionality than can be generated by using drag and drop techniques alone.

In this chapter, you'll learn more about data binding—linking a control property to a data source. You will learn how to dynamically bind properties of controls to a *DataSet* by using simple data binding. You will also learn how to use complex data binding with the *ComboBox* and *ListBox* controls. You will learn a lot more about how to design *DataSet* classes and use *DataSet* objects in code. In particular, you will learn how to use *DataSet* objects with the *DataGridView* control to update a database in an efficient manner.

Windows Forms Controls and Data Binding

Many properties of most Windows Forms controls can be attached, or bound, to a data source. After they are bound, the value in the data source changes the value of the bound property and vice versa. You have already seen data binding in action by using the *TextBox* and *DataGridView* controls in the DisplayProducts project in Chapter 23. The *controls* on the form were bound to *BindingSource* objects belonging to a *DataSet* containing records from the Suppliers and Products table in the database.

Windows Forms controls support two types of data binding: simple and complex. *Simple data binding* allows you to attach a property of a control or form to a *single value* in a data source, and *complex data binding* is specifically used to attach a control to a list of values. Simple data binding is useful for controls such as *TextBox* or *Label* that only display a single value. Complex data binding is more commonly used with controls that can display multiple values, such as *ListBox*, *ComboBox*, or *DataGridView*.

Defining a DataSet and Using Simple Data Binding

You use simple data binding to display a single value from a data source. A data source can be almost anything, from a cell in a *DataSet* to the value of a property of another control to a simple variable. You can perform simple data binding at design time by using the *Data-Bindings* property of a control. In the exercises that follow, you will define a new *DataSet* that defines a data source returning a single row, and then bind the *Text* property of a *Label* control to a *BindingSource* object for this *DataSet*.

Defining a *DataSet* class

1. In Visual Studio 2005, create a new project called ProductsMaintenance in the \Microsoft Press\Visual CSharp Step by Step\Chapter 24 folder in your My Documents folder by using the Windows Application template.

2. In the Project menu, click Add New Item.

    The Add New Item dialog box appears, displaying templates for objects that can be added to a project.

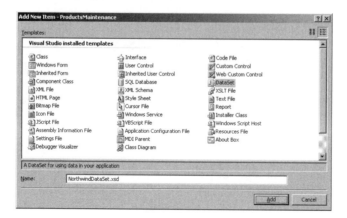

3. In the Add New Item dialog box, click the DataSet template, type
NorthwindDataSet.xsd for the name, and then click Add.

> **Note**   DataSet definitions should always be created in a file with the extension ".xsd."
> DataSet definitions are actually XML schemas, which Visual Studio 2005 uses to generate
> C# code when the application is built.

The DataSet Designer window appears.

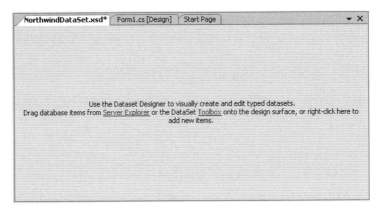

4. In the Toolbox, expand the DataSet category if necessary, and then click the Table-
Adapter tool. Click anywhere in the DataSet Designer window.

A DataTable and TableAdapter object are added to the DataSet Designer window, and
the TableAdapter Configuration Wizard appears.

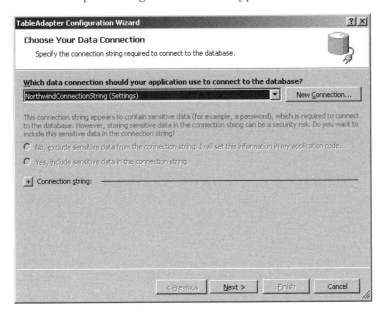

5. In the Choose Your Data Connection page of the TableAdapter Configuration Wizard, click Next.

> **Note** The Choose Your Data Connection page in the TableAdapter Configuration Wizard will either display **NorthwindConnectionString** or *YourServer***sqlex-press.Northwind.dbo** for the data connection, depending on whether you have left Visual Studio 2005 running since performing the exercises in Chapter 23, or have closed it down and restarted it. Either data connection will work for this exercise.

6. If the "Save the connection string to the application configuration file" page appears, specify that the connection string should be saved with the name Northwind-ConnectionString and click Next.

   The Choose a Command Type page appears.

7. The "Choose a Command Type" prompts you to specify how the TableAdapter should access the database. You can provide your own SQL statements, you can get the Wizard to generate stored procedures that encapsulate SQL statements for you, or you can use pre-existing stored procedures that a database developer has already created. Select Use SQL statements, and then click Next.

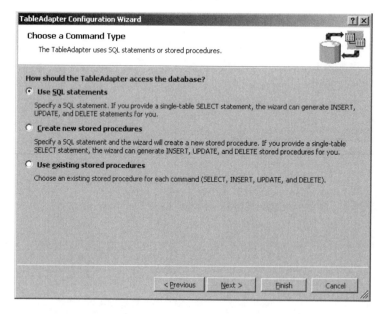

   The Enter a SQL Statement page appears.

8. Type the following SQL SELECT statement that calculates the number of rows in the Products table:

```
SELECT COUNT(*) AS NumProducts
FROM Products
```

9. Click Advanced Options.

   The Advanced Options dialog box appears.

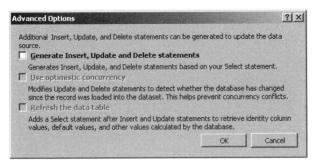

   Apart from retrieving data from the database, a *TableAdapter* object can also insert, update, and delete rows. The Wizard will generate SQL INSERT, UPDATE, and DELETE statements automatically, using the table you specified in the SQL SELECT statement (Products in this example).

10. The SQL SELECT statement used to fetch data simply counts the number of rows in the Products table. It does not make sense to generate SQL INSERT, UPDATE, or DELETE statements as this value is not directly updateable. Clear the "Generate Insert, Update, and Delete statements" check box and then click OK.

11. In the Table Adapter Configuration Wizard, click Next.

    The "Choose Methods to Generate" dialog box appears.

12. A *TableAdapter* can generate two methods for populating a *DataTable* object with the rows retrieved from the database: the *Fill* method which expects an existing *DataTable* or *DataSet* as a parameter which is filled with the data, and the *GetData* method which creates a new *DataTable* and fills it. Leave both methods selected, and then click Next.

13. The Wizard uses the information you have supplied and generates the new Table-Adapter class. Click Finish to close the Wizard.

    A *TableAdapter* class called *DataTable1TableAdapter*, and a corresponding *DataTable* class called *DataTable1*, appear in the DataSet Designer window.

14. In the DataSet Designer window, click the *DataTable1* item. Using the Properties window, change its *Name* property to **NumProductsTable**. Click the *Data-Table1TableAdapter* and change its name to **NumProductsTableTableAdapter**. The objects in the DataSet Designer window should look like the following graphic:

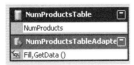

Notice that *NumProductsTable DataTable* contains a single column called *NumProducts*. This column is filled with the value of the *NumProducts* expression (the number of rows in the Products table), when the underlying SQL SELECT statement runs.

15. On the Build menu, click Build Solution.

This action generates the the code and objects for the DataSet, so that they can be used in the next exercise.

> **Tip**   You can view the code that is generated by Visual Studio 2005 by expanding Northwind-
> DataSet.xsd in the Solution Explorer, and double-clicking the file NorthwindDataSet.
> Designer.cs that appears. Be careful not to change any of this code, however.

In the next exercise, you will bind to the value retrieved by the *NumProductsTableAdapter* from the database into the *NumProducts DataTable* in the *NorthwindDataSet DataSet* to the *Text* property of a *Label* control. When the application runs, the label will display the number of rows in the Products table.

Bind to a column in a *DataTable*

1. Display *Form1* in the Design View window. In the Solution Explorer, change the file-name from Form1.cs to ProductsForm.cs. When prompted, click Yes to rename all references to Form1 in the project.

2. Using the Properties window, change the *Text* property to **Products Maintenance**.

3. Add a *Label* control to the form. Change the *Text* property of the control to **Number of Products:**, and set its *Location* property to **25, 34**.

4. Add another *Label* control to the form. Set the *Location* property of the control to **131, 34**, and change its *(Name)* property and *Text* property to **numProducts**.

5. Expand the *(DataBindings)* property for the *numProducts* label. Click the *Text* property (inside *DataBindings*), and then click the drop-down menu that appears.

A window appears displaying a tree view of data sources. Expand the Other Data Sources node, expand Project Data Sources, expand NorthwindDataSet, expand Num-ProductsTable, and then click NumProducts. This action binds the *Text* property of the *Label* control to the *NumProducts* column in the *NumProductsTable DataTable*.

Visual Studio 2005 generates an instance of the *NorthwindDataSet* class called *north-windDataSet*, an instance of the *NumProductsTableAdapter* class called *numProductsTable-Adapter*, and a *BindingSource* object called *numProductsTableBindingSource*, and adds them to the form.

6. Click the *numProductsTableBindingSource* object underneath the form. Using the Properties window, click the *DataSource* property. This property identifies the *DataSet* object that the *BindingSource* uses to connect to the database; notice that it refers to *northwind-DataSet*.

7. Click the *DataMember* property. This property specifies the *DataTable* object in *north-windDataSet* that acts as the source of the data; it is set to *NumProductsTable*.

8. Click the *numProducts* label again, and expand the *(DataBindings)* property. Examine the *Text* property again, and notice that it is set to *numProductsTableBindingSource −NumProducts*.

9. View ProductsForm.cs in the Code and Text Editor window and locate the ProductsForm_Load method.

    This method, which was generated by Visual Studio 2005, runs when the form opens. It contains the following statement:

    ```
    this.numProductsTableAdapter.Fill(this.northwindDataSet.NumProductsTable);
    ```

    From this set of objects, properties, and the code, you should be able to deduce how *label2* gets its data from the database:

    a. The *numProductsTableAdapter* object connects to the database and retrieves the number of rows in the Products in the database by executing its SQL SELECT statement.

    b. The *numProductsTableAdapter* uses this information to fill the *NumProductsTable DataTable* object in the *northwindDataSet* object when the form starts.

    c. The *numProductsTableBindingSource* object connects the *NumProducts* column in the *NumProductsTable DataTable* object in the *northwindDataSet* object to the *Text* property of label2.

10. Build and run the application.

   The *Label* control displays the number of rows in the Products table (probably 77 if you have not changed any of the data since the database was created).

11. Close the form and return to the Visual Studio 2005 programming environment.

Dynamic Data Binding

You can set the *DataBindings* property of a control by using code which executes at runtime as well as setting it statically at design time. The *DataBindings* property provides the *Add* method that you can use to bind a property to a data source. For example, you can bind the *Text* property of a *Label* control called *myLabel* to the *NumProducts* column in *numProductsTableBindingSource* like this:

```
myLabel.DataBindings.Add("Text", numProductsTableBindingSource, "NumProducts");
```

The parameters to the *Add* method are the name of the property to bind to, the name of an object containing the data to be bound to, and the member actually providing the data.

You can use the *Add* method to bind to properties of other controls. The following example binds the *Text* property of *myLabel* to the *Text* property of a *TextBox* control called *myText*:

```
myLabel.DataBindings.Add("Text", myText, "Text");
```

If you try this code, you will find that the *Label* automatically updates itself as you type text into the *TextBox*.

Using Complex Data Binding

You have seen how to use simple data binding for attaching the property of a control to a single value in a data source. Complex data binding is useful if you want to display a list of values from a data source. In the following exercises, you will use complex data binding to display the names of suppliers from the database in a *ComboBox* control and then display the SupplierID of a supplier that the user selects. You will make use of the techniques you learn here when enhancing the Products Maintenance application later in this chapter.

Tip   The *ListBox* and *CheckedListBox* controls also support complex data binding by using the same techniques that you will see in these exercises.

Create and configure the data source

1. In the Solution Explorer, double-click NorthwindDataSet.xsd to display the DataSet Designer window.

2. Using the Toolbox, add another *TableAdapter* to the *DataSet*.

    The TableAdapter Configuration Wizard opens.

3. In the TableAdapter Configuration Wizard, use the NorthwindConnectionString to connect to the database and click Next.

4. In the Choose a Command Type page, select Use SQL statements and click Next.

5. In the Enter a SQL Statement page, click Query Builder.

    The Query Builder dialog box opens.This wizard provides a convenient way for constructing SELECT statements if you cannot remember the syntax of SQL.

6. In the Add Table dialog box, select the Suppliers table, click Add, and then click Close.

    The Suppliers table is added to the Query Builder dialog box.

7. Check the SupplierID and CompanyName column. Notice that the lower pane in the dialog box displays the SQL SELECT statement that corresponds to the columns you have selected:

    ```
    SELECT SupplierID, CompanyName
    FROM Suppliers
    ```

    You can verify that this statement retrieves the rows you are expecting by clicking the Execute Query button. The results of the query are displayed in the pane at the bottom of the dialog box.

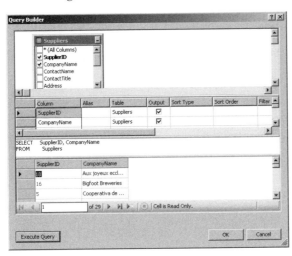

8. Click OK to close the Query Builder and return to the TableAdapter Configuration Wizard.

    The SELECT statement is copied into the Enter a SQL Statement page.

9. This application will not actually change the details of any supplier, so click Advanced Options and deselect Generate Insert, Update and Delete statements. Click OK, and then click Finish.

   A new *DataTable* class called *Suppliers*, and a *DataTableAdapter* class called *SuppliersTableAdapter*, are added to the DataSet Designer window.

10. Rebuild the solution to generate the code for the new objects.

Bind a *ComboBox* to the *DataTable*

1. Display ProductsForm in the Design View window.

2. Using the Toolbox, add a *ComboBox* control and a *Label* to the form. Set the properties of these controls by using the values in the following table.

Control	Property	Value
comboBox1	(Name)	supplierList
	Location	25, 65
label2	(Name)	supplierID
	Location	178, 70
	Text	SupplierID

3. Click the *ComboBox* control on the form. In the Properties window, click the *DataSource* property. Click the drop-down menu that appears. Expand Other Data Sources, expand Project Data Sources, expand NorthwindDataSet, and click Suppliers.

   This action binds the *ComboBox* control to the *Suppliers DataTable*, and generates a new *BindingSource* control called *suppliersBindingSource* and an instance of the *SuppliersTableAdapter* class, and adds them to the form.

4. While the *ComboBox* is still selected, set its *DisplayMember* property to *CompanyName*, and set its *ValueMember* property to *SupplierID*.

   When the form runs, it will display a list of suppliers in the combo box. When the user selects a supplier, its SupplierID will be available as the combo box value.

5. Click the Events button in the Properties window and double-click the *SelectedIndexChanged* event for the *ComboBox*.

   The code for ProductForm is displayed in the Code and Text Editor window, and a click event handler called *supplierList_ SelectedIndexChanged* is generated.

6. Add the following statements to the *supplierList_ SelectedIndexChanged* method:

```
if (supplierList.SelectedValue != null)
{
    supplierID.Text = supplierList.SelectedValue.ToString();
}
```

This block of code displays the ID of the supplier the user selects in the *supplierID* label. The *SelectedValue* property returns the *ValueMember* of the currently selected row. It is returned as an object, so you must use *ToString* if you want to treat it as a string.

7. Examine the *ProductsForm_Load* method. Notice that another line of code has been generated that populates the *Suppliers DataTable* in the *northwindDataSet* object by using the *Fill* method of *suppliersTableAdapter*.

8. Build and run the application. The combo box displays the names of all suppliers. Click a supplier. The ID appears in the label to the right of the combo box. Click other supplier names and verify that the ID displayed is updated appropriately.

9. Close the form and return to Visual Studio 2005.

Updating a Database Using a DataSet

In the exercises so far in this chapter, you have seen how to fetch data from a database. Now it's time to show you how to update data. First, however, we need to consider some potential problems and how using a *DataSet* can overcome them.

Databases are intended to support multiple concurrent users, but resources such as the number of concurrent connections allowed might be limited. In an application that fetches and displays data, you never know quite how long the user will be browsing the data, and it is not a good practice to keep a database connection open for an extended period of time. Instead, a better approach is to connect to the database, fetch the data into a *DataSet* object, and then disconnect again. The user can browse the data in the *DataSet* and make any changes required. After the user finishes, the program can reconnect to the database and submit any changes. Of course, there are complications that you need to consider, such as what happens if two users have queried and updated the same data, changing it to different values. Which value should be stored in the database? We will come back to this problem shortly.

Managing Connections

In earlier exercises, you have seen that when you define a *DataSet* you can specify a connection to use for communicating with the database. This information is embedded into the *TableAdapter* used to retrieve the data and fill the *DataSet*. When you execute the *Fill* or *GetData* methods, the code generated by Visual Studio 2005 examines the state of the connection first. If the connection to be used is already open, it is used to retrieve the data, and is left open at the end of the operation. If the connection is closed, the *Fill* and *GetData* methods open it, fetch the data, and then close it again. The *DataSet* in this case is referred to as a *disconnected DataSet* as it doesn't maintain an active connection to the database. Disconnected *DataSet* objects act as a data cache in applications. You can modify the data in the *DataSet*, and later reopen the connection and send the changes back to the database.

You can manually open a connection to a database by creating a *SqlConnection* object, setting its *ConnectionString* property, and then calling its *Open* method as shown in Chapter 23. You can associate an open connection with a *TableAdapter* by setting the *Connection* property. The following code shows how to connect to the database and fill the *Suppliers DataTable*. In this case, the database connection will remain open after the *Fill* method completes:

```
SqlConnection dataConnection = new SqlConnection();
dataConnection.ConnectionString = "Integrated Security=true;" +
                                  "Initial Catalog=Northwind;" +
                                  "Data Source=YourServer\\SQLExpress";
dataConnection.Open();
suppliersTableAdapter.Connection = dataConnection;
suppliersTableAdapter.Fill(northwindDataSet.Suppliers);
```

Unless you have a good reason to do so, you should avoid maintaining connections longer than needed; let the *Fill* and *GetData* methods open and close the connection for you and create a disconnected *DataSet*.

Handling Multi-User Updates

Earlier in this chapter, we mentioned the problem that arises if two users try and update the same data at the same time. There are at least two possible approaches you can adopt to solve this problem. Each approach has its benefits and disadvantages.

The first technique involves the Use optimistic concurrency option in the the Advanced Options dialog box in the TableAdapter Configuration Wizard.

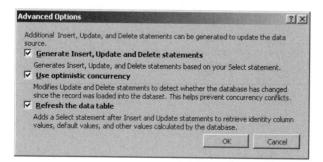

If you *deselect* this option, the rows retrieved into the *DataSet* will be locked in the database to prevent other users from changing them. This is known as pessimistic concurrency. It guarantees that any changes you make will not conflict with changes made by any other users at the expense of blocking those other users. If you retrieve a large number of rows and only update a small proportion of them, you have potentially prevented other users from modifying any of the rows that you have not changed. There is one other drawback—locking data requires that the connection used to retrieve the data remains open, therefore if you use pessimistic concurrency you also run the risk of consuming a large number of connection resources. The principal advantage of pessimistic concurrency, of course, is simplicity. You don't have to write code that checks for updates made by other users before modifying the database.

If you select the "Use optimistic concurrency" option, data is not locked, and the connection can be closed after the data has been fetched. The disadvantage is that you have to write code that ascertains whether any updates made by the user conflict with those made by other users, and this code can be quite difficult to write and debug. However, the *TableAdapter* object generated by the TableAdapter Configuration Wizard hides much of this complexity, although you must be prepared to handle the events that can be raised if conflicts occur. We will look at this in more detail in the final part of this chapter.

Using a DataSet with a DataGridView Control

Now that you have a good understanding of how to create *DataSet* objects, retrieve rows, and display data, you are going to add functionality to the Products Maintenance application to allow the user to update the details of Products in the database. You will use a *DataGridView* control for displaying and updating the data.

Add the DataGridView control to the form

1. Display ProductsForm in the Design View window. Delete the *supplierList ComboBox* control and the *supplierID Label* control from the form.

2. In the Code and Text Editor window, remove the *supplierList_SelectedIndexChanged* method from ProductsForm.cs.

3. Return to the Design View window. Resize the form; set its *Size* property to **600, 400**.

4. In the Toolbox, expand the Data category, and click the *DataGridView* control. Drop the control onto the form. Rename the *DataGridView* control as *productsGrid*. Set its *Location* property to **13, 61** and its *Size* property to **567, 300**.

5. Add two *Button* controls to the form above *productsGrid* and set their *Location* properties to **402, 22** and **505, 22**. Rename them as *queryButton* and *saveButton*. Change the *Text* property of each button to **Query** and **Save**, respectively.

The next step is to create a *DataAdapter* class and bind it to the *DataGridView* control. You will create the *DataAdapter* class by using the TableAdapter Configuration Wizard. To add a bit of variation, rather than setting the *DataSource* and *DataMember* properties of the *DataGridView* control by using the Design View window, you will bind to the *DataAdapter* by writing some code.

Create a DataAdapter for fetching Products and bind it to the DataGridView control

1. Display the DataSet Design window for NorthwindDataSet.xsd (double-click NorthwindDataSet.xsd in the Solution Explorer).

2. Add a new *TableAdapter* to the *DataSet* by using the TableAdapter Configuration Wizard for fetching the details of Products from the Northwind database. Use the information in the following table to help you.

Page	Field	Value
Choose Your Data Connection	Which data connection should your application use to connect to the database?	**NorthwindConnectionString**
Choose a Command Type	How should the *TableAdapter* access the database?	**Use SQL statements**
Enter a SQL Statement	What data should be loaded into the table?	**SELECT * FROM Products**
	Advanced Options	**Select all options**
Choose Methods to Generate	Which methods do you want to add to the *TableAdapter?*	**Select all options and use default method names**

When you complete the wizard and the *DataTable* and *TableAdapter* are generated, notice that the wizard automatically detects that the Suppliers and Products table have a relationship in the database and creates a *Relation* that links the *DataTables* together.

3. In the Build menu, click Rebuild Solution to generate the code for the new *DataTable* and *TableAdapter* classes.

4. Display ProductForm in the Design View window. Double-click the *Query Button* control.

   Visual Studio 2005 generates a click event handler for the control called *queryButton_Click* and places you in the Code and Text Editor window.

5. Add the following statements to the *queryButton_Click* method:

```
NorthwindDataSetTableAdapters.ProductsTableAdapter productsTA =
        new NorthwindDataSetTableAdapters.ProductsTableAdapter();
productsTA.Fill(northwindDataSet.Products);
BindingSource productsBS = new BindingSource(northwindDataSet, "Products");
productsGrid.DataSource = productsBS;
```

The first statement creates a new instance of the *ProductsTableAdapter* class that you defined by using the TableAdapter Configuration Wizard. Notice that this class is defined in a namespace called *NorthwindDataSetTableAdapters* (as are all the other *TableAdapter* classes for this *DataSet*). The second statement uses this object to fill the *Products DataTable* in the *northwindDataSet* object. Remember that this statement will automatically disconnect from the database after fetching the data because no prior connection had been established. The third statement creates a new *BindingSource* object for the *Products DataTable* in the *northwindDataSet* object. The fourth statement actually performs the data binding—it sets the *DataSource* property of the *DataGridView* control to refer to the new *BindingSource* object.

6. Build and run the application.

   When the application starts, the *DataGridView* control is initially empty.

7. Click Query. The *DataGridView* displays a list of Products. Verify that the number of rows in the DataGridView control matches the value displayed by the Number of Products label.

8. Click the *ProductName* column header. The rows are sorted by product name and appear in ascending order. Click the *ProductName* column again. This time the rows appear in descending order. Click the *ProductID* column to display the rows in their original order.

9. Click any cell in the *DataGridView* and overtype the data. By default, you can modify the contents of any cell other than the ProductID. You cannot change the ProductID of a row because this column is marked as the primary key of the table in the database (primary key values should never be updated as they are used to identify a row in the database).

   Try typing an invalid value into a cell—type an alphabetic string into the SupplierID column, for example. When you click away, an error dialog will be displayed. This is the default error handling dialog for the *DataGridView* control (and is rather ugly). You can replace it with your own code by trapping the *DataError* event of the *DataGridView* control. Press the Escape key to undo the change.

10. Scroll right to display the *Discontinued* column. Notice that this column appears as a check box. In the database, this column has the *bit* type, and can only contain two values (1 or 0).

11. Scroll to the end of the data in the *DataGridView* control. A row marked with an asterisk appears. You can add a new product by entering its details in this row. Notice that the ProductID is generated automatically.

12. Click in the gray margin on the left-hand side of row 76. The entire row is highlighted. Press the Delete key. The row disappears from the DataGridView control.

13. When you have finished browsing the data, close the form and return to Visual Studio 2005. No changes will be saved as you have not yet written the code to do this.

Validating User Input in the DataGridView Control

Before saving changes back to the database, we want to ensure that the changes the user makes are valid. Currently, the user can type any amount of rubbish into the *DataGridView*. In the next exercises, you will learn how to constrain the user input to eliminate some possible sources of error, and validate the data in the control.

Configure the DataGridView control to constrain user input

1. Display ProductsForm in the Design View window. Delete the Query button.

2. Display the ProductsForm.cs file in the Code and Text Editor window. Comment out the *queryButton_Click* method and its contents.

3. Return to the Design View window and click the *DataGridView* control. In the Properties window, set the *DataSource* property to the *Products DataTable* in the *Northwind-DataSet* class (in Project Data Sources, in Other Data Sources).

   The columns in the Products table appear in the DataGridView control.

4. Select the *Columns* property in the Properties window and click the ellipses button.

   The Edit Columns dialog box appears. You can use this dialog to view and set the properties of each column in the *DataGridView* control.

5. In the Edit Columns dialog box, click the ProductID column. In the list of Bound Column Properties, verify that the *ReadOnly* property is set to True. The values in this column are generated automatically, so preventing the user from changing this value eliminates one possible source of user errors.

6. Click the SupplierID column. Set the *ColumnType* property to *DataGridViewComboBox-Column* and set the *DisplayStyle* property to *ComboBox*. This will cause the column to be displayed as a combo box rather than a text box.

> **Note**   The *DisplayStyle* property does not appear until you set the *ColumnType* property.

7. Set the *DataSource* property to *suppliersBindingSource*. You will display the list of suppliers in this column by using the same technique that you saw earlier in this chapter when performing complex data binding. Set the *DisplayMember* property to *CompanyName*, and the *ValueMember* property to *SupplierID*. When the user selects a supplier from the list, the SupplierID will be used behind the scenes to supply the value for this column in the Products table. This eliminates another possible source of user errors.

8. In the Edit Columns dialog box, click OK.

You have seen how to prevent some basic errors by restricting the user input to a set of valid values. However, you still need to trap the other errors that can occur. You will achieve this by writing handlers for the *CellValidating*, *CellEndEdit*, and *DataError* events. The *CellValidating* event occurs whenever the user has changed the contents of a cell. The *CellEndEdit* event occurs after a cell has been validated, and the user attempts to move away.

Handle the CellValidating, CellEndEdit, and DataError event

1. Click the *productsGrid* control in the Design View window, and click the Events button in the Properties window.

2. Double-click the *CellValidating* event.

   Visual Studio 2005 generates the event method, *productsGrid_CellValidating*.

3. Add the following statements to the *productsGrid_CellValidating* method:

```
int newInteger;
productsGrid.Rows[e.RowIndex].ErrorText = "";
if ((productsGrid.Columns[e.ColumnIndex].DataPropertyName == "UnitsInStock") ||
    (productsGrid.Columns[e.ColumnIndex].DataPropertyName == "UnitsOnOrder") ||
    (productsGrid.Columns[e.ColumnIndex].DataPropertyName == "ReorderLevel"))
{
    if (!int.TryParse(e.FormattedValue.ToString(), out newInteger) ||
        newInteger < 0)
    {
        productsGrid.Rows[e.RowIndex].ErrorText =
                "Value must be a non-negative number";
        e.Cancel = true;
    }
}
```

This method ensures that the user types a non-negative integer into the UnitsInStock, UnitsOnOrder, or ReorderLevel columns.

The second parameter to the method, *e*, is a *DataGridViewCellValidatingEventArgs* object. This object contains a number of properties that you can use to identify the cell being edited—*e.ColumnIndex* contains the number of the column, and *e.RowIndex* contains the row number (the first column is column 0, and the first row is row 0). The first *if* statement determines which column the user is currently in. Notice that the *DataGridView* class contains a *Columns* collection holding the details of each displayed column. The value of *e.ColumnIndex* is used as an indexer into this collection, and the value of the *Name* property is used to identify the column.

The *int.TryParse* method is a useful way to determine whether a string contains a value that can be converted to an integer; it returns *true* if the operation is successful (and also passes back an *int* containing the converted value as an *out* parameter), *false* otherwise. The second *if* statement uses *int.TryParse* to determine whether the user has typed a valid integer into the current cell. If this test fails, or if the value typed is a valid *int* but is less than zero, the *ErrorText* property of the current row in the grid is set to a suitable error message. The *ErrorText* property acts like the *ErrorProvider* control you saw in

Chapter 22, "Performing Validation"—it displays an icon when an error occurs, and the user can hover over this icon with the mouse to display the error message in a tooltip. The *Cancel* property of the *e* parameter is also set; this prevents the user from being able to move away from the cell until she types in some valid data.

4. In the Design View window, click the *DataGridView* control. In the Properties window, click the Events button. Double-click the *CellEndEdit* event.

   Visual Studio 2005 generates an event handler for the *CellEndEdit* event called *productsGrid_CellEndEdit* and displays the Code and Text Editor window.

5. Add the following statement to the *productsGrid_CellEndEdit* method:

   ```
   productsGrid.Rows[e.RowIndex].ErrorText = "";
   ```

   This method is executed when the data has been successfully validated and the user moves to a different cell. The code simply clears any error message that was displayed.

6. In the Design View window, click the *DataGridView* control. In the Properties window, click the Events button. Double-click the *DataError* event.

   Visual Studio 2005 generates an event handler for the *DataError* event called *productsGrid_DataError* and displays the Code and Text Editor window.

7. Add the following statements to the *productsGrid_DataError* method:

   ```
   productsGrid.Rows[e.RowIndex].ErrorText = "Invalid input. Please re-enter";
   e.Cancel = true;
   ```

   The *DataError* event is a catch-all data validation event handler. If the user types an invalid value (such as an alphabetic string into a numeric column), that is not trapped elsewhere, the error will be caught here. This implementation simply outputs a message to the *ErrorText* property and prevents the user from moving away.

8. Build and run the application.

   The *DataGridView* control is filled as soon as the form appears.

9. Try and change a value in the ProductID column. This column should be read-only.

10. Change the SupplierID for any row by clicking the drop-down menu that appears, displaying the supplier names.

11. Type a negative number into the UnitsInStock column and then click a different cell. An error icon is displayed in the row header. Hover the mouse over this icon to display the error message. This is the message from the *CellValidating* event.

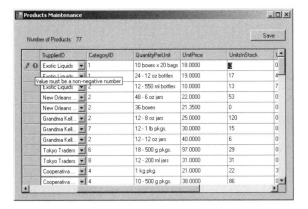

12. Type a positive integer into the UnitsIsStock column and then click a different cell. The error icon disappears and the data is accepted.

13. Type an alphabetic string into the CategoryID column and then click a different cell. The error icon appears again. Hover the mouse over the icon to display the error message. This is the message from the *DataError* event.

14. Press the **Escape** key to undo the change.

    The error icon disappears.

15. Close the form and return to Visual Studio 2005.

Performing Updates by Using a DataSet

The changes made by using the *DataGridView* control are automatically copied back to the *DataSet* acting as the data source for the control. Saving changes made to the data involves reconnecting to the database, performing any required SQL INSERT, UPDATE, and DELETE statements, and then disconnecting from the database. You must also be prepared to handle any errors that might occur. Fortunately, the *TableAdapter* classes generated for the *DataSet* contain several methods and events that can help you perform these tasks.

Before updating the database, you should ensure that the data is valid. After all, you don't want to waste a round-trip over the network to the database and all those database resources if the operation is going to fail.

Validate the changes and handle errors

1. Display ProductsForm in the Design View window. Select the Save button. In the Properties window, click Events. Double-click the Click event.

    Visual Studio 2005 generates an event method called *saveButton_Click*.

2. In the Code and Text Editor window, add the following *try/catch* block to the *saveButton_Click* method:

```
try
{
    NorthwindDataSet changes = (NorthwindDataSet)northwindDataSet.GetChanges();
    if (changes == null)
    {
        return;
    }

    // Check for errors

    //  If no errors then update the database, otherwise tell the user
}
catch(Exception ex)
{
    MessageBox.Show("Error: " + ex.Message, "Errors",
        MessageBoxButtons.OK, MessageBoxIcon.Error);
    northwindDataSet.RejectChanges();
}
```

This block of code uses the *GetChanges* method of *northwindDataSet* to create a new *NorthwindDataSet* object that contains only the rows that have changed. (The cast is necessary because the *GetChanges* method is defined as returning a generic *DataSet* object.)

Although this code is not strictly necessary, it makes updating the database quicker because the update routines do not have to calculate which rows have changed and which ones haven't. If there are no changes (the *NorthwindDataSet* object is null), the method finishes; otherwise the method checks for errors in the data and updates the database (you will write this code shortly). If an exception occurs while performing the updates, the application displays a message to the user, and undoes the changes in *northwindDataSet* by using the *RejectChanges* method.

3. In the Code and Text Editor window, replace the // Check for errors comment in the *saveButton_Click* method with the following code:

```
DataTable dt = changes.Tables["Products"];
DataRow [] badRows = dt.GetErrors();
```

The first statement extracts the Products *DataTable* in the *changes DataSet*. The *GetErrors* method of a *DataTable* object returns an array of all the rows in the table that have one or more validation errors. If there are no errors, *GetErrors* returns an empty array.

4. Replace the // If no errors then update the database, otherwise tell the user comment with the following code block:

```
if (badRows.Length == 0)
{
    // Update the database
}
else
{
```

```
    // Find the errors and inform the user
}
```

There are several strategies you can use for reporting errors to the user. One useful technique is to find all the errors and report them in a single (but possibly long) message.

5. Replace the // Find the errors and inform the user comment with the following statements:

```
string errorMsg = null;
foreach (DataRow row in badRows)
{
    foreach (DataColumn col in row.GetColumnsInError())
    {
        errorMsg += row.GetColumnError(col) + "\n";
    }
}
MessageBox.Show("Errors in data: " + errorMsg,
    "Please fix", MessageBoxButtons.OK,
    MessageBoxIcon.Error);
```

This code iterates through all the rows in the *badRows* array. Each row may have one or more errors, and the *GetColumnsInError* method returns a collection containing all the columns with bad data. The *GetColumnError* method retrieves the error message for an individual column. Each error message is appended to the *errorMsg* string. When all the bad rows and columns have been examined, the application displays a message box showing all the errors. The user should be able to use this information to correct the changes and then resubmit them.

Integrity Rules and DataSets

In this example, which uses a simple, single table *DataSet*, you are unlikely to get any validation errors reported by *GetErrors*. When the *northwindDataSet* class was generated, it also included information about primary key columns, data types for each column, integrity rules, and so on obtained from the database. A user typically makes changes to rows by using objects such as the *DataGridView* control which has its own validation mechanisms that you have already seen in this chapter. However, the data still must be validated in the *DataSet*, just in case the *DataGridView* control has not been able to trap every possible error.

For example, if the *DataSet* comprises several tables that have a foreign key/primary key relationship, it would be annoying if the user was forced to input data in a particular sequence. This situation is when the *GetErrors* method comes into its own—the method assumes that the user has finished entering data so that it can perform any complex cross-checking between *DataTables* and trap any errors.

Having said all of this, you never know when the user is going to enter something so unusual that you haven't even contemplated it. It is good practice, therefore, to write defensive code. Be prepared to trap errors whenever they can occur.

Update the database

1. Once you are certain that the data seems to be correct, you can send it to the database. Locate the // Update the database comment in the *saveButton_Click* method and replace it with the following statements:

```
int numRows = productsTableAdapter.Update(changes);
MessageBox.Show("Updated " + numRows + " rows", "Success");
northwindDataSet.AcceptChanges();
```

This code posts the changes by using the *Update* method of the *productsTableAdapter* object. When the changes have been applied, the user is told how many rows were affected, and the *AcceptChanges* method marks the changes as permanent in the *DataSet*. Notice that this code is all encapsulated within a *try/catch* block to handle any errors.

> **Important**   If another user has already changed one or more rows being updated, the *Update* method will detect this situation and throw an exception. You can then decide how to handle this conflict in your application. For example, you could give the user the option to update the database anyway and overwrite the other user's updates, or discard the conflicting changes and refresh the *DataSet* with the new data from the database.

2. Build and run the program. When the Products Maintenance form appears, change the values in the ProductName and SupplierID columns of the first two rows, and then click Save.

   The changes are made to the database and a message tells you that two rows were updated.

3. Close the form and run the application again.

   The new product name and supplier for the first two rows appear, proving that the data was saved to the database.

4. Close the form and return to the Visual Studio 2005 programming environment.

■ **If you want to continue to the next chapter**

   Keep Visual Studio 2005 running and turn to Chapter 25.

■ **If you want to exit Visual Studio 2005 for now**

   On the File menu, click Exit. If you see a Save dialog box, click Yes.

Chapter 24 Quick Reference

To	Do this
Define a new *DataSet*.	Click Add New Item in the Project menu and select the DataSet template. Give the DataSet filename an extension of ".xsd."
Add a *DataTable* and *TableAdapter* to a *DataSet*.	Open the DataSet Designer window. Using the Toolbox, add a *TableAdapter* to the *DataSet*. Use the TableAdapter Configuration Wizard to define the DataTable and the TableAdapter methods.
Use simple binding to bind a property of a control to a data source at design time.	Expand the *DataBindings* property of the control. Click the property you want to bind to and select the data source to use.
Use simple binding to bind a property of a control to a data source at run time.	Use the Add method of the DataBindings property.
	Specify the property to bind to and the data source. For example, to bind the Text property of the Button control named button1 to the Text property of the textBox1 control, use the following code:
	`myLabel.DataBindings.Add("Text", textBox1, "Text");`
Use complex binding to bind a *ListBox*, *ComboBox*, or *CheckedListBox* control to a list of values from a data source.	Set the *DataSource* property of the control.
	Specify the data to be displayed using the *DisplayMember* property, and then specify the data to be used as the value of the control by using the *ValueMember* property.
Use complex binding to bind a *DataGridView* control to a list of values from a data source.	Set the *DataSource* property of the control.
	Optionally, specify the data to be displayed and edited using the *DataMember* property.
Constrain user input in a *DataGridView* control.	Right-click the *DataGridView* control in the Design View window and click Edit Columns. Use the Edit Columns dialog box to set the *ColumnType* and *ReadOnly* properties of the control.
	If you set the *ColumnType* property to *DataGridViewComboBox*, set the *DataSource*, *DisplayMember*, and *ValueMember* properties as for performing complex binding.
Validate user input in a *DataGridView* control.	Use the *CellValidating* event to perform validation when the user modifies a cell and tries to move away.
	Use the *CellEndEdit* event to clear any error messages after the cell has been successfully validated.
	Use the *DataError* event to trap any other user input errors.
Validate the changes the user has made to the data in a *DataSet*.	For each *DataTable* in the *DataSet*, call the *GetErrors* method to find all of the rows containing errors. For each row found, use the *GetColumnsInError* method to iterate through all the columns that contain errors, and for each column, call the *GetColumnError* method to obtain the details of the error for that column.
Update the database with the information in a *DataSet*.	Run the *Update* method of the *TableAdapter* object passing the *DataSet* as the parameter. If the updates are successful, call *AcceptChanges* on the *DataSet*; otherwise call *RejectChanges*.

Part VI
Building Web Applications

Chapter 25

Introducing ASP.NET

After completing this chapter, you will be able to:

- Create simple Microsoft ASP.NET pages.
- Build applications that can be accessed from a Web browser.
- Use ASP.NET Server controls efficiently.
- Create and apply Themes

In the previous sections of this book, you have seen how to build Microsoft Visual C# applications that run in the Microsoft Windows environment on the desktop. These applications typically allow a user to gain access to a database by using ADO.NET. In this final part of the book, you will consider the world of Web applications. These are applications that are accessed over the Internet. Rather than using your desktop, Web applications rely on a Web browser to provide the user interface.

In the first three chapters of this part, you will examine the classes provided by the Microsoft .NET Framework for building Web applications. You will learn about the architecture of ASP.NET, Web forms, and Server controls. You will see that the structure of applications that execute over the Web are different from those that run on the desktop, and you will be shown some best practices for building efficient, scalable, and easily maintanable Web sites.

In the final chapter in this part, you'll learn about Web services. Web services allow you to build distributed applications composed of components and services that can be spread across the Internet (or an intranet). You will see how to create a Web service and understand how Web services are built on the Simple Object Access Protocol (SOAP). You will also study the techniques that a client application can use to connect to a Web service.

Understanding the Internet as an Infrastructure

You have heard all the hype about the Internet, and so none of it will be repeated here. However, you should consider a few points. The Internet is a big network (alright—a *really* big network) and, as a result, the information and data that you can access over it can be quite remote. This should have an impact on the way you design your applications. For example, you might get away with locking data in a database while a user browses it in a small, local desktop application, but this strategy will not be feasible for an application accessed over the Internet. Resource use impacts scalability much more for the Internet than for local applications.

Network bandwidth itself is also a scarce resource that should be used sparingly. You might notice variations in the performance of your own local network according to the time of day (networks always seem to slow down on a Friday afternoon just when you are trying to get everything done before the weekend), the applications that users in your company are running, and many other factors. But, no matter how variable the performance of your own local network is, the Internet is far more unpredictable. You are dependent on any number of servers routing your requests from your Web browser to the site you are trying to access, and the replies can get passed back along an equally tortuous route. The network protocols and data presentation mechanisms that underpin the Internet reflect the fact that networks can be (and at times most certainly will be) unreliable and that an application running on a server can be accessed by a user running one of many different Web browsers on one of many different operating systems.

Understanding Web Server Requests and Responses

A user gaining access to an application over the Internet by using a Web browser uses the Hypertext Transfer Protocol (HTTP) to communicate with the application. Applications are usually hosted by some sort of Web server that reads HTTP requests and determines which application should be used to respond to the request. The term "application" in this sense is a very loose term—the Web server might invoke an executable program to perform an action, or it might process the request itself by using its own internal logic or other means. However the request is processed, the Web server will send a response to the client, again by using HTTP. The content of an HTTP response is usually presented as a Hypertext Markup Language (HTML) page; this is the language that most browsers understand and know how to display.

> **Note** Applications run by users that access other applications over the Internet are often referred to as clients or client applications. The applications being accessed are usually called servers or server applications.

Managing State

HTTP is a connectionless protocol. This means that a request (or a response) is a stand-alone packet of data. A typical exchange between a client and an application running on a Web server might involve several requests. For example, the user can display a page, enter data, click some buttons, and expect the display to change as a result, allowing the user to enter more data, and so on. Each request sent by the client to the server is separate from any other requests sent both by this client and any other clients using the same server (and maybe running the same application) simultaneously. The problem is that a client request often requires some sort of context or state.

For example, consider the following common scenario. A Web application allows the user to browse goods for sale. The user might want to buy several items, placing each one in a virtual shopping cart. A useful feature of such an application is the ability to display the current contents of the shopping cart.

Where should the contents of the shopping cart (the client's state) be held? If this information is held on the Web server, the Web server must be able to piece together the different HTTP requests and determine which requests come from one client and which come from others. This is feasible, but might require additional processing to reconcile client requests against state information and, of course, it would require some sort of database to persist that state information between client requests. A complication with this technique is that the Web server has no guarantee; once the state information has been preserved, the client might submit another request that uses or removes the information. If the Web server saved every bit of state information for every client that used it, it could need a very big database indeed!

An alternative is to store state information on the client machine. The *Cookie Protocol* was developed to allow Web servers to cache information in cookies (small files) on the client computer. The disadvantages of this approach are that the application has to arrange for the data in the cookie to be transmitted over the Web as part of every HTTP request so that the Web server can access it. The application also has to ensure that cookies are of a limited size. Perhaps the most significant drawback of cookies is that users can disable them and prevent the Web browser from storing them on their computers, which will cause any attempt to save state information to fail.

Understanding ASP.NET

From the discussion in the previous section, you can see that a framework for building and running Web applications has a number of items that it should address. It must do the following:

- Support the standard HTTP
- Manage client state efficiently
- Provide tools allowing for the easy development of Web applications
- Generate applications that can be accessed from any browser that supports HTML
- Be responsive and scalable

Microsoft originally developed the Active Server Pages model in response to many of these issues. Active Server Pages allowed developers to embed application code in HTML pages. A Web server such as Internet Information Services (IIS) could execute the application code and use it to generate an HTML response. However, Active Server Pages did have its problems: you had to write a lot of application code to do relatively simple things, such as display a page of data from a database; mixing application code and HTML caused readability and maintenance issues; and performance was not always what it could be because Active Server Pages had to interpret application code in an HTML request every time the request was submitted, even if it was the same code each time.

With the advent of the .NET platform, Microsoft updated the Active Server Pages framework and created ASP.NET. The main features of ASP.NET include the following:

■ A rationalized program model using Web forms that contain presentation logic and code files that separate out the business logic. You can write code in any of the supported .NET languages, including C#. ASP.NET Web forms are compiled and cached on the Web server to improve performance.

■ Server controls that support server-side events but are rendered as HTML to allow them to operate correctly in any HTML-compliant browser. Microsoft has also extended many of the standard HTML controls as well, allowing you to manipulate them in your code.

■ Powerful Data controls for displaying, editing, and maintaining data from a database.

■ Options for caching client state using cookies on the client's computer, in a special service (the ASP.NET State service) on the Web server, or in a Microsoft SQL Server database. The cache is easily programmable by using code.

In the latest release of the .NET Framework supplied with Visual Studio 2005, Microsoft has further enhanced ASP.NET. A large number of improvements have been made to optimize throughput and Web site maintainability. Microsoft has also added the following features:

■ Enhanced page design and layout using Master Pages, Themes, and Web Parts. You can use Master Pages to quickly provide a common layout for all Web pages in an application. Themes help you implement a consistent look and feel across the Web site, ensuring that all controls appear in the same way if required. Web Parts enable you to create modular Web pages that users can customize to their own requirements. You will use Themes later in this chapter. Using Master Pages and Web Parts are outside the scope of this book, however.

■ New data source controls for binding data to Web pages. These new controls allow you to build applications that can display and edit data quickly and easily. The data source controls can operate with a variety of data sources, such as Microsoft SQL Server, Microsoft Access, XML files, Web services, and business objects that can return data sets. Using the data source controls provides you with a consistent mechanism for working with data, independent from the source of that data. You will make use of the data source controls in Chapter 27, "Securing a Web Site and Accessing Data with Web Forms."

■ New and updated controls. For displaying and editing data Microsoft now provides the GridView, DetailsView, and FormView controls. You can use the TreeView control to display hierarchical data, and you can use the SiteMapPath and Menu controls to assist in user navigation through your Web application. You will use the GridView control in Chapter 27.

■ Enhanced security features with built-in support for authenticating and authorizing users. You can easily grant permissions to users to allow them to access your Web application, validate users when they attempt to log in, and query user information so you know who is accessing your Web site. You can use the Login control to prompt the user for their credentials and validate them, and the PasswordRecovery control for helping users remember or reset their password. You will use these security controls in Chapter 27.

■ Improved Web site configuration and management using the ASP.NET Web Site Administration Tool. This tool provides wizards for configuring and securing ASP.NET Web applications. You will use the ASP.NET Web Site Administration Tool in Chapter 27.

In the remainder of this chapter, you will learn more about the structure of an ASP.NET application.

Creating Web Applications with ASP.NET

A Web application that uses ASP.NET typically consists of one or more ASP.NET pages or Web forms, code files, and configuration files.

A Web form is held in an .aspx file, which is essentially an HTML file with some Microsoft .NET–specific tags. An .aspx file defines the layout and appearance of a page. Each .aspx file often has an associated code file containing the application logic for the components in the .aspx file, such as event handlers and utility methods. A *tag*, or directive, at the start of each .aspx file specifies the name and location of the corresponding code file. ASP.NET also supports application-level events, which are defined in Global.asax files.

Each Web application can also have a configuration file called Web.config. This file, which is in XML format, contains information regarding security, cache management, page compilation, and so on.

Building an ASP.NET Application

In the following exercise, you will build a simple ASP.NET application that uses Server controls to gather input from the user about the details of the employees of a fictitious software company. The application will show you the structure of a typical Web application.

> **Note** You do not need to have IIS running on your computer in order to develop Web applications. Visual Studio 2005 includes its own Development Web server. When you build and run a Web application, by default Visual Studio 2005 will run the application using this server. However, you should still use IIS for hosting production Web applications after you have finished developing and testing them.

Create the Web application

1. Start Microsoft Visual Studio 2005, if it is not already running.

2. On the File menu, point to New and then click Web Site.

    The New Web Site dialog box appears.

3. Click the ASP.NET Web Site template. Select File System in the Location drop-down list box, and type **C:\Documents and Settings**YourName**\My Documents\Microsoft Press\Visual CSharp Step by Step\Chapter 25\HonestJohn** where *YourName* is your Windows login name. Set the Language to Visual C#, and then click OK.

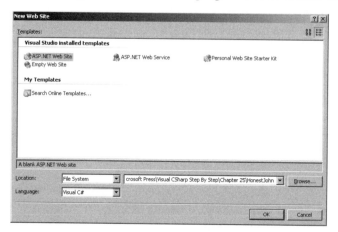

> **Note**   Setting the Location to FileSystem uses the Development Web server provided with Visual Studio 2005. You can use IIS by setting the Location to HTTP and specifying the URL of the Web Site you want to create rather than a file name.

An application is created consisting of a Web Folder called App_Data, and a Web form called Default.aspx. The HTML code for the default page appears in the Source View window.

4. In the Solution Explorer select the Default.aspx file. In the Properties window, change the File Name property of Default.aspx to EmployeeForm.aspx.

5. Click the Design button at the bottom of the form to display the Design View of the form. The Design View window is currently empty.

    In the Design View window, you can drag controls onto the Web form from the Toolbox, and Visual Studio 2005 will generate the appropriate HTML for you. This is the HTML that you see when you view the form in the Source View window. You can also edit the HTML directly if you want.

In the next exercise, you will define a style to be used by the form and add controls to the form to make it functional. Using a style enables you to ensure that all controls on the form share a common look and feel (such as color and font), as well as setting items such as a background image of the form.

Lay out the Web form

1. Click the form in the Design View window. In the Properties window, change the Title property of the DOCUMENT object to **Employee Information**.

   The value you specify for the Title property appears in the title bar of the Web Browser when you run the Web application.

2. Select the Style property and click the ellipses button.

   The Style Builder dialog box opens. This dialog box allows you to create a style for the form. (A *style* specifies the default font, color, layout, and other attributes for the Web form and its controls.)

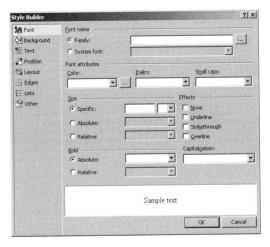

3. In the Font Name section, verify that the Family option is selected, and then click the ellipses button on the right side. In the Font Picker dialog box that opens, select Arial in the Installed Fonts list, and then click the >> button to add it to the Selected Fonts list. Click OK to return to the Style Builder dialog box.

4. In the Color drop-down list, select Blue.

5. In the left pane of the dialog box, click Background. The Background page is displayed. Select the Transparent check box.

6. Using Windows Explorer, copy the file \Microsoft Press\Visual CSharp Step By Step\Chapter 25\computer.bmp in your My Documents folder to the \Microsoft Press\Visual CSharp Step By Step\Chapter 25\HonestJohn folder.

7. Return to the Style Builder dialog box in the Visual Studio 2005 programming environment. In the Image text box, type **computer.bmp**. Click OK.

    The Web form will contain a background image of a computer.

8. Open the Toolbox and ensure that the Standard category is expanded.

    The Toolbox contains controls that you can drop onto ASP.NET forms. These controls are similar, in many cases, to the controls you have been using to build Windows forms. The difference is that these controls have been designed to operate in an HTML environment, and they are rendered using HTML at run time.

9. From the Toolbox, drag and drop four Label controls and three TextBox controls onto the Web form. Notice how the controls pick up the font and color specified by the Web form's style.

> **Note**   The controls will be automatically positioned using a left-to-right flow layout in the Design View window. Do not worry about their location just yet as you will move them after setting their properties.

> **Note**   As well as using a *Label* control, you can also type text directly onto a Web page. However, you cannot format this text so easily, set properties, or apply Themes to it. If you are building a Web site that has to support different languages (such as French or German), use *Label* controls as you can more easily localize the text they display by using Resource files. For more information, see "Resources in Applications" in the Microsoft Visual Studio 2005 Documentation.

10. Using the Properties window, set the properties of these controls to the values shown in the following table.

Control	Property	Value
Label1	*Font Bold* (expand the *Font* property)	**True**
	Font Name	**Arial Black**
	Font Size	**X-Large**
	Text	**Honest John Software Developers**
	Height	**36px**
	Width	**630px**
Label2	*Text*	**First Name**
Label3	*Text*	**Last Name**

Control	Property	Value
Label4	Text	Employee Id
TextBox1	Height	24px
	Width	230px
	(ID)	firstName
TextBox2	Height	24px
	Width	230px
	(ID)	lastName
TextBox3	Height	24px
	Width	100px
	(ID)	employeeID

11. In the Design View window, select all four labels and all three text boxes (click *Label1*, and the click the remaining controls while holding down the **Shift** key).

12. In the Layout menu, point to Position and then click Absolute.

    This setting enables you to drag the controls to an absolute position on the form rather than Visual Studio 2005 laying them out automatically.

13. Move the labels and text boxes to the positions shown on the form in the following graphic:

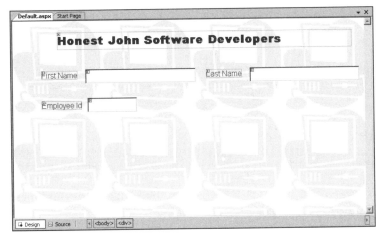

> **Tip**   You can align and space controls by using the commands on the Format menu. To align a set of controls, select them all and then, on the Format menu, click Align and select the appropriate alignment (Lefts, Centers, Rights, Tops, Middles, Bottoms). Similarly, you can space controls by selecting them and then by using the Horizontal Spacing or Vertical Spacing commands on the Format menu.

14. Click the Source button at the bottom of the form to display the HTML representation of the form and controls in the Source View window.

    The HTML should look like similar to the following code (the positions of the controls might vary slightly on your form):

```
<%@ Page Language="C#" AutoEventWireup="true"  CodeFile="EmployeeForm.aspx.cs"
Inherits="_Default" %>

<!DOCTYPE html PUBLIC "-//W3C//DTD XHTML 1.1//EN" "http://www.w3.org/TR/xhtml11/DTD/
xhtml11.dtd">

<html xmlns="http://www.w3.org/1999/xhtml" >
<head runat="server">
    <title>Employee Information</title>
</head>
<body style="background-image: url(computer.bmp); color: blue; font-family: Arial;
background-color: transparent">
    <form id="form1" runat="server">
    <div>
        <asp:Label ID="Label1" runat="server" Text="Honest John Software Developers"
style="z-index: 100; left: 96px; position: absolute; top: 24px" Font-Bold="True" Font-
Names="Arial Black" Font-Size="X-Large" Height="36px" Width="630px"></asp:Label>
        <asp:Label ID="Label2" runat="server" Text="First Name" style="z-index: 101;
left: 62px; position: absolute; top: 104px"></asp:Label>
        <asp:Label ID="Label3" runat="server" Text="Last Name" style="z-index: 102; left:
414px; position: absolute; top: 104px"></asp:Label>
        <asp:Label ID="Label4" runat="server" Text="Employee Id" style="z-index: 103;
left: 62px; position: absolute; top: 167px"></asp:Label>  
        <asp:TextBox ID="firstName" runat="server" style="z-index: 104; left: 156px;
position: absolute; top: 101px" Height="24px" Width="230px"></asp:TextBox>
        <asp:TextBox ID="lastName" runat="server" style="z-index: 107; left: 507px;
position: absolute; top: 101px" Height="24px" Width="230px"></asp:TextBox>
        <asp:TextBox ID="employeeID" runat="server" style="z-index: 106; left: 160px;
position: absolute; top: 161px" Height="24px" Width="100px"></asp:TextBox>

    </div>
    </form>
</body>
</html>
```

15. Return to the Design View window.

16. In the Layout menu, point to Position and click Auto-position Options. In the Options dialog box, expand the HTML Designer node of the tree view control if it is not already

expanded and click CSS Positioning. In the right-hand pane of the dialog box, check "Change positioning to the following for controls added by using the Toolbox, paste, or drag and drop", and select "Absolutely positioned" from the drop-down menu:

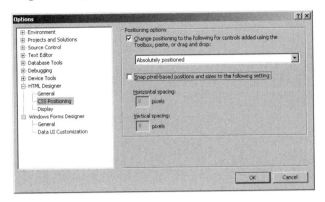

This action allows all future controls that you add to the form to be placed wherever you drag them after adding them to the form; you do not need enable absolute positioning for each one.

17. Add another Label control and four RadioButton controls to the Web form. Set the properties of these controls to the values listed in the following table.

Control	Property	Value
Label5	Text	Position
RadioButton1	Text	Worker
	TextAlign	Left
	GroupName	positionGroup
	Checked	True
	(ID)	workerButton
RadioButton2	Text	Boss
	TextAlign	Left
	GroupName	positionGroup
	Checked	False
	(ID)	bossButton
RadioButton3	Text	Vice President
	TextAlign	Left

Control	Property	Value
	GroupName	positionGroup
	Checked	False
	(ID)	vpButton
RadioButton4	Text	President
	TextAlign	Left
	GroupName	positionGroup
	Checked	False
	(ID)	presidentButton

The GroupName property determines how a set of radio buttons are grouped. All buttons with the same value for GroupName are in the same group—only one can be selected at a time.

18. Position these controls so that your Web form looks like the following graphic:

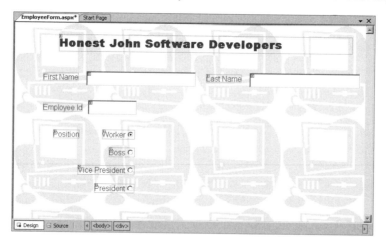

19. Add another Label control and a DropDownList control to the Web form. Set their properties to the values shown in the following table.

Control	Property	Value
Label6	Text	Role
DropDownList1	Width	230px
	(ID)	positionRole

The *positionRole* drop-down list will display the different positions that an employee can have within the company. This list will vary according to the position of the employee in the company. You will write code to populate this list dynamically.

20. Position these controls so that the form looks like the following graphic:

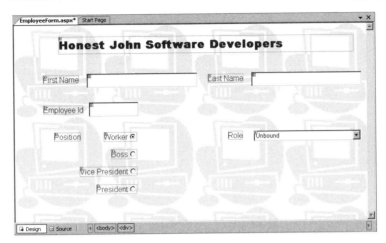

21. Add two Button controls and another *Label* control to the form. Set their properties to the values shown in the following table.

Control	Property	Value
Button1	Text	Save
	(ID)	saveButton
Button2	Text	Clear
	(ID)	clearButton
Label7	Text	leave blank
	Height	48px
	Width	680px
	(ID)	infoLabel

22.   Position the controls so that the form looks like the following graphic:

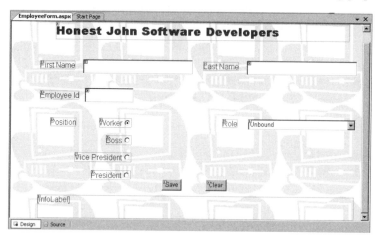

You will write event handlers for these buttons in a later exercise. The Save button will collate the information entered by the user and display it in the *InfoLabel* control at the bottom of the form. The Clear button will clear the text boxes and set other controls to their default values.

Test the Web form

1.   On the Debug menu, click Start Debugging.

Visual Studio 2005 builds the application, the ASP.NET Development Server starts, and then Internet Explorer starts and displays the form.

> **Note**   The first time you run a Web application by using the Start Debugging command, you will be prompted with a message box stating that debugging is not enabled. You can either select "Run without debugging", or select "Modify the Web.config file to enable debugging" if you really want to run in debug mode. Running in debug mode is useful initially because you can set breakpoints and single step through the code using the debugger, as described in Chapter 3, "Writing Methods and Applying Scope." However, enabling debugging will slow the application down and should be disabled before deploying the application to a production Web site. You can do this by editing the Web.config file and removing the following line: `<compilation debug="true"/>`

2.   Enter some information for a fictitious employee. Test the radio buttons to verify that they are all mutually exclusive. Click the drop-down arrow in the Role list; the list will be empty. Click Save and Clear.

3.   Close Internet Explorer and return to the Visual Studio 2005 programming environment.

Deploying a Web Site to IIS

A new feature added to Visual Studio 2005 is the Copy Web Site command on the Web-site menu, for copying a Web site from one location to another. You can use this feature to quickly deploy a Web site built and tested using the ASP.NET Development Server to a production IIS site. (You should create a new Web site, or an empty virtual directory by using the Internet Information Services management console first.)

Connect to the virtual directory on the production IIS site. You can then selectively copy individual files to or from the production Web site, or synchronize files between Web sites.

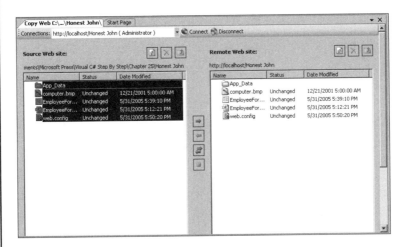

For more information, see "Walkthrough: Copying a Web Site Using the Copy Web Site Tool" and "How to: Copy Web Site Files with the Copy Web Tool" in the Microsoft Visual Studio 2005 Documentation.

Understanding Server Controls

The Web Forms controls you added to the form are collectively known as Server controls. Server controls are similar to the standard HTML items that you can use on an ordinary Web page, except that they are more programmable. Most Server controls expose event handlers, methods, and properties that code running on the server can execute and modify dynamically at run time. In the following exercises, you will learn more about programming Server controls.

Examine a Server control

1. In the Visual Studio 2005 programming environment, display EmployeeForm.aspx in the Source View window.

2. Examine the HTML code for the form. Notice that it contains the definitions for each of the controls. Look at the definition of the first *Label* control in more detail (the code won't look exactly like the following listing, which has been laid out to make it easier to read):

```
<asp:Label ID="Label1" runat="server"
  Text="Honest John Software Developers"
  style="z-index: 100; left: 96px;
  position: absolute; top: 24px"
  Font-Bold="True" Font-Names="Arial Black"
  Font-Size="X-Large" Height="36px" Width="630px">
</asp:Label>
```

There are a couple of things to observe. First, look at the type of the control: *asp:Label*. All Web forms controls live in the "asp" namespace because this is the way they are defined by Microsoft. The second noteworthy item is the *runat="server"* attribute. This attribute indicates that the control can be accessed programmatically by code running on the Web server. This code can query and change the values of any of the properties of this control (for example, change its text).

> **Note**   All controls must be properly ended with a matching *</asp:Control>* tag, where *Control* is the type of the control, such as *Label* as shown in the example.

3. Return to the Design View window.

HTML Controls

ASP.NET also supports HTML controls. If you expand the HTML category in the Toolbox, you are presented with a list of controls. These are the controls that Microsoft supplied with the original Active Server Pages model. They are provided so that you can port existing ASP pages into ASP.NET more easily. However, if you are building an application from scratch, you should use the Standard Web Forms controls instead.

HTML controls also have a *runat* attribute, allowing you to specify where event handling code should be executed for these controls. Unlike Web Forms controls, the default location for HTML controls to execute code is in the browser rather than on the server—assuming that the user's browser supports this functionality.

The EmployeeForm.aspx page requires several event handlers: a set of handlers to populate the *PositionRole* drop-down list when the user selects a position (Worker, Boss, Vice President, President); another handler to save the information entered when the user clicks the Save button; and a final handler to clear the form when the user clicks the Clear button. You will write these handlers in the next exercise.

Write event handlers

1. In the Solution Explorer, expand the file EmployeeForm.aspx.

   The file EmployeeForms.aspx.cs will appear. This is the file that will actually contain the C# code for the event handlers that you write. This file is known as a *code-behind file*. This feature of ASP.NET enables you to separate the C# code from the the display logic for a Web application (you can actually write C# code and event handlers in the EmployeeForm.aspx file by using the Source View window, but this approach is not recommended).

2. Display the HTML code for EmployeeForm.aspx in the Source View window. Examine the first line in this file. It looks like this:

   ```
   <%@ Page Language="C#" ... CodeFile="EmployeeForm.aspx.cs ... %>
   ```

   This directive specifies the file containing the program code for the Web form and the language in which it is written, in this case, C#. The other supported languages include Visual Basic and JScript.

3. In the Solution Explorer, double-click the EmployeeForm.aspx.cs file.

   The file appears in the Code and Text Editor window. At the top of the file, there is a set of *using* statements. Note that this file makes heavy use of the *System.Web* namespace and its sub-namespaces—this is where the ASP.NET classes reside. Also, notice the code itself is in a class called *_Default* that descends from *System.Web.UI.Page*; this is the class from which all Web Forms descend. Currently, it contains a single empty method called *Page_Load*. This method runs when the page is displayed. You can write code in this method to initialize any data required by the form.

4. Add a method called *initPositionRole* to the *_Default* class, after the *Page_Load* method:

   ```
   private void initPositionRole()
   {
   }
   ```

   You will use this method to initialize the *positionRole* drop-down list to its default set of values.

5. Add the following statements to the *initPositionRole* method:

   ```
   positionRole.Items.Clear();
   positionRole.Enabled = true;
   positionRole.Items.Add("Analyst");
   positionRole.Items.Add("Designer");
   positionRole.Items.Add("Developer");
   ```

   The first statement clears the list. The second statement enables the list (you will write some code shortly that disables it under certain circumstances). The remaining statements add the three roles that are applicable to workers.

6. Add the following statement to the *Page_Load* method:

```
if (!IsPostBack)
{
    initPositionRole();
}
```

This block of code will cause the positionRole drop-down list to be populated when the form appears in the user's browser. However, it is important to understand that the *Page_Load* method runs every time the Web server sends the form to the user's browser, not just the first time. For example, when the user clicks a button the form can be sent back to the Web server for processing; the Web server then responds by sending the form back to the browser for displaying when the processing has completed. You don't necessarily want the initialization to be performed every time the page appears, as it is a waste of processing and can lead to performance problems if you are building a commercial Web site. You can determine whether the *Page_Load* method is running because this is the first time the page is being displayed by querying the *IsPostBack* property of the Web page. This property returns *false* the first time the page is displayed, and *true* if the page is being redisplayed because the user has clicked a control. In the code you added, you only call the *initPositionRole* method when the form is first displayed.

7. Switch to the EmployeeForm.aspx file, and change to Design View for the form. Select the *workerButton* radio button. In the Properties window, click the Events button. Double-click the *CheckedChanged* event. This event occurs when the user clicks the radio button and its value changes. Visual Studio 2005 generates the method *workerButton_CheckedChanged* to handle this event.

8. In the *workerButton_CheckedChanged* event method, add the following statement:

```
initPositionRole();
```

Remember that the default values for the *positionRole* drop-down list are those for a worker, so the same method can be reused to initialize the list.

9. Switch to EmployeeForm.aspx in the Design View window. Select the *bossButton* radio button, and use the Properties window to create an event method called *bossButton_CheckedChanged* for the *CheckedChanged* event. When the form is displayed in Code and Text Editor window, type the following statements in the *BossChecked* method:

```
positionRole.Items.Clear();
positionRole.Enabled = true;
positionRole.Items.Add("General Manager");
positionRole.Items.Add("Project Manager");
```

These are the roles that a manager can fulfill.

10. Switch to EmployeeForm.aspx in the Design View window and create an event handler for the *CheckedChanged* event for the *vpButton* (Vice president) radio button. Add the following statements to the event method:

```
positionRole.Items.Clear();
positionRole.Enabled = true;
positionRole.Items.Add("VP Sales");
positionRole.Items.Add("VP Marketing");
positionRole.Items.Add("VP Production");
positionRole.Items.Add("VP Human Resources");
```

11. Create a final event handler for the *CheckedChanged* event for the *President* radio button. Add the following code to the event method:

```
positionRole.Items.Clear();
positionRole.Enabled = false;
```

Roles do not apply to the president of the company, so the drop-down list is disabled.

12. Create an event handler for the *Click* event of the Save button. The method would usually be used to save the information to a database, but to keep this application simple, the method will just echo some of the data in the *InfoLabel* control instead. Add the following statements to the *saveButton_Click* method:

```
string position = "";

if (workerButton.Checked)
    position = "Worker";
if (bossButton.Checked)
    position = "Manager";
if (vpButton.Checked)
    position = "Vice President";
if (presidentButton.Checked)
    position = "President";

infoLabel.Text = "Employee: " + firstName.Text + " " +
    lastName.Text + "    Id " +
    employeeID.Text + "    Position " +
    position;
```

The * * character is a non-breaking space in HTML; ordinary white-space characters after the first white-space character will normally be ignored by the browser.

13. Create an event method for the *Click* event of the Clear button. Add the following block of code to this method:

```
firstName.Text = "";
lastName.Text = "";
employeeID.Text = "";
workerButton.Checked = true;
initPositionRole();
infoLabel.Text = "";
```

This code clears the information entered by the user and then resets the role to Worker (the default value).

Test the Web form again

1. Run the Web form again.

2. Type in an employee's name and ID number (make them up). Click the Role drop-down list.

    The list of roles for a worker is displayed.

3. Change the position of your fictitious employee to Vice President, and then click the Role drop-down list box.

    Notice that the list has not changed and still displays the roles for a worker. The list hasn't changed because the *CheckedChanged* event for the Vice President radio button has not fired.

4. Close Internet Explorer and return to the Visual Studio 2005 programming environment.

5. Display EmployeeForm.aspx in the Design View window, and then select the *worker-Button* radio button. In the Properties window, set the *AutoPostBack* property to True.

    When the user clicks this radio button, the form will be sent back to the server for processing, the *CheckedChanged* event will fire, and the form can be updated to display the roles for this radio button. By default, the *AutoPostBack* property is set to *False* to avoid unnecessary network traffic.

    Set the *AutoPostBack* property to *True* for the other radio buttons: *bossButton*, *vpButton*, and *presidentButton*.

> **Tip**   You can hold down the Shift key and select all four radio buttons, and then set properties for them all at the same time in the Properties window.

6. Run the Web form again.

    This time you will find that when you click the radio buttons, there is a slight flicker while the form is submitted to the server, the event handler runs, the drop-down list is populated, and the form is displayed again.

7. On the View menu in Internet Explorer, click Source to display the source of the HTML page being displayed in the browser.

    Notepad starts and displays the HTML source for the page. Notice that there is no mention of any "asp:" Server controls in this file and no C# code. Instead, the Server controls and their contents have been converted to the equivalent HTML controls (and some JavaScript). This is one of the basic features of the Server controls—you access them programmatically like ordinary .NET Framework objects, with methods, properties, and events. When they are rendered by the Web server, they are converted into HTML, allowing you to use any HTML compliant browser to view ASP.NET Web forms at run time.

When you have finished examining the file, close Notepad.

8.   Click Save.

The *InfoLabel* control displays the details of the new employee. If you examine the source, you will see that the HTML for the *InfoLabel* control (rendered as an HTML span with an ID of "InfoLabel") contains this text.

9.   Click Clear.

The form resets to its default values.

10.   Close Internet Explorer and return to the Visual Studio 2005 programming environment.

Event Processing and Round-Trips

Server controls are undoubtedly a very powerful feature of ASP.NET, but they come with a price. You should remember that although events are raised by the Web client, the event code is executed on the Web server and that each time an event is raised, an HTTP request (or postback) is sent over the network to the Web server. The task of the Web server is to process this request and send a reply containing an HTML page to be displayed. In the case of many events, this page will be the same as the one that issued the original request. However, the Web server also needs to know what other data the user has entered on the page so that when it generates the HTML response, it can preserve these values in the display. (If the Web server only sent back the HTML that composed the original page, any data entered by the user would disappear.) If you look at the HTML source of a page generated by a Web form, you will notice a hidden input field in the form. The example shown previously had this hidden field:

```
<input type="hidden" name="__VIEWSTATE"
value="/WEPdDwxNDk0MzA1NzE0O3Q8O2w8aTwxPjs+O2w8bDxpPDE3PjtpPDE5
PjtpP DIxPjtpPDI3PjtpPDMzPjs+O2w8dDxwPHA8bDxDaGVja2VkO247bDxvPH
Q+Oz4+Oz 47Oz47dDxwPHA8bDxDaGVja2VkO247bDxvPGY+Oz4+Oz47Oz47dDxw
PHA8bDxDaGVja2U2 VkO247bDxvPGY+Oz4+Oz47Oz47dDxOPDt0PGk8Mz47QDxBbm
FseXN0O0ORlc2lnbmVyO0 RldmVsb3Blcjs+O0A8QW5hbHlzdDtEZXNpZ25lcjtE
ZXZlbG9wZXI7Pj47Pj s7Pj t0PHA8cDxsPFRleHQ7PjtsPFxlOz4+Oz47Oz47Pj
47Pj47bDxQZW9uQnV0dG9uO1BIQ kJ1dHRvbjtQSEJCdXR0b247VlBCdXR0b247
VlBCdXR0b247UHJlc2lkZW50QnV0dG9uO 1ByZXNpZGVudEJ1dHRvbjs+Pg==" />
```

This information is the content of the controls, or view state, in an encoded form. It is sent to the Web server whenever any event causes a postback. The Web server will use this information to repopulate the fields on the page when the HTML response is generated.

All of this data has an impact on scalability. The more controls you have on a form, the more state information has to be passed between the browser and Web server during the postback processing, and the more events you use, the more frequently this will happen. In general, to reduce network overhead, you should keep your Web forms relatively simple and avoid excessive use of server events, and be selective with view state to avoid sending unnecessary information across the network. You can disable the view state for a control by setting the EnableViewState property of the control to False (the default setting is True).

Creating and Using a Theme

When you first created the Web site, you defined a style for the form. This style determined the default font and color for controls on the form, and could also be used to specify default values for other attributes, such as the way in which lists are formatted and numbered (click the Lists tab in the Style Builder dialog box if you want to experiment with list formatting). However, a style defined in this way only applies to a single form. Commercial Web sites typically contains tens, or maybe hundreds of forms. Keeping all of these forms consistently formatted can be a time-consuming task (imagine if the company you work for decided to change the font on all of its Web pages, how many forms would you need to update and rebuild). This is where Themes can be very useful. A Theme is a set of properties, styles, and images that you can apply to the controls on a page, or globally across all pages in a Web site.

Note   If you are familiar with cascading style sheets (.css files), then the concept of Themes might be familiar to you. However, there are some differences between cascading style sheets and Themes. In particular, Themes do not cascade in the same way as cascading style sheets, and properties defined in a Theme applied to a control always override any local property values defined for the control.

Defining a Theme

A Theme comprises a set of skin files located in a named subfolder in the App_Themes folder for a Web site. A skin file is a text file that has the file extension ".skin". Each skin file specifies the default properties for a particular type of control using syntax very similar to that which is displayed when you view a Web form in the Source View window. For example, the following skin file specifies the default properties for TextBox and Label controls:

```
<asp:TextBox BackColor="Blue" ForeColor="White" Runat="Server" />
<asp:Label BackColor="White" ForeColor="Blue" Runat="Server" Font-Bold="True" />
```

You can specify many properties of a control in a skin file, but not all of them. For example, you cannot specify a value for the AutoPostBack property. Additionally, you cannot create skin files for every type of control, but most commonly used controls can be configured in this way.

Applying a Theme

After you have created a set of skin files for a Theme, you can apply the Theme to a page by modifying the @Page attribute that occurs at the start of the page when displayed in the Source View window. For example, if the skin files for a Theme are located in the App_Themes\BlueTheme folder under the Web site, you can apply the Theme to a page like this:

```
<%@Page Theme="BlueTheme" ...%>
```

If you want to apply the Theme to all pages in the Web site, you can modify the Web.config file and specify the Theme in the pages element, like this:

```
<configuration>
    <system.web>
        <pages theme="BlueTheme" />
    </system.web>
</configuration>
```

If you modify the definition of a Theme, all controls and pages that use the Theme will pick up the changes automatically when they are next displayed.

In the final set of exercises in this chapter, you will create a Theme for the Honest John Web site, and apply this Theme to all pages in the Web site.

Create a new theme

1. In the Visual Studio 2005 programming environment, open the Honest John Web site if it is not already open.

2. In the Solution Explorer, right-click the Honest John project folder. Point to Add ASP.NET Folder, and then click Theme.

    A new folder called App_Themes is added to the project, and a sub-folder is created called Theme1.

3. Change the name of the Theme1 folder to **HJTheme**.

4. In the Solution Explorer, right-click the HJTheme folder and then click Add New Item.

    The Add New Item dialog box appears displaying the types of file that can be stored in a Themes folder.

5. Click the Skin File template, and type **HJ.skin** for the name. Click Add.

    The skin file HJ.skin is added to the HJTheme folder, and the file is displayed in the Code and Text Editor window.

6. Add the following lines to the end of the HJ.skin file in the Code and Text Editor window (this file contains a comment with some very brief instructions):

```
<asp:TextBox BackColor="Red" ForeColor="White" Runat="Server" />
<asp:Label BackColor="White" ForeColor="Red" Runat="Server" Font-Bold="True" />
<asp:RadioButton BackColor="White" ForeColor="Red" Runat="Server"/>
<asp:Button BackColor="Red" ForeColor="White" Runat="Server" Font-Bold="True"/>
<asp:DropDownList BackColor="Red" ForeColor="White" Runat="Server"/>
```

This simple set of properties displays *TextBox*, *Button*, and *DropDownListBox* controls as white text on a red background, and *Label* and *RadioButton* controls as red text on a white background. The text on *Label* and *Button* controls is displayed using the bold font version of the current font.

> **Important**   The skin file editor is very basic and does not provide any Intellisense to help you. If you make a mistake in this file, the application will run, but entries in this file might be ignored. When you run the application later, if any of the controls do not appear as expected, ensure you have not mistyped anything in this file.

As mentioned previously, there are at least two ways you can apply a Theme to a web form: you can set the @Page attribute for each page, or you can specify the Theme globally across all pages by using an Web configuration file. You are going to use the latter approach in the next exercise. Using this mechanism will cause all new pages that you add to the site to automatically apply the same Theme.

Create a Web configuration file and apply the theme

1. In the Solution Explorer, right-click the Honest John project and click Add New Item.

    The Add New Item dialog box appears displaying the types of file that you can add to a Web site.

2. Click the Web Configuration File template, ensure the name is set to Web.config, and click Add.

    The file Web.config is added to the project and appears in the Code and Text Editor window.

3. Scroll to the end of the Web.config file, and insert a new line immediately above the </system.web> line. Type the following entry in this new line:

```
<pages theme="HJTheme" />
```

4. On the Debug menu, click Start Without Debugging.

> **Tip**   If Internet Explorer displays a list of files rather than the Web form, close Internet Explorer and return to Visual Studio 2005. In the Solution Explorer, right-click Employee-Form.aspx and click Set As Start Page. Then run the Web application again.

5. Internet Explorer appears displaying the Web form. Verify that the style of the controls on the form have changed as expected, although any text in the text boxes might be a little hard to read (you will fix this shortly). Close Internet Explorer when you have finished.

6. In Visual Studio 2005, display the HJ.skin file in the Code and Text Editor window. Modify the element defining the appearance of *TextBox* and *DropDownList* controls, as follows:

```
<asp:TextBox BackColor="White" ForeColor="Red" Font-Bold="True" Runat="Server" />
...
<asp:DropDownList BackColor="White" ForeColor="Red" Runat="Server" />
```

7. Run the form again. Notice how the style of all the *TextBox* controls (First Name, Last Name, and Employee Id) and the *DropDownList* (Role) has changed, and is easier to read. Close Internet Explorer when you have finished.

■ **If you want to continue to the next chapter**

Keep Visual Studio 2005 running and turn to Chapter 26.

■ **If you want to exit Visual Studio 2005 for now**

On the File menu, click Exit. If you see a Save dialog box, click Yes.

Chapter 25 Quick Reference

To	Do this
Create a Web application.	Create a new Web Site. Use the ASP.NET Web Site template. Specify whether you want to use the Development Web Server (specify a FileSystem location and filename), or IIS (specify an HTTP location and URL).
View and edit the HTML definition of a Web form.	Switch to Source View in the Design View window.
Create a style for a Web form.	On the Format menu, click Style. Use the Style Builder dialog box to define the style for the form.
Add Server controls to a Web form.	Switch to the Design View in the Design View window. In the Toolbox, expand the Standard category. Drag controls onto the Web form.
Add HTML controls to a Web form.	In the Toolbox, click the HTML category. Drag controls onto the Web form.
Create an event handler for a Server control.	In Design View, select the control on the Web form. In the Properties window, click the Events button. Locate the event you want to use and type the name of an event handler method. In Code and Text Editor window, write the code for the event.
View the HTML source code for a Web form at run time.	On the View menu in Internet Explorer, click Source. The HTML source will be displayed in Notepad.
Create a Theme.	Add an App_Themes folder to the Web site. Create a sub-folder for the Theme. Create a skin file defining the properties of controls in this folder.

Apply a Theme to a Web site.	Either specify the Theme using the @Page attribute of each page, like this:
	
	`<%@Page Theme="BlueTheme" ...%>`
	
	or, modify the Web.config file and specify the Theme in the pages element, like this:
	
	`<configuration>`
	`    <system.web>`
	`        <pages theme="BlueTheme" />`
	`    </system.web>`
	`</configuration>`

Chapter 26

Understanding Web Forms Validation Controls

After completing this chapter, you will be able to:

- Validate user input in a Microsoft ASP.NET Web form, by using the ASP.NET validation controls.

- Determine whether to perform user input validation at the client or the Web server.

As with Windows Forms applications, validating user input in a Web Forms application is an important part of any system. With Windows forms, you have a limited choice of where the validation should be performed—you check that the user's input makes sense by using events attached to the controls and forms of the application itself. With Web forms, there is an additional complication that you must consider: should you perform validation at the client (the browser) or at the server? In this chapter, you will examine this question and discover the options that are available to you.

Comparing Server and Client Validations

Consider the EmployeeForm.aspx page of the Honest John Web site again. The user is expected to enter the details of an employee: name, employee ID, position, and role. All the text boxes should be mandatory. The employee ID should be a positive integer.

In a Windows Forms application, you would use the *Validating* event to ensure the user typed something into the First Name and Last Name text boxes and that the employee ID value was numeric. Web forms do not have a *Validating* event, which means that you cannot use the same approach.

Server Validation

If you examine the *TextBox* class, you will notice that it publishes the *TextChanged* event. This event runs the next time the form is posted back to the server after the user changes the text typed in the text box. Like all Web Server control events, the *TextChanged* event runs at the Web server. This action involves transmitting data from the Web browser to the server, processing the event at the server to validate the data, and then packaging up any validation errors as part of the HTML response sent back to the client. If the validation being performed is complex, or requires processing that can only be performed at the Web server (such as ensuring that an Employee ID the user types in exists in a database) , this might be an acceptable technique. But if you are simply inspecting the data in a single text box in isolation (such as making sure that the user types a positive integer into an Employee ID text box), performing this type of validation of the Web server could impose an unacceptable overhead; why not perform this check in the browser on the client computer and save a network round-trip?

Client Validation

The Web Forms model provides for client-side validation through the use of validation controls. If the user is running a browser such as Microsoft Internet Explorer 4 or later, which supports dynamic HTML, these controls generate JavaScript code that runs in the browser and avoids the need to perform a network round-trip to the server. If the user is running an older browser, the validation controls generate server-side code instead. The key point is that the developer creating the Web form does not have to worry about this; all the browser detection and code generation features are built into the validation controls. The developer simply drops a validation control onto the Web form, sets its properties (by using either the Properties window or code), and specifies the validation rules to be performed and any error messages to be displayed.

There are five types of validation controls supplied with ASP.NET:

- *RequiredFieldValidator* Use this control to ensure that the user has entered data into a control.

- *CompareValidator* Use this control to compare the data entered against a constant value, the value of a property of another control, or a value retrieved from a database.

- *RangeValidator* Use this control to check the data entered by a user against a range of values, checking that the data falls either inside or outside a given range.

- *RegularExpressionValidator* Use this control to check that the data input by the user matches a specified regular expression, pattern, or format (such as a telephone number, for example).

> **Note**   You should be aware that if a user can type unrestricted text into a text box and send it to the Web server, they could type text that looks like HTML tags (<b> for example). Hackers sometimes use this technique to inject HTML into a client request in an attempt to cause damage to the Web server, or to try and break in (I am not going to go into the details here!). By default, if you try this trick with an ASP.NET Web page the request will be aborted and the user is shown the message "A potentially dangerous Request.Form value was detected from the client". You can disable this check although it is not recommended. A better approach is to use a *RegularExpressionValidator* control to verify that the user input in a text box does not constitute an HTML tag (or anything that looks like it). For more information about regular expressions and how to use them, see the topic ".NET Framework Regular Expressions" in the Microsoft Visual Studio 2005 Documentation.

■ *CustomValidator* Use this control to define your own custom validation logic and attach it to a control to be validated.

Although each control performs a single well-defined type of validation, you can use several of them in combination. For example, if you want to ensure that the user enters a value into a text box and that this value falls within a particular range, you can attach a *RequiredField Validator* control and a *RangeValidator* control to the text box.

These controls can work in conjunction with a *ValidationSummary* control to display error messages. You will use some of these controls in the following exercises.

Implementing Client Validation

Returning to the EmployeeForm.aspx Web form, you can probably see that *RequiredField Validator* controls will be required for the First Name, Last Name, and Employee Id text boxes. The employee ID must also be numeric and should be a positive integer. In this application, you will specify that the employee ID must be between 1 and 5000. This is where a *Range Validator* control is useful.

Add *RequiredFieldValidator* controls

1. In the Microsoft Visual Studio 2005 programming environment, on the File menu, point to Open, and then click Web Site. In the Open Web Site dialog box,ensure the File System option is selected, and browse to Microsoft Press\Visual CSharp Step by Step\Chapter 26\HonestJohn in your My Documents folder. Click Open.

> **Note**   You do not need to select a C# solution or project file to open a Web site for editing; just move to the folder containing the Web site files and sub-folders. Visual Studio 2005 will generate a new solution file if this folder does not contain one, and add the Web site files to it. However, this solution file is not essential to the Web site and you do not need to save it.

> **Note**   When you create a new Web site, Visual Studio 2005 creates a solution file in a solution folder in your My Documents\Visual Studio 2005 folder. If you want to open a Web site by using the existing solution file rather than generating a new one, on the File menu point to Open and click Project/Solution, then move to the solution folder and click the solution file.

2. In the Solution Explorer, right-click EmployeeForm.aspx, and then click Set As Start Page.

3. Right-click EmployeeForm.aspx again, and then click View Designer to display the Web form in the Design View window.

4. In the Toolbox, expand the Validation category.

5. Add a *RequiredFieldValidator* control to the form.

    The control appears in the upper left-hand part of the form, displaying the text "RequiredFieldValidator". Drag it and position it just below the First Name text box so it looks like the following graphic. You might need to enable absolute positioning on the form before you can move the RequiredFieldValidator control by using the Position item on the Layout menu.

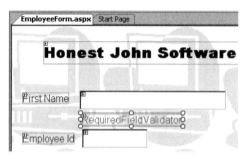

6. With *RequiredFieldValidator1* selected, click the Properties window. Set the *ControlTo Validate* property to *firstName*. Type **You must type a first name for the employee** in the *ErrorMessage* property.

    This is the message that will be displayed if the control to be validated (the First Name text box) is left blank. Notice that this message replaces the red text on the form.

7. Add two more *RequiredFieldValidator* controls to the form. Place the first control under the Last Name text box, set its *ControlToValidate* property to lastName, and type **You must type a last name for the employee** in its *ErrorMessage* property. Resize the control so that the error message appears on a single line if necessary.

    Place the second *RequiredFieldValidator* control under the Employee Id text box; set its *ControlToValidate* property to employeeID, and type **You must specify an employee ID** in its *ErrorMessage* property.

8. On the Debug menu, click Start Without Debugging to run the form and test it.

9. When the form first appears in Microsoft Internet Explorer, all the required text boxes will be empty. Click Save.

    The error messages belonging to all three *RequiredFieldValidator* controls are displayed.

    Notice that the *Click* event for the Save button did not run; and the label at the bottom of the form did not display the data summary (and the screen did not even flicker). This behavior is because the validation controls prevented the post-back to the server; they generate code that can be executed by the browser and they will continue to block posts back to the server until all the errors have been corrected.

10. Type a name in the First Name text box.

    As soon as you move away from the text box, the error message disappears. If you return to the First Name text box, erase the contents, and then move to the next text box, the error message is displayed again. All this functionality is being performed in the browser with no data is being sent to the server over the network.

11. Enter values in the First Name, Last Name, and Employee Id text boxes, and then click Save.

This time the *Click* event runs and the summary is displayed in the *InfoLabel* control at the bottom of the form.

12. Close the form and return to the Visual Studio 2005 programming environment.

Currently, you can type anything into the Employee Id text box. In the following exercise, you will use a *RangeValidator* control to restrict the values entered to integers in the range of 1 through 5000.

Add a *RangeValidator* control

1. In the Toolbox, add a *RangeValidator* control to the form and drag it under the *RequiredFieldValidator* control below the Employee Id text box. (You might need to move the Position label and radio buttons down to make space).

2. With the *RangeValidator* control selected, click the Properties window. Change the *ControlToValidate* property to employeeID. Type **ID must be between 1 and 5000** in the *ErrorMessage* property. Set the *MaximumValue* property to 5000, the *MinimumValue* property to 1, and the *Type* property to Integer.

3. Run the form again. Enter a first name and a last name, but leave the employee ID blank. Click Save.

An error message telling you that you must supply an employee ID is displayed.

4. Type **−1** in the Employee Id text box, and then click Save.

An error message telling you that the employee ID must be between 1 and 5000 is displayed.

5. Type **101** in the Employee Id text box, and then click Save.

This time the data is valid. The form is posted back to the server, the *Click* event of the Save button runs, and a summary of the information entered in the *InfoLabel* label appears at the bottom of the form.

6. Experiment with other values that are out of range or the wrong type. Try 5001 and the text "AAA" to check that the *RangeValidator* control works as expected.

7. On the Internet Explorer View menu, click Source.

The HTML source code for the Web form appears in Notepad. Scroll through the file and examine its contents. Near the end you will find a block of JavaScript code that performs the validations. This code was generated by using the properties of the validation controls. Close Notepad when you have finished browsing the HTML source code.

8. Close the form and return to the Visual Studio 2005 programming environment.

Disabling Client Validation

In the previous exercise you saw that the validations were performed by using JavaScript code running in the browser. The ASP.NET runtime generates this code automatically, depending on the capabilities of your browser. If your browser does not support JavaScript, all validation checks will be performed by using code running on the Web server instead.

If you want, you can suppress client validation and force all checks to be performed at the server. To do this, set the *EnableClientScript* property of the validation control to False. You might find it useful to do this under certain circumstances, such as those involving custom validations (by using the *CustomValidator* control) that are complex or require access to data that is available only on the server. In addition, the *Custom Validator* control also has a *ServerValidate* event that can be used to perform validation explicitly on the server, even if *EnableClientScript* is set to True.

You have seen how validation controls can validate the data that the user enters, but the error message display is not very pretty. In the following exercise, you will use a *ValidationSummary* control to change the way that the error information is presented to the user.

Add a *ValidationSummary* control

1. In the EmployeeForm.aspx Web form, select the *RequiredFieldValidator1* control under the First Name text box. In the Properties window, set the *Text* property to *.

    The message, You Must Enter A First Name For The Employee, changes to an asterisk (*) because the validation controls display the *Text* property on the form. If no value is specified for the *Text* property, it takes the value of the *ErrorMessage* property.

2. Move the *RequiredFieldValidator1* control, placing it to the right of the First Name text box.

    Now, if a validation error occurs, you will see a red asterisk appear next to the text box with the error.

3. Select the *RequiredFieldValidator2* control, set its *Text* property to *, and then move it to the right of the Last Name text box.

4. Select the *RequiredFieldValidator3* control, set its *Text* property to *, and then move it to the right of the Employee Id text box. Do the same for the *RangeValidator1* control.

5. In the Toolbox, add a *ValidationSummary* control to the form and place it in the space above the button controls and to the right of the radio buttons.

    A *ValidationSummary* control displays the *ErrorMessage* values for all of the validation controls on the Web form.

6. Leave the *ValidationSummary* control set to its default size. Verify that the *ShowSummary* property is set to True.

7. Run the Web form. When the form appears, leave the First Name, Last Name, and Employee Id text boxes blank, and then click Save.

    Red asterisks appear next to each of the text boxes, and the corresponding error messages are displayed in the *ValidationSummary* control at the bottom of the form.

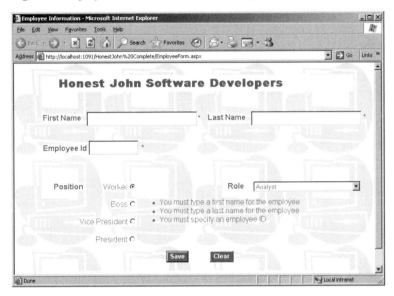

8. Enter a first name, a last name, and then type **AAA** in the Employee Id text box.

    As you move from text box to text box, the asterisks disappear from the First Name and Last Name text boxes, but another asterisk appears next to the Employee Id text box.

9. Click Save.

    The error message displayed by the *ValidationSummary* control changes.

10. Type **101** in the Employee Id text box, and then click Save.

    All error messages and asterisks disappear and a summary of the data you entered appears in the *InfoLabel* control as before.

11. Close the form and return to the Visual Studio 2005 programming environment.

Dynamic HTML and Error Messages

If you have a browser that supports dynamic HTML, you can display the validation summary data in a message box rather than on the Web form. To do this, set the *Show MessageBox* property of the *ValidationSummary* control to True. At run time, if any validation errors occur, the error messages will be displayed in a message box.

- **If you want to continue to the next chapter**

  Keep Visual Studio 2005 running and turn to Chapter 27.

- **If you want to exit Visual Studio 2005 for now**

  On the File menu, click Exit. If you see a Save dialog box, click Yes.

Chapter 26 Quick Reference

To	Do this
Perform server-side validation of user input.	Use events belonging to server controls, for example, the *TextChanged* event of the *TextBox* control.
Perform client-side validation of user input.	Use a *Validation* control. Set the *ControlToValidate* property to the control to be validated and the *ErrorMessage* property to an error message to be displayed. Verify that the *EnableClientScript* property is set to True.
Force the user to enter a value in a text box.	Use a *RequiredFieldValidator* control.
Check the type and range of data values entered into a text box.	Use a *RangeValidator* control. Set the *Type*, *MaximumValue*, and *MinimumValue* properties as required.
Display a summary of validation error messages.	Use a *ValidationSummary* control. Verify that the *ShowSummary* property is set to True.

Chapter 27

Securing a Web Site and Accessing Data with Web Forms

After completing this chapter, you will be able to:

- Secure access to a Web site by using ASP.NET Login controls and Forms-based authentication.

- Create Web Forms that present data from a database using a *GridView* control.

- Update a database from a Web form.

- Build Web applications that need to display potentially large volumes of data while minimizing resource use.

In the previous two chapters, you saw how to build a Web site that allowed the user to enter information and validate the data that was entered. In this chapter, you'll learn about creating applications that display data from a database and update the database with any changes made by the user. You will see how to do this in an efficient manner that minimizes use of shared resources, such as the network and the database.

Security is always an important issue, especially when building applications that can be accessed over the Internet. Therefore, you will also see how to configure a Web Forms application to use Forms-based security to verify the identity of the user.

Using the Web Forms *GridView* Control

When you looked at accessing databases in previous chapters, you learned how to use the Windows Forms *DataGridView* control. Web Forms have a similar control called *GridView*. It has some differences because Microsoft designed it to be used in a Microsoft ASP.NET environment, but the overall purpose is the same; to display and edit rows retrieved from a data source. One difference is related to fetching and displaying large volumes of data. In a Web Forms application, it is very likely that the client application (or the browser) will be remote from the database that is being used. It is imperative that you use network bandwidth wisely (this has been stated several times already, but it is very important and worth repeating), and you should not waste resources retrieving vast amounts of data that the user does not want to see. The Web Forms *GridView* control supports *paging*, which allows you to fetch data on demand as the user scrolls up and down through a *DataSet*.

Like the Windows Forms *DataGridView* control, the Web Forms *GridView* control is designed to be used while it is disconnected from the database. You can create an *SqlDataSource* object to connect to a database, populate a *DataSet*, and then disconnect from the database. You can bind the *DataSet* in a *SqlDataSource* control to the *GridView* control. Unlike a Windows Forms *GridView* control, the information in a Web Forms *GridView* control is presented in a grid of read-only text (rendered as an HTML table in the browser). However, properties of the Web Forms *GridView* control allow a user to enter edit mode, which changes a selected row into a set of text boxes that the user can use to modify the data that is presented. You will use this technique in the exercises in this chapter.

Managing Security

Applications built by using the Microsoft .NET Framework have a range of mechanisms available for ensuring that the users who run those applications have the appropriate privileges. Some of the techniques available rely on authenticating users based on some form of identifier and password, whereas others are based on the integrated security features of Microsoft Windows. If you are creating a Web application that will be accessed over the Internet, using Windows security is probably not an option—users are unlikely to be members of any Windows domain recognized by the Web application and might be running an operating system other than Windows, such as UNIX. Therefore, the best option to use in this environment is Forms-based security.

Understanding Forms-Based Security

Forms-based security allows you to verify the identity of a user by displaying a login form that prompts the user for an ID and a password. After the user has been authenticated, the various Web Forms that comprise the application can be accessed, and the user's security credentials can be examined by code on any page if additional authorization is needed (a user might be able to log in to the system but might not have access to every part of the application).

To use ASP.NET Forms-based security, you must configure the Web application by making some changes to the Web.config file, and you must also supply a form to validate the user. The security form will be displayed whenever the user tries to gain access to any page in the application if the user has not already been validated. The user will be able to proceed to the requested page only if the logic in the login form verifies the user's identity.

Important   It might seem, to the uninitiated, that ASP.NET Forms-based security is excessive. It's not. Don't be tempted to simply create a login form that acts as an entry point to your application and assume that users will always access your application through it. Browsers can cache forms and URLs locally on users' computers. Another user might be able to gain access to the browser cache depending on how the computer itself is configured, find the URLs of the sensitive parts of your application, and navigate directly to them, bypassing your login form. You have control over your Web server (hopefully), but you have almost no control over the user's computer. The ASP.NET Forms-based mechanism is pretty robust and, assuming that your Web server is secure, it should be adequate for most of your applications.

Implementing Forms-Based Security

In the first set of exercises in this chapter, you will create and configure a Web application. The application will ultimately enable a user to view and modify customer information in the Northwind database.

Create the Northwind Web Site

1. In the Microsoft Visual Studio 2005 programming environment, create a new ASP.NET Web site called Northwind by using the Development Web server (specify File System for the location). Create the Web site in the \Microsoft Press\Visual CSharp Step by Step\Chapter 27\Northwind folder in your My Documents folder. Make sure you specify Visual C# for the language to use.

2. In Solution Explorer, rename the Default.aspx Web form to CustomerData.aspx.

3. Right-click CustomerData.aspx and click Set As Start Page.

4. In the Source View window displaying the HTML source for the Web form, click the Design tab.

5. In the Layout menu, point to Position and click Auto-position Options. In the Options dialog box, check "Change positioning to the following for controls added using the Toolbox, paste, or drag and drop," and ensure "Absolutely positioned" is selected in the drop-down list box. Click OK.

6. From the Toolbox, add a *Label* control. Drag it to the middle of the *CustomerData* form. Type **This form will be implemented later** in the *Text* property of the label.

In the next exercises, you will build a login form to authenticate the user and configure Forms-based security for the Web application. The login form will be displayed whenever a user who has not been authenticated attempts to gain access to the application. When configured to use Forms-based security, the ASP.NET run time will redirect attempts made by an unauthenticated user to access the application to the login form instead.

Implementing a login form for Forms-based security is such a common task that Microsoft has implemented a set of Login controls to simplify matters. You will use one of these controls now.

Build the login form

1. On the Website menu, click Add New Item. The Add New Item dialog box opens. Ensure the Web Form template is selected and type **LoginForm.aspx** for the name. Verify that the language is set to Visual C#, the "Place code in separate file" box is checked, the "Select master page" box is cleared, and then click Add to create the form.

    The new Web form is created and the HTML code for the form is displayed in the Source View window.

2. Click the Design tab to display LoginForm.aspx in the Design View window.

3. In the Toolbox, expand the Login category. Add a *Login* control to the Web form. Click anywhere in the form to hide the Login Tasks menu that appears.

    The *Login* control is a composite control that comprises several labels, two text boxes for the user to type a name and a password, a "remember me" check box, and a button to click to log in. You can configure most of these items by using the Properties window for this control, and you can also modify the style of the control.

4. Drag the *Login* control to the middle of the Web form. Click the Smart Tag icon on the top edge of the control, near the right-hand corner. Click Auto Format on the Login Tasks menu that appears.

    The Auto Format dialog box is displayed. You can use this dialog to change the look and feel of the *Login* control by selecting a predefined scheme. (You can also define your own layout by creating a template using the Edit Templates option on the Login Tasks menu displayed when you click the Smart Tag for the Login control.)

5. In the Auto Format dialog box, click the Classic scheme and then click OK. Click the Smart Tag icon on the *Login* control to hide the Login Tasks menu.

6. In the Properties window, change the properties of the *Login* control by using the values in the following table.

Property	Value
DisplayRememberMe	False
FailureText	Invalid User Name or Password. Please enter a valid User Name and Password.
TitleText	Northwind Traders – Log In
DestinationPageUrl	~/CustomerData.aspx

The *DestinationPageUrl* property specifies the page the user will go to if the login attempt is successful. The "~/" prefix indicates that the page is in the top-level folder of the Web site, rather than in a sub-folder. If the login fails, the *FailureText* message will be displayed instead, and the user will have to try to log in again.

The *Login* control should look like this:

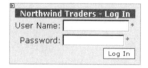

When the user clicks the Log In button, the user must be authenticated. If the user name and password are valid, the user should be allowed to proceed to the CustomerData Web form; otherwise, the error message stored in the *FailureText* property of the *Login* control should be displayed. How do you perform these tasks? You have at least two options:

■ Write code that handles the Authenticate event for the *Login* control. This event is raised whenever the Log In button is clicked. You can examine the values in the *UserName* and *Password* properties, and if they are valid, allow the user to proceed to the page identified by the *DestinationPageUrl* property. This strategy is highly customizable, but requires that you maintain your own secure list of user names and passwords to validate against.

■ Use the built-in features of Visual Studio 2005 with the ASP.NET Web Site Administration Tool to manage user names and passwords, and let the *Login* control perform its default processing to validate users when the Log In button is pressed. The ASP.NET Web Site Administration Tool maintains its own database of user names and passwords, and provides a wizard enabling you to add users to your Web site.

You will use the second option in the following exercise (you can investigate the first option in your own time).

Configure Website Security and enable Forms-based security

1.   On the Website menu, click ASP.NET Configuration.

The ASP.NET Development Server starts and displays a balloon displaying its URL—the ASP.NET Configuration command starts a Web application called the ASP.NET Web Site Administration Tool which uses its own instance of the ASP.NET Development Server, independent from your Web application. Internet Explorer starts and displays the ASP.NET Web Site Administration Tool.

This tool provides different pages allowing you to add and manage users for your Web site, specify application settings that you want to be stored in the application configuration file, and specify how security information such as user names and passwords are stored. By default, the ASP.NET Web Site Administration Tool stores security information in a local SQL Server database called ASPNETDB.MDF that it creates in the App_Data folder of your Web site, using a database provider called AspNetSqlProvider. You can configure other database providers and store security information elsewhere, but that is beyond the scope of this book.

2. Click the Security tab.

    The Security page appears. You can use this page to manager users, specify the authentication mechanism that the Web site uses, define roles for users (roles are a convenient mechanism for assigning privileges to groups of users), and specify access rules for controlling access to the Web site.

3. In the Users section, click the "Select authentication type" link.

    A new page appears asking how users will access your Web site. You have two options available: "From the internet," and "From a local network." The "From a local network" option is selected by default. This option configures the Web site to use Windows authentication; all users must be members of a Windows domain that your Web site can access. The Northwind Website will be available over the Internet, so this option is probably not very useful.

4. Click "From the internet." This option configures the application to use Forms-based security. You will make use of the login form you created in the previous exercise to prompt the user for their name and password. Click Done.

    You return to the Security page.

5. In the Users section, notice that the number of existing users that can access your Web site is currently zero. Click the Create User link.

    The Create User page appears.

6. In the Create User page, add a new user with the values shown in the following table.

Prompt	Response
User Name	John
Password	Pa$$w9rd
Confirm Password	Pa$$w9rd
E-mail	john@northwindtraders.com
Security Question	What was the name of your first pet
Security Answer	Thomas

> **Note** You must supply values for all fields in this screen. The E-mail, Security Question, and Security Answer fields are used by the *PasswordRecovery* control to recover or reset a user's password. The *PasswordRecovery* control is available in the Login category of the Toolbar, and you can add it to a login page to provide assistance to a user that has forgotten his or her password.

7. Ensure that the Active User box is checked and then click Create User.

   The message "Complete. Your account has been successfully created." appears in a new page.

8. Click Continue. The Create User page reappears enabling you to add further users. Click Back to return to the Security page. The number of existing users is now set to 1.

> **Note** You can use the Manage users link on this page to change the e-mail addresses of users and add descriptions, and remove existing users. You can enable users to change their passwords, and recover their passwords if they forget them, by adding the *Change-Password* and *PasswordRecovery* controls to the login page of the Web site. For more information, see the topic "Walkthough: Creating a Web Site with Membership and User Login" in the Microsoft Visual Studio 2005 Documentation.

9. In the Access Rules section, click "Create access rules."

   The Add New Access Rule page appears. You use this page to specify which users can access which folders in the Web site.

10. Under "Select a directory for this rule," ensure that the Northwind folder is selected by clicking it. Under "Rule applies to," ensure "user" is selected and type **John**. Under "Permission," click Allow. Click OK.

    This rule grants John access to the Web site. The Security screen reappears.

11. In the Access Rules section, click "Create access rules" again. In the Add New Access Rule page, under "Select a directory for this rule," ensure that the Northwind folder is selected. Under "Rule applies to," click Anonymous users. Under "Permission," ensure Deny is selected. Click OK.

    This rule ensures that users who have not logged in will not be able to access the Web site. The Security screen reappears.

12. Close Internet Explorer displaying the ASP.NET Web Site Administration Tool and return to Visual Studio 2005.

13. Click the Refresh button in the Solution Explorer toolbar. The database file ASP-NETDB.MDF appears in the App_Data folder, and the file Web.config appears in the project folder. Double-click Web.config to display it in the Code and Text Editor window.

This file was created by the ASP.NET Web Site Administration Tool and should look like this:

```xml
<?xml version="1.0" encoding="utf-8"?>
<configuration xmlns="http://schemas.microsoft.com/.NetConfiguration/v2.0">
    <system.web>
        <authorization>
            <allow users="John" />
            <deny users="?" />
        </authorization>
        <authentication mode="Forms" />
    </system.web>
</configuration>
```

The *<authorization>* element specifies the users that are granted and denied access to the Web site ("?" indicates anonymous users). The *mode* attribute of the *<authentication>* element indicates that the Web site uses Forms-based authentication.

14. Modify the *<authentication>* element and add a *<forms>* child element, as follows. Make sure you add a *</authentication>* element:

```xml
<authentication mode="Forms">
    <forms loginUrl="LoginForm.aspx" timeout="5"
           cookieless="AutoDetect" protection="All" />
</authentication>
```

The *<forms>* element configures the parameters for Forms-based authentication. The attributes shown here specify that if an unauthenticated user attempts to gain access to any page in the Web site, the user will be redirected to the login page, LoginForm.aspx. If the user is inactive for 5 minutes, she will have to login again when next accessing a page in the Web site. In many Web sites that use Forms-based authentication, information about the user is stored in a cookie on the user's computer. However, most browsers allow the user to specify that they don't want to use cookies (cookies can be abused by malicious Web sites and are frequently considered a security risk). Specifying *cookieless="AutoDetect"* enables the Web site to use cookies if the user's browser has not disabled them; otherwise, the user information is passed back and forth between the Web site and the user's computer as part of each request. The user information includes the user name and the password. Obviously, you don't want this to be clearly visible to everyone. You can use the *protection* attribute to encrypt this information, which is what this example does.

15. On the Debug menu, click Start Without Debugging.

Internet Explorer opens. The start page for the application is CustomerData.asps, but as you have not yet logged in, you are directed to the LoginForm.

16. Type in a random user name and password and then click Log In.

The Login page reappears displaying the error message "Invalid User Name or Password. Please enter a valid User Name and Password."

17. In the User Name field type **John**. In the Password field type **Pa$$w9rd**. Click Log In.

    The CustomerData page appears displaying the message "This form will be implemented later."

18. Close Internet Explorer and return to Visual Studio 2005.

Querying Data

Now that you can control access to your application, you can turn your attention to querying and maintaining data. You will use Web Server Data controls to connect to the database, query data, and maintain the data, in a manner similar to that used by the Windows Forms application you built in Chapter 24, "Working with Data Binding and DataSets."

Displaying Customer Information

In the following exercises, you will fetch all of the rows in the Customers table in the Microsoft SQL Server Northwind Traders database and display them in a *GridView*. The first task is to create a connection that you can use to connect to the Northwind database.

> **Note** This exercise assumes that you have completed the exercises in Chapter 23, "Using a Database," on your computer.

Create a connection to the Northwind Database

1. Display the CustomerData.aspx page in the Design View window. Delete the label displaying "This form will be implemented later."

2. In the Toolbox, expand the Data category. Add a *SqlDataSource* control to the Web form.

3. Click anywhere in the form to hide the SqlDataSource Tasks menu that appears. A control called *SqlDataSource1* is added to the Web form. The *SqlDataSource* control is a Web Server control that performs the same tasks as a data source in a Windows Forms application.

> **Note** Although the *SqlDataSource* control appears on the Web form at design time, it will not be visible when the Web form runs.

4. Using the Properties window, change the (ID) property of *SqlDataSource1* to *CustomerInfoSource*.

5. Select the *CustomerInfoSource* control on the Web Form. Click the Smart Tag icon to display the SqlDataSource Tasks menu, and then click the Configure Data Source link.

The Configure Data Source Wizard appears. This is very similar (but not identical) to the wizard you saw in Chapter 23. You will use it to create a connection to the database and fetch the data from the Customers table.

6. Click the New Connection button. Use the Add Connection page to create a new connection with the values shown in the following table. Click OK when you have finished.

Prompt	Response
Data source	**Microsoft SQL Server (SqlClient)**
Server name	*YourServer*\SQLExpress
Log on to the server	**Use windows authentication**
Select or enter a database name	Northwind

7. In the Configure Data Source Wizard, click Next.

8. In the Save the Connection String to the Application Configuration file screen, save the connection string as **NorthwindConnectionString** and click Next.

9. In the Configure the Select Statement page, ensure "Specify columns from a table or view" is selected. Select the Customers table in the Name drop-down list box. In the Columns list box, check "*".

10. Click Advanced. In the Advanced SQL Generation Options dialog box, check "Generate INSERT, UPDATE, and DELETE statements." Click OK, and then click Next.

> **Note** If you don't select "Generate INSERT, UPDATE, and DELETE statements," you will still be able to modify the data in the DataSet retrieved by the data source, but you won't be able to send these changes back to the database. You can always add commands to modify the database after creating the data source by modifying its *DeleteQuery*, *InsertQuery*, and *UpdateQuery* properties and providing the appropriate SQL statements.

11. In the Test Query page, click Test Query.

The data from the Customers table appears in the grid in the dialog box.

12. Click Finish.

13. Click the Smart Tag icon to hide the SqlDataSource Tasks menu.

In the next exercise, you will add a *GridView* control to the CustomerData Web form and bind it to the CustomerInfoSource data source.

Lay out the CustomerData Web form

1. In the Toolbox, click the *GridView* control. Drag it onto the form. Click anywhere on the form to hide the GridView Tasks menu that appears.

A *GridView* is added to the form and displays placeholder data. Resize the *GridView* so that it fills most of the form.

2. Using the Properties window, change the (ID) property of the *GridView* control to *CustomerGrid*.

3. With the *GridView* control still selected, click the Smart Tag icon to display the GridView Tasks menu. In the GridView Tasks menu, click the Auto Format link.

4. In the Auto Format dialog box, select the Classic scheme and then click OK.

> **Tip**   If you don't like any of the predefined formats available in the Auto Format dialog box, you can change the styles of the elements of a *GridView* control manually by using the properties in the Properties window. *BackColor*, *BorderStyle*, *BorderWidth*, *Footer-Style*, *HeaderStyle*, and *RowStyle* are the most commonly modified properties.

5. In the GridView Tasks menu that is still displayed, select CustomerInfoSource from the Choose Data Source drop-down list.

    The column headings for the Customers table appear in the *GridView* control on the screen.

6. Click the Smart Tag icon to hide the GridView Tasks menu.

Test the CustomerData form

1. On the Debug menu, click Start Without Debugging.

    Internet Explorer starts and displays the Log In page.

2. Log in as **John** with password **Pa$$w9rd**.

    The CustomerData page appears displaying the details of every customer in the database:

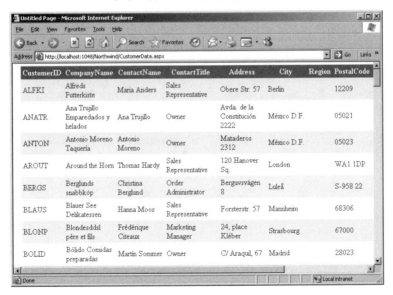

Notice that the page is currently read-only; you cannot modify any of the details displayed. You will enhance the Web form later in this chapter to enable the user to make changes.

3.   Close Internet Explorer when you have finished browsing the data and return to Visual Studio 2005.

Web Site Security and SQL Server

When you use the ASP.NET Development Server to run an application that uses Forms-based security, it executes in the context of the account you are using to run Visual Studio 2005. Assuming you used the same account to create the Northwind database, then the Web application should have no problems accessing the database.

However, if you deploy the Web site to IIS the situation changes. IIS runs applications that use Forms-based security using the ASPNET account. This account has very few privileges by default, for security purposes. In particular, it will not be able to connect to SQL Server Express and query the Northwind database. Therefore you will need to grant the ASPNET account login access to SQL Server Express and add it as a user to the Northwind database. For more details, see the *sp_grantlogin* and *sp_grantdbaccess* commands in the MSDN Library for Visual Studio 2005.

Displaying Data in Pages

Fetching the details of every customer is very useful, but suppose there are a large number of rows in the Customers table. It is highly unlikely that a user would actively want to browse thousands of rows, so generating a long page displaying them all would be a waste of time and network bandwidth. Instead, it would be far better to display data in chunks and allow the user to page through that data. This is what you will do in the following set of exercises.

Modify the *GridView* to use paging

1.   Ensure that CustomerData.aspx is displayed in the Design View window. Select the *CustomerGrid* control. In the Properties window, set the *AllowPaging* property to *True*.

A footer is added to the *GridView* containing a pair of page numbers. This footer is referred to as the *pager*. You can format the pager in many different ways. The style shown is the default format, comprising page numbers that the user can click.

2.   In the Properties window, set the *PageSize* property to *8*.

This will cause the *GridView* to display data in eight-row chunks.

3.   Expand the *PagerStyle* composite property. You can use this property to specify how the pager should be formatted. Set *HorizontalAlign* sub-property to *Left*.

The numbers in the pager move to the left marginin the *GridView* control.

4. Expand the *PagerSettings* composite property. Use the values in this property to specify how page navigation links are formatted. You can specify page navigation links in two ways: as page numbers, or as next/previous page arrows. Set the *Mode* property to *NumericFirstLast* to display page numbers with the first and last page arrows displayed to enable the user to move quickly to the start or end of the data. Set the *PageButton-Count* sub-property to 5; this will cause page links to be displayed in groups of five (you will see what this does when you run the Web application).

   If you want to use next/previous page arrows, you can change the default text displayed (">" and "<") by modifying the values of the *NextPageText* and *PreviousPageText* properties. Similarly, you can change the text displayed for the first and last page links by editing the *FirstPageText* and *LastPageText* properties. Notice that the values in these properties require encoding as HTML characters; otherwise, they will not be displayed properly (for example, the ">" symbol is specified as "&gt;"). If you prefer, you can also specify the name of an image file in the *FirstPageImageUrl*, *LastPageImageUrl*, *PreviousPageImageUrl* and *NextPageImageUrl* properties. The page navigation links will appear as buttons containing these images if supported by the browser.

5. Run the Web application.

   After logging in, the first eight rows of data and a set of page links are displayed on the CustomerData Web form. Page numbers 1, 2, 3, 4, and 5 are displayed, together with ">>" to move directly to the last page. Clicking the "..." link displays the next five page numbers together with a "<<" link for moving directly back to the first page. An additional "..." link provides access to the previous five pages.

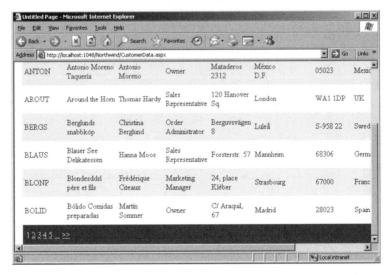

6. Click the links at the bottom of the grid to move from page to page.

7. Close Internet Explorer and return to the Visual Studio 2005 programming environment when you have finished browsing the data.

Optimizing Data Access

In this chapter, you have been using a *SqlDataSource* control to connect to the database and fetch the data. Behind the scenes, the *SqlDataSource* control creates a DataSet. When you bind a Web Server Data control such as *GridView* to a data source, Visual Studio 2005 generates code that populates the DataSet and displays it in the data control.

DataSets are very powerful objects. You have seen in earlier chapters how they can act as in-memory datastore and how you can use them to update a database. However, this power comes at a price. A DataSet that contains a large number of rows will itself be very large and can consume considerable resources. If you are using a *GridView* to simply display data rather than modify it, using a DataSet may be too cumbersome a solution. The *SqlDataSource* control has a property called *DataSourceMode* which you can set to *DataSet* (the default) or *DataReader*. Specifying a value of *DataReader* causes the data source to open an ADO.NET *DataReader* object for retrieving data. A *DataReader* implements a very efficient mechanism for fetching data as a read-only stream. For more information, see the sidebar "Firehose Cursors" in Chapter 23. However, one drawback of using a *DataReader* is that it does not support paging.

Caching Data in a Data Source

A DataSet contains a copy of the data it fetches. The longer the DataSet is held, the more out-of-date the information it holds can become. How can you make certain that the data a user sees in a Web form is the current data without continually refilling the DataSet? If you examine the *SqlDataSource* control, you will find that it has three properties that you can use to help solve this problem:

- **EnableCaching.**   Whenever you display a Web form that contains a *SqlDataSource* control, the SQL SELECT statement specified by that control is executed to populate its DataSet. By default, if you use paging to display, and the rows displayed are spread over several pages, the SQL SELECT statement will be executed whenever you move from one page to another. The SQL SELECT statement will also be executed again if you simply refresh the view of the Web form in the browser. In this way, you are always presented with a copy of the data that is up-to-date when the Web form is displayed.

  However, if none of the data actually changes between displaying or refreshing pages, you are wasting database resources by repeatedly connecting to and querying the database. If you set the *EnableCaching* property to *True*, the DataSet will act as a cache and the SQL SELECT statement will only be re-executed based on the settings of two other properties: *CacheDuration*, and *CacheExpirationPolicy*.

- **CacheDuration.**   This property specifies how frequently the SQL SELECT statement is re-executed and the cache refreshed. Its default setting of *Infinite* means that the cache never expires and so will never be refreshed. Setting it to a numeric value specifies the expiration period of the cache, in seconds.

- **CacheExpirationPolicy.** This property is used in conjunction with *CacheDuration* to determine how frequently the cache is updated. If this property is set to its default value of *Absolute*, then the cache will always be refreshed every *CacheDuration* seconds. If this property is set to *Sliding*, then the cache will only be refreshed after *CacheDuration* seconds of inactivity in the application.

> **Important** You can only set the *EnableCaching* property to *True* if the *DataSourceMode* property of the *SqlDataSource* is set to *DataSet*. If the *DataSourceMode* property is set to *DataReader*, the application will throw an exception when the page is displayed.

> **Tip** Caching can protect you from temporary database failure. If caching is disabled, the *SqlDataSource* control must connect to the database whenever a page is displayed. If the database is unavailable, this connection will fail and the *SqlDataSource* will throw an exception. However, if caching is enabled, and the data in the cache has not yet expired, you will be able to move to another page and display the cached data. If the *CacheDuration* and *CacheExpirationPolicy* properties are set to suitable values, it may even be possible to recover the database without too many users even noticing.

In the next exercise, you will see the effects of modifying the cache settings of a *SqlDataSource* control.

Investigate caching with a *SqlDataSource* object

1. Ensure that CustomerData.aspx is displayed in the Design View window. Select the *CustomerInfoSource* control. In the Properties window, set the *EnableCaching* property to *True*. Verify that the *CacheDuration* property is set to *Infinite*, and the *CacheExpiration Policy* property is set to *Absolute*.

   This combination of settings causes the DataSet generated by the *SqlDataSource* control to act as a cache that never expires. The cache will be populated when the Web form is first displayed, but will never be refreshed when moving from page to page or refreshing the Web form.

2. Run the Web application. Log in and display the first page of Customer data.

   Notice that the value in the City column of the first row (ALFKI) is Berlin.

3. Leave the Web application running, and open a Command Prompt window. In the Command Prompt window, type the following command:

   ```
   sqlcmd -S YourServer\SQLExpress -E
   ```

   Replace *YourServer* with the name of your computer. This command starts the SQL Server command line tool, allowing you to connect to a database and run SQL statements.

A 1> prompt is displayed by the sqlcmd tool.

4.   At the 1> prompt, type the following statements (the prompt will change each time you press the Enter key):

```
USE Northwind
GO
UPDATE Customers SET City = 'Bonn' WHERE CustomerID = 'ALFKI'
GO
```

The message (1 row affected) is displayed. This command changes the value of the City column for the first customer from Berlin to Bonn.

5.   Leave the Command Prompt window open and return to the Web application running in Internet Explorer. Move to page 2, and then return to page 1. Notice that the City for the first row has not changed—it is still Berlin. Close the Web application and return to Visual Studio 2005.

6.   Select the *CustomerInfoSource* control again. In the Properties window, set the *Cache Duration* property to *10* (ensure *EnableCaching* is still set to *True*).

The DataSet generated by the *SqlDataSource* control now expires after 10 seconds, and will be updated. You will see the changes if you redisplay the page after the expiration period.

7.   Run the Web application again. Log in and display the first page of Customer data. Notice that the value in the City column of the first row (ALFKI) is now Bonn (this is the change you made earlier).

8.   Return to the sqlcmd tool running in the Command Prompt window. At the 1> prompt, type the following statements:

```
UPDATE Customers SET City = 'Munich' WHERE CustomerID = 'ALFKI'
GO
```

The message (1 row affected) is displayed again. This command changes the value of the City column for the first customer from Bonn to Munich.

9.   Wait for more than 10 seconds and then return to the Web application running in Internet Explorer. Move to page 2, and then return to page 1. Notice that the City for the first row has changed to Munich as the DataSet has been refreshed. Close the Web application.

10.   Close the Command Prompt window.

Editing Data

You have seen how to use a *GridView* control to fetch and browse data. The following set of exercises concentrate on deleting and modifying data using a *GridView* control.

Deleting Rows from a *GridView* Control

The *GridView* control allows you to add buttons to the grid to indicate that a command should be performed. You can add your own custom buttons and commands, but Visual Studio 2005 supplies some predefined buttons for deleting and editing data. In the following exercise, you will add a Delete button to the *GridView* control.

Create the Delete button

1. Ensure that CustomerData.aspx is displayed in the Design View window. Click the Smart Tag icon to display the GridView Tasks menu.

2. On the GridView Tasks menu, check the Enable Deleting box.

   A hyperlink labeled Delete is added to the start of each row in the *GridView* control.

3. On the GridView Tasks menu, click Edit Columns.

   The Fields dialog box is displayed. You can use this dialog box to set the properties of the fields (columns) displayed in the *GridView* control.

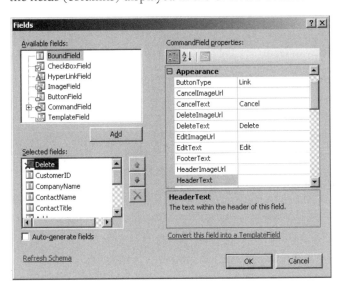

4. In the Selected fields list, select the Delete field. In the CommandField properties list, change the *ButtonType* property to *Button*. Click OK.

   The Delete link in the *GridView* control changes to a button.

5.   Run the application. Log in, and then go to page 3 of the data. Delete the customer with the ID of FISSA. This should be successful. Try to delete customer FAMIA. This will fail with an error because this customer has outstanding orders; the referential integrity rules of the Northwind Traders database forbid you from deleting a customer that has outstanding orders.

> **Tip**   The exception that is displayed is not very user-friendly (although a developer will find it very useful). If a Web form generates an exception, you can arrange for a more friendly message to be displayed by redirecting the user to another page using the *ErrorPage* attribute to the *@Page* directive in the form's source definition:
>
> ```
> <%@ Page … ErrorPage="ErrorPage.aspx" %>
> ```
>
> You can display a more comforting message to the user on this page.

6.   Close Internet Explorer and return to the Visual Studio 2005 programming environment.

Updating Rows in a *GridView* Control

You can also add an Edit button to a *GridView* to allow a user to change the data in a selected row in the *GridView*. The row changes into a set of *TextBox* controls when the user clicks the Edit button. The user can save the changes or discard them. This is achieved using two additional buttons: Update and Cancel. In the following set of exercises, you will add these buttons to the CustomerData form.

Create the Edit, Update, and Cancel buttons

1.   Display the CustomerData.aspx form in Design View. Click the Smart Tag for the *GridView* control to display the GridView Tasks menu, and then click Enable Editing.

An Edit button is added to each row in the *GridView* control.

> **Note**   The Edit button is generated to match the style of the Delete button; if the Delete button was still a hyperlink, then Edit would also appear as a hyperlink.

2.   Run the application. Log in, and then click the Edit button on the first row displayed on the CustomerData form.

The first row changes into a collection of *TextBox* controls, and the Edit and Delete buttons are replaced with an Update button and a Cancel button.

> **Note** The CustomerID column remains as a label. This is because this column is the primary key in the Customers table. You should not be able to modify primary key values in a database; otherwise, you risk breaking the referential integrity between tables.

3. Modify the data in the ContactName and ContactTitle columns, and then click Update.

   The database is updated, the row reverts back to a set of labels, the Edit and Delete buttons reappear, and the new data is displayed in the row.

4. Close Internet Explorer and return to Visual Studio 2005.

■ **If you want to continue to the next chapter**

   Keep Visual Studio 2005 running and turn to Chapter 28.

■ **If you want to exit Visual Studio 2005 for now**

   On the File menu, click Exit. If you see a Save dialog box, click Yes.

Chapter 27 Quick Reference

To	Do this
Create a login Web form.	Create a new Web form. Add a *Login* control for authenticating users.
Configure security for an ASP.NET Web site.	Use the ASP.NET Web Site Administration Tool to add and maintain users, define roles, and create access rules.
Implement Forms-based security.	Edit the Web.config file. Set the *<authentication mode>* attribute to *Forms*, provide the URL of the login form, and specify any authentication parameters required. For example: ```\n<authentication mode="Forms">\n <forms loginUrl="LoginForm.aspx"\n timeout="5"\n cookieless="AutoDetect"\n protection="All" />\n</authentication>\n```
Create a Web form for displaying data from a database.	Add a data source control to the Web form and configure it to connect to the appropriate database. Add a *GridView* control to the Web form and set its *Data SourceID* property to the data source control.
Fetch and display data in manageable chunks in a Web form.	Set the *AllowPaging* property of the *GridView* control to *True*. Set the *PagerSize* property to the number of rows to be displayed on each page. Modify the *PagerSettings* and *PagerStyle* properties to match the style of the Web form.
Use caching with a data source control.	Set the *EnableCaching* property of the data source control to *True*. Set the timeout duration of the cache in seconds using the *CacheDuration* property. Specify whether this timeout value is absolute or relative to the last piece of activity using the *CacheExpirationPolicy* property.
Modify and delete rows in a database using a *GridView* control.	Ensure that the "Generate INSERT, UPDATE, and DELETE statements" option was selected when you generated the data source using the Configure Data Source Wizard, or use the Configure Data Source Wizard to add INSERT, UPDATE, and DELETE statements to an existing data source. Using the GridView Tasks Smart Tag menu, check Enable Updating and Enable Deleting. Use the Edit Columns menu to set the display style of the Update and Delete links in the *GridView* control.

Chapter 28

Creating and Using a Web Service

After completing this chapter, you will be able to:

- Create a Web service that exposes simple Web methods.

- Test a Web service by using Microsoft Internet Explorer.

- Design classes that can be passed as parameters to a Web method, and returned from a Web method.

- Create a reference to a Web service in a client application.

- Invoke a Web method.

The previous chapters showed you how to create Web forms and build interactive Web applications using Microsoft ASP.NET. Although this approach is appropriate for applications where the client is a Web browser, you will increasingly encounter situations where it is not. As mentioned in previous chapters, the Internet is just a big network. It is possible to build distributed systems from elements that are spread across the Internet—databases, security services, financial components, and so on. The aim of this chapter is to show you how to design, build, and test components that can be accessed over the Internet and integrated into larger applications. You'll also learn how to construct an application that uses the methods exposed by a Web service.

What Is a Web Service?

A Web service is a business component that provides some useful facility to clients, or consumers. Just as Distributed Component Object Model (DCOM) is thought of as "COM with a longer wire," a Web service can be thought of as a component with a truly global reach. Web services use a standard, accepted, and well-understood protocol called HTTP to transmit data, and a portable data format that is based on XML. HTTP and XML are both standardized technologies that can be used by other programming environments outside of the .NET Framework. So, you can build Web services by using Visual Studio 2005, and client applications (called consumers) that are running in a totally different environment, such as Java, can use them. The reverse is also true; you can build Web services by using Java, and write consumer applications in C#.

You can use several different languages with Visual Studio 2005 to build Web services. Currently, Microsoft Visual C++, Microsoft Visual C#, Microsoft Visual J#, and Microsoft Visual Basic .NET are supported, and it is likely that there will be others in the future. As far as the consumer is concerned, however, the language used by the Web service, and even how the Web service performs its tasks, is not important. The consumer's view of a Web service is of an interface that exposes a number of well-defined methods. All the consumer needs to do is call these methods by using the standard Internet protocols, passing parameters in an XML format and receiving responses also in an XML format.

One of the driving forces behind the .NET Framework and future releases of Windows is the concept of the "programmable Web." The idea is that, in the future, systems will be constructed by using the data and services provided by multiple Web services. Web services provide the basic elements for systems, the Web provides the means to gain access to them, and developers glue them together in meaningful ways. Web services are a key integration technology for combining disparate systems together; they are the basis for many business-to-business (B2B) and business-to-consumer (B2C) applications.

The Role of SOAP

Simple Object Access Protocol (SOAP) is the protocol used by consumers for sending requests to, and receiving responses from, Web services.

SOAP is a lightweight protocol built on top of HTTP. It is possible to exchange SOAP messages over other protocols but, currently, only the HTTP bindings for SOAP have been defined. It defines an XML grammar for specifying the names of methods that a consumer wants to invoke on a Web service, for defining the parameters and return values, and for describing the types of parameters and return values. When a client calls a Web service, it must specify the method and parameters by using this XML grammar.

SOAP is an industry standard. Its function is to improve cross-platform interoperability. The strength of SOAP is its simplicity and also the fact that it is based on other industry standard technologies: HTTP and XML.

The SOAP specification defines a number of things. The most important are the following:

- The format of a SOAP message
- How data should be encoded
- How to send messages (method calls)
- How to process replies

For example, consider a Web service called ProductService.asmx (in the .NET Framework, URLs for Web services have the suffix .asmx) that exposes methods for accessing the Products table in the Northwind Traders database (you will build this Web service later in this chapter). One such method called *HowMuchWillItCost* allows a client to supply the name of a product and a quantity. The method queries the unit price in the database to calculate the total cost of buying the specified quantity of the product. The SOAP request sent by the client might look like this:

```
POST /NorthwindServices/Service.asmx HTTP/1.1
Host: localhost
Content-Type: application/soap+xml; charset=utf-8
Content-Length: 579

<?xml version="1.0" encoding="utf-8"?>
<soap12:Envelope xmlns:xsi="http://www.w3.org/2001/XMLSchema-instance" xmlns:xsd="http://
www.w3.org/2001/XMLSchema" xmlns:soap12="http://www.w3.org/2003/05/soap-envelope">
  <soap12:Body>
    <HowMuchWillItCost
      xmlns="http://www.contentmaster.com/NorthwindServices">
      <productName>Chai</productName>
      <howMany>39</howMany>
    </HowMuchWillItCost>
  </soap12:Body>
</soap12:Envelope>
```

The request contains two parts: a header comprising everything up to the *<soap12:Body>* tag, and the actual body of the message in the *<soap12:Body>* tag. You can see how the body encodes parameters—in this example, the name of the product is Chai and the quantity is 39.

The Web server will receive this request, identify the Web service and method to run, run the method, obtain the results, and send them back to the client as a SOAP result, like this:

```
HTTP/1.1 200 OK
Content-Type: application/soap+xml; charset=utf-8
Content-Length: 546

<?xml version="1.0" encoding="utf-8"?>
<soap12:Envelope xmlns:xsi="http://www.w3.org/2001/XMLSchema-instance" xmlns:xsd="http://
www.w3.org/2001/XMLSchema" xmlns:soap12="http://www.w3.org/2003/05/soap-envelope">
  <soap12:Body>
    <HowMuchWillItCostResponse
      xmlns="http://www.contentmaster.com/NorthwindServices">
      <HowMuchWillItCostResult>529</HowMuchWillItCostResult>
    </HowMuchWillItCostResponse>
  </soap12:Body>
</soap12:Envelope>
```

The client can then extract the result from the body of this message and process it.

What Is the Web Services Description Language?

The body of a SOAP message is XML. The Web server expects the client to use a particular set of tags for encoding the parameters for the method. How does a client know which schema to use? The answer is that, when asked, a Web service is expected to supply a description of itself. A client can submit a request to a Web service with the query string *wsdl* appended to it:

```
http://localhost/NorthwindServices/Service.asmx?wsdl
```

The Web service will reply with a description like this:

```
<?xml version="1.0" encoding="utf-8"?>
<wsdl:definitions xmlns:soap="http://schemas.xmlsoap.org/wsdl/soap/"
    ...
    targetNamespace="http://www.contentmaster.com/NorthwindServices"
    xmlns:wsdl="http://schemas.xmlsoap.org/wsdl/">
  <wsdl:types>
    <s:schema elementFormDefault="qualified"
     targetNamespace="http://www.contentmaster.com/NorthwindServices">
      <s:element name="HowMuchWillItCost">
        <s:complexType>
          <s:sequence>
            <s:element minOccurs="0" maxOccurs="1"
                       name="productName" type="s:string" />
            <s:element minOccurs="1" maxOccurs="1"
                       name="howMany" type="s:int" />
          </s:sequence>
        </s:complexType>
      </s:element>
      <s:element name="HowMuchWillItCostResponse">
        <s:complexType>
          <s:sequence>
            <s:element minOccurs="1" maxOccurs="1"
                       name="HowMuchWillItCostResult" type="s:decimal" />
          </s:sequence>
        </s:complexType>
      </s:element>
    </s:schema>
  </wsdl:types>
  ...
</wsdl:definitions>
```

This is known as the Web Service Description (a large chunk has been omitted to save space), and the schema used is called Web Services Description Language (WSDL). This description provides enough information to allow a client to construct a SOAP request in a format that the Web server should understand. The description looks complicated but, fortunately, Microsoft Visual Studio 2005 contains tools that can parse the WSDL for a Web service in a mechanical manner, and then use it to create a proxy object that a client can use to convert method calls into SOAP requests. You will do this later in this chapter. For now, you can concentrate on building a Web service.

Web Services Enhancements

Not long after Web services became a mainstream technology for integrating distributed services together, it became apparent that there were issues that SOAP and HTTP alone could not address. These issues include:

- **Security**. How do you ensure that SOAP messages that flow between a Web service and a consumer have not been intercepted and changed on their way across the Internet? How can you be sure that a SOAP message has actually been sent by the consumer or Web service that claims to have sent it, and not some "spoof" site that is trying to fraudulently obtain information? How can you restrict access to a Web service to specific users? These are matters of message integrity, confidentiality, and authentication, and are fundamental concerns if you are building distributed applications that make use of the Internet.

  In the early 1990s, a number of vendors supplying tools for building distributed systems formed an organization that later became known as the Organization for the Advancement of Structured Information Standards, or OASIS. As the short-comings of the early Web services infrastructure became apparent, members of OASIS pondered these problems and produced what became known as the WS-Security specification. The WS-Security specification describes how to secure the messages sent by Web services. Vendors that subscribe to WS-Security provide their own implementations that meet this specification, typically by using various encryption mechanisms and certificates.

- **Policy**. Although the WS-Security specification provides enhanced security, developers still need to write code to implement it. Web services created by different developers can often vary in how stringent the security mechanism they have elected to implement is. For example, a Web service might use only a relatively weak form of encryption which can easily be broken. A consumer sending highly confidential information to this Web service would probably insist on a higher level of security. This is one example of policy. Other examples include the quality of service and reliability of the Web service. A Web service could implement varying degrees of security, quality of service, and reliability, and charge the client application accordingly. The client application and the Web service can negotiate which level of service to use based on the requirements and cost. However, this negotiation requires that the client and the Web service have a common understanding of the policies available. The WS-Policy specification provides a general purpose model and corresponding syntax to describe and communicate the policies of a Web service.

- **Routing and addressing**. It is useful for a Web server to be able to re-route a Web service request to one of a number of servers. For example, many scalable systems make use of load-balancing; requests sent to a server are actually redirected by that server to other computers to spread the load across those computers. The server can use any number of algorithms to try and balance the load. The important point is that this redirection is transparent to the client making the Web service request. Redirecting Web service requests is also useful if an administrator needs to shut down a computer to perform maintenance. Requests that would otherwise have been sent to this computer can be re-routed to one of its peers. The WS-Addressing specification describes a framework for routing Web service requests.

What does all this mean if you are developing Web services using Visual Studio 2005? Well, Microsoft provides its own implementation of the WS-Security, WS-Policy, and WS-Addressing specifications in its Web services Enhancements package (WSE). You can download this package free of charge from the Microsoft Web site, at *http://msdn.microsoft.com/webservices/building/wse/default.aspx*. When you install it, it integrates itself into the Visual Studio environment and adds additional project templates and assemblies that you can use. For Visual Studio 2005, you need to download WSE 3.0.

Note None of the exercises in this chapter require you to install WSE 3.0.

Building the ProductService Web Service

In this chapter, you will create the ProductService Web service. This Web service will expose two Web methods. The first method will allow the user to calculate the cost of buying a specified quantity of a particular product in the Northwind Traders database, and the second method will take the name of a product and return all the details for that product.

Creating the ProductService Web Service

In the first exercise, you will create the ProductService Web service and implement the *HowMuchWillItCost* Web method. You will then test the Web method to ensure that it works as expected.

Create the Web service

1. In the Microsoft Visual Studio 2005 programming environment, create a new Web site using the ASP.NET Web Service template. Make sure you specify File System as the Location, and Visual C# for the Language. Create the Web site in the \Microsoft Press\Visual CSharp Step by Step\Chapter 28\NorthwindServices folder in your My Documents folder.

Important Ensure you select the ASP.NET Web Service template and not the ASP.NET Web Site template.

Visual Studio 2005 generates a Web site containing folders called App_Code and App_Data, and a file called Service.asmx. The .asmx file contains the Web service definition. The code for the Web service is defined in the *Service* class, stored in the file Service.cs in the App_Code folder, and displayed in the Code and Text Editor window.

2. In the Solution Explorer, click the NorthwindServices project. In the Properties window, set the *Use dynamic ports* property to *False*, and set the *Port number* property to *4500*.

   By default, the Development Web server provided with Visual Studio 2005 picks a port at random to reduce the chances of clashing with any other ports used by other network services running on your computer. This feature is useful if you are building and testing ASP.NET Web sites in a development prior to copying them to a production server such as IIS. However, when building a Web service it is more useful to use a fixed port number as client applications need to be able to connect to it.

3. In the Service.cs file in the Code and Text Editor window, examine the *Service* class; it is descended from *System.Web.Services.WebService*. Scroll to the bottom of the class. A sample Web service method called *HelloWorld* is provided by the Visual Studio 2005 template. This method simply returns the string, "Hello World." Notice that all methods that a client can call must be tagged with the *[WebMethod]* attribute. Comment out the *HelloWorld* method and the *[WebMethod]* attribute; you will not need this method in this exercise.

4. Above the *Service* class you can see two more attributes: *[WebService]* and *[WebServiceBinding]*. The *[WebServiceBinding]* attribute identifies the level of the Web services interoperability specification that the Web service conforms to. You can ignore this attribute in this chapter and leave it set to its default value. The *[WebService]* attribute indicates the namespace used to identify the Web service. Change the value of this attribute, as shown below:

```
[WebService(Namespace="http://www.contentmaster.com/NorthwindServices")]
[WebServiceBinding(ConformsTo = WsiProfiles.BasicProfile1_1)]
public class Service : System.Web.Services.WebService
{
    ...
}
```

5. Right-click the NorthwindServices project in the Solution Explorer, and then click Add New Item. In the Add New Item dialog box, click the Web Configuration File template. Make sure the name of the file is set to Web.config and then click Add.

   This action adds a Web configuration file to your project, containing default settings. The Web.config file appears in the Code and Text Editor window.

6. Modify the *<connectionStrings/>* element in the Web.config file. Add the following *<add>* sub element that defines a new connection string that you will use for connecting to the

Northwind database. Replace *YourServer* with the name of your computer. Make sure you add a *</connectionStrings>* element:

```
<connectionStrings>
    <add name="NorthwindConnectionString"
        connectionString="Data Source=YourServer\SQLExpress; Initial Catalog=Northwind;
Integrated Security=True"
            providerName="System.Data.SqlClient"/>
</connectionStrings>
```

7. Display the Service.cs file in the Code and Text Editor window. Add the following method to the *Service* class, underneath the commented-out *HelloWorld* method:

```
[WebMethod]
public decimal HowMuchWillItCost(string productName, int howMany)
{
}
```

This method expects the client to pass in the name of a product found in the Products table in the Northwind Traders database, and a quantity of that product. The method will use the information in the database to calculate the cost of supplying this quantity of the product and pass this cost back as the return value of the method.

8. Add the following *using* statements to the top of the file:

```
using System.Configuration;
using System.Data.SqlClient;
```

This *System.Configuration* namespace contains classes that you can use for reading configuration settings from the Web.config file. The *System.Data.SqlClient* namespace contains the Microsoft ADO.NET classes for accessing Microsoft SQL Server.

9. In the *HowMuchWillItCost* Web method, type the following statements:

```
SqlConnection sqlConn = null;



try
{
    ConnectionStringSettings cs =
        ConfigurationManager.ConnectionStrings["NorthwindConnectionString"];
    string connString = cs.ConnectionString;
    sqlConn = new SqlConnection(connString);
    SqlCommand sqlCmd = new SqlCommand();
    sqlCmd.CommandText = "SELECT UnitPrice FROM Products " +
        "WHERE ProductName = '" + productName + "'";
    sqlCmd.Connection = sqlConn;
    sqlConn.Open();
    decimal price = (decimal)sqlCmd.ExecuteScalar();
    return price * howMany;
}
catch(Exception e)
```

```
{
    // Handle the exception
}
finally
{
    if (sqlConn != null)
        sqlConn.Close();
}
```

This code the connection string called *NorthwindConnectionString* from the Web.config file by using the static *ConnectionStrings* property of the *ConfigurationManager* class. This property returns the corresponding entry from the Web.config file. The entry contains information such as the name of the connection string, the provider, and the connection string itself. You can extract the connection string from this entry by using the *ConnectionString* property.

The code then connects to the Northwind Traders database and runs a SQL *SELECT* statement to retrieve the UnitPrice column for the selected product in the Products table. The *ExecuteScalar* method is the most efficient way of running a *SELECT* statement that returns a single value. The UnitPrice column is stored in the *price* variable, which is then multiplied by the *howMany* parameter that is passed in to calculate the cost.

> **Note**   Refer back to the section "Using ADO.NET Programmatically" in Chapter 23, "Using a Database," if you need to refresh your memory on using ADO.NET to access a SQL Server database.

The Web service uses a *try...catch* block to trap any runtime errors, although it does not validate the parameters passed in (for example, the client might supply a negative value for the *howMany* parameter). You can add the necessary code to validate the parameters yourself.

It is important to make sure you close the connection to the database, even after an exception. That is the purpose of the *finally* block.

If an exception occurs, you should capture the details somewhere. It is usually not advisable to send the details of the exception back to the user as it might not mean much to them, and there can also be security concerns if too much information about the internal workings of your Web service is reported back to the user (details such as the names and addresses of databases are just the sort of things that hackers trying to break into your system will find useful). However, the administrator for the Web site should be very interested in this information. The ideal place to capture details of Web service exceptions is the Windows Event Log.

10.   Add the following *using* statement to the top of the file:

```
using System.Diagnostics;
```

This is the namespace that contains the classes for interacting with the event logs.

11. Add the following method to the *Service* class. Notice that this is a local, private method and is not tagged with the *[WebMethod]* attribute:

```
private void handleWebException(Exception e)
{
    EventLog log = new EventLog("Application");
    log.Source = "NorthwindServices";
    log.WriteEntry(e.Message, EventLogEntryType.Error);
}
```

These statements add an entry to the Windows Application event log containing the details of the exception passed in as the parameter, flagging it as an error (you can also store warnings and informational messages in the event log).

However, writing to any Windows event log is a privileged operation, and requires that the Administrator for your computer has granted you the appropriate access rights. You will see how to grant these rights in the next exercise.

12. In the *catch* block for the *HowMuchWillItCost* Web method, remove the comment and type the following statements. The first statement calls the *handleWebException* method, passing it the exception that occurred as its parameter. The *throw* statement throws an empty exception, which simply causes an "HTTP 500 – Internal server error" page to be displayed in the user's browser:

```
catch(Exception e)
{
    handleWebException(e);
    throw new Exception();
}
```

13. On the Build menu, click Build Web Site to compile the Web service.

The Structure of a Web Service

Web services in the .NET Framework are similar to ASP.NET Web applications inasmuch as they consist of two parts: the .asmx file which defines the Web service, and a C# code file with the suffix .cs. The .cs file actually contains the C# code for the methods that you add to the Web service, and is the file displayed in the Code and Text Editor window by default. This file is located in the App_Code folder of the Web site. You can see this file in the Solution Explorer if you expand the App_Code folder.

You can view the .asmx file by double-clicking the file in the Solution Explorer. The .asmx for the NorthwindServices Web service looks like this:

```
<%@ WebService Language="C#" CodeBehind="~/App_Code/Service.cs" Class="Service" %>
```

It is highly unlikely that you will need to modify this file.

Web Service Namespaces

A Web service should use a unique namespace to identify itself so that client applications can distinguish it from other services on the Web. By default, Web services created with Visual Studio 2005 use http://tempuri.org. This is fine for Web services that are under development, but you should create your own namespace when you publish the Web service. A common convention is to use your company's URL as part of the namespace, together with some other form of identifier. You should note that the namespace does not have to be an existing URL—its purpose is only to uniquely identify the Web service.

Grant Access Rights to use the Windows Event Log

> **Important**   You will require the password for the Administrator user on your computer to perform the tasks in this exercise.

1. On the Windows Start menu, point to All Programs, point to Accessories, and then right-click Command Prompt. Click Run As. In the Run As dialog box, click "The following user." Type **Administrator** for the User name, type the password, and then click OK.

    A Command Prompt window opens. This window is running as Administrator, and you can do anything an administrator can do—be careful.

2. In the Command Prompt window, type **regedit**.

    The Registry Editor starts. This tool allows you to configure your computer. Be very careful as you can easily cause serious problems that require you to reinstall your operating system.

3. In the tree view in the left-hand pane, expand My Computer\HKEY_LOCAL_MACHINE\ SYSTEMCurrentControlSet\Services\Eventlog.

4. Right-click the Application node, point to New, and then click Key. A new key called New Key #1 appears in the left-hand pane. Overwrite this name with the text **NorthwindServices**.

> **Tip**   If you mistype the name, you can change it by right-clicking the key, and then clicking Rename. Do not rename any other keys.

5. Close the Registry Editor, and then close the Command Prompt window.

Test the Web method

1. Return to Visual Studio 2005. In the Solution Explorer, right-click Service.asmx and then click View in Browser.

    The ASP.NET Development Web Server starts and displays a message indicating that the Web service is available at the address http://localhost:4500/NorthwindServices .

    Internet Explorer starts and moves to the URL http://localhost:4500/NorthwindServices/Service.asmx, displaying the Service test page.

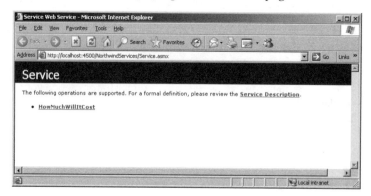

    The test page allows you to view the WSDL description by clicking the Service Description hyperlink or to test individual Web methods (in this example, there is only one: *HowMuchWillItCost*).

2. Click the Service Description hyperlink.

    The URL changes to http://localhost:4500/NorthwindServices/Service.asmx?WSDL, and Internet Explorer displays the WSDL description of your Web service.

3. Click the Back button in the Internet Explorer Toolbar to return to the test page. Click the *HowMuchWillItCost* hyperlink.

    Internet Explorer generates another page that allows you to specify values for the parameters and test the *HowMuchWillItCost* method. The page also displays sample SOAP requests and responses.

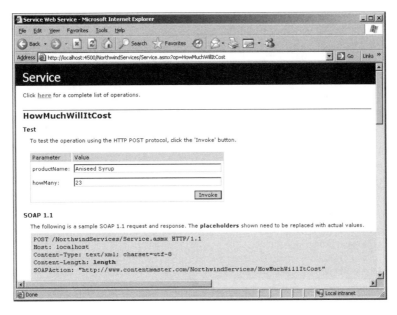

4. In the *productName* text box, type **Aniseed Syrup**, and then type **23** in the *howMany* text box. Click Invoke.

    The Web method runs, and a second Internet Explorer window opens and displays the response in SOAP format.

5. Close both Internet Explorer windows and return to the Visual Studio 2005 programming environment.

Handling Complex Data

SOAP enables you to pass complex data structures between a client and a Web service as input parameters, output parameters, or return values. To do this, the data structures themselves are converted into a format that can be tranmitted over the network and reassembled at the other end. This process is known as *serialization*. For example, in the following exercise, you will build a class that holds information about a product in the Northwind Traders database. The class will contain many properties, including *ProductID*, *ProductName*, *SupplierID*, and *CategoryID*. You will then create a Web method that returns an instance of this class. The

SOAP serialization process will convert the class into XML, send the serialized version across the network using SOAP, and reconstruct the class from the XML at the other end (a very simple marshalling technique). The following structure shows an example of how the class will be serialized for transmission:

```xml
<?xml version="1.0" encoding="utf-8" ?>
<Product xmlns:xsi="http://www.w3.org/2001/XMLSchema-instance"
  xmlns:xsd="http://www.w3.org/2001/XMLSchema"
  xmlns="http://www.contentmaster.com/NorthwindServices">
  <ProductID>1</ProductID>
  <ProductName>Chai</ProductName>
  <SupplierID>1</SupplierID>
  <CategoryID>1</CategoryID>
  <QuantityPerUnit>10 boxes x 20 bags</QuantityPerUnit>
  <UnitPrice>18.0000</UnitPrice>
  <UnitsInStock>39</UnitsInStock>
  <UnitsOnOrder>0</UnitsOnOrder>
  <ReorderLevel>10</ReorderLevel>
  <Discontinued>false</Discontinued>
</Product>
```

The serialization process is automatic and largely transparent as long as you follow a few simple rules when defining the class. In particular, serialization can only be used when transmitting classes that contain public fields and properties. If an object contains private members that do not have corresponding *get* and *set* property accessors, it will not transfer correctly; the private data will not be initialized at the receiving end. Also note that all properties must have both *get* and *set* accessors. This is because the XML serialization process must be able to write this data back to the object after it has been transferred. Additionally, the class must have a default (with no parameters) constructor.

It is common to design classes used for SOAP purely as containers for transmitting data. You can then define additional functional classes that act as facades providing the business logic for these data structures. Users and applications would gain access to the data by using these business facades.

If you want, you can customize the serialization mechanism using the various SOAP attribute classes of the *System.Xml.Serialization* namespace or define your own XML serialization mechanism by implementing the *ISerializable* interface of the *System.Runtime.Serialization* namespace.

Define the *Product* class

1. In the Solution Explorer, right-click the App_Code folder, and then click Add New Item. In the Add New Item dialog box, click the Class template, and then type **Product.cs** for the name of the new class. Click Add to create the class.

> **Note**   It is conventional to place source code files for an ASP.NET Web site in the
> App_Code folder.

2. In the Solution Explorer, expand the App_Code folder if it is not already expanded.
    Double-click the file Product.cs to display it in the Code and Text Editor window.

3. Add the following private variables to the *Product* class, above the constructor. There is
    one variable for each of the columns in the Products table in the database:

    ```
    private int productID;
    private string productName;
    private int supplierID;
    private int categoryID;
    private string quantityPerUnit;
    private decimal unitPrice;
    private short unitsInStock;
    private short unitsOnOrder;
    private short reorderLevel;
    private bool discontinued;
    ```

4. Create a read/write property called *ProductID*. The property provides access to the pri-
    vate *productID* variable:

    ```
    public int ProductID
    {
        get { return this.productID; }
        set { this.productID = value; }
    }
    ```

5. Add properties to provide read/write access to the remaining variables. You can achieve
    this task in at least two different ways: you can manually write each *get* and *set* accessor,
    or you can get Visual Studio 2005 to generate them for you.

    To use Visual Studio 2005 to generate a property for the *productName* variable, double
    click the *productName* variable in the code to highlight it. On the Refactor menu, click
    Encapsulate Field. In the Encapsulate Field dialog box, ensure the Property name is set
    to ProductName, clear the "Preview reference changes" check box, and then click OK, as
    shown in the following graphic:

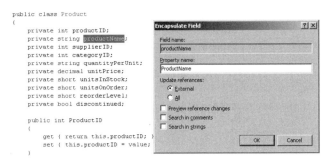

The following property is added to the *Product* class:

```
public int ProductName
{
    get { return productName; }
    set { productName = value; }
}
```

Repeat this process for the remaining fields.

Properties and Field Names: A Warning

Although it is a commonly accepted practice to give properties and private fields the same name that differ only in the case of the initial letter, you should be aware of one drawback. Examine this code:

```
public int CategoryID
{
    get { return this.CategoryID; }
    set { this.CategoryID = value; }
}
```

This code will compile perfectly well, but it results in the program hanging whenever the *CategoryID* property is accessed. This is because the *get* and *set* accessors reference the property (upper-case C) rather than the private field (lower-case c), which causes an endless recursive loop. This sort of bug is very difficult to spot!

Create the *GetProductInfo* Web method

1. Return to the Service.cs file in the Code and Text Editor window. Add a second Web method called *GetProductInfo* that takes a product name (a string) as its parameter and returns a *Product* object:

```
[WebMethod]
public Product GetProductInfo(string productName)
{
}
```

2. Add the following statements to the *GetProductInfo* method (replace *YourServer* when calling the *SqlConnection* constructor with the name of your SQL Server computer):

```
Product product = new Product();
SqlConnection sqlConn = null;
try
{
    ConnectionStringSettings cs =
        ConfigurationManager.ConnectionStrings["NorthwindConnectionString"];
    string connString = cs.ConnectionString;
    sqlConn = new SqlConnection(connString);
    SqlCommand sqlCmd = new SqlCommand();
```

```
       sqlCmd.CommandText = "SELECT * FROM Products " +
           "WHERE ProductName = '" + productName + "'";
       sqlCmd.Connection = sqlConn;
       sqlConn.Open();
       SqlDataReader productData = sqlCmd.ExecuteReader();
       if (productData.Read())
       {
           product.ProductID = productData.GetInt32(0);
           product.ProductName = productData.GetString(1);
           product.SupplierID = productData.GetInt32(2);
           product.CategoryID = productData.GetInt32(3);
           product.QuantityPerUnit = productData.GetString(4);
           product.UnitPrice = productData.GetDecimal(5);
           product.UnitsInStock = productData.GetInt16(6);
           product.UnitsOnOrder = productData.GetInt16(7);
           product.ReorderLevel = productData.GetInt16(8);
           product.Discontinued = productData.GetBoolean(9);

       }
       else
       {
           throw new ArgumentException("No such product " + productName);
       }

       productData.Close();
       return product;
   }

   catch(ArgumentException e)
   {
       handleWebException(e);
       throw e;
   }

   catch(Exception e)
   {
       handleWebException(e);
       throw new Exception();
   }

   finally
   {
       if (sqlConn != null)
           sqlConn.Close();
   }
```

These statements use ADO.NET to connect to the Northwind Traders database and retrieve the details for the specified product from the database.

This method uses the same approach as the *HowMuchWillItCost* method to handle most exceptions. However, if no product with the specified product name exists, this information is useful to the client and probably does not compromise security. In this situation, the method throws an *ArgumentException*. To prevent this exception being filtered out by the generic exception handler, the *ArgumentException* handler re-throws the same exception, passing its details back to the client.

3. Build the Web Site. Run the Web service by right-clicking Service.asmx in the Solution Explorer and clicking View in Browser. When Internet Explorer displays the test page, click the *GetProductInfo* hyperlink.

The *GetProductInfo* test page appears, enabling you to test the *GetProductInfo* method.

4. In the *productName* text box, type **Aniseed Syrup** and then click Invoke.

The Web method runs, fetches the details for Aniseed Syrup, and returns a *Product* object. The *Product* object is serialized as XML and displayed in Internet Explorer.

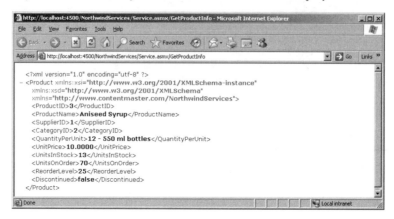

5. Close the Internet Explorer windows.

Web Services, Clients, and Proxies

You have seen that a Web service uses SOAP to provide a mechanism for receiving requests and sending back results. SOAP uses XML to format the data being transmitted, which rides on top of the HTTP protocol used by Web servers and browsers. This is what makes Web services so powerful—HTTP and XML are well understood (in theory anyway) and are the subjects of several standards committees. SOAP itself is going through the standardization process and has been adopted by most companies that want to make their services available over the Web. A client that "talks" SOAP can communicate with a Web service. The client and the Web service can be implemented in totally different languages, running on otherwise incompatible systems. For example, a Microsoft Visual Basic client running on a handheld device can communicate with a Web service being hosted on an IBM 390 mainframe running UNIX.

So how does a client "talk" SOAP? There are two ways: the difficult way and the easy way.

Talking SOAP: The Difficult Way

In the difficult way, the client application must perform a number of steps:

1. Determine the URL of the Web service running the Web method.

2. Perform a Web Services Description Language (WSDL) inquiry using the URL to obtain a description of the Web methods available, the parameters used, and the values returned. This is an XML document. (You saw an example in the previous chapter.)

3. Convert each Web method call into the appropriate URL and serialize each parameter into the format described by the WSDL document.

4. Submit the request, along with the serialized data, to the URL using HTTP.

5. Wait for the Web service to reply.

6. Using the formats specified by the WSDL document, de-serialize the data returned by the Web service into meaningful values that your application can then process.

This is a lot of work to just invoke a method, and it is potentially error-prone.

Talking SOAP: The Easy Way

The bad news is that the easy way to use SOAP is not much different from the difficult way. The good news is that the process can be automated because it is largely mechanical. Many vendors supply tools that can generate proxy classes based on a WSDL description. The proxy hides the complexity of using SOAP and exposes a simple programmatic interface based on the methods published by the Web service. The client application calls Web methods by invoking methods with the same name in the proxy. The proxy converts these local method calls into SOAP requests and sends them to the Web service. The proxy waits for the reply, de-serializes the data, and then passes it back to the client just like the return from any simple method call.

Consuming the ProductService Web Service

You have created a Web service call that exposes two Web methods: *GetProductInfo* to return the details of a specified product, and *HowMuchWillItCost* to determine the cost of buying *n* items of product *x* from Northwind Traders. In the following exercises, you will use this Web service and create an application that consumes these methods. You'll start with the *Get-ProductInfo* method.

Create a Web service client application

1. Start another instance of Visual Studio 2005. This is important. The ASP.NET Development server stops if you close the NorthwindServices Web service project, meaning that you won't be able to access it from the client (an alternative approach you can use is to create the client application as a project in the same solution as the Web service). When you host a Web service in a production environment by using IIS, this problem does not arise because IIS runs independently from Visual Studio 2005.

2. In the second instance of Microsoft Visual Studio 2005, create a new project using the Windows Application template. Name the project **ProductInfo** and save it in the \Microsoft Press\Visual CSharp Step By Step\Chapter 28 folder in your My Documents folder.

3. Change the filename of the Form1.cs file to **ProductForm.cs**.

4. Change the size of the form to 392, 400. Set its *Text* property to *Product Details*.

5. Add 10 labels to the form, evenly spaced down the left side. From top to bottom, set the *Text* property of each label using the following values: Product Name, Product ID, Supplier ID, Category ID, Quantity Per Unit, Unit Price, Units In Stock, Units On Order, Reorder Level, and Discontinued.

6. Add nine text boxes to the form adjacent to the first nine labels. Clear the *Text* property for each text box. Set the *Name* property of each text box from top to bottom using the following values: *productName*, *productID*, *supplierID*, *categoryID*, *quantityPerUnit*, *unitPrice*, *unitsInStock*, *unitsOnOrder*, and *reorderLevel*.

7. Add a check box to the form next to the *Discontinued* label and below the *reorderLevel* text box. Set its *Name* property to *discontinued*, and then clear its *Text* property.

8. Add a button to the form, to the right of the *productName* text box. Change the name of the button to *getProduct*, and then set its *Text* property to *Get Product*.

    The completed form should look like the following graphic:

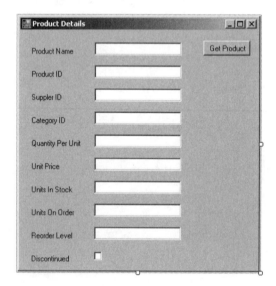

Add a reference to the Web service

1. On the Project menu, click Add Web Reference.

    The Add Web Reference dialog box opens.

This dialog box allows you to browse for Web services and examine the WSDL descriptions.

2. Type the URL of the NorthwindServices Web service in the Address text box at the top of the dialog box: **http://localhost:4500/NorthwindServices/Service.asmx**. Click Go.

> **Tip**   If the Web service is hosted by IIS on your computer, you can click the "Web services on the local machine" hyperlink in the left pane of the dialog box rather than typing the address in manually. In our case, the Web service is hosted by the ASP.NET Development server and won't appear if you click this hyperlink.

The Web service test page displaying the *GetProductInfo* and *HowMuchWillItCost* methods appears. Change the value in the Web reference name text box to *NorthwindServices*, as shown in the following graphic:

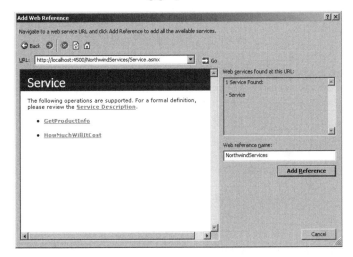

3. Click Add Reference. Look at the Solution Explorer. A new folder called Web References is added that contains an item called NorthwindServices. Click the NorthwindServices Web reference and examine its properties in the Properties window. You will notice the Web Reference URL property, which contains the URL of the Web service.

Execute a Web method

1. Display ProductForm.cs in the Code and Text Editor window. Add the following *using* statement to the list at the top of the file:

```
using ProductInfo.NorthwindServices;
```

When you add a Web reference to a project, the proxy generated by the Web service is placed in a namespace that is named after the Web service reference—in this case, *NorthwindServices*.

2. Create an event method for the *Click* event of the *getProduct* button called
    getProduct_Click. In the *getProduct_Click* method, create the following variable:

    ```
    Service northwindService = new Service();
    ```

    Service is the proxy class that provides access to the Web service (the proxy will always
    be named after the Web service). It resides in the *NorthwindServices* namespace. To use
    the Web service, you must create an instance of the proxy, which is what this code does.

3. Add code to execute the *GetProductInfo* Web method to the *getProduct_Click* method.
    You are probably aware of how unpredictable networks are, and this applies doubly to
    the Internet. Create a *try/catch* block below the statement that creates the *northwind
    Service* variable. Remember that the Web service will also throw an exception if you
    try to access a non-existent product.

    ```
    try
    {
        // Code goes here in the next steps
    }
    catch (Exception ex)
    {
        MessageBox.Show("Error fetching product details: " +
            ex.Message, "Error", MessageBoxButtons.OK,
            MessageBoxIcon.Error);
    }
    ```

    Add the following statement to the *try* block:

    ```
    Product prod = northwindService.GetProductInfo(productName.Text);
    ```

    The proxy object (*northwindService*) makes the call to the *GetProductInfo* Web method
    look like an ordinary local method call. The information returned by the *GetProductInfo*
    method is assembled into an instance of the *Product* class. The WSDL description of the
    Web service provides enough information to define the structure of this class, and you
    can use it in your client application as shown here.

4. Add the following statements, which extract the details from the *Product* object and
    display them on the form, to the *try* block:

    ```
    productID.Text = prod.ProductID.ToString();
    supplierID.Text = prod.SupplierID.ToString();
    categoryID.Text = prod.CategoryID.ToString();
    quantityPerUnit.Text = prod.QuantityPerUnit;
    unitPrice.Text = prod.UnitPrice.ToString();
    unitsInStock.Text = prod.UnitsInStock.ToString();
    unitsOnOrder.Text = prod.UnitsOnOrder.ToString();
    reorderLevel.Text = prod.ReorderLevel.ToString();
    discontinued.Checked = prod.Discontinued;
    ```

Test the application

1. Build and run the project. When the Product Details form appears, type **Aniseed Syrup** in the Product Name text box and click Get Product.

   After a short delay while the client instantiates the proxy, the proxy marshals the parameter and sends the request to the Web service. The Web service reads the database, creates a *Product* object, marshals it as XML, and then sends it back to the proxy. The proxy unmarshals the XML data and creates a copy of the *Product* object, and then passes this copy to your code in the *getButtonClick* method. The details for Aniseed Syrup then appear in the form as shown by the following graphic:

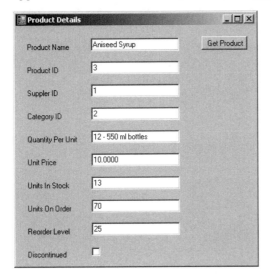

2. Type **Tofu** in the Product Name text box, and then click Get Product.

   You will probably find that the details are displayed more quickly this time.

3. Type **Sticky Toffee** in the Product Name text box, and then click Get once more.

   Because this product does not exist, the Web service will throw an exception that is passed back to your application. If you look closely, you will see the "No such product Sticky Toffee" message.

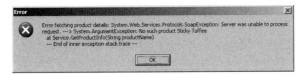

4. Click OK to acknowledge the error. Close the Product Details form and return to the Visual Studio 2005 programming environment.

Web Services, Anonymous Access, and Authentication

When you create a Web service client using Visual Studio 2005, the client application executes Web services using anonymous access by default. This might be fine when building and testing Web services in a development environment using the ASP.NET Development Web server, but in a production environment using IIS you might want to restrict access to authenticated clients only.

You can configure the authentication mechanism for a Web service hosted by IIS using the Internet Information Services console, available from the Administrative Tools folder in the Control Panel. If you expand the Default Web Site node, select your Web service, and click Properties from the Action menu, you can change the Directory Security settings by clicking the Edit button under Anonymous Access And Authentication Control. Make sure the Anonymous Access box is checked to permit unauthenticated access—the accepted convention is to use the local IUSR account for such access; the Web service will execute using this identity, which must be granted access to any resources used by the Web service, such as a SQL Server database.

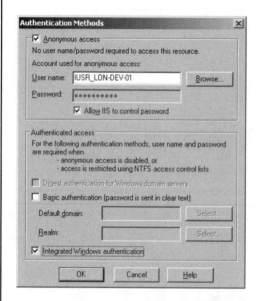

The alternative to using anonymous access is using authenticated access. If you clear the Anonymous access check box and select one or more of the authenticated mechanisms (Digest, Basic, Integrated Windows), you can restrict access to clients that supply a valid user name and password. For more information on the differences between the authenticated access modes, consult the Internet Information Services documentation (click Help in the Authentication Methods dialog box).

You can supply the information needed to authenticate the client application by setting the *Credentials* property of the Web service proxy at run time. This property is a *NetworkCredential* object (the *NetworkCredential* class is located in the *System.Net* namespace). The following code creates a *NetworkCredential* object for the user "John," with the password "JohnsPassword" and sets the *Credentials* property of the *productService* Web service proxy:

```
using System.Net;
…
private void getProduct_Click(...)
{
    Service northwindService = new Service();
    try
    {
        NetworkCredential credentials =
            new NetworkCredential("John", "JohnsPassword");
        productService.Credentials = credentials;
        Product prod = productService.GetProductInfo(...);
        …
    }
    …
}
```

The user name and password must be valid for the Windows domain (a different Windows domain can be specified as an optional third parameter to the *NetworkCredential* constructor), and the specified account must be granted access to the various resources used by the Web service if it is to function correctly.

Chapter 28 Quick Reference

To	Do this
Create a Web service.	Use the ASP.NET Web Service template. Use the *WebService* attribute to specify the namespace used to uniquely identify the Web service to the outside world. Tag each method you want to expose with the *WebMethod* attribute.
Test a Web service.	Right-click the .asmx file in the Solution Explorer and click View in Browser. Internet Explorer runs, moves to the Web service URL, and displays the test page. Click the link corresponding to the Web method you wish to run. On the Web method test page, enter values for the parameters and click Invoke. The Web method will run and generate a SOAP response that will be displayed in Internet Explorer.
Pass complex data as Web method parameters and return values.	Define a class to hold the data. Ensure that each item of data is accessible either as a public field or through a public property that provides *get* and *set* access. Ensure that the class has a default constructor (which might be empty).
Add a Web reference to an application and create a proxy class.	On the Project menu, click Add Web Reference. Either type the URL of the Web service in the Address text box at the top of the dialog box, or click the "Web References on local Web server" link and locate the Web service. Click Add Reference to create the Web service proxy.
Invoke a Web method synchronously.	Create an instance of the proxy class; it will reside in a namespace named after the Web server hosting the Web service unless you changed it when adding the Web reference. Run the Web method using the proxy class.

Index

NOTE: Page numbers in *italics* refer to illustrations

Symbols and Numbers

-= (compound assignment) operator, 76
− operator, 38
!= (inequality operator), 60, 336–337
; (semicolon), for terminating statements, 23
& (ampersand) character, for menu item access, 371
& (ampersand) operator
  for bit manipulation, 260
  for variable address, 147
! (NOT) operator, 60
&& (AND) operator, 61
  short circuiting, 62
% (percent sign), as remainder operator, 33
%= (compound assignment) operator, 76
* (asterisk), to identify variable as pointer, 147, 148
*= (compound assignment) operator, 76
. (dot) operator, 228
/= (compound assignment) operator, 76
/* (slash with asterisk), for multi-line comments, 9
// (slashes), for comments, 9
@Page attribute, 480
[ ] (square brackets), 37
  for arrays, 169
\ (back-slash), as escape character, 73
^ (XOR; exclusive or) operator, 261
{ } (braces), 37
  for array values, 171
  for scope definition, 47–48
  for statement blocks, 64–65
| (bitwise OR) operator, 260
|| (OR) operator, 61
  short circuiting, 62
~ (tilde)
  for destructor, 228
  as unary operator, 260
+ (plus sign), arithmetic addition vs. string concatenation, 164–165

+= (compound assignment) operator, 76
  for delegate, 276
  for event, 283
++ operator, 37–39
  in if statement, 63
< (less than) operator, 60
<< bit manipulation operator, 260
<= (less than or equal to) operator, 60
= (equal sign) as assignment operator, 26
  vs. == (equality) operator, 60
== (equality operator), 60, 336–337
> (greater than) operator, 60
>= (greater than or equal to) operator, 60
0 (zero), as array size, 171

A

abstract classes, 213–216
abstract keyword, 215
  and operators, 331
  valid and invalid combinations, 224
AcceptChanges method, 452
access keys (shortcut keys), for menu item access, 371, 374
accessibility, 116–117
  protected keyword, 208–209
accessing individual array elements, 172
Active Server Pages, 459–460
ActiveControl property, 354
ActiveX Data Objects (ADO), 409
adapter method, 281
Add Connection dialog box, 413, *413*
Add New Item dialog box, 432, *432*
  Class Diagram template, 223
  for Web site, 480
Add Reference dialog box, Projects tab, 307–308
Add Web Reference dialog box, 532–533, *533*
addClick method, 365–366
AddExtension property, for *SaveFileDialog* control, 385
additive operators, precedence order, 36
addValues method, 44
  calling, 45, 46–47

ADO.NET databases, 409–422. *See also DataSets*
  DataSets, *DataTables* and *TableAdapters*, 417–418
    displaying data, 418–422
  Northwind Traders database, *410*, 410
    accessing, 411–415
    creating, 410–411
  programmatic use, 422–429
    closing connections, 428
    connecting to database, 423–424
    disconnecting from database, 427–428
    fetching and displaying data, 425–426
    null values in database, 428–429
    querying table, 424–425
    SQL Server authentication, 424
  quick reference, 430
Advanced Build Settings dialog box, 101
Advanced Options dialog box, 435, *435*
  optimistic concurrency, 442, 443
Aggregates project, vi
alignment handles for controls, 17
AllowPaging property, of *GridView* control, 504–505
Alt key, for menu item access, 371
ampersand (&) character, for menu item access, 371
ampersand (&) operator
  for bit manipulation, 260
  for variable address, 147
AND (&&) operator, 61
  short circuiting, 62
anonymous methods, 280–282
anonymous users
  for Web services, 536–537
  Web site access, 500
application configuration file, 416
Application Programming Interface (API), 274
Application.Run statement, 353
applications. *See* console application; Windows forms application
ArgumentException, 195, 529
argumentList for method, 45
ArgumentOutOfRangeException class, 104

539

About the Author

John Sharp is a Principal Technologist at Content Master, part of CM Group Ltd, a technical authoring and consulting company in the United Kingdom. There he researches and develops technical content for technical training courses, seminars, workshops, guidance, books, and white papers. Throughout his development career, John has been active in training, developing, and delivering courses, and he currently writes full time. He writes on subjects ranging from UNIX Systems Programming to SQL Server Administration to Enterprise Java Development. He has used his experience to create a broad range of training materials covering many subjects. John is deeply involved with .NET development, writing courses, building tutorials, and delivering conference presentations covering Visual C# .NET development and ASP.NET. He lives in Tetbury, Gloucestershire in the United Kingdom.

Additional Resources for Web Developers

Published and Forthcoming Titles from Microsoft Press

Microsoft® Visual Web Developer™ 2005 Express Edition: Build a Web Site Now!
Jim Buyens • ISBN 0-7356-2212-4

With this lively, eye-opening, and hands-on book, all you need is a computer and the desire to learn how to create Web pages now using Visual Web Developer Express Edition! Featuring a full working edition of the software, this fun and highly visual guide walks you through a complete Web page project from set-up to launch. You'll get an introduction to the Microsoft Visual Studio® environment and learn how to put the light-weight, easy-to-use tools in Visual Web Developer Express to work right away—building your first, dynamic Web pages with Microsoft ASP.NET 2.0. You'll get expert tips, coaching, and visual examples at each step of the way, along with pointers to additional learning resources.

Microsoft ASP.NET 2.0 Programming
Step by Step
George Shepherd • ISBN 0-7356-2201-9

With dramatic improvements in performance, productivity, and security features, Visual Studio 2005 and ASP.NET 2.0 deliver a simplified, high-performance, and powerful Web development experience. ASP.NET 2.0 features a new set of controls and infrastructure that simplify Web-based data access and include functionality that facilitates code reuse, visual consistency, and aesthetic appeal. Now you can teach yourself the essentials of working with ASP.NET 2.0 in the Visual Studio environment— one step at a time. With *Step by Step*, you work at your own pace through hands-on, learn-by-doing exercises. Whether you're a beginning programmer or new to this version of the technology, you'll understand the core capabilities and fundamental techniques for ASP.NET 2.0. Each chapter puts you to work, showing you how, when, and why to use specific features of the ASP.NET 2.0 rapid application development environment and guiding you as you create actual components and working applications for the Web, including advanced features such as personalization.

Programming Microsoft ASP.NET 2.0
Core Reference
Dino Esposito • ISBN 0-7356-2176-4

Delve into the core topics for ASP.NET 2.0 programming, mastering the essential skills and capabilities needed to build high-performance Web applications successfully. Well-known ASP.NET author Dino Esposito deftly builds your expertise with Web forms, Visual Studio, core controls, master pages, data access, data binding, state management, security services, and other must-know topics—combining defini-

tive reference with practical, hands-on programming instruction. Packed with expert guidance and pragmatic examples, this *Core Reference* delivers the key resources that you need to develop professional-level Web programming skills.

Programming Microsoft ASP.NET 2.0
Applications: *Advanced Topics*
Dino Esposito • ISBN 0-7356-2177-2

Master advanced topics in ASP.NET 2.0 programming—gaining the essential insights and in-depth understanding that you need to build sophisticated, highly func-tional Web applications success-fully. Topics include Web forms, Visual Studio 2005, core controls, master pages, data access, data binding, state management, and security considerations. Developers often discover that the more they use ASP.NET, the

more they need to know. With expert guidance from ASP.NET authority Dino Esposito, you get the in-depth, comprehensive information that leads to full mastery of the technology.

Programming Microsoft Windows® Forms
Charles Petzold • ISBN 0-7356-2153-5

Programming Microsoft Web Forms
Douglas J. Reilly • ISBN 0-7356-2179-9

CLR via C++
Jeffrey Richter with Stanley B. Lippman
ISBN 0-7356-2248-5

Debugging, Tuning, and Testing Microsoft .NET 2.0 Applications
John Robbins • ISBN 0-7356-2202-7

CLR via C#, Second Edition
Jeffrey Richter • ISBN 0-7356-2163-2

For more information about Microsoft Press® books and other learning products,
visit: **www.microsoft.com/books** *and* **www.microsoft.com/learning**

Additional Resources for Database Developers
Published and Forthcoming Titles from Microsoft Press

Microsoft® SQL Server™ 2005 Express Edition
Step by Step
Jackie Goldstein • ISBN 0-7356-2184-5

Teach yourself how to get database projects up and running quickly with SQL Server Express Edition—one step at a time! SQL Server Express is a free, easy-to-use database product that is based on SQL Server 2005 technology. It's designed for building simple, dynamic applications, with all the rich functionality of the SQL Server database engine and using the same data access APIs such as Microsoft ADO.NET, SQL Native Client, and T-SQL. With *Step by Step*, you work at your own pace through hands-on, learn-by-doing exercises. Whether you're new to database programming or new to SQL Server, you'll learn how, when, and why to use specific features of this simple but powerful database development environment. Each chapter puts you to work, building your knowledge of core capabilities and guiding you as you create actual components and working applications. You'll also discover how SQL Server Express works seamlessly with the Microsoft Visual Studio® 2005 environment, simplifying the design, development, and deployment of your applications.

Programming Microsoft ADO.NET 2.0
Applications: *Advanced Topics*
Glenn Johnson • ISBN 0-7356-2141-1

Get in-depth coverage and expert insights on advanced ADO.NET programming topics such as optimization, DataView, and large objects (BLOBs and CLOBs). Targeting experienced, professional software developers who design and develop enterprise applications, this book assumes that the reader knows and understands the basic functionality and concepts of ADO.NET 2.0 and that he or she is ready to move to mastering data-manipulation skills in Microsoft Windows. The book, complete with pragmatic and instructive code examples, is structured so that readers can jump in for reference on each topic as needed.

Microsoft ADO.NET 2.0
Step by Step
Rebecca Riordan • ISBN 0-7356-2164-0

In Microsoft .NET Framework 2.0, data access is enhanced not only through the addition of new data access controls, services, and the ability to integrate more seamlessly with SQL Server 2005, but also through improvements to the ADO.NET class libraries themselves. Now you can teach yourself the essentials of working with ADO.NET 2.0 in the Visual Studio environment—one step at a time. With *Step by Step*, you work at your own pace through hands-on, learn-by-doing exercises. Whether you're a beginning programmer or new to this version of the technology, you'll understand the core capabilities and fundamental techniques for ADO.NET 2.0. Each chapter puts you to work, showing you how, when, and why to use specific features of the ADO.NET 2.0 rapid application development environment and guiding as you create actual components and working applications for Microsoft Windows®.

Programming Microsoft ADO.NET 2.0
Core Reference
David Sceppa • ISBN 0-7356-2206-X

This *Core Reference* demonstrates how to use ADO.NET 2.0, a technology within Visual Studio 2005, to access, sort, and manipulate data in standalone, enterprise, and Web-enabled applications. Discover best practices for writing, testing, and debugging database application code using the new tools and wizards in Visual Studio 2005, and put them to work with extensive code samples, tutorials, and insider tips. The book describes the ADO.NET object model, its XML features for Web extensibility, integration with Microsoft SQL Server 2000 and SQL Server 2005, and other core topics.

Programming Microsoft Windows Forms
Charles Petzold • ISBN 0-7356-2153-5

Programming Microsoft Web Forms
Douglas J. Reilly • ISBN 0-7356-2179-9

Inside Microsoft SQL Server 2005: The Storage Engine (Volume 1)
Kalen Delaney • ISBN 0-7356-2105-5

Debugging, Tuning, and Testing Microsoft .NET 2.0 Applications
John Robbins • ISBN 0-7356-2202-7

Microsoft SQL Server 2005 Programming *Step by Step*
Fernando Guerrero • ISBN 0-7356-2207-8

Programming Microsoft SQL Server 2005
Andrew J. Brust, Stephen Forte, and William H. Zack
ISBN 0-7356-1923-9

For more information about Microsoft Press® books and other learning products,
visit: **www.microsoft.com/books** *and* **www.microsoft.com/learning**

Additional Resources for C# Developers

Published and Forthcoming Titles from Microsoft Press

Microsoft® Visual C#® 2005 Express Edition: Build a Program Now!

Patrice Pelland ● ISBN 0-7356-2229-9

In this lively, eye-opening, and hands-on book, all you need is a computer and the desire to learn how to program with Visual C# 2005 Express Edition. Featuring a full working edition of the software, this fun and highly visual guide walks you through a complete programming project—a desktop weather-reporting application—from start to finish. You'll get an unintimidating introduction to the Microsoft Visual Studio® development environment and learn how to put the lightweight, easy-to-use tools in Visual C# Express to work right away—creating, compiling, testing, and delivering your first, ready-to-use program. You'll get expert tips, coaching, and visual examples at each step of the way, along with pointers to additional learning resources.

Microsoft Visual C# 2005 *Step by Step*

John Sharp ● ISBN 0-7356-2129-2

Visual C#, a feature of Visual Studio 2005, is a modern programming language designed to deliver a productive environment for creating business frameworks and reusable object-oriented components. Now you can teach yourself essential techniques with Visual C#—and start building components and Microsoft Windows®–based applications—one step at a time. With *Step by Step*, you work at your own pace through hands-on, learn-by-doing exercises. Whether you're a beginning programmer or new to this particular language, you'll learn how, when, and why to use specific features of Visual C# 2005. Each chapter puts you to work, building your knowledge of core capabilities and guiding you as you create your first C#-based applications for Windows, data management, and the Web.

Programming Microsoft Visual C# 2005 Framework Reference

Francesco Balena ● ISBN 0-7356-2182-9

Complementing *Programming Microsoft Visual C# 2005 Core Reference*, this book covers a wide range of additional topics and information critical to Visual C# developers, including Windows Forms, working with Microsoft ADO.NET 2.0 and Microsoft ASP.NET 2.0, Web services, security, remoting, and much more. Packed with sample code and real-world examples, this book will help developers move from understanding to mastery.

Programming Microsoft Visual C# 2005 *Core Reference*

Donis Marshall ● ISBN 0-7356-2181-0

Get the in-depth reference and pragmatic, real-world insights you need to exploit the enhanced language features and core capabilities in Visual C# 2005. Programming expert Donis Marshall deftly builds your proficiency with classes, structs, and other fundamentals, and advances your expertise with more advanced topics such as debugging, threading, and memory management. Combining incisive reference with hands-on coding examples and best practices, this *Core Reference* focuses on mastering the C# skills you need to build innovative solutions for smart clients and the Web.

CLR via C#, Second Edition

Jeffrey Richter ● ISBN 0-7356-2163-2

In this new edition of Jeffrey Richter's popular book, you get focused, pragmatic guidance on how to exploit the common language runtime (CLR) functionality in Microsoft .NET Framework 2.0 for applications of all types—from Web Forms, Windows Forms, and Web services to solutions for Microsoft SQL Server™, Microsoft code names "Avalon" and "Indigo," consoles, Microsoft Windows NT® Service, and more. Targeted to advanced developers and software designers, this book takes you under the covers of .NET for an in-depth understanding of its structure, functions, and operational components, demonstrating the most practical ways to apply this knowledge to your own development efforts. You'll master fundamental design tenets for .NET and get hands-on insights for creating high-performance applications more easily and efficiently. The book features extensive code examples in Visual C# 2005.

Programming Microsoft Windows Forms
Charles Petzold ● ISBN 0-7356-2153-5

CLR via C++
Jeffrey Richter with Stanley B. Lippman
ISBN 0-7356-2248-5

Programming Microsoft Web Forms
Douglas J. Reilly ● ISBN 0-7356-2179-9

Debugging, Tuning, and Testing Microsoft .NET 2.0 Applications
John Robbins ● ISBN 0-7356-2202-7

For more information about Microsoft Press® books and other learning products,
visit: **www.microsoft.com/books** *and* **www.microsoft.com/learning**

Additional Resources for Visual Basic Developers

Published and Forthcoming Titles from Microsoft Press

Microsoft® Visual Basic® 2005 Express Edition: Build a Program Now!
Patrice Pelland • ISBN 0-7356-2213-2

Featuring a full working edition of the software, this fun and highly visual guide walks you through a complete programming project—a desktop weather-reporting application—from start to finish. You'll get an introduction to the Microsoft Visual Studio® development environment and learn how to put the lightweight, easy-to-use tools in Visual Basic Express to work right away—creating, compiling, testing, and delivering your first ready-to-use program. You'll get expert tips, coaching, and visual examples each step of the way, along with pointers to additional learning resources.

Microsoft Visual Basic 2005 *Step by Step*
Michael Halvorson • ISBN 0-7356-2131-4

With enhancements across its visual designers, code editor, language, and debugger that help accelerate the development and deployment of robust, elegant applications across the Web, a business group, or an enterprise, Visual Basic 2005 focuses on enabling developers to rapidly build applications. Now you can teach yourself the essentials of working with Visual Studio 2005 and the new features of the Visual  Basic language—one step at a time. Each chapter puts you to work, showing you how, when, and why to use specific features of Visual Basic and guiding as you create actual components and working applications for Microsoft Windows®. You'll also explore data management and Web-based development topics.

Programming Microsoft Visual Basic 2005 *Core Reference*
Francesco Balena • ISBN 0-7356-2183-7

Get the expert insights, indispensable reference, and practical instruction needed to exploit the core language features and capabilities in Visual Basic 2005. Well-known Visual Basic programming author Francesco Balena expertly guides you through the fundamentals, including modules, keywords, and inheritance, and builds your mastery of more advanced topics such as delegates, assemblies, and My Namespace. Combining  in-depth reference with extensive, hands-on code examples and best-practices advice, this *Core Reference* delivers the key resources that you need to develop professional-level programming skills for smart clients and the Web.

Programming Microsoft Visual Basic 2005 Framework Reference
Francesco Balena • ISBN 0-7356-2175-6

Complementing *Programming Microsoft Visual Basic 2005 Core Reference*, this book covers a wide range of additional topics and information critical to Visual Basic developers, including Windows Forms, working with Microsoft ADO.NET 2.0 and ASP.NET 2.0, Web services, security, remoting, and much more. Packed with sample code and real-world examples, this book will help developers move from understanding to mastery.

Programming Microsoft Windows Forms
Charles Petzold • ISBN 0-7356-2153-5

Programming Microsoft Web Forms
Douglas J. Reilly • ISBN 0-7356-2179-9

Debugging, Tuning, and Testing Microsoft .NET 2.0 Applications
John Robbins • ISBN 0-7356-2202-7

Microsoft ASP.NET 2.0 *Step by Step*
George Shepherd • ISBN 0-7356-2201-9

Microsoft ADO.NET 2.0 *Step by Step*
Rebecca Riordan • ISBN 0-7356-2164-0

Programming Microsoft ASP.NET 2.0 *Core Reference*
Dino Esposito • ISBN 0-7356-2176-4

For more information about Microsoft Press® books and other learning products,
visit: **www.microsoft.com/books** *and* **www.microsoft.com/learning**

What do you think of this book?
We want to hear from you!

Do you have a few minutes to participate in a brief online survey? Microsoft is interested in hearing your feedback about this publication so that we can continually improve our books and learning resources for you.

To participate in our survey, please visit:

www.microsoft.com/learning/booksurvey

And enter this book's ISBN, 6-2129-2. As a thank-you to survey participants in the United States and Canada, each month we'll randomly select five respondents to win one of five $100 gift certificates from a leading online merchant.* At the conclusion of the survey, you can enter the drawing by providing your e-mail address, which will be used for prize notification *only*

Thanks in advance for your input. Your opinion counts!

Sincerely,

Microsoft Learning

Learn More. Go Further.

To see special offers on Microsoft Learning products for developers, IT professionals, and home and office users, visit: *www.microsoft.com/learning/booksurvey*

* No purchase necessary. Void where prohibited. Open only to residents of the 50 United States (includes District of Columbia) and Canada (void in Quebec). Sweepstakes ends 6/30/2006. For official rules, see: *www.microsoft.com/learning/booksurvey*